THE ELIZABETHANS

A. N. WILSON

arrow books

Published by Arrow Books 2012

2 4 6 8 10 9 7 5 3 1

This book is a work of non-fiction.

First published in Great Britain in 2011 by
Hutchinson
Random House, 20 Vauxhall Bridge Road,
London SW1V 2SA

www.rbooks.co.uk

Addresses for companies within The Random House Group Limited can be found at: www.randomhouse.co.uk/offices.htm

The Random House Group Limited Reg. No. 954009

A CIP catalogue record for this book is available from the British Library

ISBN 9780099547143

Typeset in Sabon MT by Palimpsest Book Production Limited,
Falkirk, Stirlingshire

Printed and bound in Great Britain by CPI Group (UK) Ltd, Croydon CR0 4YY for

KATHERINE DUNCAN-JONES,

Elizabethan *sans pareil*

Acknowledgements

Gillon Aitken was the 'onlie begetter' of this book. It was his idea that I should write it, and I am deeply grateful for all his encouragement, with this and other projects, and for his friendship over many years. Many thanks, too, to Emma Mitchell, Paul Sidey, Mandy Greenfield and George Capel who all gave support and advice. Thanks to Simon Thurley, Anna Keay, David Starkey, and Roy Strong, all experts in a field where I am an amateur, who guided my steps and suggested further reading. Georgie Wilson helped with Elizabethan Highgate and with the Armada chapter, and Ruth Guilding with the architecture. I finished the book at Lamorna Cove, Ruth's brainchild, looking at the sea and imagining the Armada sailing by. My greatest debt, in writing this book and in understanding many others, is expressed in the dedication.

Oak Apple Day, 2011

List of illustrations and credits

Elizabeth I, 'The Ditchley Portrait', by Marcus Gheeraerts the Younger, c.1592. National Portrait Gallery, London: NPG 2561

An Allegory of the Tudor Succession: The Family of Henry VIII, c.1589–95 (oil on panel), English School, (16th century) / Yale Center for British Art, Paul Mellon Collection, USA / The Bridgeman Art Library

Sir Francis Walsingham c.1532–1590 English statesman and spymaster for Queen Elizabeth I. From the book 'Lodge's British Portraits' published in London, 1823. (Photo by Universal History Archive/Getty Images) © Getty Images

William Cecil, 1st Baron Burghley (1520–98) English statesman. Lord High Treasurer to Elizabeth I from 1572. Engraving. (Photo by Universal History Archive/Getty Images) © Getty Images

G.11631.B.L. Title Page with a Portrait of Shakespeare, from 'Mr. William Shakespeare's Comedies, Histories and Tragedies', edited by J. Heminge and H. Condell, engraving by Droeshout, 1623 (engraving) © British Library Board. All Rights Reserved

Interior of schoolroom where William Shakespeare was educated, Stratford-upon-Avon, Warwickshire, England, UK, Europe © Peter Scholey

Mary Herbert Countess of Pembroke, nee Mary Sidney, 1561–1621. English patroness of the arts and translator. From the book 'Lodge's British Portraits' published London 1823. (Photo by Universal History Archive/Getty Images) © Getty Images

Circa 1590, English poet Edmund Spenser (c. 1552–1599). With Sir Philip Sidney and Dyer, he formed the literary club 'Areopagus,' and invented the Spenserian stanza in poetry. Original Artwork: Engraving by Thomson. (Photo by Archive Photos/Getty Images) © Getty Images

Robert Dudley (1532–88) 1st Earl of Leicester, c.1560s (oil on panel), Meulen, or Muelen, Steven van der (fl.1543–68) / Yale Center for British Art, Paul Mellon Collection, USA / The Bridgeman Art Library

Kenilworth Castle, Warwickshire, England © David Hughes

Portrait of Sir Francis Drake (1540–1596) 1591 (oil on panel) © Marcus Gheeraerts the Younger

Portrait of British Naval commander Sir John Hawkins. (Photo by Time Life Pictures/Mansell/Time Life Pictures/Getty Images)© Time & Life Pictures/Getty Images

Circa 1600, A naval and military battle in which the English fleet engages the Spanish Armada at Cadiz. (Photo by Hulton Archive/Getty Images) © Getty Images

Circa 1570, English poet, courtier and soldier Sir Philip Sidney (1554–1586) who typified the Elizabethan gentleman. Original Artwork: Engraved by E Scriven. (Photo by Hulton Archive/Getty Images) © Getty Images

View of Penshurst Place from the east over a wilderness of weeds in the kitchen garden. (Photo by Ian Smith/Time Life Pictures/Getty Images) © Time & Life Pictures/Getty Images

The funeral cortege of Sir Philip Sidney (1554–1586) on its way to St. Paul's Cathedral, 1587, engraved by Theodor de Bry (1528–1598) (engraving), English School, (16th century) / Private Collection / The Stapleton Collection / The Bridgeman Art Library

Stage and seating (photo), / Shakespeare's Globe, Southwark, London, UK / © Peter Phipp/Travelshots / The Bridgeman Art Library

Queen Elizabeth I (1533–1603) at a stag hunt, plate from 'Noble Art of Venerie and Hunting' by George Turberville, 1575 (woodcut) (b/w photo) by English School, (16th century) British Library, London, UK/ The Bridgeman Art Library

Sir Henry Lee (1533–1611), 1568 (panel), Mor, Sir Anthonis van Dashorst (Antonio Moro) (1517/20–76/7) / National Portrait Gallery, London, UK / The Bridgeman Art Library

Elizabeth Knollys, Lady Layton, 1577 (oil on panel), Gower, George (1540–96) (attr. to) / Montacute House, Somerset, UK / The Phelips Collection National Trust Photographic Library/Derrick E. Witty / The Bridgeman Art Library

A pair of embroidered gloves belonging to Queen Elizabeth I, 19th May 1953. They were presented to her during a visit to Oxford in 1566, and are on display at an exhibition of Treasures of Oxford at Goldsmith's Hall, London. (Photo by T. Marshall/Topical Press Agency/Getty Images) © Getty Images

Queen Elizabeth I Feeds the Dutch Cow. Oil on panel, 39.4 × 49.5, artist unknown

Spring Cleaning Takes Place At Longleat © Getty Images

Hardwick Hall © English School

Robed lawyers dine under carved beams in Middle Temple's Great Hall, Inns of Court, London, England (Photo by Willis D. Vaughn/National Geographic/Getty Images) © National Geographic/Getty Images

Tomb of Pope Saint Pius V in Santa Maria Maggiore Rome

The tomb of Mary Queen of Scots, south isle of the Lady Chapel, c.1612–13 (marble), Cure, Cornelius (d.1607) and Cure, William (d.1632) / Westminster Abbey, London, UK / Photo: James Brittain / The Bridgeman Art Library

Britain's Queen Elizabeth II (R) and Ireland's President Mary McAleese stand together during a wreath laying ceremony at the Irish War memorial Garden at Islandbridge in Dublin, Ireland on May 18, 2011. Queen Elizabeth II Wednesday visited a memorial to the 49,400 Irish soldiers killed fighting for Britain in World War I in a highly-charged ceremony on the second day of her historic visit to Ireland. © PAUL ELLIS/AFP/Getty Images) AFP/Getty Images

Portrait of John Dee (1547–1608) (oil on canvas), English School, (17th century) / Ashmolean Museum, University of Oxford, UK / The Bridgeman Art Library

Great Britain, England, Devon, Exeter, Exeter Cathedral, marble statue of theologian Richard Hooker © Nigel Hicks

Portrait of Queen Elizabeth I – The Drewe Portrait, late 1580s (oil on panel), Gower, George (1540–96) (attr. to) / Private Collection / Photo © Philip Mould Ltd, London / The Bridgeman Art Library

Contents

Preface

We have lived to see the Elizabethan world come to an end. This makes *now* a very interesting time to be reconsidering the Elizabethans, but it also makes for some difficulties. As human societies and civilisations change, it is natural for them to suppose that what they do, what they think, what they eat and drink and believe is superior to what went before. While the Elizabethan world was still going on – and in some respects it was still continuing, in modified form, until the Second World War – British and American historians were able to see the reign of Queen Elizabeth I as a glory age. This was how the Elizabethans saw themselves. Their great poet, Edmund Spenser, named his Faerie Queene (who was a projection of Elizabeth herself) Gloriana, and her capital, an idealised London, he named Cleopolis – the Greek for 'Glory-ville'. Modern historians from, let us say, James Anthony Froude (1819–84) to A.L. Rowse (1903–97) wrote about the Elizabethan Age with celebratory *brio*. They noted, correctly, that this was the age when the history of modern England (and Wales) really began. With the other British nations, Scotland and Ireland, the tale was perhaps more complicated. This was when England, having put civil wars and the superstitions of the Middle Ages behind it, emerged into the broad sunlit uplands. This was the age that saw the origins of English sea-power. In consequence, if not in Elizabeth I's own day, America – the future United States – became an English-speaking civilisation. This was the great age when British explorers went out to every corner of the known world. Modern geography began, and the colonial expansion that was the foundation of later British power and prosperity.

This was the age of Renaissance humanism – a humanism that was not the preserve only of a few intellectuals, as had been the case at the close of the fifteenth century, but which, through the grammar schools founded in the reigns of Edward VI and Elizabeth, disseminated learning and a reasonable attitude to life throughout the land. Shakespeare himself was the product of this grammar-school education. And merely to name Shakespeare is to remind us that the Elizabethan age was indeed a glory age – some would say *the* glory age – of English literature. The reign (especially its last fifteen years) saw a prodigious literary flowering. Who could not revel in times that produced so rich a variety of books as Richard Hakluyt's *Principall Navigations*, Thomas Nashe's hilarious, scabrous fictions such as *Pierce Penilesse* or *The Unfortunate Traveller*, the poems and songs of Thomas Campion, the translations by Chapman of Homer, by North of Plutarch, by Harington of Ariosto – even before you mention the poems of Spenser, Sidney and Donne; Sidney's two prose romances of *Arcadia*; and the dramas of Christopher Marlowe, Ben Jonson and William Shakespeare himself?

Add to this the music of John Dowland, William Byrd and Thomas Tallis, and glory is added to glory. Think of the architecture! Apart from the splendour of the great houses – Kirby Hall, Longleat, Hardwick – there were innumerable manor houses of incomparable beauty. So much survives: Elizabethan tombs in small country churches, gatehouses, lodges, schools, guildhalls and corn exchanges, towers, staircases, colleges, often quirky, never ugly.

In this book I hope we shall be basking together in wholehearted appreciation of all this; but it is no longer possible to do so without a recognition of the Difficulty – hence my title for the opening chapter. The Difficulty is really a moral one: things which they, the Elizabethans, regarded as a cause for pride, we – the great majority of educated, liberal Western opinion – consider shameful. Things of which they boasted, we deplore. Earlier generations of British writers looked back at the Elizabethans and either saw simple causes of celebration in their legal, political, naval and military and ecclesiastical achievements. Or, as Virginia Woolf did, in her camp comedy *Orlando*, they saw merely a fancy-dress parade. The best way of blinding oneself to the Difficulty was to write solely from an aesthetic or literary viewpoint. C.S. Lewis did this in his highly readable and scholarly *English Literature in the Sixteenth Century Excluding Drama*, first published in 1954. He sidesteps all controversy, unless you consider it controversial that this Ulster Protestant refers throughout his book to Roman Catholics as 'Papists'. Of Spenser's *A View of the Present State of Ireland*, Lewis, who was a great Spenserian and who did more than any twentieth-century scholar to help us enjoy *The Faerie Queene*, fights shy of examining the contents of this prose work by the chief poet of the age. 'The morality of [Spenser's] . . . plan for the reduction of Ireland has been shown to be not so much indefensible as quotations might make it appear, but any stronger apologia would be a burden beyond my shoulders.'[1]

Such an attitude could not easily be struck by a writer of our generation. We need neither condemn nor construct an 'apologia' for Spenser's programme for the Irish, but merely speaking of his 'plan for the reduction of Ireland' scarcely gives to a modern reader who has not read *A View* much idea of what it contains. A modern Irish historian has not unfairly paraphrased Spenser's book as a programme for the complete destruction of Ireland's existing political structure. 'Only when that had been achieved and the Irish had been reduced, through mass starvation, exemplary killing and the imposition of full military repression, to a state of being without a culture at all, could the process of educating them in the ways of the superior English culture commence.'[2]

The Irish question will never go away, but it could be said that it is only in our generation that the English have finally rid themselves of the Elizabethan mindset – namely, that Ireland was a beautiful island whose inhabitants would be unable to learn the habits of civilisation until taught them by the English.

Here is a vivid example of what I mean by my suggestion that we – this generation – have lived to see the Elizabethan world come to an end. And here is a vivid example of what I call the Difficulty. It is no longer an option for any Englishman to write as Froude or Rowse did: that is, *defending* the Elizabethan attitude to Ireland and the Irish. On the other hand – and this is what I mean by the 'Difficulty' – I do not want this book to be a tedious and anachronistic exercise in judging one age by the standards of another. We have so far, so very far, left the Elizabethan Age behind us that today only the deranged would share, let us say, Sir Francis Walsingham's views on capital punishment, Sir John Hawkins's views on Africans or, come to that, Marlowe's and Shakespeare's implied views on Jews. But we would paint a poor portrait of the Age if all we did was to hold our noses and point fingers of scorn. Because we can see not merely a continuation, but an ending of the Elizabethan story, in our own day, our danger is to be too dismissive, too unimaginatively judgemental. And yet some judgement is inescapable.

In this opening part I have chosen to write first about two areas of life in which the Elizabethan story has continued into living memory, but has now come to a definite end. Each of these areas will be illustrations of the fact that we are both close to the Elizabethans and infinitely far away; we are their heirs, but we have put our ancestry behind us. When these illustrations are complete, we will be in a stronger position to see the Elizabethan world with clear eyes – and that will be the aim of the remaining parts of the book.

Part One

The Early Reign

Part One

The Difficulties

After [illegible] and more than [illegible]
of Nemo [illegible] agreed in the [illegible]
first [illegible] had [illegible]
[illegible]

[illegible] specifically [illegible]
the end [illegible] the rebel [illegible]
O'Donnell [illegible] as champions [illegible]
religion [illegible]. The [illegible]
[illegible]

[illegible]

I

The Difficulty

After thirty years of fighting and more than 3,000 deaths in the province of Northern Ireland, peace was agreed. In the first decade of the twenty-first century the Northern Ireland Assembly held democratic elections.

There have been sporadic outbursts of violence since, but most people, in the Republic of Ireland, in Northern Ireland and in the rest of Britain, seem to think that peace has come, and that the compromises on all sides have been worth the peace. The Republic has, in effect, abandoned its claim over the six counties of the North. It has accepted the partition of Ireland. The peoples of the six counties now enjoy, in effect, self-government, with power shared between Catholics and Protestants. The government in Westminster, while keeping a toe-hold in the province, and while retaining a special Minister for Northern Ireland, has given up any notion of 'making Ireland British' against its will.[1]

Ireland was Britain's first, and least willing, colony, the most unsuccessful of all British colonial experiments. The pattern of Elizabethan failure in Ireland was to be replicated at other periods of history: first an attempt to woo the Irish, to persuade the people themselves to adopt laws and customs that were alien to them. Next, this wooing having known only partial success, or abject failure, an attempt at coercion; and one method of such coercion was a resettlement of Irish land by English, Welsh or Scottish incomers. Third, when neither gentle persuasion nor dispossession achieved the desired result – viz. the rule of English law on Irish soil – there was a resort to outright violence and massacre.

It was not, initially at least, a specifically religious matter, though by the end of the sixteenth century the rebels Hugh O'Neill and Hugh O'Donnell could see themselves as champions of 'Christ's Catholic religion' against the English heretics. The fundamental point of contention, though, was English interference in Irish affairs: English attempts to make Ireland less Irish. As a matter of fact, in the early stages of the Reformation, the Irish went along with Henry VIII's religious revolution more peaceably than the English did. There was no Pilgrimage of Grace, there were no Irish martyrs for the faith, no Irish Thomas More[2] or Bishop Fisher. More than 400 Irish monasteries and abbeys were sold to Irish laymen during the reigns of Henry VIII and Elizabeth I.

The Irish did not protest when Henry VIII made George Browne the Archbishop of Dublin – that was, the former Augustinian friar who performed the marriage ceremony between the King and Anne Boleyn. Perhaps, if a Gaelic Bible and Gaelic Prayer Book had been made available in Ireland, as a Welsh Bible and Prayer Book were in Wales by 1567, Ireland might have remained Protestant. It was not until the beginning of James I's reign that the Prayer Book appeared in Irish.[3]

Outside the Pale – that is, the small area twenty miles to the east and north of Dublin that was English-speaking – Ireland had its own language, literature, culture. The Reformation bishops were bidden to preach to the people in English,[4] a language understood by Irish congregations no better than they understood Latin. But it was not Protestantism *per se* that the Irish rejected, it was English cultural imperialism, which had been just as strong in the reigns of Henry VIII, Edward VI, Queen Mary and Queen Elizabeth. It was in 1521 that the Earl of Surrey, as Lieutenant of Ireland, had first proposed *plantation* as a means of subduing the recalcitrant island. That is, removing the Irish from their land and replacing them with English or Scots. George Dowdall, the Catholic appointed as Archbishop of Armagh by Mary Tudor, urged a continuation of the policy. The only solution to the Irish 'problem' was, according to the archbishop, to get rid of the Irish: either expel them or kill them, and give their land to the English.[5]

What made Ireland so ungovernable, so anarchic – not merely in the eyes of English colonists, but also in the eyes of many Irish people themselves?[6] Central to the problem was the Irish method of determining both *succession* and property-ownership. Conn Bacach O'Neill (*c.*1482–1559) was proclaimed The O'Neill – that is, head of his tribe or sept – though he was actually the younger son of Conn More O'Neill, chieftain and lord of Tyrone. The English never came to grips with this system of *tanistry*, whereby the clans or tribes chose the new leader on grounds of quality rather than those of primogeniture.

Henry VIII made Conn O'Neill Earl of Tyrone in exchange for his submission to English law and English ideas of land ownership, or as his own people saw it: 'O'Neill of Oileach and Eamhait, the king of Tara and Tailte has exchanged in foolish submission his kingdom for the Ulster Earldom'[7]. When Conn O'Neill died, Shane – his youngest son, by his second wife, Sorcha – was elected O' Neilll by his sept. By English law, the earldom of Tyrone passed to Conn's eldest son Matthew, but Shane argued that as head of the sept he should receive the earldom. Queen Elizabeth (anything for a quiet life, as far as her view of Ireland was concerned) wanted her Deputy in Ireland, Thomas Radcliffe, Earl of Sussex, to recognise Shane's claim. This Sussex was extremely unwilling to do, with the result that within the first year of the Queen's reign the English Pale was being raided by Shane's troops, many of them mercenaries from Scotland; and Ulster, the Northern Kingdom, was an anarchy of warring O'Neills, fighting one another.

So within a year of Elizabeth becoming queen were to be seen, in the clash between Shane O'Neill and the Earl of Sussex, many of the key ingredients of the Irish phenomenon. There was the fact, for example, that chiefs such as O'Neill were able to command large private armies of gallowglasses from the Western Isles of Scotland and Redshanks – unsettled mercenaries who sailed the coasts in their galleys plying for hire as soldiers, either in Irish quarrels among themselves or in their wars against the English. In the last years of Mary's reign and the first of Elizabeth's, Sussex had secured the consent of the Crown to make naval attacks on the Hebrides to try to cut off the supply of gallowglasses at source.[8]

While Sussex attempted out-and-out defeat of O'Neill and extirpation of the enemy, the Queen was undermining him by attempting to pacify O'Neill. Here is another ingredient of the Elizabethan story of Ireland: a perpetual tension between the Englishmen on the ground, trying to defend the interests of the Crown, and the Crown itself wishing to avoid trouble and expense. In all this, during Elizabeth's reign, there was also a strong element of misogyny. Sir Henry Sidney, for example, complained to Walsingham, 'Three tymes her Majestie hath sent me her Deputie into Ireland, and in everie of the three tymes I susteyned a great and a violent rebellion, everie one of which I subdued and (with honourable peace) lefte the country in quiet.' Yet he felt himself undermined by the Queen's allowing herself to be bamboozled – as Sidney thought – by the Earl of Ormond.

(Yet another ingredient in the anarchic mix there! The clash between the old families such as the Ormonds and Desmonds, descended from *Norman* settlers in Ireland and tending to identify with Irish septs and Gaelic culture, and the *new* English settlers.)

Sidney looked back nostalgically to the days when their monarch was male. He had been a courtier to the boy king, Edward VI. 'Sondry tymes he bountifully rewarded me . . . Lastly, not only to my own still felt grief, but also to the universal wo of England, he died in my armes.'[9] Sidney was less overtly misogynistic and disrespectful of the Queen than a later Deputy, Sir John Perrot, a notoriously choleric figure who exclaimed with fury, 'Silly woman, now she shall not curb me, she shall not rule me now.' Taking orders from the Queen was, he intemperately believed, 'to serve a base bastard piss kitchen woman.'[10] As one who was himself spoken of as a bastard son of Henry VIII, Perrot was perhaps a pot calling a kettle black.

Sir Henry Sidney was one of the prime movers in bringing Reform to Ireland: in confirming the Protestant Reformation, in introducing the rule of law to replace the more anarchic Gaelic traditions relating to inheritance and property, in inaugurating a system of education. Elizabeth allowed him to summon an Irish parliament upon his arrival in 1566, the first Irish parliament to meet for six years. Every single reform that Sidney proposed met with opposition from the Palesmen, from the English-speaking parliamentary representatives. They rejected his proposal for an Irish university – it was not until 1592 that Trinity College, Dublin, was established. They rejected his attempts to set up grammar schools all over Ireland. They were deeply suspicious of trial by jury being introduced to Ireland. Sidney had two terms as Deputy: 1566–71 and 1575–8. Like those of the other Elizabethan deputies, his Irish career ended in failure. In 1577 his son, Philip, aged twenty-three, wrote a defence of his father's career in Ireland. It was also a job application to succeed him as Deputy. He told the Queen that she had three options when it came to attempting to rule Ireland. The first was military conquest – not an option, as he realised, not least because the parsimonious monarch would have deemed it far too expensive. Second was the path of complete military withdrawal. Again, this was not an option, for it would lead to the loss of Ireland altogether. The only other option, the third way, was to raise revenue in Ireland itself to meet the costs of extended government. The rebellions of 'Shane O'Neill and all the Earl of Ormond's brethren' must be put down by the Irish themselves. Of course Ireland and its inhabitants were 'in no case to be equalled to this realm [of England]'. Of course one symptom of this was the 'ignorant obstinacy in papistry'. But they would never forget 'the fresh remembrance of their lost liberty', 'until by time they find the sweetness of due subjection'.[11]

Funnily enough, the Irish never did find due subjection as sweet as the young Philip Sidney believed that they should. But the matter is more complicated than we should suppose, when viewing it from the perspective of today. Ireland is today at peace. It could be said that it is at peace because it has at last got rid of English interference. Another way of describing the current, early twenty-first-century picture of Ireland, however, is that, for the first time in 400 years, Ireland is governed by a rule of law *accepted by all sides*. The secularised values of modern Ireland derive from the Renaissance and Reformation, which the English Elizabethan deputies were trying to persuade the Irish to adopt. After the scandals of child abuse and the decline in priestly and religious vocations, Ireland has abandoned its 'papistry'. The days of de Valera's Ireland, in which it was impossible to purchase a copy of James Joyce's *Ulysses* in the city that inspired it, have gone for ever.

This has led to a divergence among the Irish historians themselves. On the one hand, there are those who do not baulk at comparisons between the Elizabethans in Ireland and the butchers of the Third Reich.[12] On the other hand, there are more moderate voices among Irish historians[13] who argue that Celtic, or Gaelic, Ireland was in any event dying in the sixteenth century. It had to be replaced by *something*. An historian such as Patricia Coughlan (*Spenser and Ireland*) has some sympathy with the actual administrators in Ireland itself during this period, and blames the failure on a 'loss of nerve' in London – by the Queen and her court. The planters were, Coughlan argued,[14] constantly urging London, from the 1540s onwards, not to abandon Ireland, not to give up helping the Irish emerge from a collapsing Gaelic community of life.

But – is it true that Gaelic culture in Ireland was collapsing? True, Ireland was an outpost, in a changing Europe, of a way of life that was totally unlike the mercantile, urbanised world of Elizabethan London, or the city states of Italy. But how much did the English colonists *know* of Irish culture? How much, come to that, do modern historians know of it? Edmund Spenser was unusual among the English in Ireland. His antiquarian curiosity led him to obtain translations of old Irish poems. And he learned a smattering of Gaelic.

A much more typical Elizabethan picture of Ireland came from the famous traveller Fynes Moryson – chief secretary to Sir Charles Blount, Lord Mountjoy – in 1600 Lord Deputy of Ireland and younger brother of Sir George Moryson, Vice President of Munster 1609–28. Fynes Moryson, who in 1616 published An *itinerary* of travels in places as far afield as Turkey and Poland, gave what was the stereotypical view of Ireland. The Irish speak 'a peculiar language, not derived from any other radical tongue (that ever I could hear, for myself neither have nor ever sought to have any skill therein)'. He regarded the Irish, of whatever degree, as no better than savages. 'They willingly eat the herb shamrock, being of a sharp taste, which, as they run and are chased to and fro, they snatch like beasts out of the ditches . . .'

> Many of these wild Irish eat no flesh, but that which dies of disease or otherwise of itself, neither can it scape them for stinking . . .
>
> I trust no man expects among these gallants any beds, much less feather beds and sheets, who like the nomads removing their dwellings, according to the commodity of pastures for their cows, sleep under the canopy of heaven, or in a poor house of clay, or in a cabin made of the boughs of trees and covered with turf, for such are the dwellings of the very lords among them.[15]

Edmund Campion, later a Jesuit, wrote a *History of Ireland*, in ten weeks in 1571, and dedicated it to his patron the Earl of Leicester.[16] It was in part intended as a defence of Sir Henry Sidney. It is doubtful whether Campion ever went beyond the Pale, and he based his frequently satirical picture of the Irish on the writings of Giraldus Cambrensis – whose visit to Ireland was in 1185–6. Typical in tone is Campion's account: 'In Ulster thus they used to Crowne their king, a white cow was brought forth, which the King must kill, and seeth in water whole, and bathe himself therein stark naked. The sitting in the same Caldron, his people about him, together with them, he must eat the fleshe, and drinke the broath, wherein he sitteth, without the cuppe or dish or use of his hand.'[17]

In fact there is no particular evidence for any so-called 'decline' in the clan system in Ireland during the sixteenth century when the Elizabethans decided to abolish it – just as the London government waged its war on the Scottish clans in the eighteenth century, and systematically attempted to eliminate tribal structures in Africa in the nineteenth and twentieth centuries.[18] 'The Gaelic way of life stood in the path of Progress.' Those who have studied sixteenth-century Ireland from a non-imperialist viewpoint for example, in the lands belonging to the Desmonds, found 'an organized State, with an elaborate fiscal system, providing a settled annual revenue for the sovereign and his various sub-chiefs. This revenue was definitely assessed on certain areas of land. It postulates fixed metes and bounds, a considerable amount of tillage. Every clan, every sub-sept, had its own territory; and on this territory the amounts due for the support of the hierarchy of chiefs were systematically applotted.'[19]

This is very different from the barbarous anarchy seen by the Elizabethan deputies, their assistants and their sympathetic English, usually male, historians. They did not trouble to learn Gaelic, so they were hardly in a position to know whether or not the Gaelic culture was 'in decline'. In fact, the bardic poets were a group detested by the Elizabethan governments because of the influence they exercised over the Gaelic aristocracy. Sir Henry Harrington, seneschal and chief English officer of the O'Byrne territory in County Wicklow in 1579, was instructed to 'make proclamation that no idle person, vagabond or masterless man, bard, rymor, or other notorious malefactor, remain within the district on pain of whipping after eight days, and of death after *twenty days*.'[20] In the same year, 1579, Hugh MacShane O'Byrne died, Gaelic chieftain and leader of the resistance in Wicklow. You can read his Poem Book and see the vigour with which the bards responded to the Elizabethan Reform movement:

> Who buyeth a piece of nine verses,
>   Even though he get the purchase thereof?
> To the men of Leinster, though high their repute,
>   I know that is a difficult question.

The answer the O'Byrnes make us is:
'Let not the verses, eight or nine, be heard;
Until the Sasanachs have retired overseas
We shall pay for neither poem nor lay.

He who never bowed to Foreigner's custom
Hugh MacShane, of comeliness renowned
It is with him I have tried my fortune
With a piece in verses eight or nine.'[21]

In fact there is a great deal of manuscript evidence that a vigorous bardic tradition survived in sixteenth-century Ireland. Nor could even the most repressive of the settlers always manage to sustain the classic justification for colonialism the world over – namely, that the natives existed in an anarchy from which imperialism alone could rescue them. In 1556 the O'Moore lands in Leix were confiscated by settlers. For fifty years the O'Moores and their supporters resisted plantation and carried on their old tribal way of life unless interrupted by English attempts to civilise them. In 1600 Lord Deputy Mountjoy raided Leix. It was none other than Fynes Moryson who left the desperate account:

> Our captains, and by their example (for it was otherwise painful) the common soldiers, did cut down with their swords all the rebels corn, to the value of 10,000 and upwards, the only means by which they were to live, and to keep their bonaghts [hired soldiers]. It seemed incredible that by so barbarous inhabitants the ground should be so manured, the fields so orderly fenced, the towns so frequently inhabited, and the highways and paths so beaten, as the Lord Deputy here found them. The reason whereof was, that the Queen's forces during these wars, never till then came among them.[22]

Edmund Spenser did not like the conclusion to which his *View of the Present State of Ireland* drove him: that it was the introduction of English law – that bedrock of English stability – that made Ireland in fact anarchic and ungovernable. Yet he and all his fellow planters and administrators were:

. . . in blood
Stepped in so far that, should I wade no more,
Returning were as tedious as go o'er.[23]

In the early seventeenth and eighteenth centuries, the Munster plantations served as a model for settlements in Virginia and the Carolinas.[24]

In the sixteenth century, as the Irish seemed less and less amenable to 'the sweetness of due subjection', we can now see that as there was so little chance of subduing the Irish by persuasion, it had to be done by coercion. And for this the English looked for role models among the Spanish Conquistadors in the New World. It was an unhappy example to follow, but entirely compatible with Elizabethan attitudes to cultures that got in their way of progress, or people who could if necessary be reduced to sub-human or non-human status for the sake of commercial gain. And it is to the painful subject of slavery and its relation to colonisation that we must now turn.

2
The New World

When, drifting in the morning calm of 26 July 1588, the Lord Admiral of the Fleet, Howard of Effingham, conferred knighthoods upon six Elizabethan seamen, there was probably none more deserving of the honour than John Hawkins of Plymouth. As Treasurer to the Royal Navy, Hawkins had done more than any man to ensure the invincibility of the English fleet and, in the defeat of the Spanish Armada, his seamanship and skill had just been ably demonstrated. After ten days of bitter fighting against the huge Spanish navy, not one English ship had fallen out for sea damage or the enemies' shot.[1] That was a collective achievement of course, but it would not have been possible without Hawkins, who learned about ships not simply from his ship-owning father – William Hawkins, Mayor of Plymouth – but from his very active career as a young man on the high seas.

How shall we classify that career? As a 'privateer'? As a cut-throat pirate? As a spy, a double-agent, a confidence trickster and thief? A case could be made for making such a description of this brave desperado. And I think it must be said at the outset that if you find *nothing* to admire about John Hawkins, or about his cousin Francis Drake – nothing to enjoy in their outrageous careers – then the Elizabethan Age will remain for ever a place of incomprehensible nightmare for you.

To King Philip II of Spain he was 'the English pirate named John Hawkins, who has gone through the Indies committing great robberies and destruction'. When trying to con his way into the Spanish pearl fishery of Borburata (in present-day Venezuela) he had told the Spanish officials that he was a personal friend of Philip's. 'I knowe the [King of] Spaine your mr unto whome alsoe I have bene a servaun.'[2] A few years later a Spaniard called Juanos de Urquiza was stating as a fact that Hawkins was the first man knighted by Philip II when he came to England.[3]

Hawkins's coat of arms tells his story quite shamelessly. All Elizabethans who were not already gentlemen or gentlewomen – or aristocrats born – aspired to rise. They wanted to formalise their 'gentle' status, and for this, a coat of arms, supplied by the College of Arms, the heralds, was necessary. William Garvey, Clarenceux King of Arms, granted Hawkins his coat, having decided that Hawkins was 'lineally descended from his ancestors a gentilman' of 'courageous worthe and famious enterprises'.[4]

The coat of arms consists of a shield, with a seashell in the top left-hand corner – symbolic of his maritime life; and a rampaging lion of gold (or) pacing the waves – symbolic no doubt not merely of Hawkins's prowess at sea, but of Elizabethan aspirations to make the country rich by sea-power. It is the crest of the coat of arms that is so arresting: it is a naked black person of indeterminate sex with golden earrings, bound with rope. Hawkins knew that his wealth and his practical maritime skill derived from his years, as a young man, of sailing to the Canaries, and to West Africa. At first he contented himself with stealing slaves who had already been captured by Portuguese traders. Soon he was penetrating into West Africa and making raiding parties himself, capturing Africans and transporting them, either to mid-Atlantic slave markets or to the Caribbean, where they could be sold direct to Spanish and Portuguese buyers. He pursued this gruesome trade, not with the mere connivance of his monarch; Queen Elizabeth actually invested in the enterprise and gave him the largest ship in the Royal Navy, the *Jesus of Lübeck*, to transport the slaves to the New World.

Neither Hawkins himself nor his English contemporaries invented slavery. It is an institution as old as humanity – anyway as old as urban humanity. Nor did they invent the modern Atlantic slave trade, which began when a young Portuguese tax official called Lançarote de Freitas imported 235 West African slaves to the Algarve in August 1444.[5] Those who today bask in the holiday sunshine of the Canary Islands perpetuate his memory every time they buy a ticket to Lanzarote. The Portuguese themselves – we must further acknowledge – did not invent the slave trade. It was fully alive in West Africa when they went there. Hugh Thomas, modern historian of the slave trade, opines that in fifteenth-century West Africa 'slaves seem to have been the only form of private property recognised by African custom'.[6] Thomas also reminds us – and it is a useful mental corrective that is necessary, to keep sixteenth-century slave traders in perspective – that, compared with the slave trading that went on in the late seventeenth and eighteenth centuries, 'the slave trade to the Americas in the 16th and early 17th centuries – until the 1640s, when sugar took over from tobacco in the Caribbean plantations – was still on a fairly small and relatively human, if not humane, scale. It was probably still smaller in many years than the Arab trans-Saharan trade in black slaves.'[7] In the whole of the fifteenth and sixteenth centuries some 70,000 slaves were brought to Portugal. In the last quarter of the seventeenth century, 175,000 African slaves were imported to the British Caribbean and in the same period some 350,000 Africans were trafficked to Brazil.[8]

Against these truly gruesome numbers, and the hundreds of thousands of human beings forcibly transported from West Africa to Barbados, Jamaica and South Carolina during the eighteenth century, the Elizabethan traders were dealing with tiny numbers. But the later slave trade followed the early pioneers.

John Hawkins's involvement with the slave trade was tangential. If he could have made the same sort of money, on his expeditions, trading in pearls or hides or parrots as he did with his dubiously acquired slave cargoes, he would doubtless have done so. But the crest on his coat of arms cannot lightly be forgotten. He was not yet thirty when he had made voyages to the Canary Islands and learned 'that negroes were very good merchandise in Hispaniola, and that they might easily be had upon the coast of Guinea'.[9]

In consideration of Ireland, the 'Difficulty' was convoluted. Nearly all the problems of Ireland in modern times stemmed from their Elizabethan origins – from the Elizabethan belief that if the Irish were recalcitrant, they could be replaced on their own soil by planters. And yet the paradox is that peace came to Ireland towards the close of the twentieth century because the Irish themselves, though for un-Elizabethan reasons, accepted two of the key Elizabethan propositions: the necessity of the rule of law, and the effectual discarding of Roman Catholicism.

Turning to the careers of the great Elizabethan privateers and seafaring men, we are confronted at once by the problem of slavery. There is no escaping the horrible fact, whatever aspect of early Atlantic history we explore. From the very beginning, the European experiment of crossing the Atlantic was tainted by the readiness of Europeans to treat the lives of the indigenous populations of the Americas with contempt, and to use slave labour as a way of enhancing their wealth, whether in mines or plantations. Christopher Columbus himself has been described as 'a product of the new Atlantic slave-powered society'.[10] He lived for a while on Madeira with its many slaves, and he married the daughter of Bartolomé Perestrello, a fellow Genoese, who was the protégé of Henry the Navigator, the Portuguese prince who drove forward the origins of the modern Atlantic slave trade.

Shakespeare's Caliban in *The Tempest* snarls:

> This island's mine by Sycorax my mother,
> Which thou tak'st from me.

Prospero odiously counters this with:

> Thou most lying slave,
> Whom stripes may move, not kindness! I have used thee –
> Filth as thou art – with humane care.[11]

It would be comforting to say that all-knowing and all-feeling Shakespeare *sees* quite how odious Prospero's behaviour to Caliban really is, but this would be sentimental. The sad truth is that Shakespeare probably saw no more harm than did Sir John Hawkins or Sir Francis Drake in a European addressing a member of an enslaved race in this way.

The 'Difficulty', with both the question of Ireland and of the seafarers, is one of perspective. The Irish story, from the beginning, was one of unrelenting tragedy of which the Elizabethans themselves were aware. Spenser saw that, short of genocide – the replacement of the population of the island with people who were not Irish – the only alternative was English withdrawal from Ireland, with all the subsequent loss of national security when/if Ireland were in turn taken over by the French or the Spanish. Our difficulty, as moderns, is to avoid anachronistic declarations of *blame* of the Elizabethans, while not wishing to whitewash the enormity of the Irish conflict.

With the Atlantic story, the problem of perspective is surely a little different. The establishment of English colonies in the Caribbean and Virginia, and the subsequent history of the English-speaking peoples, would not have been possible without the piratical activities of Hawkins and Drake in the early decades of the reign, and their subsequent enlargement and strengthening of the Royal Navy. Although the abhorrent slave trade is something that cannot be ignored as we relive the story, the 'difficulty' here is in making it central to the story. That is our 'difficulty' of perspective. The slave trade would have been part of transatlantic history if Hawkins and Drake had never left England. Without them, however, there would not have been an English-speaking civilisation in America. For it was they, in their piratical lives – albeit in a tiny way initially – who challenged and broke the Portuguese and Spanish domination of the Atlantic and of the New World.

In 1493 the second of the Borgia popes, Alexander VI, opened a map of the world and drew a line across it. On one side of the line there was to be Portuguese dominion; on the other side of the line, Spanish. The division set a line 270 leagues west of the Cape Verde Islands, a key place for slave markets off the Guinea Coast of West Africa. The papal division was hotly contested between the Spanish and Portuguese for centuries. When John Hawkins made raids on the Cape Verde Islands in 1564, the Portuguese would have seen nothing more than a spectacularly bold individual in charge of a pirate operation. Quarter of a century later, Portuguese-Spanish domination of the Atlantic had been broken. Spain, ambivalent in its attitude towards Elizabethan England at the beginning of the reign, had become its implacable foe.

Richard Hakluyt, the geographer and chronicler of early English exploration, tells us that old William Hawkins of Plymouth had 'made the voyage to Brasill . . . in the yeere 1530'.[12] William's son John had a great seagoing exemplar in his father, the Mayor of Plymouth, and evidence from the size and wealth of his father's house that there was money to be made as a privateer. Even while Mayor of Plymouth, old William (he had a son William, as well as John) was summoned before the Privy Council to answer charges of piracy. He did not appear, and was eventually sentenced by the Admiralty Court to imprisonment unless he returned the plunder to a French ship that he had robbed.

William died in 1554. His son William became prosperous trading with the Canaries – mainly in sugar and Canary wine. John Hawkins, his brother, was twelve years his junior. In 1556, when he was twenty-four, John Hawkins seized a French ship, the *Peter*, and sailed with it to the Canaries, trading English textiles for Canary sugar with a family of Canarian merchants, the Solers. On their way home they sailed into the harbour at Santa Cruz, stole a Spanish merchant vessel and sailed it home to Plymouth.[13]

It was another family of Canarian merchants, the Pontes, who offered John Hawkins the chance to sail the slave coasts of Africa and thence to the ports of the Indies.[14] He set out from Plymouth in October 1562 with four small ships – the largest of them was the 140-ton *Salomon*. He kept his crew to a minimum, 100 men or fewer, aware of the dangers of overcrowding and sickness on a slave ship. This first trip to the West Indies was not without its hazards, but it was spectacularly successful from a commercial viewpoint. There was a second expedition, no less profitable, in 1566. At Sierra Leone, Hawkins managed to capture some half-dozen Portuguese ships, laden with slaves. He loaded one of the ships with cloves, wax, ivory, sugar, wine and coins, and this vessel was sailed home to England by Hawkins's young cousin, Francis Drake. Hawkins sailed off to the Indies with ships laden with African goods, Canary sugar and wine, and the 400 slaves. Crammed in the holds of the ships and fed on beans and water, the slaves suffered horribly. Nearly half of them died on the journey. Hawkins hastily sold as many of the survivors as possible at bargain prices to the Spanish on the Caribbean island of La Española. He was playing a dangerous game, trading on a Spanish island without a licence. Amazingly, in exchange for most of his remaining slave cargo, Hawkins sweet-talked his way into the confidence of the Spanish officer from Santo Domingo in charge of the case. Having loaded *three ships* with gold, silver, pearls, ginger, sugar, hides and other goods, Hawkins had more than he could transport to London. Even when he lost one of the vessels at Seville – it was seized as contraband – his return to Plymouth caused a sensation. The sheer scale of the booty brought handsome profits to his London investors. Another voyage was immediately planned.

This was the third 'troublesome . . . sorroweful voyadge' (Hakluyt's words) of Hawkins as a slave trader. Hakluyt wrote a somewhat 'improved' version of the tale, though quite unapologetic about the object of the voyage – which was an adventure by Englishmen who had decided 'that Negroes were very good merchandise'.[15] The Cotton MS account of the voyage is a desperate attempt at self-exculpation – but for the moral turpitude of the slave trade, a turpitude to which Hawkins and his men were blind, not for the disaster of losing the Queen's ship. The manuscript of Hawkins's frantic account was bought by Sir Robert Cotton (1571–1631) and survived (just) the fire in that antiquary's library. (It was the fire in 1731 in Ashburnham House, Dean's Yard, Westminster, where Cotton's priceless collection was then housed, that nearly destroyed our only copy of *Beowulf*!) The charred edges of the frantically written (dictated to a secretary?) pages make the manuscript itself one of the most exciting objects in the British Library. Here in the middle of modern London is this extraordinary account of Elizabethan Englishmen, afloat on the Atlantic Ocean, an utterly alien group of individuals, performing deeds of extraordinary baseness, and bravery. Unlike Hakluyt and the subsequent generations of English patriots, we would also wish to set beside this account the Spanish version of the 'troublesome voyage' – which sees the Elizabethan hero as 'Don Juan Hawkins, the enemy of God and of Our Christians'. The Ponte family, Canary merchants, were prime backers, and Queen Elizabeth herself was now an investor. She let Hawkins use one of the largest ships in her navy, the *Jesus of Lübeck*.

Henry VIII had bought the 700-ton ship from the Hanseatic League in 1545, but she had been sadly neglected during the reigns of Edward VI and Queen Mary. Ships built from newly felled timber 'began to rot from the day they were launched,'[16] and it was probably for this reason that the *Jesus* was in such a poor state. There had been talk of scuppering her in King Edward's reign, so Elizabeth's offer of the ship to piratical Hawkins need not be seen as too recklessly generous. As for the moral ambivalence of the Queen – what a good example there was of it, when she expressed the hope that when he did find slaves in Africa, they would not be carried off without their consent, a thing 'which would be detestable and call down the vengeance of heaven upon the undertakers'.[17] She cannot really have supposed that Africans would have walked aboard a slave ship willingly, but no left hand was more adept than Queen Elizabeth's at ignoring the gestures of the right. The *Jesus of Lübeck* had capacity for carrying an enormous human cargo – she was built to house a crew of 300 men.

She was a typical mid-sixteenth-century warship, and her inadequacies taught Hawkins a great deal about ships – knowledge he would put to good use in middle age when, as Treasurer of the Navy, he streamlined the ships that would defeat the Armada. The *Jesus* was broad in the beam, to provide balance for the great height of the poop and the forecastle. These two vast wooden forts, constructed at either end of the ship, were separate. Boarders could only enter the ship in the waist, which made them immediately vulnerable to crossfire between poop and forecastle. On the broadside were a few great guns. Above them, guns of medium size, and higher up yet were small firearms, mounted on a swivel and designed to fire hailshot and dice at point-blank range. There were four masts: the fore and main each carried a course and a topsail, the mizzen and bonaventure mizzen each had a single lateen sail. We can see what it looked like from a sketch in the Pepys Library at Magdalene College, Cambridge, and our modern eyes would at first take in a construction of great beauty, its pinnaces and banners fluttering from the masts, its port-holes and gun-holes making a picturesque fretwork in old German wood.

The reality of life on the *Jesus* was hellish. She began to spring leaks during the first Atlantic gale that she encountered in October 1567. Of the six ships and 400 men accompanying Hawkins on that expedition, some seventy men were destined to return. From the squadron of six ships, only the *Minion* (300 tons) and the *Judith* (50 tons) made it home.

Hawkins took his squadron to Sierra Leone. Along the way he commandeered a French pirate ship, the *Don de Dieu*. The Portuguese claim that in the neighbourhood of the Cabo Rojo and the Rio Grande he captured or looted seven Portuguese ships. He had stolen various slaves from ships encountered along the way, and in Africa itself he rounded up some 500 more for transport to America. Probably some sixty or so were lost in the course of battles and skirmishes.

The 500 or so slaves were kept in the hold of the *Jesus of Lübeck*. It was not possible to bring them on deck for necessary bodily functions, so the smell and condition down there can readily be imagined. It seems (from the various accounts of the voyage) that Hawkins sold 325 of these slaves, which leaves well over 100 lost through sickness.

Above deck, the modern reader is especially struck by two features of life on this rotting, creaking sailing ship, with its cargo of suffering humanity.

One is the unforgettable image of Hawkins himself at table, being entertained by a group of five or six musicians, playing the fiddle. The leader of the group was William Low. When he was captured by the Inquisition and incarcerated in a monastery, the friars guessed the age of this freckly English boy to be seven or eight. In fact he was twenty years old when the *Jesus* set out.

Another feature of life that we should find striking, were we to spend twenty-four hours on that 'troublesome voyage', would be the religious observances. Morning and evening prayer, a truncated version of the services in the Church of England's *Book of Common Prayer*, were strictly observed. When I say strictly, I mean that Thomas Williams, Second Mate, went round the ship with a whip driving the crew to attend the reading of the Psalms appointed for each morning and evening of the month, and a recitation of the Creed and the Lord's Prayer. On Sunday mornings they would be assembled for an hour, hearing the Epistle and Gospel of the Day, followed by a reading by Hawkins himself of the *Paraphrases* of Erasmus. When, on the *Minion*, a man was unguarded enough to make the sign of the cross before taking the helm, he was roundly abused. William Saunders, mate of the *Minion* said, 'There are on this voyage such evil papist Christians, that we cannot avoid having a pestilence visited on this Armada.'[18]

Whatever the cause, the third voyage of Hawkins from Africa to the Caribbean was indeed disastrous. By the time he left Sierra Leone he had ten ships. He managed to trade at seven ports in the Spanish Indies before a storm drove him to take refuge at San Juan de Ulúa, the port of landing for the inland journey to the city of Mexico. By now, the *Jesus* was in a terrible way.

> The *Jesus* was brought in such case that she was not able to bear the sea longer, for in her stern on either side of the sternpost the planks did open and shut with every sea. The seas . . . without number and the leaks so big as the thickness of a man's arm, the living fish did swim upon the ballast as in the sea. Our general, seeing this, did his utmost to stop her leaks, as divers times before he had . . . about her. And truly, without his great experience had been, we had been sunk in the sea in her within six days after we came out of England, and, escaping that, yet she had never been able to have been brought hither but by his industry, the which his trouble and care he had of her may be thought to be because she was the Queen's Majesty's ship and that she should not perish under his hand.'[19]

By the time the *Jesus* put in to San Juan de Ulúa, Hawkins had made unsuccessful applications to the Spanish authorities to be allowed to trade. In the Spanish pearl fishery of Borburata he had made the claim, already quoted, of personal acquaintanceship with Philip I ('I know the [King of] Spaine your mr'). In the Venezuelan port of Rió de la Hacha the Spanish governor Castellanos was told by Hawkins that he was a 'Catholic Christian', but the English buccaneers, led by Lovell (like Drake, a relative of Hawkins), commander of the *Minion*, marauded and took hostages. Hawkins left behind seventy-five sick and dying slaves by way of compensation. It was in an attempt to reach Florida that the fleet was blown off-course and compelled to take shelter at the Mexican port of San Juan de Ulúa. Once in the harbour, they were attacked by the Spaniards. Drake, in the *Judith*, did the sensible thing – he got his ship out of harbour as soon as possible, and was able to sail back to England. 'The *Judith* forsoke us in our greate miserie,' said Hawkins. Five ships of Hawkins's fleet were abandoned, four were captured and one was destroyed. Hawkins himself got away on the *Minion*, according to the Spanish Viceroy, Enríquez. Hawkins managed to escape with 'the greater part of his possessions and loot'.[20]

The greatest loss was the loss of life. Drake got home with about a dozen men on the *Judith*. Another ship in the fleet, the *William and John*, which had not accompanied them to Mexico, probably had another fifteen or twenty. And a dozen or so were on board the *Minion* with Hawkins when, on 24 January 1569, it landed in the chill of a Cornish morning at Mount's Bay. What a sight for them as they opened their frosty windows in St Michael's Mount, or in the fishing villages of Newlyn and Mousehole! In Vigo, on the Portuguese coast, a few days earlier, Hawkins and his men had come ashore. A Portuguese merchant described the appearance of this thirty-six-year-old Englishman who had been so battered and humiliated by near-shipwreck, by storms at sea, by battle and by Spanish guns. Was he bedraggled, careworn, spectral? Hawkins was, according to his Portuguese observer, 'dressed in a coat trimmed with marten skins, with cuffs of black silk. He had a scarlet cloak, edged in silver and a doublet of the same material. His cape was silk, and he wore a great gold chain around his neck.'[21]

The fates of the men who fell into the hands of the Spaniards, left behind in Mexico, were often gruesome. Some were sent to Spain. Others remained in Mexican prisons, comparatively well treated until the arrival in Mexico in 1571 of the Holy Inquisition, of which the two merciless officers were Moya de Contreras and Fernandez de Bonilla.

Eleven of the English prisoners were younger than sixteen at the time of the battle of San Juan. The Inquisitors treated the juveniles, who had been small children when Elizabeth came to the throne and had therefore had no chance of instruction in the Catholic faith, with some mercy. Miles Philips, for example, eighteen in 1572, was sentenced to three years in a Jesuit house in Mexico. But the older men were considered mature enough to be Catholics who had lapsed into heresy. They were kept for a long time in prison by the Inquisition, and in February 1574 the following sentences were pronounced: William Collins, of Oxford, age forty, seaman, ten years in the galleys; John Burton, of Bar Abbey, twenty-two, seaman, 200 lashes and six years in the galleys; John Williams, twenty-eight, of Cornwall, 200 lashes and eight years in the galleys; George Dee, thirty, seaman, 300 lashes and eight years in the galleys. The following year John Martin of Cork, otherwise known as Cornelius the Irishman, was burned at the stake.

When John Hawkins set out on his first transatlantic voyage, with its shocking cargo, Philip II of Spain, the Queen of England's brother-in-law, was inclined to see England as a potential ally against the machinations of the French. By the time of the third voyage of Hawkins, Anglo-Spanish relations were badly damaged. Neither Drake nor Hawkins can be said to have behaved well on this voyage, but they had displayed great skills as seamen, and extraordinary resourcefulness. These qualities could not alone break the power of the two mighty maritime empires, the Portuguese and the Spanish. But thanks to the Elizabethan privateers, the world was no longer simply divided, as it had been by a Borgia pope, between the Iberian superpowers. The barbarous cruelty of the Spanish Inquisition to the English sailors left behind by Hawkins in Mexico was not forgotten. Within twenty years the sea-dogs would take their revenge on the Spanish Armada. An anti-Catholic mindset remained ingrained in English national consciousness until the advent of multiculturalism in the late twentieth century. Even then it was not obliterated. Rather, instinctive hatred of religious bigotry controlled from abroad remained, with the objects of obloquy being now not Catholics so much as Muslims.

The *Jesus of Lübeck* had fallen into the hands of Spain. The image of it at sea, however, with its slaves in the hold, its velvet-clad captain at table above, and its ageless boy-musicians, remains in our mind as emblematic of its times – something we should be unlikely to encounter in any era before or after the new times ushered in by the reign of Elizabeth. Perhaps it is as good an image as any to hold in our minds as we try to focus on that most extraordinary age.

3

Ceremonial – Twixt earnest and twixt game

Elizabeth's reign began with ceremony. Even by the ritualistic standards of sixteenth-century Europe, England stood out for its love of formal ceremonies. The Venetian Ambassador to the court of Henry VIII had been astonished to see Princess Elizabeth kneel three times before her father in the course of one interview.[1] All foreign observers noted the ceremony with which the English royalty and nobility surrounded their existence. As an old lady, Elizabeth was watched passing to chapel at Greenwich, on a Sunday in 1598. 'As she went along in all this state and magnificence she spoke very graciously to foreign ministers, in English, French and Italian. Whosoever speaks to her, kneels; now and then she raises someone with her hand. Wherever she turned her face, as she was going along, every one fell on their knees.'[2]

In November 1558 it was only to be expected, then, that pageantry of the greatest possible extravagance should advertise to the people of England that an era of marvels was about to begin. National morale was low. England had just been defeated in a humiliating war against the French. Its last hold on French soil – the port of Calais – had been lost. The last Queen of England, Elizabeth's half-sister Mary, had been married to Philip II, King of Spain, and England had therefore been caught up with the Franco-Spanish rivalry that was the chief political fact of contemporary Europe. And this had not been to England's advantage. Philip, who had never been close to his wife, had not been in England for months when Mary died. There was every reason to fear that the French would press home their victory over Calais and make a bid for the English throne itself. Why not make the Dauphiness of France, Mary Stuart, Queen of England? Mary was the great-granddaughter of Henry VII, and although the will of Henry VIII, anticipating the threat of the French, forbade any foreigner from inheriting the English throne, she did at least have the claim of legitimacy; whereas Elizabeth, in many eyes, did not. Elizabeth's mother, Anne Boleyn, had given birth to her when Henry's queen, Catherine of Aragon, was yet living. Anne Boleyn's eruption into Henry VIII's heart had provoked what, for many English men and women of 1558, was the ultimate tragic disaster – the severance of the English Church from Rome, the splintering of Catholicism, the Dissolution of the monasteries, the end of the old religion. Elizabeth had been declared a bastard by the Pope, but even in English law the annulment of Henry's marriage to Catherine was highly questionable. Moreover, after the disgrace and beheading of Anne Boleyn, Elizabeth's mother, and his remarriage to Jane Seymour and the birth of Edward VI, Henry VIII had himself declared Elizabeth to be a bastard. Even though, by his will, he had declared that the succession should pass, as it did, first to Edward, then to Mary, and next (if they both died childless) to Elizabeth, the declaration of her illegitimacy had never been revoked in law. There was much debate among the lawyers and political classes about the wisdom of raising this matter in Parliament. Apart from the considerable danger of enraging the new monarch (and she was Henry VIII's daughter, quite capable of flying into rages and dispatching her subjects to the block), there was also the propaganda danger of rehearsing her technical illegitimacy. Nicholas Bacon, the Lord Keeper, decreed that the 'Crowne, once worne, taketh away all defects whatsoever'.[3]

Yet if the Protestantism that had been brought in by Anne Boleyn's adultery scandalised the Catholic majority, the attempt at a Counter-Reformation by Henry's daughter Mary Tudor, during her short reign (1553–8) had antagonised many of her subjects. Against the advice of her husband, she had introduced the hated heresy-hunts of the Inquisition, and more than 300 people had been roasted alive for their thought-crimes. There must have been very many conservative-minded English men and women in 1553 who had their doubts about the Reformation; who regarded Sir Thomas More, Lord Chancellor of England, as a fine man who had been wrongly executed by King Henry; who deplored the wreckage of the monasteries, and even more, detested the bullying persecution of such saintly figures as the monks of the London Charterhouse; who yet disliked the fanaticism of continental Calvinists and missed the outward trappings of old Catholic England – May poles, Mystery Plays, Corpus Christi processions – and who felt revulsion at the human bonfires of Smithfield. Mary Tudor, in her zeal for the Catholic faith of the Counter-Reformation, made many a convert to the fledgling Church of England.

Yet, as the young Queen Elizabeth knew, and her close advisers perhaps knew even better, she was a ruler of questionable legitimacy, becoming the queen of a realm divided against itself. The ceremonies that were put in hand from the very hour of her accession were therefore designed to reinforce in the populace a sense of reassurance, a sense of national unity, a sense of her sacred place in the life of a revivified nation.

The news came to her at Hatfield House in Hertfordshire, some twenty miles from the capital. It was 17 November 1558. Elizabeth Tudor was twenty-five years old: she had been born at Greenwich on 7 September 1533. Her appearance is more familiar, perhaps, than any other character in English history, and one of the reasons for this is that her ritualised portraits were painted so often, and their messages were so carefully plotted. The coronation portrait, for example, of which a copy survives in London's National Portrait Gallery, shows her holding orb and sceptre, and crowned in state. Her robe is emblazoned with Tudor roses. This is a picture that is almost all regalia. It is stating her claim to continue the dynasty begun by her 'good grandfather', as she called him (not everyone would have applied that epithet to the brilliantly devious Welshman Henry Tudor), Henry VII. But the regalia are not all that we remember from the portrait. We remember the long, red-gold hair, fine and loose over her ermine-clad shoulders. We remember the very distinctive long, white hands (the genes shared with Mary, Queen of Scots produced the same attractive feature, which often seems to accompany high intelligence); and there is the face. She was very recognisably Henry VIII's daughter, with the same aquiline nose, the same shape of brow; but the shape of the face, long and oval, was much more like her mother, Anne Boleyn. Whereas Anne had been dark and sallow, however, Elizabeth had all the Tudor Welsh lightness of skin. One observer – Robert Johnston in *Historia Rerum Britannicarum* – noted that her skin was more than white, it was of a glowing paleness. Her eyes were golden, too, and large-pupilled from short-sight – exacerbated from much reading. She read and spoke fluently in Latin, Greek, French, Spanish, Italian and English and had a little Welsh.

This was a formidably clever, and slightly frightening, young person who had never fully opened her heart to anyone – not to her terrifying monster of a father; not to Catherine Parr, who had been such a wise stepmother, and certainly not to Parr's reprehensible husband Thomas Seymour, whose scandalous cuddlings and attempts to make love to the young princess had caused public outrage. Nor had Elizabeth ever opened her heart to her brother, her sister or her tutors. From the moment of her accession she would rely, with a mixture of profound intelligence, flirtatious recklessness and Welsh canniness, on a succession of differing, nearly always male, advisers. But there was never one person who could claim to be her sole educator, her one love or her only counsellor. The deftly captured coronation portrait by Guillim Stretes, though it survives only in a copy, reveals a face that is alive with intelligence. England – like most other countries – has flourished when governed by intelligent people. Queen Victoria's prime ministers, from Peel to Salisbury, were some of the cleverest men in the country. The only other period of comparable expansion and prosperity in English history is the reign of Elizabeth, when the head of state, and her surrounding court, were first-class brains.

By the time the Council had reached Hatfield, Elizabeth was waiting for them – the 'news' having evidently been broken to her by an earlier outrider. She was walking in the park, and stood beneath a leafless oak when they told her that she was the Queen of England. She knelt down in the grass and said, '*A domino factum est et mirabile in oculis nostris*', a quotation from the 118th Psalm – 'It is the Lord's doing and it is marvellous in our eyes.' When she stood, the councillors could see that she was 'indifferent tall, slender and straight.'

As well as being one of the most intellectually accomplished rulers who had ever occupied the throne of England, Elizabeth was also gifted with a peculiar political intelligence and the ability to empathise with, and understand, and manipulate, crowds. Her poor sister Mary, with her rather gruff mannish voice, her poor skin, her tiny eyes and her shyness, totally lacked these qualities. She had never engaged with the People at all. From the moment of her appearing in the London streets, Elizabeth knew how to work the crowd. The economy of England had been left, by Mary Tudor's incompetence and by the failures in the French wars, in a terrible condition. There were debts of more than £266,000[4]. Elizabeth – one of her least amiable characteristics – was extremely parsimonious and 'retentive', unwilling to spend, even when national emergency depended upon it. But in this matter of selling herself to the people, she was prepared to part with more than £20,000 for the ceremonies alone. Yet it is not fair to think of her solely as a skinflint in economic terms. Early in the reign, 1560–1, she would issue a new coinage, which restored the value of the currency.[5] Walsingham considered this her finest achievement.

Six days after her accession there was the first of the great processions, from Hatfield to London. It was a cavalcade of more than a thousand people. She stayed a fortnight at Lord North's House and, among other things, received the foreign ambassadors. It was here that she received, via Gomez Suarez de Figuerosa, Count de Feria, the Spanish Ambassador, a proposal of marriage from her brother-in-law, the King of Spain. She could have done worse than accept this honour. It would have avoided much political speculation, and it would have aligned England with the greatest power in the world against France, the second-greatest. But she declined the honour. When de Feria expressed Philip's hope that she would be very careful in her handling of religion, she gave the equivocal reply that it would be very bad of her to forget God, who had been so good to her. So Catholics and Protestants were left none the wiser about the direction of her religious policy.

When she met the judges of England, she proclaimed, 'Have a care over my people . . . they are my people. Every man oppresseth them and spoileth them without mercy. They cannot revenge their quarrel nor help themselves. See unto them, see unto them, for they are my charge'.[6]

Then, on 28 November, she moved in slow procession, so that as many Londoners as possible could see her, from Lord North's house to the Tower – her old prison, now her bastion. The journey was broken by several pauses.

When the Recorder of London presented her with a purse containing 1,000 gold marks, she said:

> I thank my Lord Mayor, his brethren and you all. And whereas your request is that I shall continue your good lady and Queen, be ye ensured that I will be as good unto you as ever Queen was unto her people. No will in me can lack, neither do I trust shall there lack any power. And persuade yourselves that for the safety and quietness of you all I will not spare if need be to spend my blood. God thank you all.[7]

What made this an electrifying speech was that it was true. Elizabeth, like her father, was every inch a political creature. She could be devious, stubborn, difficult. But (unlike her political rival, Mary, the Scottish queen) she was in many ways very straightforward. She did, passionately, want to be the queen of England, to be a good queen; and it was her primary wish. She would do anything to be a good queen, and she did have the interests of the country at heart. One of the reasons for her prodigious success as a political ruler was that she would undoubtedly have been prepared to die in order to be queen in her own way and on her own terms. Her own mother had died on the block. She knew that she was living in an age when this would be the price of failure – either a failure to keep at bay the threat of foreign invasion, or the failure to stave off any rival claimants to the throne. She was lucky enough to have only one plausible rival, in Mary.

By open chariot she was driven to Cripplegate, preceded by the Lord Mayor, who carried her sceptre, and by the Garter King of Arms beside him; next came Lord Pembroke, carrying the sword of state in a gold scabbard laden with pearls. Then the sergeants-at-arms surrounding the tall, pale redhead, who was dressed in a purple velvet riding habit. At fixed points along the route children's choirs burst into song. In the distance, the roar of cannon had already begun to thunder out from the Tower. The first splash of pageantry, and the first showing of herself to the people, had been triumphantly successful. They loved her.

From the Tower she sent her favourite, and childhood friend, Lord Robert Dudley, to the mathematician and astrologer Dr John Dee to determine the most propitious day for her coronation. The answer came back from the Sage of Mortlake that it should be held on 15 January 1559.

Before the crowning itself in Westminster Abbey, there was a series of highly elaborate pageants and ceremonies in the City of London, designed as ritualised manifestos for the coming reign.[8] Lest the meaning of these ceremonies should be missed, the Corporation of London – largely Protestant, and representative of the mercantile class who would determine how well the country came out of the grave financial crisis of Mary's reign – commissioned the MP for Carlisle, Richard Mulcaster, to write an account of them. Mulcaster, an Old Etonian and a Renaissance humanist, whom we shall meet in a later chapter as an eminent grammarian and educationalist, was paid forty shillings for his work, which was first published nine days after the coronation and was so popular that it was reprinted soon afterwards. The publisher was Richard Tottel, who paid the licence fee of two shillings and fourpence to print the work, at the Hand and Star, situated on Fleet Street within the Temple Bar. Throughout the Tudor period, but especially in the reign of Elizabeth, publication was strictly under the control of the state and nothing could be printed without licence. *The Passage of our most drad Soveraigne Lady Quene Elyzabeth through the citie of London to Westminster the day before her coronacion* gives us the most vivid sense not only of those heady few days, but also of the huge importance to the Elizabethans of ceremonial. Shakespeare's Henry V could ask before his Coronation, 'And what art thou, thou idol ceremony?' Cranmer, at the coronation of the nine-year-old Edward VI, could remind the adults present that the oil of anointing 'if added is but a ceremony'.[9] But the Elizabethans, and especially the Protestants, who were inventing new ceremonies rather than merely re-enacting the medieval ceremonials of the Church, rediscovered the enormous importance of ritual.

In his pageant allegory-poem about his own age, *The Faerie Queene*, Edmund Spenser describes the coronation of Una in Booke One:

> Then on her head they sett a girlond greene
> And crowned her twixt earnest and twixt game.[10]

This is the perfect phrase for the successful use of ceremony which has marked its place in English public life from the reign of the first Queen Elizabeth to the reign of the second. There is always a small element of playfulness in it, so that, for example, the Victorian lampoons of public ceremony in the operettas of Gilbert and Sullivan are only just lampoons, and are certainly nothing so strong as satire. They merely bring out some of the inherent absurdity in rituals that are 'but a ceremony'. Nevertheless, ceremonies can make statements which remain in the memory, which stir the eye and the heart. And this was something that Queen Elizabeth I and her advisers understood through and through.

Mulcaster's *The Passage of . . . Quene Elizabeth* presents Elizabeth's ride through London, with its many pauses to watch plays and tableaux, as a piece of theatre, 'So that if a man should say well, he could not better tearme the citie of London that time, than a stage wherein was showed the wonderfull spectacle of a noble hearted princesse toward her most loving people.' So she set off, this consummate actress and political genius, on the afternoon of Saturday, 14 January 1559, from the Tower of London. She was dressed in a cloth-of-gold robe. Her hair streamed over her shoulders. On her head she wore a small circlet of gold. She sat on cloth-of-gold cushions in a rich, satin-lined litter, open at all sides with a canopy at the top, carried by the four barons of the Cinque Ports. As she entered the City by Fenchurch Street she was greeted by the first pageant, a child in costly apparel, welcoming her from a 'richely furnished' stage. Then, on to Gracechurch Street, where she saw a pageant of the uniting of the Houses of Lancaster and York. This highly elaborate display depicted the Queen's descent. It had representations of her father Henry VIII, her mother Anne Boleyn and herself, wearing the Imperial Crown. And on it went, and at each stopping post, attended by huge crowds, there would be a little play or display, here representing the Virtues, there the Beatitudes in St Matthew's Gospels. At the Little Conduit at the bottom of Cheapside there had been erected two hills. On one was a ruinous state – a *Respublica Ruinosa*. On the other, a well-founded state, the *Respublica bene instituta*, there was a cave. Old Father Time came out of the cave, leading his daughter Truth. This child presented Elizabeth with a Bible on which was inscribed '*Verbum Veritatis*' – the Word of Truth.

Mulcaster, in his commentary on all these events, was intent to bring out their meaning for the readers. It is Mulcaster, and not the script of the pageant (which survives), who brings out the Protestantism of this scene – that it is an English Bible.

> When the childe had thus ended his speache, he reached hys boke towards the Quene's majestie, which a little before, Trueth had let downe unto him from the hill, whiche by maister Parrat was received, and delivered unto the Quene. But she as soone as she had received the booke, kissed it, and with both her hands held up the same, and so laid it upon her brest, with great thankes to the cities therefore'.[11]

Like the great schoolmaster he was to become, Mulcaster made the 'passage' a learning process, not only for the readers, and for the crowds witnessing the ceremonies, but also for the Queen herself, who, in his narrative, does not move on from one spectacle to the next until she makes it clear that she has grasped its meaning.

Moreover, this series of secular pageants – seen by a far greater number than those who would file into the Abbey to witness the coronation – provided intelligible ceremonial with a very distinct religious and political agenda: Elizabeth, in all her new and gorgeous garment majesty, was to be the protectress of the rising generation of the Protestant mercantile class; she would support learning, she would uphold virtue and justice. The highly popular text is not propaganda. It was a manifesto that one very powerful, and very new, section of society was presenting to the Queen and hoping she would follow. Mulcaster is distinctly a parliamentarian rationalist humanist. For example, in the pageant representing the Old Testament judge Deborah, the chronicler Richard Grafton sees it as signifying Deborah's gender – 'This was made to encourage the Quene not to feare though she were a woman: For women by the spirite and power of Almightye God, haue ruled both honourably and politiquely, and that a great tyme, as did Debora, whiche was there sett forth in Pageant'; but Mulcaster interpreted the pageant to mean that Deborah was a good ruler who listened to her parliaments.

Elizabeth was quite intelligent enough to realise that monarchy, even that of an absolute monarch such as herself, was a matter of contract. It was not possible for one individual to impose her will on the people unless she were to carry with her a sufficient group of the Powerful, and unless she had the good will of the people too. The crucial few weeks and months at the beginning of her reign triumphantly made her popular with the people of London, and she would be able to exercise this charm over crowds throughout her reign. She was a monarch much on the move, showing herself to the people; and had she ever travelled north of the Trent, the story of her reign might have been very different. Her often-vaunted popularity, which is widely attested, whenever she appeared before crowds, was a southern phenomenon. Protestantism, if that is a satisfactory word for the religion that the City of London hoped she would espouse and promote, was primarily a religion of the South.

The ceremony of the coronation itself in the Abbey would provide the first test, and a very crucial test, of how Elizabeth could reconcile the warring Protestants, who had supported the full-blown continental-style Reformation of Edward VI's reign, and the Roman Catholics, who had rejoiced at the return of the Latin Mass, and perhaps even rejoiced at the smell of roasting human flesh and the screams of dying heretics who were burned alive near the butchers' market in Smithfield. This most contentious question lay at the nub of the Abbey service. Would it be

Roman Catholic? Would it be Protestant? Would the new Queen show her hand?

The Archbishop of Canterbury, Reginald Pole, had died shortly after Mary Tudor and not been replaced. The Archbishop of York, Nicholas Heath, had declined to crown her. The ceremonies were in the hands of the Bishop of Carlisle, Owen Oglethorpe. Already at Christmas there had been something of a stir in the Royal Chapel. The Mass had been conducted in the traditional form, in Latin; but the Queen had left in the middle – at the Offertory.

She could scarcely walk out halfway through the coronation ceremony. Here was an occasion when she would have to make clear, in emblematic and symbolic style, whether she intended to preserve the old religion or go with the Reformers. She had given Oglethorpe various directions for adapting the ceremony. The Epistle and the Gospel were to be read in English as well as Latin. With this stipulation, the Bishop complied. He was also told that he must not elevate the Host at the time of Consecration: that is, at the moment of the Mass when traditionally minded people might have believed that the bread changed its substance and became the Body of Christ, Oglethorpe was not to hold it up for veneration. He defied Elizabeth in this request. But where was she while he was doing it? At this point in the ceremony she had withdrawn into the Closet, a curtained area in the transept of the Abbey where she would receive Communion. Such is the Welsh ambiguity of Elizabeth's situation that to this day no one quite knows what happened at this stage of the ceremony, with some maintaining that she did receive Communion, but in both kinds – that is, she received both the Host and the Chalice (Roman Catholic custom decreeing that she should only receive the Host); others maintaining that she did not receive Communion at all.[12]

She had managed to get away with a coronation ceremony which gave out the signals that she wanted the people to read, and not the signals that the Church wanted. That is, the coronation said: I am your Sovereign Lady the Queen. I shall maintain the stability and strength of the realm, and as for religion – well, wait and see. Was there really so much difference between my coronation Mass and that of my sister? Would the skies really fall if I continue to maintain the religion of my father Henry VIII – Catholicism without the Pope?

These were the cunning questions posed by the coronation ceremony of Queen Elizabeth I.

An older school of historical and political thinking liked to speak as if the Protestant Establishment, or Queen Elizabeth herself, somehow cunningly substituted the Cult of the Virgin Mary for the Cult of the Virgin Queen, offering to the Mariolatrous multitude the worship of

Elizabeth as a substitute for Our Lady of Walsingham, rather as addicts in 'rehab' might be offered methadone as way of breaking the heroin habit. The picture suggests, perhaps, a populace that is more docile than any crowd has ever been.

What happened was perhaps more subtle, and more interesting. From the very beginning, the ceremonial surrounding Elizabeth became ever more inventive. It became a way of expressing what the Queen and those around her hoped was going to grow out of the reign. It grew out of reading, and it also grew, as it were, organically – the ceremonies of tilt, masque, procession and drama having an almost organic life of their own: what 'worked' on one ceremonial occasion becoming part of the repertoire and feeding the mythology, the symbolism. So Elizabeth, in portraiture, in drama, masque, political pamphlets and songs, was to become Cynthia, the Moon Goddess, she would be Diana the Virgin Huntress, she would be Gloriana and Belphoebe.

From pagan times, Europeans had believed in Four Ages of history. Ovid tells of them in his *Metamorphoses*, for example: the Golden Age was that of humanity's springtime; followed by a Silver Age, a Brass Age and an Age of Iron, when war, tyranny and chaos were unleashed upon the historical scene. During this Iron Age, the Virgin Justice left the Earth and took up her position in the sky as the constellation Virgo. Spenser in *The Fairie Queene*, during the procession of the months, tells us:

The sixt was August, being rich arrayd
In garment all of gold downe to the ground
Yet rode he not, but led a lovely Mayd
Forth by the lilly hand, the which was cround
With eares of corne, and full her hand was found;
That was the righteous Virgin, which of old
Liv'd here on earth, and plenty made abound;
But after Wrong was lov'd and Justice solde,
She left th' vnrighteous world and was to heauen extold.[13]

Astraea, the Virgin symbol of Justice, was also a figure of Empire. In the many ceremonial ways in which Elizabeth presented herself, and in which the people responded to her, they wished to see her as the Virgin who had left the Earth with the coming of the Age of Iron. Her reign would usher in a time of righteousness and justice, but also of 'British Empire' – it was the age in which this phrase was first used, and it was a coinage of her astrologer, Dr Dee.

So, rather than thinking of the pageants as some kind of con-trick played on the people, or as a substitute for religion, it is perhaps more helpful to think of them as an extraordinarily public display, in that age of displays, of England's emerging self-consciousness; England being guided in part by the acute intelligence of its monarch. It is England set to music, England tripping a fantastic dance, England making a tableau. Into this picture of a country coming to life – after a century of civil war, confusion, economic depression – comes this vision of a young Virgin Sovereign who can lead it on to a different existence: an existence where it expands beyond the seas, where it plumbs new areas of learning, where it builds great houses, where it pioneers new literary forms. Much of the ritual was done as a conscious parody of, or imitation of, the imperialist rituals surrounding the Emperor Charles V on the continent,[14] but this was itself a revelation: rather than seeing itself as dependent upon the great empires of the world, Elizabethan England saw itself as a fledgling empire.

Elizabeth, with her ceremonies, her tournaments, her progresses, brought a palpable sense of optimism to her people, an extraordinary sense that, as a whole, the nation was now capable of creativity and expansion that had somehow previously not been possible.

This was apparent with the Accession Day Tilts, which became an annual ceremony every November of the reign. On these occasions, every detail was charged with symbolism. The colours worn by the Queen for masques and pageants would have had significance. Red symbolised prowess, yellow joy, white innocence, green hope . . .[15] The jewels presented to the Queen by courtiers, especially the jewels given as New Year gifts, reflected the classical origins of her cult – a miniature by Nicholas Hilliard shows her wearing a jewelled crescent moon in her hair, to show her as Diana the Virgin Huntress; Sir Francis Drake once gave the Queen a fan 'of fethers, white and red, the handle of gold inamuled, with a halfe moone of mother-of-perles, within that a halfe moone garnished with sparkes of dyamondes, and a few seede perles on thone side, having her Majesties picture within it, and on the backside a device with a crowe over it'. Once again, the crescent moon emphasising her virgin status. Other mythological subjects reflected in her jewellery would have been Elizabeth as Astraea, or Elizabeth as a Vestal Virgin.

In the Second Book of Sidney's revised *Arcadia* we read of the elaborate annual jousts held on the anniversary of the marriage of the Iberian queen. Young knights from the court of Queen Helen arrive. Of her, we are told:

> For being brought by right of birth, a woman, a yong woman, a faire woman, to governe a people, in nature mvtinously prowde, and always

> before so used to hard governours, as they knew not how to obey without the sworde were drawne. Yet could she for some years, so carry her selfe among them, that they found cause in the delicacie of her sex, of admiration, not contempt; and which was notable, even in the time that many countries were full of wars . . . yet so handled shee the matter, that the threatens ever smarted in the threatners . . . For by continuall martiall exercises without bloud, she made them perfect in that bloudy art.[15]

Sidney was describing in more or less precise detail the tilts in which he himself took part and which were choreographed by his friend Sir Henry Lee, the Queen's Champion – who appears in the *Arcadia* as Lelius. The games were indeed a paradoxical expression of a 'bloudy art' for peaceable means. The Elizabethan governing classes – the aristocracy, the gentry, the higher clergy, the emerging merchant class, the universities – were all united with their queen in wanting to live in peace and prosperity. There were a number of significant threats to this hope: from Ireland, from Scotland, from France, and ultimately from Spain. But the greatest threat was from within. As Shakespeare's great historical dramas would rehearse in the last decade of the reign, England had taken a long time to learn how to be governed. Tudor statecraft had been a hit-and-miss affair with King Edward, much of the time, a child monarch ruled by rival aristocratic cliques every bit as dangerous and unpopular as those who fought in the fifteenth-century civil wars. Mary's reign had been a disaster of a rather different kind – Mary just was a very bad queen, with poor advisers and worse luck: under her supervision, Ireland erupted into even worse chaos than usual, the French war was lost, the populace at large was poised for a civil war on religious lines. The pageantry of Elizabeth's reign, from the very beginning, wanted to say that a new page had been turned. But it would require great patience and skill to emerge from the mistakes of the past. Governance was an art, and much would depend upon Elizabeth's choice of political advisers.

4

Men in Power

One of the most celebrated titles of a sixteenth-century prose work is John Knox's *The First Blast of the Trumpet against the Monstrous Regiment of Women*. Indeed, it is one of those works, such as *On Grand Central Station I Sat Down and Wept*, whose titles are so powerful that the contents could never hope to match their promise. Rendered into modern English, the phrase 'Monstrous Regiment of Women' would be 'the unnatural government of women'. For what John Knox was arguing was that the very idea of allowing a woman to rule over men is unnatural – monstrous. 'To promote a woman to bear rule, superiority, dominion, or empire above any realm, nation or city is repugnant to nature, contumely to God, a thing most contrarious to His revealed will and approved ordinance and finally, it is the subversion of good order, of all equity and justice.'[1]

John Knox (*c*.1514–72), a Scottish clergyman, born at Giffordgate, Haddington (near Edinburgh), was a clever controversialist whose eloquence had so impressed the Duke of Northumberland in 1551 that the Protector had him appointed a chaplain to King Edward VI. Knox was offered the bishopric of Rochester, but turned it down, and while in England he never relented in his zeal to make the court, and the new National Church, conform more fanatically to the Calvinist norms of Geneva. He tried to outlaw the custom of kneeling to receive Holy Communion, but the moderate Archbishop of Canterbury, Thomas Cranmer, quietly insisted that this devotional custom remained. (Cranmer aptly described Knox and friends as 'unquiet spirits').[2]

Naturally, when Catholic Mary I came to the throne of England, Knox was obliged to go abroad, where, among a large expatriate community of discontented English and Scottish Protestants, first in Frankfurt, later in Geneva, he poured forth a flood of sermons and controversial prose works. (While in Geneva, he came to realise 'how small was my learning' and began a study of Greek and Hebrew.[3])

While Scotland (and especially today's Scottish Nationalists) will continue to debate Knox's legacy in his native land – weighing, for example, his encouragement of education against the unfortunate stereotyping of Presbyterian fervour, which Knox's rants encouraged – he will always be, for the rest of the world, the man who wrote *The First Blast of the Trumpet*; the man who took on, and beat, Mary, Queen of

Scots; who denounced with equal and impartial loathing her mother-in-law, the Scottish regent, Mary of Guise, and her namesake and cousin, Queen Mary Tudor – 'Our mischievous Maries' as he called them. Whereas Deborah, the female Judge of Israel in the Bible was a ruler 'under whom were strangers chased out of Israel', the mischievous Maries had *delivered* their respective countries into strangers' hands. 'England, for satisfying the inordinate appetites of that cruel monster Mary (unworthy by reason of her bloody tyranny of the name of a woman), betrayed, alas, to the proud Spaniard; and Scotland, by the rash madness of foolish governors and by the practices of a crafty dame, resigned likewise, under the title of marriage, into the power of France.'[4]

Knox wrote his diatribe in Dieppe, and it was published in 1558. Hindsight might suggest that he was unfortunate with his timing. He published his denunciation of female governance in the very year that England gained as its ruler Elizabeth I, perhaps the most successful, the most triumphantly intelligent, ruler the country ever had. You might add to that judgement the postscript that the two periods of history in which England enjoyed not merely commercial and cultural prosperity, but something akin to pure glory, were the long reigns of two women: Elizabeth and Victoria.

But in 1558 most dispassionate readers of Knox's pamphlet, whether Catholic or Protestant, while perhaps smiling at its intemperate mode of expression, would have found its arguments persuasive. The regency of Mary of Guise had been a disastrous period for Scotland. As for England, five years of Mary Tudor's reign had brought a catastrophic war with France, the humiliation of the loss of Calais (until then an English outpost on the continent) and a period of gruesome religious persecution – with its 300 Protestant martyrs burned for heresy – which for many Christians in England, and for many generations, would make not merely the King or the Inquisition of Spain, and not merely the Pope, but the very notion of Catholicism a hated thing. Militarily vanquished, diplomatically disgraced, socially divided, spiritually in torment, England after five years of female rule did not have any reason to doubt Knox's views.

There would be few today, outside the worlds of Islam or extreme Christian evangelicalism, who would endorse Knox's view that 'woman in her greatest perfection was *made* to serve and obey man, not to rule and command him'.[5]

For that reason, we need to remind ourselves that on this point, however much they deplored Knox's intemperate and revolutionary views of the Church, his contemporaries were very largely agreed. It was against nature – in their view – for women to rule men. Moreover, as modern feminist history shows, Knox, far from being reactionary, was in the vanguard of political thought here. The early Renaissance had, in a few enlightened areas, foreseen a feminist future, whereas the realpolitik of the seventeenth century very decidedly put a stop to this. So at the turn of the fifteenth century Christine de Pisan (born in Venice around 1364) could envisage in *Le Livre de la cité des dames* a great city of ladies built entirely by and for women. But 250 years later the feminist aspirations of Anne Marie-Louise d'Orléans, Duchesse de Montpensier, could only conjure up, in her letters with Françoise Bertaut de Motteville, a rural republic where she could rule as queen (the correspondence dates from 1660–1). Whereas Queen Mary I ruled (however badly) as a monarch in her own right (1553–8), Queen Mary II refused any settlement that did not make her husband, William of Orange, King in 1689. She ruled as the 'and Mary' appendage in 'William and Mary'. Queen Christina of Sweden abdicated in 1654 in favour of a man. Queen Elizabeth I named a male as her successor. When Knox wrote in 1558, he was setting an agenda that history would follow. Elizabeth was the great exception to a rule that Western society would, broadly speaking, endorse until the generation of Margaret Thatcher and Golda Meyer.[6]

There is, moreover, one crucial sense in which Elizabeth's reign was a paradoxical vindication of Knox's *First Blast*. We can smile at what appears to be Knox's grotesquely poor timing, in sounding his *First Blast* in a year that saw the beginning of the great Elizabeth's political success story. We can smile further when we read that Knox was surprised that Queen Elizabeth did not appreciate his pamphlet. 'He had advanced proofs from scripture; if they were invalid, let them be answered. If not, as he wrote to her in 1559, "Why that youre grace be offendit at the authore of such ane work, I can perceive no just occasion."'[7]

But in one sense Elizabeth was to take the message of Knox's argument very seriously. For Knox – as for all Elizabeth's political advisers, every member of her government, her councils and her parliaments – the word 'woman' meant, in practical terms, someone married to a man. Even if it did not mean precisely this, it denoted one who could, potentially, be married to a man. Because they were obsessed with the succession question, and dreaded the prospect of another Wars of the Roses, with different factions dividing England with civil conflict about the most basic question of who was in charge, these men saw the young Princess Elizabeth as breeding stock. The body that had been clothed in gold and set upon a throne in January 1559 was not simply a political leader. It was a womb that could be filled with a safe succession of Protestant and, it was to be hoped, male heirs, who could confirm the reformation of Church and state begun by Henry VIII, confirmed by Edward VI and interrupted with such calamitous effect by Mary I.

One of the persistent themes of Knox's political pamphlets is that royal marriages, so often contracted with foreign princes, allow the foreign power to usurp that of the native-born. 'Yet most of their glory be transferred to the house of a stranger', as he put it, not in the *First Blast*, but in his belligerent *Letter to the Regent of Scotland* – that is, to the mother of Mary, Queen of Scots. Scotland, thanks to the death of James V and the marriage of the surviving daughter to the Dauphin of France, was doubly linked to Catholic France and the House of Guise. England, because of the marriage of 'that cursed Jezebel' to the Habsburg King of Spain, was likewise automatically subservient.

All manner of reasons have been adduced for Elizabeth's refusal to marry. They have ranged from the psychological to the brutally anatomical. It has been (plausibly) noted that the daughter of a six-times-married tyrant would not have had a happy role model to follow into the married state, not least when we remember that her own mother's head had been chopped off. The dread of penetration that has been attributed to Elizabeth must remain a matter of (rather pointless) speculation. That she was, as she so often claimed to be, a lifelong virgin must be accepted as the overwhelmingly probable truth. To remain unmarried had, for her, two powerful political advantages.

First, for all her protestations of love for England, which were no doubt genuine as far as they went, she could always feel, for as long as she was single: *après moi, le déluge*. If England was to have not merely stability, but the sort of stability glimpsed by the Protestant new money, by the 9,000-and-more-strong clergy, by the squires and the merchants, which had begun to come to them with the Reformation, they needed *her*. The very precariousness of the fact – that her death could plunge the country into total anarchy – enormously increased her personal political significance. And if she died and if the anarchy came, then that would be England's nightmare, not the dead Elizabeth's.

For as long as she lived, however, she was guided by the very same argument that lay at the basis of Knox's *First Blast*. 'Wonder it is that the advocates and patrons of the right of our ladies did not consider and ponder this law before that they counselled the blind princes and unworthy nobles of their countries to betray the liberties thereof into the hands of strangers.'[8] This was something Elizabeth would never do. There is almost an echo of Knox's *First Blast* in Elizabeth's great speech at the time of the Armada, when she had been on the throne thirty years. For political purposes she would have the spirit and stomach of a man – virginity would allow her, in effect, to be a man; to hold men at home in constant suspense, and to hold the princes of Europe at bay.

With a flair that still dazzles at a distance of five centuries, Elizabeth, aged twenty-five, while using all the charm and caprice of a clever young woman, decided to rule *as if she were a man.* 'I know I have the body of a weak and feeble woman but I have the heart and stomach of a King.' It would take maturity and a great national crisis in the summer of 1588, when she had reigned thirty years, to bring forth these words. But they had always been true, and the weak and feeble woman paid a great price for possessing that King's heart and stomach. The very sight of other women having husbands and children was sometimes enough to drive her into frenzies of jealousy and rage. She would say that she wanted to marry, and she would passionately, as a weak and feeble woman, mean it. Yet the King whom she became – and . . . 'a King of England, too' – would not allow her to weaken.

All successful political leaders in history, from Julius Caesar to Napoleon, have based their success on believing themselves to be in touch with the *people*, and this Elizabeth did with extraordinary panache from the very beginning. But she also had the politician's instinct for knowing how the business of government worked. The progresses and visits to different parts of the country, as well as defraying the expenses of the court, enabled her to visit as many areas as possible (in the South), and actually to be seen by as many of her people – I nearly wrote her 'public' – as possible. As we shall see at the end of this part of the book, when the magic failed to work and her public did not adore her, she behaved with paranoid ruthlessness.

The system worked, in England and in Wales. Both monarch and people knew that. For as long as the peace held, at home and abroad, England was, in the Prayer Book words, 'godly and quietly governed'. The country at large was administered by the gentry and the landowners. By modern standards the population was tiny. Even by medieval standards it was small. (The Black Death reduced a population of 4.5–6 million inhabitants to 2 million. In 1547, the year Henry VIII died, it was still only 2.8 million, rising to around 4 million by the close of Elizabeth's reign in 1603).[9] Most of this population was rural. The instruments of control, apart from hunger and the need to work, were found in local law-enforcement – the parish constables – Shakespeare's Dogberry and the Justices of the Peace, the Justice Shallows. The country was in effect administered by these Justices, who were usually squires, small landowners, owing their allegiance in quasi-feudal fashion to the greater landowners.

Parliament was an important element in Elizabethan governance, but we should not imagine that they had a parliamentary system of government such as began to develop in the following century. 'Parliaments were called for only the greatest occasions and purposes; at the accession of the sovereign, to give warrant for some great change in national policy, as for example, in religion, or to give support in waging war, and always for the purpose of voting supplies.[10]

The England of Elizabeth was governed by its Council. At the end of Mary's reign this had numbered thirty-nine. Elizabeth immediately reduced this number by twenty. Of the nineteen Council members, she retained only ten who had served her sister. Committed Roman Catholics were excluded. She kept seven great noblemen: the Marquess of Winchester, the Earls of Arundel, Derby, Pembroke and Shrewsbury, Lord Clinton and Howard of Effingham. The peerage of Elizabethan England was small and, unlike her father, Elizabeth created very few new noblemen. Of the 250 or so peerages (many of the titles held by the same person), seventy-three were Scottish peerages and thirty-six were Irish; so in reality there were only about 150 noblemen in Elizabethan England.[11]

It was a small country governed by a tiny élite.

The principal officer of Elizabeth's state and household was the Lord Chancellor, Nicholas Bacon in 1558 (succeeded in turn by Sir Thomas Bromley in 1579, Christopher Hatton in 1587, Sir John Puckering in 1592 and Sir Thomas Egerton in 1596). Many Elizabethan Lords Chancellor also occupied the great medieval administrative office of Lord Keeper of the Great Seal.

The major change that Elizabeth made to the way the country was governed was in her elevation of the status of Principal Secretary. Until 1558 this had been an office of the royal household and was not necessarily of any political significance. Elizabeth gave this office to her trusted friend William Cecil and thereafter the Secretary became 'the natural channel for exercising the Queen's prerogative for superintending communications between the Crown and the Privy Council and for co-ordinating the activities of the Queen's foreign secretaries and ambassadors, becoming in effect the Secretary of State for Foreign Affairs'.[12]

This meant, in practice, that from the moment of her accession Elizabeth was an absolute monarch and, for that reason, near-absolute power was exercised by the men in whom she placed the greatest trust.

Two men, from the very beginning of the reign, were of central importance to Elizabeth, and to the Elizabethan Age. Both men were present at Hatfield House to watch Queen Mary's seal of office, the great emblem of authority, being surrendered, the day after the accession, to the new Queen. But both men, as well as being extremely strong characters in their own rights, were emblems. One was William Cecil, who had already been working as secretary to the twenty-five-year-old Elizabeth for weeks at Hatfield House. He would become her Secretary in office and would remain at the heart of office and power in Elizabethan England for the next forty years. The other was Robert Dudley, a young nobleman who had known Elizabeth since childhood, had ridden to Hatfield immediately after Mary I's death mounted on a snow-white horse and beautifully and extravagantly attired. Dudley was not made a member of the Council in 1558. He was appointed Master of the Horse, a role in the household which ensured that he would need almost daily contact with the Queen. His dark, flirtatious eyes made it natural for her to nickname him 'Two-eyes', and he would often write to her signing himself simply ōō. But his were not the only sharp eyes at court.

The older man, Cecil, was measured, calculating, seeming older than his thirty-eight years. His sharp, dark, intelligent eyes beneath those quizzical, almost triangular eyelids saw everything, gave little away. His very long, almost anteater nose was a symbol of his ability to sniff out intrigue, mischief and danger to his royal heroine. He had studied at Cambridge with the scholar John Cheke. He had married Cheke's sister, though she was only the daughter of a poor wine-seller and it was, as Mandell Creighton drily remarked, 'the only trace of romance in Cecil's life'.[13] She died after only three years and his second wife, Mildred, was a decidedly unromantic-looking woman, with a thin humourless face, a rat-trap mouth and a pointed chin – the daughter of a lawyer and courtier. From his mid-twenties William Cecil had played the dangerous role of a public servant to the Tudor dynasty. He had been in the entourage of Protector Somerset in the reign of Edward VI. At Edward's court he learned the business of government, and came to love it. When Elizabeth acceded to the throne, Cecil, her Secretary and right-hand man, knew intimately how government worked, and he would be the man, more than any other, who taught her the day-to-day business of statecraft. A trimmer he was, when political expediency required it. A coward he was not. He had the political ability to take risks for genuinely held principles and the political nous to abandon, or *appear* to abandon, his principles if his neck was in danger.

Such was his commitment to the Protestant cause that, when King Edward died, Cecil had been one of those who swore allegiance, not to Queen Mary, but to Lady Jane Grey. With the collapse of the attempted Protestant coup, however, in the summer of 1553, Cecil had cunningly managed to distance himself from the hardcore Jane-ites. He submitted himself to Queen Mary with 'all lowliness that any heart can conceive'. Unafraid to ditch his former friends at this point, he had told Mary that he might 'feel some difference from others that have more plainly offended and yet be partakers of her highness's bountifulness and grace'. He kissed Queen Mary's hand ('a tiresome bluestocking' according to the Spanish Ambassador de Feria).[14] Feria was right when he wrote in his dispatches back to Spain that Cecil would be 'secretary to Madame Elizabeth. He is said to be a virtuous man, but a heretic.'[15] Quite so.

Cecil was part of the delegation sent to bring back Reginald Pole (pronounced Pool), the great-nephew of Edward IV, to serve as (England's last – as it happened) Roman Catholic Archbishop of Canterbury. As high steward of Cardinal Pole's manor of Wimbledon in Surrey, Cecil and his wife Mildred were careful to be seen going to confession and receiving Communion at Easter. Cecil let it be known that he had paid for the bread, wine, tapers and oil necessary for the Easter ceremonies at Wimbledon, and Lady Mildred very publicly went down the Thames by barge to St Mary Arches Church in the City of London to hear Pole preach. Yet although Cecil was a consummate politician, the Catholics were undeceived, and there was never really any variation in Cecil's core beliefs. These were: the need for a stable monarchy; the forwarding of the Protestant Reformation; the protection of the realm of England from incursion by the French. From these stemmed all his patient exposition of foreign and domestic policy to his new queen – his suspicions of Scotland and his growing obsession with a desire to get rid of the Scottish queen; his preparedness to form alliances with the Catholic power of Spain, if it kept France in check; his suspicion of the Catholic nobility. Every day of his life Mr Secretary Cecil, as he had now become, was Elizabeth's political manager. Especially over the question of Scotland, her apparent lack of caution made him consider resignation. But in reality he was the rock on which her strength as a political leader of genius depended. His spidery handwriting survives in hundreds – possibly thousands – of memos and documents, ranging from the approval of minor appointments to major statements of policy, from draft letters to the Queen of theatrical sycophancy to tersely destructive character-assessments of his rivals, either to her affection or, same thing, to political power. The spidery hand is the reverse of weak. It is forward-thrusting, indicative of an absolute and very male confidence. There is, in Cecil's life, much deft use of retreat as well as advance; an astute mastery of the art of when to bow, as well as when to make a display or when to insist. But never for an instant do we sense him doubting himself. He had the ultimate strutting male self-confidence disguised beneath the Polonius manners, the quasi-clerical dark gowns and scholar's black caps.

He was supremely and unmistakably Welsh, the most successful member of what Dr David Starkey calls 'the Tudor Taffia'.

It was a good time to be Welsh. Elizabeth possessed immediately recognisable Welsh features. On market day in a Welsh town you will pass between ten or twenty women with something of a 'look' of Queen Elizabeth. She herself owed her temperamental similarity to 'my good grandfather', as she called that canny Welshman Henry VII. Elizabeth's household was dominated by the Welsh. As a young princess she had entrusted her cofferer,

Welshman Thomas Parry, with some of her closest secrets and missions – he was the man who had to defend her to the Council when she was accused of improper conduct with Lord Admiral Seymour. Parry's daughter Blanche was chief Gentlewoman of the Bedchamber, one of the Queen's closest intimates. Her apothecary was Welshman Hugh Morgan.

The Tudor Age saw the rise of the great Welsh dynasty of Herberts. The legitimate line of Herbert Earls of Pembroke had perished in the Wars of the Roses. Henry VIII had elevated the illegitimate line, making them Earls of Pembroke of the second creation and settling them at Wilton, where we shall meet them later in this book – the 2nd Earl, and his wife Mary, sister of Sir Philip Sidney, the nexus of a great literary world; writers and poets themselves and patrons of such as Ben Jonson, George Chapman and Shakespeare. The larger family produced Lord Herbert of Cherbury, George Herbert the poet-priest, and many less famous but distinguished figures.

And in this age so conducive to the advancement of Welshmen we see the rise of the Cecils, or Sitsylt as they still spelt the name when David Sitsylt resided at Alltyrynys, a Welsh-speaking area of south Herefordshire. He had done well out of the Wars of the Roses and fought on the side of his fellow Welshman, Henry Tudor, at the Battle of Bosworth (1485). He settled at Stamford in Lincolnshire where, a little mysteriously, he accumulated considerable riches. His son Richard Cecil continued the rise in wealth and fortune; he was a minor figure at the court of Henry VIII, present at the Field of the Cloth of Gold as a 'yeoman of the chamber'; Keeper of Warwick Castle and – eventually – a Member of Parliament. He had a house in Cannon Row, Westminster, and estates in Rutland and Lincolnshire.

Like many members of the new rich in the Tudor Age, the Cecils had profited from the coming of Protestantism. When the nunnery, the priory and the friary in Stamford were wound up at the behest of Henry VIII, Richard Cecil was able, in 1544, to buy most of their land at a concessionary price. The Cecils literally had a vested interest in the Reformation. Richard sent his son William Cecil to Cambridge, where he came under the Protestant influence of John Cheke, followed by a spell studying law at Gray's Inn in London, before entering the service of the Protector Somerset in the reign of Edward VI.

Costive, devious, patient, the master of detail, all but humourless, and dependably sensible, William Cecil was the lynchpin of Elizabeth's administration. And as a male – and one who dreaded above all things an undoing of the Reformation and the inevitable takeover by Mary, Queen of Scots, and the French, and the Pope – Cecil was the most persistent of those voices that urged the young Queen to marry and to produce an heir. This would undoubtedly have been the 'sensible' course of action, though as we have seen, in our reflections upon John Knox, marriage would mean subservience or compromise with some foreign power. For so long as she did not marry, Elizabeth could not sustain her emotional life by sensible political deliberations with that dry stick Cecil alone.

Like a great artist, Queen Elizabeth was a multifaceted personality. The men and women who were important in her life drew out different aspects of her mercurial nature, and almost became symbols of her self-contradictions. If her realm, and her court, depended for their security on the patience, common sense, piety, deviousness and doggedness of Cecil, they found much of their colour, exuberance, callowness, energy and display exemplified in the figure of Robert Dudley – Lord Robert Dudley as he would become, as soon as he was able to reclaim the titles of which the previous queen had deprived him.

For his father, John, the Duke of Northumberland, had been executed for treason on 22 August 1553 by Mary Tudor, for attempting to place on the throne of England his daughter-in-law, Lady Jane Grey. The children of aristocrats arraigned for treason are automatically stripped of their titles. John Dudley had effectively been in charge of Edward VI's government, and it made sense to speak of the Dudleys as 'the uncrowned Kings of England'.[16] Guildford Dudley – Robert's brother – would have become King, had the coup been successful that attempted to make Guildford's wife, Lady Jane, the Protestant queen. Guildford, like his father Duke John, paid the price with execution. And on Palm Sunday 1554 the Princess Elizabeth was brought to the Tower of London and made – under vigorous protest – to pass through Traitors' Gate, although she denied any part in the rebellion of Sir Thomas Wyatt the younger, which (in the absence of Lady Jane Grey) had tried to make Elizabeth the Protestant queen.

When she was imprisoned in the Tower she was twenty-one years old, very much enfeebled by a recent illness and reduced to a nervous collapse. When her frail condition was reported to the Council, the young Elizabeth was permitted to get fresh air and exercise by walking upon the leads of the roof of the Bell Tower where she was immured. Tiptoeing between her armed escort in the narrow trough between the battlements, on the one side, and the gables of the King's House and the Yeoman Gaolers' house on the other, she would have been able to look out over London, the unbuilt-upon stretches of Thames shoreline and the clear stretches of the Essex marshes. As she turned, however, she would be only a few feet away from the ever-locked door of the Beauchamp Tower, where Queen Mary had imprisoned the surviving sons of John Dudley – John, former Viscount Lisle, Earl of Warwick; Ambrose, who would inherit these titles after John was executed; Henry; and Robert. To beguile the time before he was beheaded, John carved a pareil bordered with leaves and flowers and representing the heraldic beasts that had supported their former devices: the bear and the ragged staff, the double-tailed lion.

> Yow that these beasts do wel behold and se
> May deme with ease wherefore her made they be
> with borders eve wherein [there may be found]
> 4 Brother's names who list to serche the ground.

He carved roses for Ambrose, honeysuckle for Henry, gillyflowers for Guildford and oak leaves (Latin *robur* = oak) for Robert. The brothers in the Tower were under sentence of death for fourteen months until Philip II, Mary's husband, persuaded her to release them.

There were many bonds that tied Elizabeth and Robert Dudley together. He was electrifyingly attractive – tall, dark, dashing and with the unashamed braggartry of the 'wide boy'. He dressed fashionably and extravagantly. In later years he admitted, 'I have lived always above any living I had.'[17] In youth he had already developed the exuberant dress sense that we find in an order to Antwerp in the late 1570s: 'touching the silks I wrote about, I wish you to take up and stay for me 4,000 crowns worth of crimson and black velvet and satins and silvers of other colours. And if there be any good cloth of tissue or of gold or such other pretty stuff, stay for me to the value of £300 or £400, whatever the charge shall be . . .'[18] He dazzled, and added to the young Queen Elizabeth's early court a fizz and an air of danger that it would certainly have lacked, if it had been dominated entirely by Cecil or by the old aristocrats on the Council. Deeper, perhaps, than the sexual frisson that Elizabeth and Dudley enjoyed exhibiting to shocked or prurient old observers was the sense of what they had been through together during Mary I's reign. Elizabeth would say that she had been Daniel in the lion's den while her unsympathetic sister was on the throne. Even if she and Dudley did not actually meet during the nine weeks of Elizabeth's imprisonment in the Tower (she was later transferred to effectual house-arrest at Woodstock), it was a shared experience. During the years when Cecil had been a trimmer to the Catholic regime of Mary, Dudley had been a marked man, and Elizabeth a marked woman. It had only been King Philip II's desire to build up the Anglo-Spanish alliance (against France) that had tempered Queen Mary's implacable distrust and saved Elizabeth and Robert Dudley from the block. They could both live from now on like birds that had escaped the snare of the fowler.

They had not grown up together, but they had known one another long before their spell as gaol-birds in the Tower.

They were the same age. 'I have known her better than any man alive since she was eight years old,' he would later claim.[19] When Henry VIII contracted his final marriage, to Catherine Parr, the small ceremony was witnessed by the new Queen's friend, Jane Dudley – Robert's mother. When Catherine Parr took in hand the education of Princess Elizabeth, and introduced her to the Cambridge dons – Cheke, Grindal, Ascham and Buckley – who taught her children of the courtiers joined these 'royal schools' and Robert Dudley was taught alongside the Princess. He learned mathematics with her (though she was far cleverer than he was), he learned riding and dancing with her.[20] At the age of thirteen he officially joined the household of her brother, Edward VI. At seventeen he married Amy, daughter of a Norfolk squire named Sir John Robsart, and Princess Elizabeth was present at the wedding. (So too in all likelihood was a twenty-nine-year-old lawyer, William Cecil, now a member of Edward VI's court, who dismissed Dudley's union to Amy as 'a carnal marriage, begun for pleasure and ended in lamentation'.[21])

So Robert and Elizabeth had been very close from childhood. Of course, he would not have been a Dudley if he had not made full political capital out of this. In their long and complicated relationship, much of which was played out – with deliberate exhibitionism on both sides – in public, they both depended upon, and exploited, one another.

From the first, Elizabeth's easy intimacy with her favourite caused rage among those courtiers who automatically distrusted a Dudley, and – to a wider circle, spreading by rumour throughout Europe – scandal. Dudley was a very handsome young man (*giovane bellissimo*), reported the Venetian Ambassador, 'towards whom in various ways the Queen evinces such affection and inclination that many persons believe that if his wife, who has been ailing for some time, were to die, the Queen might easily take him for her husband.'[22]

Count de Feria, the Spanish Ambassador, wrote to Philip II, who, when married to Mary Tudor, had expressed his lust for his sister-in-law Elizabeth:

> Lord Robert has come so much into favour that he does whatever he likes with affairs and it is even said that her Majesty visits him in his chamber day and night. People talk of this so freely that they go so far as to say that his wife has a malady in one of her breasts and the Queen is only waiting for her to die to marry Lord Robert. I can assure your Majesty that matters have reached such a pass that I have been brought to consider whether it would not be well to approach Lord Robert on your Majesty's behalf, promising him your help and favour and coming to terms with him.[23]

The gossip about the Queen and Dudley, and more specifically the widely held view that they were waiting for his neglected young wife to die, reached an unpleasant crisis when on Sunday, 8 September 1560, Dudley's wife Amy died, aged twenty-eight. She was found lying dead at the bottom of the staircase at Cumnor Place, near Oxford. It is a curious incident and it is worth recording the facts of the case, in so far as they are known.

First, perhaps, one should note that Amy Dudley fell down a single flight of not particularly steep stairs, and that this broke her neck. This suggests that the cause of death was a 'spontaneous' or 'pathological' fracture of the spine.[24] Amy Dudley was too young for this to have been caused by ageing or osteoporosis, but it is possible that she had cancerous deposits in her bones, which made them brittle. The Count de Feria, the Spanish Ambassador, in the letter just quoted of 18 April 1559, used the Spanish phrase *enferma y mala de un pecho*; the use of the indefinite article – *a* breast – suggesting that a mammary gland was intended, not the chest in general.

Second, attention should be drawn to the positioning of Cumnor Place. It was not a large house. It had been a sanatorium for the monastery in Abingdon. It belonged to William Owen, whose father had been one of Henry VIII's doctors (hence, perhaps, his getting the sanatorium when the monastery was dissolved). Owen let it to Anthony Forster, who was the Chief Controller of Robert Dudley's household and a personal friend. Amy moved in during the early part of 1560, having previously rented a house at Denchworth, near Abingdon, from a Mr Hyde.

Cumnor Place might well have been divided into separate dwellings, but the household there consisted of Mrs Odingsells (a widowed sister of Mr Hyde), Mrs Owen (wife of the owner, who acted as a housekeeper) and Mr and Mrs Forster. The house was therefore occupied by a group of friends. It was not a remote,[25] lonely country place, but a village house, easily accessible from the church and from another building that adjoined it. It was built around a small quadrangle, and the fateful staircase led from the first floor of one wing – the west wing – of the building.

In other words, if anyone had wished to murder Amy Dudley, they would have been taking a considerable risk (screams, someone entering the house unannounced) if they had done so by attacking her at Cumnor Place; and a flight of gradual wooden stairs would not be an obvious place to secure the victim's death. This would not be like pushing the victim off a cliff. By far the likeliest explanation is that she tripped on a trailing dress and – suffering from cancer as she probably did – broke her neck spontaneously. This was the opinion of the coroner's jury, which convened instantly.

There were, however, a few oddities in the case, and it is inevitable, given the intense gossip and speculation circulating about Dudley and the Queen, that the worst possible interpretations should have been placed upon the tragedy. One is that in the morning of Sunday, 8 September, Lady Robert directed her whole household to attend Abingdon Fair. Mrs Odingsells fussily remonstrated, apparently thinking it unsuitable that Amy be left alone. Amy dismissed all the servants – who did attend the fair – and she dined alone with Mrs Owen. One should like to have cross-examined Mrs Odingsells about this. Was she simply a tiresome fusspot? Had Amy Dudley promised herself a few quiet hours *alone*, and was it merely the officiousness of Mrs Odingsells that made Amy Dudley lose her temper, as she apparently did? Or were the women aware that Amy was ill? Were they *fussing* over her? Or – and here one enters the realm of pure speculation – did Amy have a lover? This would be the normal explanation for a young woman of twenty-eight wishing to dismiss even the servants who would clear away a meal. We shall never know precisely what happened. One modern biographer of Dudley comes close to hinting that William Cecil might have had a hand in her death. 'The only person in England who might have gained from such a tragedy was William Cecil,'[26] wrote Derek Wilson in *Sweet Robin* in 1997.

Certainly the Spanish Ambassador, Bishop de Quadra, making much of the bad relations between Cecil and Dudley, claimed that Cecil had confided in him. On 11 September the gossiping old bishop wrote to the Duchess of Parma that the Queen was, yet again, shilly-shallying over the question of marriage:

> She had promised me an answer about the marriage by the third instant, and said she was certain to marry, but now she coolly tells me she cannot make up her mind and will not marry. After this I had an opportunity of talking to Cecil, who I understand was in disgrace, and Robert was trying to turn him out of his place. After exacting many pledges of strict secrecy he said the Queen was conducting herself in such a way that he thought of retiring. He said it was a bad sailor who did not enter port if he could when he saw a storm coming on, and he clearly foresaw the ruin of the realm through Robert's intimacy with the Queen, who surrendered all her affairs to him and meant to marry him . . . He ended by saying that Robert was thinking of killing his wife, who was publicly announced to be ill, although she was quite well, and would take very good care they did not poison her. He said surely God would never allow such a wicked thing to be done.'

In the adjacent paragraph the bishop went on: 'the next day the Queen told me as she returned from hunting that Robert's wife was dead or nearly so, and asked me not to say anything about it. Certainly this business is most shameful and scandalous and withal I am not sure whether she will marry the man at once or even if she will marry at all as I do not think she has her mind sufficiently fixed. Cecil says she wishes to do as her father did.'[27]

A month later de Quadra was writing in slightly less frantic terms. This time to the King of Spain that 'the Queen had decided not to marry Lord Robert'.[28]

Clearly, the death of Amy Robsart in such shady circumstances *did* make it impossible, in the short term, for Elizabeth to marry Robert Dudley, and *did* greatly strengthen Cecil's hand. For, at court, when Dudley was down, Cecil was up. The Spanish bishop, like most addicts of gossip, perhaps passed on rumours *because* they made an exciting story rather than because they were true. But perhaps the ever-fluctuating rumour-machine reflected the flickering compass-needle of Elizabeth's heart. Possibly she did, with a part of herself, wish to marry Robert Dudley and, with another part of herself, to marry the King of Spain. When Cecil said that she 'wishes to do as her father did', he perhaps expressed a genuine dread that she would become a female Henry VIII, a violent serial monogamist, who was capable of wedding on a whim and sending the unfortunate spouse to the block when the marriage hit the rocks. This might have been possible had she limited her spouse-victims to the English nobility, but she would have been faced with diplomatic difficulties if she had married a foreign prince and ended the relationship by murder.

Perhaps, however, it was not chance, but some instinct of common sense, that kept her single. If the death of Amy Dudley reduced the likelihood of Elizabeth's marriage with her widower, it did not make Robert Dudley in the long term a less important figure in her life, nor did the powerful Dudleys diminish in their significance, as figures in Elizabeth's life. In 1562, in common with many of her subjects, the Queen succumbed to the epidemic of smallpox that was sweeping through the southern counties of England. Elizabeth was at Hampton Court when symptoms of fever began. It was believed by medical opinion, or at any rate by Bishop de Quadra quoting the most pessimistic medical opinion,[29] that so long as the eruptions did not come out, the patient was in mortal danger. He wrote to the Duchess of Parma, on 16 October, 'Cecil was hastily summoned from London at midnight. If the Queen die, it will be very soon, within a few days at latest, and now all the talk is to be told her successor. Lord Robert has a large armed force under his control and will probably pronounce for his brother-in-law the Earl of Huntingdon.'

Though de Quadra's medical diagnosis was premature, he was probably right in his political analysis. The Earl of Huntingdon, married to Dudley's sister Catherine, was much the strongest Protestant candidate for the throne. In a minute to Philip II (15 October 1560) de Quadra quoted Cecil's opinion that 'they were devising a very important plan for the maintenance of their heresies, namely to make the earl of Huntingdon King in case the Queen should die without issue, and that Cecil had told the Bishop that the succession belonged of right to the earl as he was descended from the house of York'.[30] Reading this letter, one could be back a hundred years in the Wars of the Roses and one sees what a nightmare would have ensued, had Elizabeth died of the smallpox in 1562. Had Cecil – and Dudley – declared for the Earl of Huntingdon on the grounds of his descent from that fifteenth-century Duke of Clarence drowned in malmsey wine by Richard III, it is equally likely that the rival claims of Jane Grey's sister, Lady Catherine, would have been pressed.

By the terms of Henry VIII's will, if his three children died without issue, Lady Catherine would be the next in succession, being a granddaughter of Henry's sister, the Duchess of Suffolk. Catherine had been married (aged perhaps fifteen) to Henry Herbert, afterwards 2nd Earl of Pembroke, in the year (1553) that Northumberland had tried to make her sister, Lady Jane Grey, queen. This marriage had been purely part of Northumberland's power-brokering – to consolidate aristocratic support around the Grey–Dudley axis. During Mary's reign, Herbert was embarrassed by the alliance and, since the marriage was unconsummated, it could easily be annulled.

By the time Elizabeth became Queen, Lady Catherine Grey would have been in her late teens, probably nineteen. She was a scatter-brained, rather petulant girl, easily swayed by her emotions and by those who wished to manipulate her. Count de Feria, the Spanish Ambassador, found that she was 'discontented and offended' because she had not been given the official status of heir presumptive. Or was she discontented because his line of questioning had made her so? Clearly, Catherine took the very foolish risk of not behaving obsequiously at court. De Feria noted with satisfaction that Catherine had spoken 'very arrogant and unseemly words in the presence of the Queen'. Time was, only five years before, when Catherine had seen her mother, the Duchess of Suffolk, given greater status than the Queen, and witnessed Princess Elizabeth obliged to walk out of a room after the Duchess.

This duchess, Frances, was, during the opening years of Elizabeth's reign, in the last stages of illness. With recklessness that defies belief, she encouraged Catherine in a secret courtship with the young Earl of

Hertford, who was probably no more than her age, possibly a year younger. Hertford was the son of the late Protector Somerset. He was almost ridiculously short of stature, but this is not always unattractive to women. His sister, Lady Jane Seymour, was one of Elizabeth's favourite maids of honour. It was (still is) forbidden for any near-heir to the throne to marry without the sovereign's permission. The Duchess wrote to the Queen that the marriage was 'th' onlie thinge that shee desired before her death and shold be an occasion to her to die the more quietlie'.[31] It seems as though Duchess Frances died before completing this letter.

Jane Seymour continued to act as the lovers' friend, and it was Jane who arranged their clandestine and, by definition, treasonable marriage in December 1560. She found a clergyman to read the marriage service (no one else present appeared so much as to catch his name). It was Jane who organised a secret wedding breakfast – 'comfects and other Banquetting meates and beare and wyne'. No sooner had these been consumed than the young couple 'unarrayed themselves' and 'went into naked bedd in the said Chamber where they were so married'. Once in bed they had 'Companie and Carnall Copulation . . . divers tymes' . . . and 'laie sometimes on th' outside of the Bedd and sometymes on th' other'. The lightly pornographic nature of the testimony suggests it is invented or half-invented, based on servants' tittle-tattle, but it gives the flavour of contemporary gossip about Lady Catherine. Similar gossip circulated, inaccurately, about the Queen and Dudley. But in that case it was not true, and this must have heightened Elizabeth's jealous hatred of Catherine when, inevitably, the story leaked out. It is even quite possible that the whole union between these easily led, highly sexed teenagers was politically engineered by Dudley's enemies when it was feared he would marry the Queen. That was what Bishop de Quadra thought. 'Cecil was at the bottom of it.'[32]

For a few weeks the couple kept the marriage a secret, but they could not do so for long. When Cecil came to hear of it he warned the young earl that there were rumours of 'good will' between him and Catherine. Hertford denied it. Soon all the women of the court were jabbering of it. It was said (perhaps the story is apocryphal) that Blanche Parry, the Queen's trusted Welsh attendant and lady-in-waiting, did her best to warn Catherine by telling her fortune and claiming to see in her palm that 'the lines say, madam, that if you ever marry without the Queen's consent in writing, you and your husband will be undone, and your fate worse than that of my Lady Jane [Grey]'.[33]

Catherine Grey was now pregnant. The Earl of Hertford had serious reason to panic. This was not just the usual panic that would afflict any boy of less than twenty who had got his girl 'into trouble'. Even he, idiotic as he must have been, would now realise that what he had been doing was treasonable; that in a Tudor court, people had been beheaded for less than this. His own father had been beheaded on Tower Hill for treason, and the Seymours had been deeply distrusted as the enemies of the Dudleys and the Tudors ever since all the post-Reformation power-brokering of Edward VI's reign. It was arranged that Hertford should be sent to France with Thomas Cecil, son of Mr Secretary Cecil. In every major crisis of Elizabeth's reign there is William Cecil, trying to save the Queen, which often meant saving her from herself. There was much unconscious Polonius-like comedy in Cecil sending his son Thomas abroad with Hertford. This was the child he had had with his first wife, Mary Cheke. By now, Thomas was nineteen years old. Though Mildred, the thin-lipped bluestocking second wife, had borne him three children (two daughters and a son), only one – a daughter, Anne – had survived infancy. But in May 1561 she had a second son. (This was Robert, destined to succeed his father as Secretary.)

'I have foreborne to send my son Thomas Cecil out of the realm for that I had no more [sons], and now that God hath given me another I am disposed to send him abroad, meaning only to have him absent about one year, so as, at his return, if God so grant, to see him married for that he shall then be full 20.' So, Mr Secretary Cecil to Sir Nicholas Throckmorton, the British Ambassador in Paris. Cecil was candid enough to add, 'I never showed any fatherly fancy to him but in teaching and correcting.'[34] Cecil had the idea of making his son reside with Admiral Coligny, where it was hoped he would master French, as well as improving his horsemanship, playing the lute, dancing and perfecting his tennis. To the boy himself he imparted a tedious list of instructions, above all insisting upon the habit of daily prayer. 'My meaning is that you shall use the manner of the Church of England in Latin.'

It goes without saying that Thomas Cecil did not heed much of this advice. By the end of a year his father felt obliged to catalogue his son's vices as 'slothfulness in keeping his bed, negligent and rash in expenses, careless in his apparel, an immoderate lover of dice and cards; in study, soon weary, in game never'.

In later years, the bad influence of the tiny Earl of Hertford was blamed for these habits of dissipation, unjustly according to the writer Thomas Seccombe.[35] Cecil remained in Paris after the Earl had left, and found plenty of others with whom to indulge his juvenile tastes. Throckmorton kept his eye upon him, and took him into his own household. In July 1561 Throckmorton presented Cecil (and Hertford?) at the French court. It was just six months since King Francis II had died. His widow, not yet twenty years old, was still in France. Her mother, Mary of Guise, the

Regent of Scotland, had died the previous year. Thomas Cecil was presented to her – Mary, Queen of Scots: tall, with a beautifully modulated voice and an instantaneous sexual appeal. Perhaps it was for this moment that William Cecil had really dispatched his son to Paris, for Cecil was obsessed by the Scottish queen and the danger she posed to Elizabeth's power.[36]

Mary, having lost her young husband, felt sidelined in the French court by the new queen, Catherine de' Medici. In her Scottish kingdom the Protestants who held power barely acknowledged her. In England, it was otherwise. Although she had no legal claim to the court – the will of Henry VIII did not mention her as a successor – she was the focus of hopes for those who wished to see England revert to Catholicism, and from the moment of Mary Tudor's death, Mary Stuart, a great-granddaughter of Henry VII, declared herself to be the rightful Queen of England.

Meanwhile, Hertford was by now the father of a rival claimant to the throne of England, and in August the young man returned to London to face the awful consequences.

Things had not gone well for his wife, even though, before he left for France, Hertford had given Catherine a deed of jointure and settled on her £1,000 per annum. The first catastrophe was that Hertford's sister, Lady Jane Seymour, died in 1561. The Queen was distraught and ordered a lavish funeral in Westminster Abbey. The sole surviving witness to Catherine Grey's marriage to the Earl of Hertford was thereby buried, while Thomas Cecil and the Queen were on a progress through Suffolk and Norfolk. At Norwich, the Queen complained of the squalid conditions to which the presence of wives and children had reduced the cathedral close. She immediately drafted an ordinance to the Archbishops of Canterbury and York forbidding cathedral-clergy to marry. It was plainly contrary to the intentions of the founders.

Meanwhile, an exhausted Catherine Seymour, in the entourage of the Virgin Queen, was seven months pregnant. The Queen was seen to have taken a great dislike to Catherine, and she had probably heard the rumours. But she allowed the young fool to sweat it out. Desperate, Catherine confided in another of the women of the court, Elizabeth St Loe, always known as Bess, who wept, and reprimanded her for her foolishness, saying that 'she was sorrie therefore because that shee had not made the Queene's Majestie pryvie thereunto'.[37]

That night Catherine, disturbed by Bess St Loe's failure to take her side, crept into the bedroom of her kinsman, Robert Dudley, and threw herself on his mercy. It was a fatally stupid thing to do. He could not possibly keep such information to himself, and when he was obliged to tell the Queen, not only of the circumstances, but of how, where (his bedroom) and when (midnight) he knew them, it was an occasion for a Tudor hysterical outburst of gale force.

Catherine Seymour was dispatched at once to the Tower, where her child was born. So was Bess St Loe. Catherine, who had got herself into all this trouble by seriously considering herself worthy to take over the cares of government from the great Queen Elizabeth, now found that she had mislaid the essential deed of jointure from her husband. She could not remember the name of the clergyman who had married her. The one witness – Jane Seymour – was dead. When the Earl of Hertford returned from France he was also sent to the Tower. Their second child, rather touchingly named Thomas, after the Earl's fellow Parisian reveller, was born on 10 February 1563. (The godfathers were two warders in the Tower.[38]) Elizabeth had the marriage, if it ever had been a legal marriage, annulled by the Archbishop of Canterbury. The children were declared bastards and the Earl of Hertford was fined a ludicrous £15,000, later commuted to £10,000. Rather like an extortioner of the modern criminal underworld, the Queen, ever avid for cash, in the event accepted £1,000 down.

This is the pair – the hopeless Catherine Grey and her diminutive earl – who would have been declared Queen of England and Consort, had Elizabeth died of smallpox in 1562. But she pulled through.

Dudley's sister, Lady Mary Sidney, was the chief victim of that crisis. She, and Sybil Penne, the Queen's childhood nurse, tended Elizabeth during the illness. Though the Queen was all but unscarred, Mary Sidney was less lucky. Her husband, Sir Henry Sidney, could recall, 'I lefte her a full faire Ladye in myne eye at least the fayerest, and when I returned I found her as fowle a ladie as the smale pox could make her, which she did take by contynuall attendance of her majesties most precious person (sicke of the same disease) the skares of which (to her resolute discomforte) ever syns hath doss and doth remayne in her face.'[39]

Sir Henry Sidney remained a just-about loyal, if often exasperated, servant of the Queen, both in Wales and Ireland. When one remembers his wife's fate, Sidney's ambivalence about Elizabeth is understandable. The Queen's infatuation with Sidney's brother-in-law, Robert Dudley, went on unabated, though with many a tiff and storm to make the relationship more exciting.

When she recovered from her smallpox, though it was Mary Dudley/Sidney who bore the scars, it was her brother Robert who reaped the reward. She appointed Robert Protector of the Realm, with the enormous salary of £20,000. This meant that in the event of her death he would be, like his father before him, the effective Regent. She also gave his body-servant, Tamworth, a salary of £500. This was the man who slept in Dudley's bedchamber, and who would know the truth, if any, of the rumours circulating that the Queen visited Dudley by night.[40] Good hush-money? If she did so, she would never have been such a fool as Lady Catherine Grey and become accidentally pregnant. So it must be assumed that, if in any physical sense they were lovers, the intimacies stopped short of total intimacy.

In October 1562, to Cecil's chagrin, Elizabeth appointed Dudley, and the Duke of Norfolk, to the Council. In 1563 she granted him possession of the castle and estates of Kenilworth in Warwickshire – it had briefly belonged to his father and was in the heart of Dudley country. In 1564 she created him the Earl of Leicester.

The primary reason for this, however, was not to deepen their intimacy. Indeed, the ennoblement reminds us of the impenetrable paradox of the relationship between Elizabeth and her 'sweet Robin'. He was made into a great earl so that he could be a plausible husband – not for the English, but for the Scottish queen. However deeply her heart was engaged with Dudley, she never stopped being the political operator. If Dudley married Mary Stuart, he would neuter the Scottish queen's power, and strengthen the power of the Protestant government in Edinburgh. Neither Dudley nor the Scottish queen were enthusiasts for the idea, but Elizabeth seriously considered it.

One advantage, from her point of view, was that it would skewer the prospects of another Stuart, Henry, Lord Darnley, whose fervently ambitious mother, Lady Margaret Lennox, longed for her son to marry Mary Stuart and become in effect the King of Scotland. Henry VII's daughter Margaret married, first, James IV of Scotland. Her son, James V, married Mary of Guise, and their child was Mary Stuart, now Queen of Scots. Margaret Tudor had married *en secondes noces* the Earl of Angus, Archibald Douglas. His daughter, Lady Margaret Douglas, married Matthew Stuart, Earl of Lennox, and their child was Henry Stuart – Mary, Queen of Scots's cousin, Lord Darnley.

Darnley and his parents were brought to London and kept under close supervision; not quite house-arrest, but under the eye of Elizabeth and her court. And they were present during the great court spectacular, when Robert Dudley was made Earl of Leicester on Michaelmas Day 1564. Elizabeth knew what was passing through all the minds of the key players in this great piece of political theatre. She knew that Lady Margaret Lennox and her son Lord Darnley could easily be the grandmother and father of English kings. And so they were destined to become. 'Thou shalt get kings though thou be none'[41] as the third of the weird sisters tells Banquo in that Scottish play, perhaps performed at the court of Darnley's son, James I.[42] Elizabeth knew that Cecil wanted Dudley to marry Mary Stuart, partly for religious and diplomatic reasons, partly to get his hated rival out of London. She knew that, little though 'sweet Robin' wanted to marry Mary Stuart from an emotional or sexual point of view, no Dudley would give up the chance of fathering a line of kings.

And so the great ceremony took place, and there they all were to witness it: Sir James Melville, Mary, Queen of Scots's representative; Lady Margaret Lennox, who must have squirmed uncomfortably throughout; wily Cecil; and the ambassadors of France and Spain, with the Council and all the court. Lord Darnley entered the Presence Chamber in front of the Queen, nineteen years old, and for this ceremony the official sword-bearer to the monarch. This was a nice touch by Elizabeth, reminding Lord Darnley's mother that if she had control of events, he would do no more than be an attendant lord. But Elizabeth did not have control over the future, and the fates had a cruel and unhappy destiny in store for this youth and his descendants. He would, in the event, marry the Scottish queen and she would murder him. As he carried the sword in front of Queen Elizabeth, Henry Darnley had not three years to live. His future wife, Mary, Queen of Scots, would perish on the block at Fotheringay in 1587; his grandson, Charles I, would die, our English royal martyr, by beheading on 30 January 1649; his great-grandson, James II, would be sent into exile; and the doomed cause of the House of Stuart would be the ruin of many an English and Scottish life in the first half of the eighteenth century before the Young Chevalier, Bonnie Prince Charlie, died his sordid alcoholic death in Rome in 1788. With the death in 1807 of his brother, Henry Benedict Maria Clement, Cardinal of York (styled by loyalists Henry IX), the extraordinary Stuart tapestry may be deemed finally to have unravelled.

We see it being woven in that Westminster ceremony on 29 September 1564 when the Queen, in her splendour, entered the chamber to raise her beloved Eyes, her sweet Robin, to the earldom of Leicester. He knelt before her and she, always very physical in her expressions both of love and anger, fixed his ermine robe about him. As she did so, she tickled his neck and turned to the Scottish Ambassador, Melville. 'How like you my creation?' she asked. The ambassador was nonplussed and murmured diplomatic niceties. Pointing to the lanky teenager, Henry Darnley, Elizabeth answered for him, and for the bloody future, 'And yet you like better of yonder long lad.'[43] She said it jokingly, but perhaps with an inkling of the stormy future that lay ahead for the long lad and his heirs.

5
Which Church?

It is time to speak of the Church, that subject of such minimal importance to a majority in England today, of such centrality to men and women of the sixteenth century.

Christianity, institutional Christianity, has taken a tremendous battering since the time of the Napoleonic Wars in the West. Religious conservatives would wish this had not been so, but so it is. In this chapter, we will be concerned with that branch of Christianity known as the Church of England. It was during the reign of the first Queen Elizabeth that this institution took its particular and distinctive shape. It was during the reign of the second Elizabeth that this Church, as originally conceived in the sixteenth century, was seen to unravel. This is to comment upon a fact, not to make any kind of partisan 'point'. So much has it unravelled that it will be necessary, if the reader is to make any sense either of it in particular or of the Elizabethan age in general, to spell out (at the risk of stating the obvious) what the Church of England was intended to be.

Technically, it does, at the time of writing, still survive. Bishops still sit in the House of Lords, the second legislative chamber of the English Parliament. The Queen – Elizabeth II – is supreme governor of the Established Church. The cathedrals and medieval parish churches of England are the property of this Church. The old colleges at Oxford and Cambridge all subscribe to this Church. Many of England's schools are Church of England schools – the majority of primary schools have this status. But you only have to read a newspaper account of any of these phenomena to realise how little the average journalist or member of the public understands what the Church of England is.

Many speak of the Church of England schools, for example, as 'faith schools', as though they were items on a multicultural menu, to which various alternatives – Roman Catholic, secular, Muslim schools – could be offered to parents wondering where to send their children. Likewise, the bishops of the Church are spoken of as *Anglican* bishops. The word 'Anglican', deriving from dog Latin or Church Latin for 'English', was technically in existence in the seventeenth century, but did not really gain widespread usage until the nineteenth century, when many English Christians decided to become Roman Catholics and it became semantically necessary to distinguish between those who believed in bishops, the sacramental life, and so on, and did belong to the Church of England (Anglicans) and those who had decided to leave the Church of England for that of Rome. The *Oxford English Dictionary* records Charles Kingsley, author of *The Water Babies*, as the first, in 1838, to use the word 'Anglicanism'. In the sixteenth century there was no such thing as Anglicanism, which is why people did not need a word for it. Queen Elizabeth was not an Anglican, nor were her bishops. They believed themselves to belong to the Church of Christ, the Church that Christ had founded. Historically speaking, the oldest branches of this Church were in the East: in Antioch, in Alexandria, in Jerusalem, in Constantinople, where the various patriarchates took local titles. The Patriarch of Constantinople came to be seen as the senior of these Eastern Churches and some, such as the Copts of Egypt, were separated from the others on the grounds of doctrine, but they all regarded themselves as members of the Church of Christ – what the Prayer Book of Edward VI called 'the blessed company of all faithful people'.

In the England of Elizabeth, only the very learned or the far-travelled (that is, a small minority) would have been aware of the Church in its oriental manifestations. For them, the arguments boiled down to whether or not they accepted the Roman Catholic authority or followed one of the Reformers – Luther or Zwingli or Calvin.

No one in the sixteenth century, in all its disputes, controversies and wars about religion, said, 'I don't like *this* Church, let's go and start *another*.' The fact that, as a result of the Reformation, and the fissiparous nature of Protestantism, there are many 'denominations' in today's Western world, confuses the modern observer into such anachronism as speaking of the Elizabethan Church as 'Anglican'. The 'Puritans' – those who wished the Church to follow the path it had done in Zwingli's or Calvin's Switzerland or Luther's Germany – are seen as proto-Presbyterians, Baptists or some other denomination, whereas those who could not in conscience take the oath swearing allegiance to the Queen as Governor of the Church of England are seen as members of yet another 'denomination': the Catholics.

But it was not like that. There was one Church that in the West had suffered the sort of crisis which had divided the Eastern Churches in the past – but never so radically. Since the twelfth century the popes had asserted, with increasing boldness, their quasi-monarchical status. When the separation and quarrels with Eastern Churches became an actual Schism in the twelfth century, the Roman Popes made ever more confident claims to jurisdiction over the entire Church – claiming the right to temporal as well as spiritual power.

It was really in these political quarrels – between the papacy and the

East, the papacy and the Western (usually German) emperors, and the papacy and the Kings of France, between 1200 and 1500 – that the seeds of the *religious* quarrels of the Reformation began. In the East, which had made the Emperor Constantine into a saint, it was perfectly imaginable that a secular ruler could be the Church's Governor on Earth. In the West, where popes had quarrelled with almost all the monarchs of Europe at some time or another, on precisely this issue, it was seen by many Christians as improper for any but the Pope to appoint bishops or authorise liturgies. Henry VIII's quarrel with the Pope about divorce in 1529 was far less radical than, say, the outright rejection of Christianity by the Emperor Frederick II (died 1250) or Philip the Fair of France's rejection of papal taxes and the Pope's right to appoint bishops.

What was new in the sixteenth century was an upsurge of *intellectual* enquiry about what the Church was. Luther did not nail his Treatise to the great doors of the abbey at Wittenberg because he wanted to start a Lutheran Church as a rival show to the Roman Catholic Church. He did so because he believed that late-medieval Christianity – with its sales of indulgences, its use of the Eucharistic Sacrament as a sort of bargaining tool or bribe to shorten a dead person's time in Purgatory, its lax sexual morals in monasteries, its papal politicking – was grossly failing to be the Church: the Church that Christ wanted it to be. Luther believed he had rediscovered the very Gospel itself. This was the Gospel of Justification by Faith Only, obscured and encrusted for centuries by superstition, and by attempts to win God's favour by 'good works', pilgrimages, requiem Masses, and the like. Calvin's view was different. For him, the key to all mythologies was predestination. Those who followed Calvin were (like Marxists and Darwinists) in that long tradition of thinkers who believe humanity is *programmed* (by God, by the materialist forces of history, by inheritance and DNA) to be as it is. Nothing can alter it. The concept of grace is severely limited by such a theology. But all these thinkers (who revolutionised the way Christians think and who blew to smithereens any chance of one undivided European Church acknowledging the supremacy of the Pope) believed they were trying to persuade the Church to find its true nature.

One of the most eloquent expressions of this yearning for the Church to find its true nature, and to find unity on Earth, was written by John Donne (1572–1631). Donne was brought up in a family that would not accept the Church of England. Two of his uncles were Jesuit priests. In 1593 a Roman Catholic priest, William Harrington, was found in the rooms of Donne's brother Henry. Both were arrested and imprisoned in the clink prison in Southwark. Harrington was hanged, drawn and quartered for treason. Donne was not yet twenty-one. He is noted for his extraordinary satires and tautly rendered erotic lyrics. But he also, in middle age, took Holy Orders. By now he had abandoned the Romanist sympathies of his family and he became Dean of St Paul's in London.

We do not know exactly when he wrote the sonnet which so eloquently encapsulates the sixteenth-century yearning not simply for unity and concord among Christians, but for truth. Helen Gardner glossed this poem as follows, and it might help the reader to follow her prose 'translation' before reading the poem itself:

> Make visible, dear Lord, the Church as she is described in Scripture. Can she be either the insolent, proud Church of Rome, or the mourning and desolate Protestant Church of Germany and here? Am I to believe that for a thousand years or more there was no true Church on earth? Or, that a Church claiming to be the truth itself, yet constantly erring – both innovating and deserting what she formerly held – can be she? Am I to believe that now, as of old, and in future, as long as the world lasts, she is to be found in one place only – here, or there, or elsewhere? Am I to believe that she is to be found here on earth, or am I to hold that only in heaven, after our pilgrimage, can we see her as she is? Lord, do not thus hide thy Bride from our sight, but let me woo the gentle spouse of thy marriage song, who is most faithful to Thy will and most pleasing to Thee when the greatest number of men seek and receive her embraces.

> Show me deare Christ, thy spouse, so bright and cleare.
> What, is it she, which on the other shore
> Goes richly painted? Or which rob'd and tore
> Laments and mournes in Germany and here?
> Sleepes she a thousand, then peepes up one yeare?
> Is she selfe truth and errs? Now new, now outwore?
> Doth she, and did she, and shall she evermore
> On one, on seaven, or on no hill appeare?
> Dwells she with us, or like adventuring knights
> First travaile we to seeke and then make Love?
> Betray kind husband thy spouse to our sights,
> And let myne amorous soule court thy mild Dove,
> Who is most trew, and most pleasing to thee, then
> When she is embrac'd and open to most men.[1]

It really was the aim of Elizabeth, when she came to the throne, to enable the Church to be 'open to most men' – and women, of course. That is, rather than adhering to her sister's policy of burning many heretics at the stake, or to her brother's highly divisive continental Protestantism, she aimed to create an ecclesiastical polity that was inclusive. There was great intellectual seriousness about her aim, and that of her first Parliament, to get the formula right: to arrange the Government of the Church, its rites and liturgies, in such a way that the majority of (ideally all) men and women could in conscience subscribe to it. It was necessary to cast the net as broadly as possible, since, once the formula had been decided, there was no room *politically* for dissent. The Church of England was not conceived as a religious denomination for 'Anglicans'. It was the Church for all the People of England. A failure to get it right would alienate large quantities of people, and create such a lack of sympathy between monarch and subjects as had obtained in Mary Tudor's reign. Such alienation of sympathy was not something that Elizabeth, politically, could afford.

The situation of the English Church at the beginning of Elizabeth's reign was one of complete chaos, a chaos heightened by the Queen's subtle and ambivalent attitude, her attempts not merely to adopt, but to explain, the religious position of her father Henry VIII in his last days. Was England to go Protestant, as the 'wolves of Germany' hoped, those thoroughgoing Lutherans or Calvinists who had gone into European exile during the reign of Mary? By no means, said Elizabeth. Within six weeks of her accession she had issued a proclamation (three days after Christmas 1558) forbidding all preaching, but permitting the Gospel and Epistle to be read in English at Mass. So the Roman Catholics had reason to be optimistic? Not so, since Elizabeth's first Parliament swept away all Mary's legislation, gave supreme power over the national Church to the Crown, brought back the second Prayer Book (the more Protestant version – Elizabeth herself preferred the first) of King Edward VI's reign, and made it a treasonable offence, punishable by death, to make written or oral defence of the 'authority of a foreign prince, prelate or potentate within her majesty's dominions' – that is, to accept the Pope as a higher *religious* authority than the Queen. All clergy, judges, justices, mayors, royal officials and persons wishing to take a degree at one of the universities were obliged to take the Oath of Supremacy, which declared the Queen to be the 'only supreme governor of this realm, as well in all spiritual and ecclesiastical things or causes as temporal'. She did not claim, as Henry VIII had done, to be 'the only supreme head on earth of the Church of England', but her defiance of papal authority put Catholics in an awkward position.

In Westminster Hall, at the end of March 1559, she had commanded a public debate about such matters as the Eucharist. Elizabeth herself, when once quizzed by her Catholic sister about her beliefs, had replied with the theologically impeccable, but brilliantly ambivalent quatrain of her own composition:

Christ was the Word that spake it,
He took the bread and brake it,
And what His words did make it,
That I believe and take it.

Only the word *did* is dubious from a Catholic viewpoint, since it implies a questioning of the sacerdotal power to summon Christ to the altar with each and every offering of the Eucharistic sacrifice.

But where did it leave the English churchgoer who, in one generation, had lived through the Henrician Reformation, the Edwardian Reformation and the Marian Counter-Reformation? Henry had abolished monasteries, cut off the English Church from the Pope and placed in every parish church what Catholics deemed to be an heretical translation of the Bible. But he had insisted upon the very presence of Christ in the Mass. He had retained Catholic Holy Orders – bishops, priests and deacons – and he had insisted that those who wished should go to confession to a priest and receive absolution. Edward VI's advisers were much more Protestant and, without the restraining influence of the ambivalent Cranmer, the mellifluous compiler of the new Prayer Books, might easily have introduced a system of Presbyterianism in which bishops and priests were abolished and the Eucharist declared unambiguously to be no more than a memorial meal, its elements merely bread and wine.

Mary had come to the throne and she had never wavered from the position for which Henry VIII's greatest Lord Chancellor, Sir Thomas More, had died: that a Catholicism that tried to separate itself from its parent stem, the Holy See of Rome, was an impossibility. But in her fervent desire to restore Catholicism she had burned heretics at the stake, including Elizabeth's godfather, Archbishop Cranmer.

Elizabeth's desire was, in the words of the Lord Keeper, Sir Nicholas Bacon, 'to secure and unite the people of the realm in one uniform order to the glory of God and to general tranquillity'.[2] This might have been her desire, but the reality was the reverse either of order or tranquillity.

The Venetian observer Il Schifanoya noted that the Bishop of London, Edmund Bonner, defiantly continued to have the old Roman Mass at St Paul's Cathedral up to St John the Baptist's Day (24 June) 1559. When the Council summoned him, he robustly answered, 'I possess three things, soul, body and property: of the two last you can dispose at your pleasure, but as to the soul God alone can command me.'[3] He was eventually imprisoned in the Marshalsea, where he died of an illness. Elizabeth had a particular hatred of Bonner, who had been a leading enthusiast for the incineration of (live) heretics at Smithfield. (He had, however, accepted Henry VIII's claim to be the head of the English Church and he had not followed the path of More or Fisher to martyrdom or recusancy.) Equally, however, Elizabeth would have disapproved of the Puritan louts who rioted within yards of St Paul's. 'These accursed preachers,' wrote the Venetian:

> who have come from Germany, do not fail to preach in their own fashion, both in public and in private, in such wise that they persuaded certain rogues to forcibly enter the church of St Mary-le-Bow in the middle of Cheapside, and force the shrine of the most Holy Sacrament, breaking the tabernacle, and throwing the most precious consecrated body of Jesus Christ to the ground. They also destroyed the altar and the images, with the pall and church linen, breaking everything into a thousand pieces.

Equally baffling to the Italian was the fact that in the Chapel Royal, 'Mass was sung in English, with the Communion being given in both kinds.' (Among the Roman Catholics it was only the custom – and still is the custom in most churches – to give the Host, reserving the Chalice for the celebrant priest alone.) The Venetian was fascinated to learn that the Mass had been sung by a priest wearing Catholic vestments, but that to distribute Communion he had divested himself and wore just a surplice – *la semplice cotta*.[4]

To impose order on this anarchy was no easy task, and it would require a new Archbishop of Canterbury. Mary, astonishingly for one who cared so much about the Church, had an ageing and enfeebled collection of bishops. You would have expected her, and her Archbishop, Reginald Pole, to urge upon the Pope the necessity of the swift replacement of dead or decrepit diocesans, but at the time of her death there were no fewer than nine vacant sees, whose bishops had died in the last year of her reign. Pole himself had died at the same time as Mary herself, so Elizabeth did not have the painful task of removing him. The Archbishop of York, Nicholas Heath, was urged to accept the Elizabethan settlement of the Church, but he was unable to do so, and was permitted to retire to Surrey. Of the remaining diocesan bishops, only Anthony Kitchin of Llandaff took the oath to Elizabeth. This left no more than ten who at first tried to block the religious reforms in the House of Lords and were then removed from office. None of them were killed, still less burned at the stake as Cranmer had been.

Guided no doubt by Cambridge-obsessed William Cecil, the Queen appointed a don as the new Archbishop of Canterbury. This was the prodigious scholar and bibliophile Matthew Parker, Master of Corpus Christi College and Vice Chancellor of Cecil's old university. Elizabeth herself had reason to love Parker. He had been her mother's chaplain, and when Anne Boleyn was about to be beheaded she urged the Protestant Dr Parker to give spiritual guidance to her little daughter. He had preached before the 'lady Elizabeth' at Hatfield.[5] A diffident man unused to the machinations of courts or the hurly-burly of politics, Parker seemed at first an improbable pilot for the fledgling Church of England. He himself certainly thought so, confiding to his diary, '*17 Decembr, Ann. 1559.* CONSECRATUS *sum in Archiepiscopum Cantuarien. Heu! Heu! Domine Deus, in quae tempora servasti me? Jam veni in profundum aquarum, et tempestas demersit me.*' (17 December 1559. I was consecrated Archbishop of Canterbury. Alas! Alas! Lord God, for what times has thou kept me? For now I am plunged into the depth of the waters and the storm has overwhelmed me.)[6]

It is worth noting – since it was questioned subsequently by controversialists with an axe to grind – that Parker's consecration could leave no doubt of its Catholic and Apostolic intentions. That is, the bishops who took part in the ceremony believed their authority to derive in an unbroken line, by the laying-on of hands, back to the Apostles of Christ himself. The bishops who consecrated Parker were William Barlow, former Prior of Bisham, who had been made a bishop in Henry VIII's reign and was Bishop of St David's until deprived of his see by Mary; Hodgkins, another bishop consecrated in Henry VIII's time; and two bishops of Edwardian vintage, Miles Coverdale and John Scory. The consecrating bishops invoked the Holy Spirit with the words of the Apostle Paul: 'Take the Holy Ghost, and remember that thou stir up the grace of God that is in thee by imposition of hands.'[7] It cannot be doubted that all those present would have seen this as much more than a mere form of words, and that they would have shared William Cecil's view that English bishops 'had been apostolically ordained and not merely elected by a congregation like Lutheran or Calvinist heretics.'[8] Forty-five years passed before the concoction of the so-called Nag's Head Fable, first published in Antwerp, in 1604. This claimed that the deprived Catholic bishops had been summoned to the Nag's Head tavern in Cheapside and asked to consecrate Parker and the other new Elizabethan bishops. When they refused, pressure was put upon Scory, 'an apostate monk', to do so, even though he was not – according to the fable – himself consecrated; and 'they all rose up Bishops' after Scory had merely waved a Bible over their heads. This scurrilous yarn would not be worth denying, were it not for the fact that so many, even down to the twentieth century, were persuaded by it.

Though the Nag's Head Fable is no longer believed, there has been a tendency, even among academic historians of our own day, to speak as if Parker's consecration was somehow unreal or invalid. Kenneth Carleton, in *Bishops and Reform in the English Church, 1520–1559*, wrote, 'the day 17 December 1559 was a watershed in the history of the English Church. More than any other event, the consecration of Matthew Parker marked the final and definitive split from the Western Catholicism which subsisted in the Church of Rome and drew its unifying principle from communion with the Pope'. This is on a surface level self-evidently true, but even this statement needs qualifying. When the Council of Trent reassembled (it rumbled on, redefining doctrine and making European liturgy uniform for nearly twenty years, from 1545 to 1563), the Pope invited Elizabeth I to send representatives of the English Church, and William Cecil (no papalist he) felt that the Church 'could not refuse to allow the presidency of the Pope, provided it was understood that the Pope was not above the Council, but merely its head; and its decision should be accepted in England if they were in harmony with Holy Scripture and the first four Councils' – that is, of the early Church.[9]

That is why some readers could be misled by Carleton's conclusion: 'from Parker onwards, it could truly be said that the Anglican Church possessed a Protestant episcopate'. It could not be truly said, for the reasons already rehearsed in this chapter: namely, no such body as 'the Anglican Church' existed and, although Parker would appoint some Protestant-minded clergymen as bishops, none of them would have recognised such a phenomenon as 'a Protestant episcopate'.[10] There is in fact no such thing. Either there is an episcopate, whose bishops are bishops of the universal Church, or there is no episcopate. How important it was to have bishops, whether you could have a Church without bishops – these were matters that the Elizabethans discussed keenly. But a bishop, was (is) a bishop, whether he calls himself a Copt or a Russian, an Englishman or an Italian.

Parker then set to work filling the many sees that had become vacant owing to Pole's negligence or the resignation of their conservative occupants. Many of the new bishops were far more Protestant than the Queen, but she insisted that they dress in the same outfits as had been worn by the Catholic bishops of Mary's reign – a rochet, or long surplice with gathered cuffs, over which they wore a chimere, a sleeveless tabard, which reached to their ankles. Bishops of the Church of England still wear this rig in Parliament to this day. The clothes of the ordinary clergy were no less important to Elizabeth, as they were to many of her contemporaries. The apparel oft proclaims the man, and clothes in church have a symbolic significance that was not lost on the controversialists of those overheated times. To celebrate Mass, a priest in the Western Church wears a chasuble, a sleeveless garment like a poncho, thrown over the head. Its historical origin was in the *pinula* or *planeta* of the late classical world. Early chasubles were simply the 'Sunday best' of a Roman man in the fourth century. But what had been simply a sign that the president at the Eucharist wished to look smart, *endimanché*, became in time a symbol of the accumulations of Catholic doctrine surrounding the liturgy at which the garment was worn. To wear a chasuble meant that you believed Christ came to the altar. It meant the Real Presence. It meant a Catholic understanding of the Sacrament. The Queen, whose father wrote theological treatises, whose sister had burned heretics at the stake and whose closest adviser was the religiously Protestant Cecil, did not, surely, ask her bishops and priests to wear vestments simply because they looked pretty. She wanted the ministers of the Sacrament in the Church of England to wear chasubles at the Eucharistic table because she wanted Henry VIII's Anglo-Catholic religion – Catholicism translated into English, Catholicism without the Pope – to be the norm. John Jewel, a learned and godly man who had gone into exile during Mary's reign, returned and was made Bishop of Salisbury.

Jewel wrote the first major theological treatise of the reign, *An Apology of the Church of England* (published in 1562). He maintained that the Church of England, far from departing from Catholic tradition, was in fact returning to it. It was Rome that had departed 'from God's word, from Christ's commandments, from the apostles' ordinances, from the primitive church's examples, from the old fathers and councils orders'. The church orders decreed by Elizabeth and her advisers were *not* an innovation, still less a new denomination. England had 'returned to the apostles and old Catholic fathers'.[11]

But the Church of England had no hope of succeeding, no hope of uniting the doubting Catholic with the fervent Puritan, unless it was prepared to compromise. Elizabeth herself was forced to climb down over the question of chasubles. Jewel gently reminded her that 'touching the knowledge of God's word and cases of religion certain it is the King is inferior to a bishop'.[12] Chasubles were discarded – only to be revived by nineteenth-century ritualists. In cathedrals and colleges it was required that the clergy wore copes (cloak-like vestments). In ordinary parishes a surplice was all that was needed. Elizabeth's request that churches should keep their crucifixes – that is, an image of the cross with a statue of the suffering Christ upon it – was largely ignored, and in especially Protestant places, such as the City of London, bonfires were lit in Cheapside to burn 'all the roods and Maries and Johns and many other of the church goods.'[13]

Elizabeth wished to revert to the Catholic idea of a celibate clergy. She succeeded (largely) in banning women from cathedral closes, and was unpardonably rude to clergy wives when she encountered them. Archbishop Parker's wife, Margaret Harlestone, committed a triple offence in the Queen's eyes. Not only was she married to an archbishop, something Elizabeth abhorred, but she was also a beautiful woman – far more beautiful than the Queen. Worse still, perhaps, Margaret was a clever woman who conversed fluently in Latin and Greek. When the Parkers entertained the Queen at Lambeth Palace, the Queen thanked the archbishop effusively, but then turned to Mrs Parker: 'And you – Madam I may not call you, and Mistress I am ashamed to call you, so I know not what to call you, but yet I do thank you.'[14] This anecdote still has the power to make the reader cringe on Elizabeth's behalf.

The Parkers, the first married couple to reside at Lambeth Palace, were prodigiously hospitable. The Great Hall was hung with Flemish tapestries of harmonious colours. Food was served on silver and gold. There were no forks in those days – guests ate with knives and fingers. And we can see what they ate from a book in the archbishop's library, preserved in Corpus Christi, Cambridge – 'A Proper newe booke of Cookerye', which Mrs Parker purchased in 1560. The recipes appropriately follow the liturgical calendar. 'Brawn is beste from a fortnight before Mychalemas tyll lente, mutton is good at all times, but from Easter to Mydsommer it is worste' . . . 'A Pollard is speciall good in Maye, at Mydsommer he is a bucke and is verye good tyll holye Rood daye' (a pollard is a stag without horns).[15]

So the Church, in its prayers and feasts, its meals as well as its liturgy, maintained the old Catholic calendar: Advent, Christmas, Candlemas, Lent, Easter, Pentecost. Yet in other ways the Church of England at this date seemed intolerantly, even belligerently, Protestant. Protestant were its 39 Articles – a sort of manifesto of belief and practice to which the clergy must subscribe. Protestant was its vandalism. In the episcopal registry at Lincoln there is a parchment manuscript volume upon whose vellum cover is inscribed INVENTARIUM MONUMENTORUM SUPERSTITIONIS. It describes how, in parish after parish, the church wardens systematically destroyed the beautiful outward signs of Catholic devotion:

> Thorpe in P'rochie de Heyther – Wittiam Smyth church warden, 8 April 1566. Itm we had no Roode nor other Imageis but that were painted on the wall and thei ar defaced and put oute anno pmo Eliz. John psonne beinge churchwarden.
>
> Itm two vestments a sepulchre cloth two banner clothes and a crosse clothe sold to Wittm Cressie about e a moneth sens 1565 wch was

defaced before he brought them. Itm one mass boore burnte yesterdaie.

As this item shows, the actual service book in this remote Lincolnshire parish continued to be the old Mass book until 1566, a full eight years after Elizabeth came to the throne. In the same year we find 'ASBYE IUXA SLEFORD [that is Sleaford Abbey, Lincolnshire][16] William Daunce and Robert Cranwell 26 April 1566 Imprimis or Images of the Rood mary and Jhon wth all other Images – burned Ao iijo Elizabethe. Itm iij papistical books – wch did belonge to Mr Yorke who had defaced them Ao quarto Elizabethe the other were stole awaie in queene maries reign.'[17] The Yorkes had been settled at Ashby-de-la-Laund since the Wars of the Roses. Why did Mr Yorke deface his 'papistical books' in the fourth year of Elizabeth's reign? History cannot tell us. All over the country we find the same thing happening. In another parish we find Thomas Waite and Thomas Stevenson, church wardens, 29 April 1566: 'The rood marie and Johnne and all other Imagies of papistrie – were burnte by a plu'mer in a 1562 . . . Itm two vestements were cut in pieces yeterdaie and sold to Thomas Waite and George Holmes and theye have put them to prophane use.'[18] At Somersby, where in the nineteenth century Alfred Tennyson's father would be the alcoholic rector: 'Itm iij candellstickes a crose a hollie water fatt censors and a sacring bell – sold to a puterer of Lincoln at Grantham faire this year by the said churchwardens'.[19] And at Grantham – one day destined to be Margaret Thatcher's home town:

> ffurst we present that the Roode loft stode vpe in carved work in the ffurst yeare of the Queenes maiestie Reigne that nowe is and was broken downe and sold and the mony to the use of the poore and paying wages for taking downe to carpenters and masons and of the surplasage accompt was made by John Taylyer then being churche warden to master Bentham master ffleetwod and mast everyngton then beying visitors.[20]

At Grantham, too, we find them selling 'a silver and copper shrine called senet Wulffran shrine' . . . 'and bought wythe the pyrce thereof a silver pott pcell Glyt an [*sic*] an ewer of silver for the mynistracion of the holye and most sacred supper of our lorde Jesus Crist called the holye comanyon'.[21]

These visitations, and the enforcement of the injunctions, should not be seen in purely religious terms. It is true that many of the Elizabethan bishops, and the enforcers they employed to visit parishes and ensure the destruction of the 'monuments of superstition', were motivated by

Protestant zeal. But during a decade when Mary, Queen of Scots was seen as a constant threat to Elizabeth's throne, the government was terrified by the political implications of Catholicism. It did not want a repetition of what had happened upon the death of Edward VI when, for example, at Cratfield the reredos of a medieval high altar had been brought out of hiding from the vicarage barn; or at Long Metlow, or Morebath, where much-loved vestments, statues, reliquaries and Mass books came out from hiding upon the accession of Mary Tudor.[22] It was essential, from a political point of view, for Cecil and Parker to drive forward a much more thorough-going destruction of the outward signs of Catholic piety. To this extent, some of the vandalism – the ripping-up of copes and chasubles and the use of missals to line pudding basins – should be seen in the light of those patriotic enthusiasts in 1939–40 who turned signposts the wrong away round to confuse any Nazi storm-troopers who might have come marching down the English roads. The Queen of Scotland, or the armies of France, would *not* find an England secretly eager to reinstate reliquaries or to reclothe their clergy in Mass vestments, which were by now indelibly associated with intrusions upon the political as well as the religious liberties of the English.

The *piety* of those for whom holy water stoups, crucifixes or coloured stoles were valuable did not vanish as easily as broken stained glass or a shredded frontal. John Cosin, chaplain to the royalist court in exile during the 1650s and subsequently Bishop of Durham in 1660, looked back on his time as chaplain to Bishop Overall of Norwich (1560–1619) and remembered, for example, how that bishop ignored the Protestantising rubrics of the Settlement and used (as did the Queen herself in the Chapel Royal) the more Catholic order of the 1549 liturgy.[23] Bishop Lancelot Andrewes (1555–1626), who received a supposedly Protestant education from Richard Mulcaster at Merchant Taylors' School (see Chapter 6), when he became Bishop of Ely had 'an altar with two silver candlesticks on it. A silver gilt canister for the wafers . . . A chalice with Christ engraven on it' and other tokens of the belief, expressed in his *Preces Privatae*, in the:

> Catholic Church
> Eastern, Western, British.

To a Roman cardinal, Andrewes would write, 'Our Bishops have been ordained in each case by three bishops and by true bishops. I say by true bishops for they were ordained by yours, unless yours are not true bishops.' Archbishop Laud, in the reign of Charles I, could insist that 'The altar is the greatest place of God's residence upon earth, for there it is . . . This is my body.'[24] And again:

> In the sacrament is the very true and natural body and blood of Christ, even that which was born of the Virgin Mary which ascended into heaven, which sitteth at the right hand of God the Father, which shall come to judge the quick and the dead: only we differ 'in modo' [from Roman Catholics] in the way and manner of being we confess all the one thing to be in The Sacrament, and dissent in the manner of being there.[25]

What Hilaire Belloc called 'the Catholic thing' – Mass, the recitation of the hours of prayer, confession – continued within the Church of England, as did the Catholic order of bishops, priests and deacons, even if there were times when it became an underground stream invisible from the surface. It is often assumed, by Roman Catholic or secularist historians, that idleness and cowardice explained the fact that so few clergy and laity stood out against the Elizabethan Settlement. 'Out of 9,400 clergy in England only 192 refused the oath of supremacy.'[26] One reason for this could have been that, whatever Protestant resolutions were being passed in London, and whatever was demanded by bishops and official busybodies, the people of England continued to find Catholic sustenance in their national Church. A modern historian asks how 'one of the most Catholic countries became one of the least.'[27] One answer to this is that it did not, but that its Catholicism found it could survive, under the Protestant dispensation of the Elizabethan Church. Another answer is that the Reformation took a very, very long time. Yet another answer is that only a minority of zealots – and those chiefly in the North – felt it was necessary to ally themselves with the Queen of Scots or the King of Spain or the Pope of Rome in order to worship God in an English church; and the more these foreign potentates threatened England, the more entrenched the Protestantism of the English became.

But, as the parish visitations to the diocese of Chichester revealed, as late as 1569 the Reformation was not greeted with enthusiasm in all areas of the national Church. In the cathedral itself was one William Weaye, appointed by the Henrician Bishop Sherburne to a clerkship and summoned before the dean and chapter on 13 October 1569. It was charged that he had in his possession certain Catholic theological and devotional books and a portable altar. He did not deny it, and when asked what he thought of Purgatory, the veneration of the saints, the Mass and transubstantiation, he admitted that he 'lyketh of these'. 'He believes as the Catholic Church does, whereof he thinks the Pope to be head, or else there should be many heads if every prince were supreme governor in their own realm.' Poor old Weaye was deprived of his clerkship and fined thirty shillings 'out of hand',[28] but for every case brought before the courts there must have been hundreds where a blind eye was turned to Catholicism being practised within the Church of England.

The archbishop's commissary, visiting in 1569, concluded sadly:

> except it be about Lewes and a little in Chichester, the whole diocese is very blind and superstitious for want of teaching.
>
> They use in many places ringing between morning and the litany, and all the night following All Saints' day, as before in time of blind ignorance and superstition taught by the pope's clergy.
>
> Many bring to church the old popish Latin primers, and use to pray upon them all the time when the lessons are being read.
>
> Some old folks and women used to have beads in the churches, but these I took away from them but they have some yet at home in their houses.[29]

In the country parishes of Sussex there was little contact with the outside world. For much of the year the few existent roads were impassable. No wonder that twelve years after they had been made illegal in London, the tiny Sussex parish of Tarring should still be using 'vestments and the old mass book'.

Eamon Duffy, a modern historian of the sixteenth-century Church, ended his haunting account *The Stripping of the Altars*, which is the story of the Reformation: 'Cranmer's sombrely magnificent prose, read week by week, entered and possessed their minds, and became the fabric of their prayer, the utterance of their most solemn and their most vulnerable moments.'[30] But this was not something that happened overnight. The outward events of the political world had far more to do with this than the often Cambridge-educated Lutheran or Calvinist preachers sent to unresponsive congregations from London to the remoter corners of England. If the English stopped praying from Latin primers or muttering over beads (and not all did), it was not necessarily because they had been bossed by home-grown Protestants. It was because if there was anything they resented more than the busybodydom of an 'archbishop's commissary', it was the threat to their own queen's authority by the Queen of Scotland or some other foreign power. The successive popes did far more to make England Protestant. At home, the system of double-think, of turning a blind eye, of nodding and winking, which has often made English life so confusing for social observers, left their inner and religious life rather more ambiguous, rather less easy to categorise than the busy-bodies would have liked. This was certainly true of the 1560s before events made life for crypto-Catholics much more difficult. For the first dozen years of the reign it was perfectly in order to pay lip service to the new Church order and, if challenged, to offer a bribe or a fine, to carry on regardless.

'As for the commissaries court,' opined *The Admonition to the Parliament* of 1572, 'that is but a pettie little stinking ditche, that floweth oute of that former great puddle, robbing Christes church of lawfull pastors, of watchfull Seniors and Elders, and carefull Deacons.'[31]

But it would give a misleading impression to end this chapter on so vinaigrous or negative a tone.

Mandell Creighton, in his superb biography of Queen Elizabeth (1896), said, of the Elizabethan Settlement, 'England was again independent. Its Church was again free to work out its own problems. Its system has not changed from that day to this.'[32]

It is hard to imagine any member of the Church of England in the twenty-first century who would be able to echo the great Victorian bishop's words. Since the advent of a multicultural Britain, the 'C of E' has become one sect among many, even though its technical and legal status might remain still as it was in the reign of the first Elizabeth. Although, wearing Elizabethan costume, Church of England bishops still, at the time of writing, sit as of right in the British Parliament, this cannot be for long. Their presence there can scarcely be justified to the great majority of citizens who do not share their faith. This is one of the most fundamental signs that the England created in Elizabeth's reign has been brought to an end. Nevertheless, as we have seen, the Elizabethan Settlement in the Church was not a wholly spiritual thing. Elizabeth's national Church was a coalition. It was not tolerant of those, such as Roman Catholics or Puritans, who denied its grounds for existence. It did, however, for the huge majority of citizens, teach the necessity of two incompatible parties learning to live together. To this degree, it is possible to see in the workings of the Elizabethan Church the ancestry of a later 'consensus' politics.

6

The New Learning

Richard Mulcaster, the observant recorder of the pageantry and celebrations on Queen Elizabeth's coronation day, was a northerner and an Old Etonian. His father was one of the two Members of Parliament for Carlisle, and Mulcaster himself would serve in the same capacity in the first of Elizabeth's parliaments.[1]

In 1561 he was chosen as the first headmaster of the newly founded Merchant Taylors' School in the City of London. The building selected for the grammar school, at the expense of the Merchant Taylors' Company, was a house formerly belonging to the Dukes of Buckingham at the Manor of the Rose in the parish of St Lawrence-Poultney. In Shakespeare's *Henry VIII*, the duke's ownership of the house is still remembered:

> Nor long before your highness sped to France
> The Duke, being at The Rose, within the parish
> St Lawrence Poultney, did of me demand
> What was the speech among the Londoners
> Concerning the French journey . . .[2]

The Merchant Taylors' School – destined to become, almost instantaneously, one of the most prestigious of English Renaissance schools – was only one of dozens that were founded, or reconstituted, in these times. John Colet (1467–1519), friend of Erasmus and Sir Thomas More, had led the way with the foundation of St Paul's School in London in 1509 – with the trustees being the Mercers' Company. With the coming of the Reformation and the removal of monastery schools and charity schools, the need to found new educational establishments became urgent. The monasteries were dissolved between 1536 and 1541. The Charities Act of Henry VIII left many a teacher in a charity school penniless. For example, Libeus Byard, the chantry chaplain at Stamford, Lincolnshire, earned his living as the teacher of young boys, such as William Cecil, the future Secretary to Elizabeth I.[3] Some of the educational damage done by the removal of Church teachers was repaired in Henry VIII's own time, with the foundation of fine schools such as the Royal Grammar School, Newcastle-on-Tyne. The school song, composed in the 1920s by the school's historian and history master, J.B. Brodie, was historically accurate when it proclaimed:

Horsley, a Merchant Venturer bold,
Of good Northumbrian strain,
Founded our rule and built our school
In bluff King Harry's reign . . .[4]

Yet though Henry promised to raise a subsidy through Parliament to fund schools, he did little about it, and most educational initiatives of the time came from benevolent private means, such as those of Robert Thorn, a Spanish oil merchant and soap-maker who – as it says on his Latin monument in the Temple Church in London – 'devised certain property for the erection, foundation, continuance and support of a Free Grammar School to be established in Bristol', his home town.[5]

Even more schools were rescued, reconstituted or founded in the reign of Edward VI: famous establishments such as Sherborne and the King Edward VI School in Birmingham, as well as many smaller ones. Protector Somerset did much to undo the damage of Henry VIII's Chantries Act and to re-endow local schools. 'He should be regarded,' wrote one historian, 'as the true patron saint of the Grammar Schools of Grantham and Louth, and Morpeth, of Birmingham and Macclesfield, and of the Public Schools of Sedbergh, Shrewsbury and Sherborne.' (Of course the distinction between grammar schools and 'public schools' is a Victorian one. In the Tudor age Sir Philip Sidney [Shrewsbury] and William Shakespeare [Stratford-upon-Avon Grammar School], whatever differences in the social status of their families, would have made none between their schools.)

There is a natural tendency to see the Tudor passion for education as a Protestant phenomenon, but the distinction is not necessarily a fair one. Colet, after all, was a Catholic. In regions where Catholicism persisted during or after the landmark dates of the Reformation, there was no less zeal than in Protestant regions for maintaining or founding schools. Sir Richard Towneley, for example, a devoted Catholic, together with the families of Haydock, Habergham, Woodneff and Whitacre, was among the founders and first governors of the grammar school at Burnley in Lancashire. 'The school which was refounded was possibly intended to keep alive the Catholic Faith.'[6] The founder of the grammar school at Appleby, in Westmorland – Robert Langton, Archdeacon of Dorset – became a monk of the Charterhouse in London and an Elizabethan headmaster of the school. And John Boste, Master of the school, was a convert to Catholicism who was canonised in 1970 as one of the forty English and Welsh martyrs steadfast to death for their beliefs.

Even within the Merchant Taylors' Company itself, with which we began, there was by no means a simple religious mono-culture. The school's founder is usually named as Sir Thomas White, a Catholic Merchant Taylor who, during the reign of Mary Tudor, had founded St John's College, Oxford.[7] The real founder of the school, however, was a Merchant Taylor of a very different complexion, Richard Hilles. A convinced Protestant, Hilles had taken a leading part in the nomination of Lady Jane Grey as Queen. (He was lucky to receive a pardon from the Queen.) For ten years (1539–49) Hilles had lived in Strasbourg and absorbed the tenets of Calvinism. During Mary's reign, he had maintained contacts with English Protestant exiles on the continent – men such as Miles Coverdale, the translator of our unforgettable Psalter, as still sung daily in England 'in quires and places where they sing'; or Edmund Grindal, later Bishop of London and Archbishop of Canterbury under Elizabeth. When Hilles set in train the foundation of the Merchant Taylors' School he had it in mind to establish a distinctly Protestant school. The Elizabethan schools were nurseries in which the Reformation could be planted and nurtured.

The letters of the Queen's Council to the Archbishop of Canterbury were silent on the subject of any intellectual training for schoolmasters, or on the details of secular life in the schools. What mattered was 'That all teachers of children shall stir and move them to live and do reverence to God's true religion now truly set forth by public authority' and that 'every parson, vicar and curate shall upon every holy day and every second Sunday in the year hear and instruct the youth of the parish for half an hour at least before evening prayer in the ten commandments, the Articles of the Belief, and the Lord's Prayer, and diligently examine them and teach the Catechism set forth in the book of public prayer'.[8]

Just as for the brief years of Mary Tudor's reign the Catholics had attempted to further their ideas among children, so with the accession of Elizabeth there was a systematic insistence that the children be imbued not only with new learning, but also with the faith of the Reformation. To some extent they went together. Sir John Cheke, Provost of King's College, 'Who once taught Cambridge and King Edward Greek'[9] (as Milton wrote in a sonnet), was ardent for the Reformation. Mulcaster was at Cheke's college in Cambridge from 1548 to 1553 and, as well as a mastery of Greek, Latin and Hebrew, which he passed on so successfully to his pupils, he also shared Cheke's passion for the religion of the continental Reformers.

When the arch-Protestant Bishop of London, Edmund Grindal, made a 'solempne visitacon' to the Merchant Taylors' School, he brought with him as examiners learned Protestants who had gone into exile during Mary's reign, as he had done himself: in 1562, David Whitehead, Canon Calfhill of Christ Church, and Archdeacon Watts; in 1564, Dean Nowell of St Paul's and Miles Coverdale himself. They found the children competent in Latin, Greek and Hebrew – Mulcaster had 'moche profited the schollers there & there for worthy of greate comendacon'. The only feature of Mulcaster's education to which they took exception was his North Country accent, something shared with the ushers or assistant masters, who 'therefore did not pronounce so well as those that be brought up in the schools of the south pites of the realme'.[10]

The pupils who did such credit to their headmaster included Edmund Spenser, who entered the school aged nine in 1561 and would go on to write *The Faerie Queene*, and Lancelot Andrewes, the incomparable prose stylist who oversaw the Authorized Version of the Bible. By the time he left the school in 1586, Mulcaster had also taught Thomas Kyd, author of *The Spanish Tragedy*; Thomas Lodge, one of the medics among *littérateurs* (with Keats and Bridges and Anton Chekhov), a fine lyric poet; James Whitlocke, who as well as being one of the great judges and law-men of Elizabethan England, was also, thanks to Mulcaster, a fine Hebraist (the Merchant Taylors' School had a Hebrew master until the 1950s). 'He red unto me all Jobe,' Whitlocke remembered, 'and twenty Psalmes, and a part of Genesis, and after I had taken my lecture from him, which was after five of the clock that I went from school, I wolde daly, after supper, make a praxis of that I had herd, and set it down in writing'.[11]

The daily curriculum of an Elizabethan grammar school was demanding. Shakespeare, the product of such an education at the grammar school in Stratford-upon-Avon, looked back on his childhood self:

> The whining schoolboy, with his satchel
> And shining morning face, creeping like snail
> Unwillingly to school . . .[12]

The day began early. At Highgate, founded in 1562 by Sir Roger Cholmeley, but with the enthusiastic blessing of Grindal – who gave the land for the school – they started at 7 a.m. with prayers, the boys 'devoutly kneeling down on their knees', and it continued until 5 p.m. in winter, 6 p.m. in summer.[13] The Highgate boys had it comparatively easy. At Winchester, a boarding school, the day began at 5 a.m. with a prefect shouting '*Surgite*' (Latin for 'get up!' – and the children were praying in the chapel by 5.30. Similar routines were expected of the boys at Eton. At Westminster, Ben Jonson's old school, it was up at 5.15, say Latin prayers, wash in the cloister and in school by 6 a.m., with lessons lasting through a seven-hour day.

Eighteenth-century prints of the Merchant Taylors' schoolroom at

Suffolk Lane show what would have been commonplace in schools all over England: one large hall with benches and desks arranged down the sides. The whole school would have been taught in the same space, divided into different 'forms' – that is, literally forms or benches – according to age or ability. St Paul's had one of the larger schoolrooms: 122 feet by 33 feet. Manchester Grammar had a schoolroom that measured 96 feet by 30 feet. The average grammar school would have consisted of a room 50–60 feet long by 20 feet broad, and it would have held fifty to eighty boys. It would have been cold in winter and, at any time of year, extremely uncomfortable.

The room would have been kept clean by a 'poor scholar'. At St Paul's the admission fee of fourpence was waived for a poor scholar 'that sweepeth the school and keepeth the seats clean'. At the Merchant Taylors' School the admission fee was paid to one who had 'to sweep the school and keep the court of the school clean, and see the streets nigh to the school gate cleansed of all manner of ordure, carrion, or other filthy or unclean things, out of good order, or extraordinarily there thrown'.[14] Was this the job of Edmund Spenser, described in the Towneley Hall MSS transcribed by the Rev. A.B. Grosart in 1877 as one of the 'poor scholars' to whom 'gownes' were given (the Merchant Taylors' also paid Spenser ten shillings 'at his gowinge to pembrocke hall in chambridge').[15]

Keeping order in the schoolroom was not always easy. At the worst schools there must have been uproar much of the time. Discipline was maintained, if at all, by physical chastisement. (When a student took a degree as master of grammar in medieval Cambridge he was given as symbols of his office a birch and a psalter.[16]) There were complaints at the Merchant Taylors' School from 'cockering mothers' and 'indulgent fathers' that he should mitigate his severity, but Mulcaster was impenitent about thrashing the boys. 'If that instrument be thought too severe for boys, which was not devised by our time, but received from antiquity, I will not strive with any man in its defence if he will leave us some means for compelling obedience where numbers have to be taught together.' On the other hand, Mulcaster was, by the standards of the age, soft-hearted enough to consider that the 'continual and terrible whipping' in other schools was deplorable, and that 'beating must only be for ill behaviour, not for failure in learning'. [Mulcaster, Elementarie]

Not all teachers at other schools were so restrained. In July 1563 a teacher named Penred beat a boy with a belt buckle 'that left no skin on his body'. This was too much, even by Elizabethan standards, and Penred was prosecuted. The thrasher was given a punishment even more sadistic than his own mistreatment of schoolboys. He was pilloried at the Standard in Cheapside, his neck, hands and feet fastened to a stake with iron cuffs while the Beadles of the Beggars whipped him. Sometimes as many as three beadles at a time beat him. The Lord Mayor of London came to watch, and the victim of Penred's cruelty, the half-flayed boy, was also displayed on the pillory, his bare torso gashed and bruised. Henry Machyn, a London draper who kept a diary, said that the sight of the child was the most pitiful he could imagine.[17]

In that same year of 1563 the Queen was dining with her old tutor Roger Ascham, Sir William Cecil and Sir Richard Sackville. The conversation turned to some Eton boys who had lately run away from the school because of excessive beating. Ascham argued that children were sooner allured by love than driven by beating to good learning. The schoolhouse, in general a place of torment, should, argued Ascham, be 'a refuge against fear'. Sackville, a Boleyn cousin of the Queen through his mother, and the father of Thomas Sackville, was silent, but after dinner he drew Ascham aside, saying how much he agreed and how he lamented his own harshness as a parent. 'Surely, God willing, if God lend me life, I will make this my mishap some occasion of good hope to little Robert Sackville my son's son. For whose bringing up I would gladly if it so please you, use specially your good advice. I hear say you have a son much of his age [Ascham had three sons]: we will deal with this together.'[18]

This was the origin of Ascham's book *The Schoolmaster*, dedicated to William Cecil, but left incomplete at Ascham's death (in 1568) and published by his widow in 1570. The little dinner table of these extremely clever people – Ascham, Cecil, the Queen – reminds us, if reminder were required, that the Queen herself was the direct beneficiary of the revival in learning. When her tutor William Grindal died in 1548, when she was still fourteen, he was replaced immediately by his mentor Roger Ascham – 'not only the greatest teacher of the age; he was also one of its most notable gossips'.[19] Ascham, like William Cecil, like so many other influential Elizabethans, had learned Greek at Cambridge from John Cheke. He was a Fellow of St John's College, and thirty-four years old, when he joined the Princess's household in Chelsea. Their mornings together began with the study of the Greek New Testament, a book that was in effect for the sixteenth century a Protestant text. In classical Greek they read Sophocles, Isocrates and Demosthenes. In the afternoons they read the Roman historian Livy and the statesman-rhetorician Cicero. Among the Greek texts of late antiquity they read the North African Cyprian, Bishop of Carthage. Cyprian among the ancients, and Philipp Melanchthon, the Protestant reformer, among the moderns, were studied because they 'convey pure doctrine in elegant language'. It has been questioned whether Ascham admired the Princess's prose style,[20] but he did admire her proficiency in the classical tongues. Oral Greek she spoke 'frequently, willingly and moderately well'.

Because of the educationalists' emphasis on repetition and on the 'correct' pronunciation of Latin and Greek – Erasmus had pioneered the reconstruction of what ancient Greek *sounded* like[21] – and because many of the educationalists and grammarians were also advocates of spelling reform, they have left behind abundant evidence of how Elizabethan English was spoken.

As in modern English, there was a huge variety of pronunciation. But in London, and at court, there was a Received Pronunciation as there was throughout the period of English cultural self-confidence, 1550–1950. Sir Walter Raleigh's Devon accent was *noted* at court.[22] Something that would strike any modern time-traveller, if transported back to Elizabeth's court, or Grindal's church, or Shakespeare's theatre, would be the differences in vowel-sounds. Words that we now pronounce [i:] while spelling *ea* would all, in Elizabeth's reign, have been rendered [e:] or [eI], as would many words with the long *a* vowel. By extension the [e:] or [eI] pronunciation was used for *conceive*, *receive*, *deceive*, *feature*, *supreme*. The vowels in these words would have been all but identical to the *a* in father – [fayther]. The long [a], so noticeable a feature of *southern* RP in modern English, with its *bahth, plahstic*, and so on, barely existed in early modern or Elizabethan English. Even foreign names and loan-words were assimilated into an English *ay* sound.

So we find Milton, in the middle of the seventeenth century, punning on the word *Gaza*. 'Eyeless in Gaza' for him, as for Queen Elizabeth, would have sounded like the cruel paradox of a blind man in a place that sounded like *Gazer*. Some modern Roman Catholics pronounce 'Mass', the monosyllabic synonym for the Eucharist, *marce* to rhyme with *farce*. For an Elizabethan the vowel would have been short (as for the French from which it derived in Middle English – *messe*) and scarcely distinguishable from *mess*. Had the Elizabethans lengthened the vowel, they would have pronounced it *mace*. *Marce* is a Victorian Irishism (cf. some modern Irish pronunciation of *gas* as *garce*).

If we owe to the Elizabethan schoolmasters and grammarians a knowledge of how they spoke, we also owe to them the immense growth in English vocabulary that occurred in the decades before and during Shakespeare's acquisition of the language. True, much of the vocabulary enrichment derived from trade. During the marriage of Mary Tudor and Philip II the English for the first time adapted and adopted the words *sherry*, *anchovy*, *comrade*, *carrot*, *flotilla*, *castanet* and *guitar*. Portuguese trade made them familiar not only with the words *coco-nut* and *molasses*, but also with such Africanisms as *yam* and *palaver*. Travellers in Italy made the English familiar for the first time with *volcano*, *bandit*, *casino*, *broccoli* and, as architects copied Italian taste, they needed the words *balcony*, *arcade*, *colonnade* and *loggia*. From Turkey they introduced *caviar* and *kiosk*, while Persian traders introduced *caravan* and *divan*. But by far the greatest number of loan-words came to English by literary means. Those London schools that introduced the boys to elementary Hebrew were responsible for the much wider number of English speakers for whom *myrtle*, *jubilee*, *mammon* and *leviathan* were part of their word-hoard. The Renaissance passion for Greek made it natural for English to speak of *irony*, *alphabet*, *drama*, *tome*, *dilemma*, *idea*, *enigma*, *cynic*, *labyrinth*, *scheme*, *chorus*, *bulb* or *nausea*. But the greatest number of foreign words absorbed into the English language during the Renaissance period came from Latin. A century and more ago two great philologists stated, 'we are safe in asserting that our language has appropriated a full quarter of the Latin vocabulary, besides what it has gained by transferring Latin meanings to native words'.[23] To the Renaissance humanists the English are indebted for their *cadaver*, *arbiter*, *genius*, *cornea, acumen, folio, alias, area, exit, peninsula, quietus, pus, miser, circus, interim, vacuum, species, hiatus* and *decorum*.[24]

7

A Library at Mortlake

Fifteen years before Elizabeth became the Queen of England, there died in Frauenberg (now Frombork, Poland), a clergyman-mathematician named Mikolaj Kopernik (1473–1543). This scholarly canon of Wroclaw is known to history by his Latin name of Copernicus; and he is one of those rare beings – to be named with Newton, Darwin, Einstein and Rutherford – who changed the way humanity viewed the whole of life: on the planet, and in the cosmos.

Legend has it that, a few days before he lost consciousness, from a stroke, Copernicus had placed in his own hands a copy of that world-changing book that he had completed – *Six Books Concerning the Revolutions of the Heavenly Orbs* (*De revolutionibus orbium coelestium libri vi*). Copernicus possessed no powerful telescope. He was not, in the modern sense, an astronomer so much as he was a theoretical mathematician and physicist. His revolution in thought was a simple one, and perhaps the most outstanding achievement of Renaissance humanism. Hitherto, the human race had believed itself to live in a geocentric universe. The Earth was the centre and the Sun and the Moon and the other planets, according to this theory, revolved around it. Copernicus posited something very different: a heliocentric universe. We lived in a solar system with the Sun at its centre.

Such was the danger of this revolutionary notion that, although it was printed in the most free-thinking of European cities, Nuremberg (the German Athens[1]), it was felt necessary to publish Copernicus's revolution as if it were a fiction illustrated with numerous woodcuts. And a preface was attached to the book, written by a clergyman named Andreas Osiander, pointing out that Copernicus's version of astronomy was only a theory, and might well be untrue.[2] It was simply a mathematical theorem, not a picture of the universe as it actually was.

This was to enable the printers to escape any dangerous consequences, for the revolution was an absolute one. Goethe wrote:

> of all discoveries and opinions, none can have exercised a greater effect on the human spirit than the teaching of Copernicus . . . never, perhaps, has mankind had a greater demand made upon it. For this discovery, so many things vanished in mist and smoke. Whatever happened to

our Garden of Eden, our world of Innocence, piety and poetry: the testimony of our senses, the certainties of poetic-religious faith?[3]

Suddenly, the world, rather than being a fixed thing, the still centre of the universe where we all knew our place, became a thing of flux. The world of physics posited by Aristotle and Ptolemy – and which the Catholic Church had enshrined not simply as a scientific idea, but as a doctrine of faith – had in fact been dismantled. Dante's still Earth in the early fourteenth century, surrounded by a hierarchy of moving planets, had been surrounded in turn by a sphere of perfect stillness. God himself inhabited the next sphere, which could, technically at least, be envisaged as a physical location. Copernicus changed all that. The future belonged not to the clergy who preserved the old doctrines, but to mathematicians, scientists and (same thing in many sixteenth-century cases) mages. That is to say, Nature, instead of being a reality to which humanity was asked to submit, became an object that humanity could potentially set out to master, to explore, to control.

Humanity was not going to absorb the Copernican revolution overnight. (When Hermann Kesten wrote his biography of Copernicus in 1948, he pointed out that the book had seen five printings in 400 years: at Nuremberg in 1543, Basel in 1566, Amsterdam in 1617 – the first edition to admit that Copernicus did not write the Preface and to concede that the theory was seriously advanced – Warsaw in 1854 and Torun in 1873. Though it was translated into German, Polish, French and Italian, it had not been translated into English – Kesten was wrong, but only by a year, the first English translation being made by J.F. Dobson for the Royal Astronomical Society in 1947.)[4]

In 1596, a twenty-seven-year-old lawyer at the Middle Temple registered with the stationers a poetic work entitled *Orchestra, or, A Poeme of Dancing*, in which he invoked the old idea of the music of the spheres and saw the universe itself as a dance – as Dante had done in the *Paradiso*. For poetic purposes, John Davies holds fast to the pre-Copernican universe, as Dryden would do a hundred years later, a fixed geocentric universe guided by heavenly harmony. But Davies the skilful lawyer knew that the fiction would not last for ever. The dance would last their time out, but thereafter science had drawn a less-certain universe:

> Only the earth doth stand for ever still,
> Her rocks remove not now her mountains meet,
> (Although some wits enrich with learning's skill
> Say heav'n stands firm and that the earth doth fleet

And swiftly turneth underneath their feet):
Yet, though the earth is ever stedfast seen,
On her broad breast hath dancing ever been.

In Elizabethan England one of the 'wits' most abundantly 'enricht with learning's skill', and one of the first in England to absorb the ideas of Copernicus, was a Welsh mathematician, priest and magus named John Dee. For him, as for nearly all of his contemporaries, the importance of Copernicus was that he opened the possibility of returning to ancient sources of wisdom, and to systems of thought that many Christians dreaded as pagan.

Modern historians of science see the Copernican revolution as the moment in history when all the old ideas were scrapped. For the Elizabethans, Copernicus provided them with the excuse to revive ideas of the universe that were even older. Aristotle and the Middle Ages were discarded, but not in favour (or for them at least, not yet) of Newton and Hubble, but for the mystic doctrines of Hermes Trismegistus, the Thrice-Great Prophet identified with the Egyptian god Thoth, considered by many Renaissance humanists to be the equal of Moses. Copernicus opened the way to ancient sun worship. Trismegistus had regarded the sun as the Visible God, and mathematics, for those such as Copernicus and John Dee, were in alignment with philosophy. Numbers were not merely abstract. They carried meaning, clues about the nature of things.

When, in November 1572, a new star appeared in the Heavens, it seemed – to that age that had only the most primitive observing instruments – like a confirmation of Copernicus's theory. Dee was in Denmark at the time of its appearing with his friend Tycho Brahe, one of the great Renaissance astronomers. They were in a monastery that was in the process of being purged of its Catholic past, and Brahe had a small laboratory in one of the outhouses. Looking at the bright W of the constellation Cassiopeia, Brahe saw the two bright stars, Schedar and Caph, that form the last upward stroke. He then saw that there was a bright point of light suspended over the second V, equal to Venus, the Evening Star, in brilliance. There, in the middle of the Milky Way, was a new star.

Back in England, the new star was being observed by Dee's friend and assistant, Thomas Digges. Digges's *A Perfit Description of the Caelestiall Orbes* (1576) contains many long passages of Copernicus rendered into English and was an overt homage to the Polish astronomer, 'according to the most aunciente doctrine of the PYTHAGOREANS, latelye reuiued by COPERNICVS and by Geometricall Demonstrations approved'.

Digges and Dee were both from time to time encouraged in their researches by William Cecil – and it was to Cecil that Digges wrote:

> I cannot, here, set a limit to again urging, exhorting and admonishing all students of *Celestial Wisdom* with respect to how great and how hoped-for an opportunity has been offered to Earthdwellers of examining whether the *Monstrous System* of Celestial globes . . . has been fully corrected and amended by that divine *Copernicus* of more than human talent, or whether there still remains something to be further considered. This I have considered cannot be done otherwise than through most careful observations, now of this *Most Rare Star*, now of the rest of the wandering stars and through various regions of this dark and obscure *Terrestrial Star*, where, wandering as strangers, we lead, in a short space of time, a life harassed by varied fortunes.[5]

It has been justly argued that Digges, himself the son of an eminent mathematician, Leonard Digges, was seen at the time as one of the leading English Copernicans. Robert Burton, for instance, in his preface to the *Anatomy of Melancholy*, never fails to mention Digges's name when he discusses those who believe in the Copernican theory, not just as a mathematical hypothesis, but as a physical reality.[6]

The new star was visible for a few months and then faded from view – disappearing completely by March 1574. Whether it was a comet or a meteor, with a tail too small to be seen with the naked eye, it is impossible to say. Throughout Europe at the time, opinion was divided between those who were prepared to concede the implications of the new star and those who were not. Conservatives who had not believed, let alone absorbed, the teaching of Copernicus, had to believe that the star had been there all along, and had only now become momentarily visible because condensation on one of the spheres carrying the planets had cleared. Such a view was advanced by Valesius of Covarrubias, Philip II's physician; in Italy, Girolamo Cardano, an ancient and distinguished mathematician, argued that it was the Star of Bethlehem that had reappeared, full of portent.

Most European astronomers, however, dismissed this view. And that would mean that the universe in which men and women had believed since the time of Aristotle was no longer there. The fixed, enclosed universe, with the Earth at its centre, was – as humanity was slowly about to discover – limitless. All they knew so far was that they were living in a new order.

What we call applied science began as magic; applied science and magic both seek to impose the human will on Nature. To this extent, medicine and the cures of witchcraft both have the same aim. Alchemy might differ from later chemistry in being fuller of chicanery, but it has comparable aims – to transform matter by laboratory experiments.

The Renaissance scholars who looked back to the sun-centred mysteries of Hermes Trismegistus were the ancestors of modern experimental scientists, but it is not surprising that they should also be seen as magicians. Mathematics was regarded as a form of magic. The obsession with alchemy – the turning of base metal into gold – was shared by many a serious academic. Yet the ability to summon up spirits (a skill that in our day is quite distinct from physics and chemistry) was in Elizabethan times a necromantic art that would be half-expected of the mathematician or the astrologer.

When drama emerged as the great art-form of Elizabethan literature, it was not surprising that the scientific preoccupations of the age should be projected onto two mythic figures: Faust and Prospero.

The original Faust was an inconsiderable, fraudulent scholar. Dr Georg Faust was banished as a soothsayer from Ingolstadt in 1527. Dr Faust – 'the great sodomite and necromancer' – was refused a safe-conduct by the city of Nuremberg on 10 May 1532. Is he the same as Johannes Faust who was granted his BA in the Faculty of Theology in Heidelberg in 1509?[7] In a sense it does not matter. The original Faust(s) laid claim to magic power because of his learning. He was ripe to be turned into a potent symbol of his times; Christopher Marlowe probably read an English translation of Faust's life in 1588.[8] Although Marlowe's play *Dr Faustus* ends with the protagonist's supposed damnation – he has sold his soul to the Devil in exchange for forbidden knowledge – the scholar-necromancer is really a hero to Marlowe, whose conquests of knowledge, like Tamburlaine's conquests of territory in Marlowe's other (two-part) hit play, wowed audiences in the 1590s with their picture of moral defiance. Marlowe no more expects his audience to succumb to a Christian or moral view of the world, having seen the downfall of Dr Faustus, than the fans of 1970s rock bands would be deterred from a wild way of life by one of their idols taking an overdose or dying a violent death. The terrible end is part of the hero's daredevil thrill.

Dr Faustus probably owed something to the character of Dr Dee, about whom all sorts of wild stories circulated from his earliest years, but then, as John Aubrey charitably remarked in his *Brief Lives*, 'in those dark times, astrologer, mathematician and conjuror were accounted the same things'. In another place, Aubrey says, "Twas had a sin to make a Scrutinie into the Waies of Nature.'[9]

Aubrey considered Dee 'a mighty good man'.[10] He did not deny Dee's magical powers, or that 'the Children dreaded him because he was accounted a Conjuror . . .' 'Meredith Lloyd . . . told me of John Dee etc., conjuring at a poole in Brecknockshire, and that they found a wedge of Gold; and that they were troubled and indicted as Conjurors at the Assizes; that a mighty storme and tempest was raysed in harvest time, the country people had not known the like.'

When Dee was a Fellow of Trinity College, Cambridge, and a mere nineteen years old, he demonstrated what appeared to be supernatural powers. During a production of Aristophanes' play *Peace*, Dee laid on some spectacular special effects. In the play, Trygaeus, a vine-dresser, wishes to consult Zeus about the military prospects of his fellow citizens in Athens. He takes a ride on a giant dung-beetle. Dee somehow managed to create just such a flying machine, to the wonder and bewilderment of the Cambridge audience. He had seen such flying automata on his continental travels: 'for in Nuremberg a fly of iron, being let out of the Artificer's hand did (as it were) fly about the gates . . . and at length, as though weary, return to his master's hand again . . .'[11]

When Mary Tudor became Queen, Dee was arrested and charged with 'calculating', 'conjuring and witchcraft', on the grounds that he had drawn up horoscopes for the Queen and for Princess Elizabeth. He managed to avoid being prosecuted, however, even though they deprived him of his living – he was the vicar of Upton-upon-Severn. With an admirable capacity to bob up again when stricken with misfortune, he became chaplain to the Bishop of London, Edmund Bonner, who master-minded the burning of so many heretics at Smithfield. It is possible that Dee had been planted in this role by Protestants (he had formerly been part of Protector Northumberland's household). He certainly was involved in espionage in various capacities. He was identified by a double agent as 'Prideaux', a Catholic spy. (Did this suggest the name of Jim Prideaux in John Le Carré's Cold War thriller *Tinker, Tailor, Soldier, Spy*?)

Queen Elizabeth, always willing to favour her fellow Welsh, had none of her half-sister Mary's objections to Dee's alleged activities as a 'conjuror'. He had been a favoured member of the Dudley entourage in the reign of Edward VI and, with Elizabeth's accession, Dee returned to favour. He was actually asked to choose the most auspicious date for Elizabeth's coronation. He selected 15 January 1559, Jupiter then being in Aquarius – which suggested the possible emergence of such great statesmanlike qualities as impartiality, independence and tolerance; and Mars being in Scorpio, which would provide the new ruler with passion and commitment. When he had made this calculation, Dee was taken by Dudley to Whitehall Palace for an audience with the Queen. It took place in the Great Hall, built by Cardinal Wolsey. Dee, a tall Merlin-like figure, with 'a very faire cleare rosie complexion' and a long beard, wore 'a Gowne like an Artist's gowne, with hanging sleeves, and a slitt'.[12] He was led up to the Queen by Robert Dudley and by a leading member of the Taffia, the Earl of Pembroke. She merrily told him that 'where my brother hath given him a crown, I will give him a noble',[13] a joke that could have meant she intended to pay him a gold coin (worth two silver crowns). It could also have meant she was flirtatiously hinting that she would like to have ennobled him. Dee tells us that his father was a gentleman-server, *antesignanus dapiferorum*, to Henry VIII and in no fewer than three pedigrees he claimed ancestry through the Lord Rhys, Rhys ap Gruffudd to Rhodri Mawri and Coel Hen. If he hoped for preferment from the Crown, Dee was to be largely disappointed. He hoped in vain to become Dean of Gloucester. In old age he was obsessed by his pursuit of a sinecure. His application to become Master of the Hospital of St Cross, Winchester, to this day a refuge for indigent rogues and those of unsound mind, was unsuccessful, and he ended by having to be content with a less lucrative wardenship of a collegiate church in Manchester. Those who wish to cast him in a Faustian mould have had to contrive an end for Dee that was a disgrace, even a 'hell', but the truth is that he never fell into disgrace with the Queen. She simply was not as generous to him as she might have been. In the early 1580s she consulted him about the possibility of changing over to the Julian Calendar. He had been asked to give her advice about the new star in 1572; he even acted as one of her medical advisers in 1571 and 1578; and in the 1570s and 1590s he was asked for legal advice about Elizabeth's titles to foreign lands.[14]

Clearly there always were, and always will be, those for whom Dee's wizardry was the most interesting thing about him.

Beside Dee's dabbling with alchemy, his interest in astrology and his fondness for crystal-gazing, we must also remember his friendship with the spurious wizard Edward Kelley, and his claim to have seen angels and summon up spirits. Undoubtedly it is as a wizard that his reputation survives in the scholarly writings of Frances Yates. He is known to have been a hero to the preposterous master of the Dark Arts, Aleister Crowley (self-styled wickedest man in the world), and he probably contributed to the character of Voldemort in the *Harry Potter* stories. He also turns up as a character in Charlie Fletcher's *Stoneheart* trilogy for children, as a wholly malign worker of black magic.

Yet this is the man to whom Queen Elizabeth gave a modest church living as a clergyman in Manchester, and who as late as August 1592 was having dinner two nights running with Lord Burghley and his sons, Robert and Thomas, mulling over the chances of church preferment. In spite of the 'jentle answer' he received from Cecil, there was not much money forthcoming, but the sober, respectable and religious Cecil would never have had dinner with an evil wizard. He would, however, have delighted in the company of Dee the well-travelled scholar, whose lectures on Euclid at 'Rhemes College' in Paris had been received by enormous, rapturous audiences; who knew the courts of Bohemia and Poland, and the scholars of many of the most distinguished universities in Europe.

One reason that Dee was always poor was that he was irresistibly drawn to the acquisition of books and manuscripts. This was a passion he shared with Archbishop Parker, who also had a prodigious collection. The Dissolution of the monasteries during the reign of Henry VIII had led to the destruction of untold, unguessable numbers of treasures. Parker had a particular interest in the discovery and preservation of Anglo-Saxon manuscripts, but in the vandalistic mayhem of the 1530s there is no knowing how many *Wanderer* or *Seafarer* poems were used to line pudding basins or how many epics of the quality of *Beowulf* were used as lavatory paper. Nor was the vandalism confined to bumpkin monasteries in the country. The universities were just as gleefully anxious to destroy the past. Richard Layton, the King's visitor to Oxford in September 1535, delighted in the spectacle of the front quadrangle at New College thick with the leaves of scholastic manuscripts that his assistants had thrown out of the library. They were collected by a Buckinghamshire gentleman to use as scarecrows.[15]

Dee's collection of books and manuscripts was one of the most significant of Renaissance collections in England – significant, that is to say, for what antiquarian interest sought to salvage from the past, and in what scientific and other directions he chose to expand learning. Some of Dee's manuscript collection was lost through vandalism. During one of his absences abroad in 1589, his house in Mortlake was attacked by burglars. John Davies the pirate (not to be confused with the lawyer-poet of *Orchestra*) was believed by Dee to be responsible. His pupil Nicholas Saunder also appears to have stolen from him.[16]

Some of the books and manuscripts were sold by Dee himself or were bought by other scholars or libraries from his collection after he died. These were catalogued in 1921 by M.R. James – he of the *Ghost Stories* – and the bulk of the manuscript collection identified by James is to be found in Corpus Christi College, Oxford. As for the books, stray volumes were acquired by such varied libraries as Pepys, Harley and Lambeth Palace.[17]

What M.R. James demonstrated was that Dee's library was not merely a private antiquarian fad, or an accumulation of old junk by an obsessive collector. His library was possibly as large as 3,000 or even 4,000 volumes.

It was far bigger than any university or college library at this date, and it was rich in learning that was all but unknown in universities. 'The whole Renaissance is in this library,' said Frances Yates.[18] F.R. Johnson, the American historian of science, wrote that Dee's circle and his Mortlake library constituted the scientific academy of Renaissance England.[19] There were works here in twenty-one different languages, and covering every branch of learning. It was much consulted by those who wished to share in Dee's learning, not only in science as we should now term those branches of knowledge that relate to outer space and the natural world and mathematics, but also to navigation. Dee was the first man to use the phrase the 'British Empire' and he was one of those who encouraged the Queen and her government to expand their interests beyond Europe and colonise the New World. In short, the books and manuscripts that filled room after room at Mortlake ('4 or 5 Roomes in his house fild with Bookes', according to the antiquary Elias Ashmole, 1617–92) were the library of Prospero.

Faust is a myth of knowledge as power. Prospero is a myth of knowledge as imagination. Like Dee, Prospero was a magician and a book man and, in his treatment of Caliban and his assumption of lordship over the island, an early exemplar of 'the British impire'. His library 'was dukedom large enough',[20] but this is not a self-abnegating saying, since he achieves more power through knowledge and magic than he would have done through politics.

When we light our eyes on Dr Dee, what was memorably called the Elizabethan World Picture[21] comes into focus. Dee's library, salvaged as it was from the wastes of monasteries, as well as being replenished from the new printing presses of Europe, represents a continuation just as much as it represents a break with the past. Dee and his contemporaries – Catholic or Protestant – had far more in common with the Middle Ages, and indeed with the classical past, than they do with us. They took for granted a fluency in Latin, for one thing. They regarded astrology as a science rather than a chicanery. They might have disapproved of summoning up angel-spirits, but of the reality of angels they had no doubt. Heaven had been shifted by Copernicus, but God was still there. The planets still shed their influence.

8

The Northern Rebellion

North of Trent was another land. If Elizabeth made herself loved by royal progresses and pageants in Berkshire, Hertfordshire, East Anglia or Warwickshire, she was never in the North. During the whole of her reign she limited her travels to the Midlands and the South.

In spite of Cecil's preoccupation with the threats to the government of the realm by Scotland or the Scottish queen, he overlooked warnings sent from the country in between – the North of England – that not everyone was happy.

In October 1561 the new Bishop of Durham, a learned and Protestant-minded man named James Pilkington, wrote in distraught tones to Cecil, 'I am afraid to think what may follow if it be not foreseen. The worshipful of the shire' – that is, the aristocracy and the gentry – 'is set and of small power, the people rude and heady and by these occasions most bold.' A month later Pilkington was continuing to warn Cecil, 'for the nature of the people I would not have thought there had been so forward a generation in this realm . . . I am grown into such displeasure with them . . . that I know not whether they like me worse or I they. So great dissembling, so poisonful tongues and malicious words I have not seen . . . where I had little wit at my coming, now have left me almost none.'[1]

The extent of the bishopric of Durham, the actual landed wealth of the bishop, was enormous. He was by far the biggest landowner in the region, owning whole manors, boroughs, towns and hamlets, and commanding rents of £2,500 per annum.[2] Next to the bishop in landed wealth was the cathedral itself – formerly a great Benedictine monastery, and now a corporation (chapter) of canons, presided over by a dean. The leading lay magnate of the region was the Earl of Westmorland, who owned almost as much as the cathedral – as well as lands in Northumberland and Yorkshire, he commanded the lordships of Brancepeth, Raby, Eggleston and Winlaton. The Earl of Westmorland, of the family of Neville, was the greatest magnate of the Durham bishopric, with other aristocratic and gentry families – Lord Lumley, the Bowes of Streatlarn, the Hiltons of Hylton, the Tempests, the Lambtons – themselves owning much land and owing an almost feudal obedience to the Nevilles. The tensions between the Durham landowners and the new government in London should have alerted Cecil to the potential dangers of a clash with the North. But Durham is a very long way from London. Even in the eighteenth century, after the invention of stagecoaches, the journey from London to York took four days, with a further two from York to Newcastle. The ride made by Sir Robert Carey in 1603 from London to Edinburgh, to tell James VI that he was now the King of England, took a prodigiously brief three days, but this meant averaging a ride of 150 miles per twenty-four hours. Anything that required the movement of luggage, or goods, or military supplies took much, much longer. The only main road was the Great North Road, leading from York to Newcastle and onward to the Scottish border.

The sheer difficulty of communications between North and South did not, however, as is sometimes supposed, cut off the northerners from the South. For example, the coal-mining industry and the coal trade flourished in the sixteenth century (and greatly increased) towards the end of the reign – rising from 56 to 139 tons from 1590 to 1630 – shipped from the Tyne to London. Northern clergy, northern magistrates and northern landowners remained fully aware of what was going on in London and quite often had good reason to resent it. When parliaments were summoned, northern constituents sent members. The great northern magnates were represented in the Council. The problem was not that the North was out of touch with the South, so much as that the South was out of touch with the North, never bothering to go there or to sound out the feelings of those – high and low, urban and rural, landed and mercantile – who lived there.

In 1536 there had occurred one of the great conservative mass movements against the Tudor regime. Sir Robert Aske, a Yorkshire lawyer, drew together an enormous mass protest against the Dissolution of the monasteries: the Pilgrimage of Grace. More than 30,000 pilgrims began to march southwards. It was almost entirely a religious rebellion, though this inevitably – given the nature of the times – was a political gesture against the influence of Thomas Cromwell, and against the extension of the King's rights to raise taxes. The Pilgrimage of Grace was a failure. The leaders of the movement were put to death: some 216 hangings or executions.[3]

In the thirty years that passed after the Pilgrimage of Grace, the North changed. The principal, and crucial, change was in York and urban Yorkshire. When Elizabeth became Queen in 1558 the city of York was laid waste by plague. In 1561 she established the Northern Council, one of whose aims was to reverse the economic decline of the region. From now on there was a palpable increase in the city's prosperity – more inns, more bakers, more tailors, drapers and clothiers. The increase of prosperity and the combined efforts of the Northern Council and Commission 'made York a miniature Westminster'.[4] When the rebellion of the northern earls occurred in 1569–70, York had completely reversed its position as the champion of Catholic reaction. Not only did York accommodate 3,000-odd of those 14,000[5] soldiers who were used to suppress the rebellion, but the citizens of York gave a short-term loan of more than £1,000 to supply the soldiers' wages.[6]

Lancashire, more rural, was much more religiously conservative than Yorkshire in Elizabeth's reign. Only thirteen priests in the county[7] were actually deprived of their livings for refusing to take an oath to Queen Elizabeth. These included the warden and Fellows of Manchester College – of which John Dee would eventually become the warden. It is difficult to judge, however, which priests and congregations were 'church papists', outwardly conforming to the Elizabethan Settlement while secretly wishing to realign the Church of England with Rome, and how many were, with greater or lesser degrees of muddle, High Church – or content to recognise the Church where they found it. In the later decades, from the 1570s onwards, we shall begin to see the emergence of recusancy, of a refusal to accept the Elizabethan Church and an allegiance, secret or overt, to the Pope and the old religion. Lancashire, was a stronghold of recusancy. This was not to deny that there was some Protestantism in Lancashire, but it was mainly imposed upon them from above by interfering visitations. These visitors often discovered to their consternation that when they descended upon Lancashire parishes, it was 'business as usual'. In 1564 they found the curate of Farnworth shriving (that is, hearing confessions, as the Prayer Book entitled him to do) and 'suffering candles to be burned in the chapel upon Candlemas Day, according to the old superstitious customs'.[8]

The vicar of Huyton (later in history, Harold Wilson's parliamentary constituency) was found using holy water and persuading people to 'pray in the old ways'. In Wigan they were still using holy water in 1584. Bells were tolled for the dead at Preston in 1574, and at Manchester, Walton and Whalley in 1571. In 1573 it was still found customary in Lancashire for the congregations to make offerings and to keep up the old ceremonies – the kissing of the celebrant's hands after he had consecrated the holy bread, and so on – at a priest's First Mass.[9] None of this exactly suggests an upsurge of Protestant fervour from the Lancashire 'grass roots'.

When it came to supporting the Northern Rebellion of 1569, however, there is no doubt that the hard core of belligerent reaction – those actually willing to take up arms against the government – came from the lands and manors of the Earl of Westmorland himself and of those gentry who supported him. Only 20 per cent of them, however, had feudal links with these landlords. It seems as though they responded to calls to the muster when the earls took up arms. Thirsk, Northallerton,

Richmond, Yarm, Darlington and most of County Durham were the places where the diehards were thick on the ground. But before describing the progress of the rebellion, it is necessary to trace its causes and set it in context.

Throughout the 1560s the major threat to Elizabeth's security as head of state came from the figure of Mary, Queen of Scots. The will of Henry VIII may have been passed into Act of Parliament. This, technically, meant that, in the event of Elizabeth's death, Lady Catherine Grey would be Queen. Mary Stuart was not even mentioned in the will and the law made no provision for her to succeed Elizabeth. Everyone knew that in reality, however, Mary was seen as the obvious and natural alternative to Elizabeth: alternative, not simply successor. There were plenty of people in England who would have been happy to have Mary as Queen, and to restore the old religion. The paradox is that there were probably more people in England who wanted Mary as their queen than there were such people in Scotland. Though always, and rightly, known as Mary, Queen of Scots, she was only partially Scottish. Her real ambition was to be the Queen of England. Even though the Treaty of Edinburgh, negotiated by Cecil with the French on 5 July 1560, agreed upon the withdrawal of French troops from Scotland, and an assurance that Mary would recognise Elizabeth's title as Queen of England, Mary would not ratify the treaty. (The previous year Cecil had noted in his diary, 'On January 16, 1559, the Dauphin of France and the Queen of Scots his wife did, by the style and title of King & Queen of England and Ireland, grant to Lord Fleming certain things.')

When she was the widowed Queen of France, Mary married Darnley. They were both great-grandchildren of Henry VII and the match strengthened her claim to the English Crown. And he provided her with an heir: the future James VI. In no other respect was he a suitable King of Scotland, or husband. Drunken and idle, he was an object of Mary's hatred, and was hated too by her Council of Protestant lords. Mary consoled herself with an Italian musician named David Rizzio – 'Seigneur David' as the Scots mockingly called him. The swaggering, conceited figure, who sat at dinner beside the Queen without removing his hat, was soon not merely her intimate, but a figure of political power. It was decided by the Protestant lords that Rizzio must go and, for once, they saw eye-to-eye with Darnley, who burst in on Rizzio with the Queen on 9 March 1566 while they were having dinner. Accompanied by the gaunt Earl of Ruthven who was clad in full armour, Darnley dragged Rizzio away from Mary. The Italian tried to hold on to Mary's skirts as he was taken into a neighbouring room and stabbed fifty-six times. When told Rizzio was dead, Mary chillingly remarked, 'No more tears. I will think upon a revenge.'[10]

The revenge was violent indeed. The following spring – 11 February 1567 – Darnley, who had suffered during the previous months from smallpox, was asleep at a mean house at Kirk o' Field, in an Edinburgh suburb. Mary had by now taken another lover, the Earl of Bothwell. In the small hours of that February night, Edinburgh was shaken by a huge explosion. The house was blown up by gunpowder, but Darnley's body, far from being destroyed by the blast, was thrown into the garden, where he was found to have been strangled.[11]

Mary's folly in getting involved in such a crime – quite apart from its lack of morality – gave her enemies in Scotland the excuse they needed to depose her. The 'trial' of Bothwell made matters even worse for Mary. Mounted on Darnley's horse, Bothwell rode out of Holyrood Palace to go to court; the Queen was seen waving him goodbye from a window. He had arranged for a huge gang of supporters, some said as many as 4,000, to throng the streets outside the courthouse. So intimidated was the 4th Earl of Lennox (who was supposed to be prosecuting) that he did not even appear and the 'trial' ended with a cry of 'Not guilty!' Bothwell then returned to Holyrood and carried off Mary. There followed her alleged 'rape' and her marriage by Protestant rites.

By now, the Protestant lords and the people of Scotland had had enough. They took up arms and, at Carberry Hill, Mary's forces disbanded without a fight. Bothwell abandoned her on the battlefield, and she was arrested and brought back to Edinburgh, to face an angry mob chanting, 'Burn the whore!' The next morning she was taken to the seclusion of Lochleven Castle on an island in the middle of a lake, and there she was immured. Lennox became the Regent of Scotland.

Mary's marital career was her sordid undoing; but even when her singularly poor taste in men has been admitted, her story was an object lesson in the dangers of marriage for a female head of state. The lesson was not lost on Elizabeth. While her closest advisers – Cecil, the Council, parliaments of both houses – all wanted her to marry, and while she in part desired it herself, she could see its dangers. Marry a foreign prince, and he would almost certainly be a Catholic. If she had married the Archduke Charles, for example, which would in many ways have looked like a sensible political move, strengthening England's alliance with the Holy Roman Empire, it would have antagonised all Elizabeth's Protestant-minded subjects. In Scotland and in France, the spectre of religiously motivated civil war provided Elizabeth with a fearsome example that she was determined *not* to follow. To marry a foreigner was to risk stirring up religious hatred. To marry an English nobleman was to risk joining a faction.

To marry off the Scottish queen to an English nobleman, however, was a very different matter. That was why Elizabeth had favoured Mary's marriage to Robert Dudley – and made him Earl of Leicester for the purpose. But that was in 1564, and in a remarkably short space of time Mary had changed from a potential menace, mismanaging the kingdom of Scotland north of the border, to a political refugee on English soil. For she escaped from Lochleven. With a small band of supporters – Lord Herries, Lord Fleming and eighteen others – she took a boat across the Solway Firth and landed on the coast of Cumberland, at Workington.

Elizabeth's attitude was one of genuine ambivalence. Her cousin Mary was, after all, the rightful Queen of Scotland, and the Deed of Abdication that she had been forced to sign on her island prison could not but shock the Queen of England. Elizabeth wrote to Mary congratulating her on her escape from Lochleven, and promising assistance so long as she did not appeal to France for help as well. The letter never arrived.

From Carlisle, Mary wrote to Elizabeth to say that she had no clothes other than those she stood up in, and asking her cousin to supply the deficiency, and to meet. Meanwhile she held court in the northerly English town, where the local gentry streamed in to pay their respects. (Four years earlier, Cecil had been told by a spy, Christopher Rokesby, the Scottish queen had a list of English families from whom she could expect support if she made a bid for Elizabeth's crown.)[12]

The significance of clothes in Elizabeth's personal mythology can never be exaggerated. She herself had been crowned wearing a dress belonging to her sister. No portrait ever appeared of Elizabeth in which the dress she was wearing did not make an eloquent public statement about her. Mary had asked for her to send raiment worthy of a queen.

Elizabeth put the matter in the hands of Sir Francis Knollys, Vice Chamberlain of the Queen's Household. He was dispatched to Carlisle, and told one of the waiting women to make up a parcel of clothes. There was a misunderstanding, and the maid merely brought two worn-out chemises, a length of black velvet and a pair of shoes – apparently thinking clothes were required for some other waiting woman. By the time this insulting parcel was opened, Mary had been supplied with 'two or three suits made in black velvet', tailored in Carlisle. Meanwhile, her base-born brother, the Earl of Murray, had dispatched some of the Scottish queen's jewels to London as a present for the Queen of England: six ropes of extremely fine pearls strung on a knotted thread, and twenty-five separate pearls of enormous size, whose tinge was 'like that of black muscat grapes'.

Sir Francis Knollys, meanwhile, had to break the news to Mary that she must be under custody. She was to be moved from Carlisle to Bolton Castle and to be placed under the supervision of the Earl of Shrewsbury.

'I have made great wars in Scotland – I pray to God I make no trouble in other realms also!' she exclaimed. But her very existence on English soil was a trouble.

Her arrival coincided with an especially difficult juncture in political affairs for Elizabeth and Cecil down in London. Ireland, as nearly always, was in trouble, with a revolt by Fitzmaurice in Munster. Relations with the French were in the process of being brought to a difficult peace. Sir John Hawkins's adventures in the Caribbean had begun a sharp deterioration in Anglo-Spanish relations, which would, from now on, descend from bad to worse. There was a feeling at court that Cecil was not up to the job of running the nation's affairs.

The Council was divided into squabbling factions, some loyal to Elizabeth, others not. The idea was mooted that Thomas Howard, the 4th Duke of Norfolk, England's premier peer, should be married to the Queen of Scots. It was suggested by Secretary Maitland, one of the Scottish regent (Murray)'s commissioners who came down to York to discuss Mary's future. And there were friends of Elizabeth who saw advantages in the idea. Robert Dudley, Earl of Leicester, for example, and Sir Nicholas Throckmorton, former English Ambassador in Paris, saw it as a way of *containing* Mary, securing the succession and making peace with the Catholic powers, France and Spain.

Elizabeth challenged Norfolk to deny the rumour, which he fulsomely and insincerely did:

> What! Should I seek to marry her, being so wicked a woman, such a notorious adulterer and murderer? I love to sleep upon a safe pillow. I count myself, by your Majesty's favour, as good a prince at home in my bowling-alley at Norwich, as she is, though she were in the midst of Scotland. And if I should go about to marry her, knowing as I do, that she pretendeth a title to the present possession of your Majesty's crown, your Majesty might justly charge me with seeking your own crown from your head.'[13]

Even as he said the words, she only half-believed him. But on Ash Wednesday 1569, Leicester went to Elizabeth and told her not only to dismiss, but to behead, Cecil. She dismissed the suggestion furiously, but it meant that in the matter of the Norfolk–Mary Stuart marriage plot Elizabeth was momentarily isolated, unable to rely on either of her stalwarts at court. Again, she confronted Norfolk. Again, he denied it. At this stage of things the court was in progress. Pleading illness, Norfolk retreated to his East Anglian estates at Kenninghall. Since he did so without permission, it was taken as an admission of guilty connivance in the conspiracy that was now coming to light. Norfolk sent desperate messages north to his brother-in-law, Westmorland, telling him not to rise against Elizabeth, but by then events were out of Norfolk's hands. By October he was in the Tower.

For months now an Italian banker, Roberto Ridolfi, had been acting as go-between between the southern nobility and the Pope. De Spes, the Spanish Ambassador, urged Philip II to marry Mary and was wholly optimistic about the success of a rebellion. Some of the northern peers, most notably Thomas Percy, 7th Percy Earl of Northumberland, were doubtful about the Norfolk–Mary match, for Norfolk was Church of England – by their standards, a heretic. Whatever the political ramifications of the Northern Rebellion, it was seen by the leadership as essential to draw upon the powerful Catholic feelings of northerners who, it was hoped, would be enlisted to a movement that could bring the Church of England to an end and restore the country to papal obedience.

It cannot be doubted that the clumsy and insensitive ultra-Protestant attacks on Church rites and buildings were deeply offensive to many people. Although the Queen hoped that her Church of England could contain both Catholics and Protestants, the Protestants made the loudest noise and, at this stage, the most damage. Elizabeth, for example, specifically excluded funerary monuments from destruction by the Reformers, but William Whittingham, the rigidly Calvinist Dean of Durham, hacked at tombs in the cathedral if they bore imagery offensive to his prejudices. Whittingham had been an army chaplain who had initially refused to use the Prayer Book, as smacking too pungently of Romish superstition. Meanwhile, his wife Katherine scandalised local opinion by organising the burning of the ancient banner of St Cuthbert, the patron saint of Durham, who lies in the cathedral. The dean was much hated for this act of gratuitous vandalism.[14]

So it was with a real sense of a region getting its own back on southern interference, and of men and women expressing their love of their saint and their creed, that the northerners followed the Earl of Westmorland (Charles Neville, 6th Earl) and the Earl of Northumberland (Thomas Percy, 7th Earl) in their rebellion. The clumsy, southern, Protestant vandalism of the dean and Mrs Whittingham were but the outward and visible signs of resentment felt by various levels of society in Durham and North Yorkshire. Robert Tempest of Holmside, one of the landed gentry who rallied to the earls, had been displaced as sheriff of the county and lost valuable leases to the new bishop who had taken his land. John Swinburne of Chopwell (ancestor of the great poet) and Sir George Bowes were other landowners who, long before actual persecution of recusant Catholics had begun, had lost out, in material ways, to the new

Protestants. Swinburne, for instance, had lost valuable coal-producing land to the bishop at a juncture when the coal fields of the North-East were increasing in production and value.[15] Nor was it simply a question of the old feudal system surviving in the North, and the great lords having the power to 'call in' their tenancy to take up arms. A survey of the 6,000 men who instantly answered the earls' call, and took up arms, shows that the bulk of them were not the earls' tenants. This was not a medieval case of peasants blindly following, because they knew 'no prince but a Percy'.[16] On the contrary, locally it was an expression of widespread opinion at all levels. Religion was its focus.

On 14 November 1569 they marched on Durham. They occupied the cathedral and destroyed the prayer books, bibles and the Communion table set up by the dean and Mrs Whittingham; 794 people were counted by worried government observers crowding in to hear Mass sung once more.[17] But it was not just in the cathedral, or just in Durham, that people took matters into their own hands. At Sedgefield, for example (later in history Tony Blair's parliamentary constituency), they re-erected the stone altar in the church. (They had done so once before in 1567 and it had been destroyed by visitors.)[18] The government of Elizabeth and Cecil in London faced the nightmare possibility of a religiously enflamed civil war, such as had torn apart Scotland and France. And the woman who had been queen of both of these countries was now in the North of England, with an army willing to fight to make her their queen also. Only two things could save Elizabeth's position now: the weakness of the rebels' power-base, especially in the South; and a complete ruthlessness in securing out-and-out defeat of the rebellion.

As we have seen, Norfolk caved in before the rebellion even started. Even those you might expect to have supported it were lukewarm in their enthusiasm. The recusant priests in exile – Robert Parsons, the Jesuit, and Cardinal Allen – were dubious about the prospect of putting Mary Stuart on the English throne at this point.[19] Richard Norton was an old veteran of the Pilgrimage of Grace, when he had worn the badge of the Five Wounds of Christ. He was wearing the old badge again at Durham for the rebels' Mass in the cathedral. Norton it was who wrote a letter to Northumberland 'leaking' the fact that Spanish troops were on their way to reinforce the northerners. It was designed to strengthen morale and – for he knew the letter would be intercepted – to worry the government. It merely insured for Norton, when the rebellion was over, a particularly grisly end at Tyburn. The rebels' hopes, that Philip II would supply them with military aid, were a groundless fantasy. Philip did not want the daughter-in-law of the hated Guise family as Queen of England.

Mary herself, at this point, did not wish it, being far more concerned to be released from her imprisonment.[20]

In the event, when they saw that their cause was lost, the rebels were dispersed almost without a fight. They marched south to rescue Mary from her incarceration at Tutbury, but by the time they reached Tadcaster, they found she had already been transferred to Coventry. By the end of November, Northumberland and Westmorland had fled over the border to Scotland.

The army that marched north to put down the rebellion was under the command of the Earl of Sussex, who as President of the Northern Council was responsible for the security of the North of England. The most the rebels could muster was 4,000 foot-soldiers and 1,800 horsemen. The government was eventually to assemble an army of more than 12,000 men, under the command of the Earl of Warwick and Lord Clinton. Their armies could get the pickings of victory without having to fight for it. 'Others beat the bush and they have had the birds,' said the Governor of Berwick, Lord Hunsdon.[21]

He was the only government commander who saw any really dangerous fighting. Henry Carey, as he was born, was a first cousin to the Queen, and one of the very few men she ennobled – she made him Baron Hunsdon two days before her coronation, and he became a Knight of the Garter on 18 May 1561. His mother, Mary Boleyn (married to Henry III's Esquire of the Body, William Carey), and Elizabeth's mother, Anne Boleyn, were sisters. The governorship of Berwick was among the many privileges, manors and estates that Elizabeth gave him, and at the time of the earls' rising he was in his mid-forties (his probable date of birth was 1524).

It was after the Earls of Westmorland and Northumberland had fled that the London government, and Hunsdon, realised there was one major troublemaker left: Leonard Dacre. For most of the autumn of 1569 he had been in London fighting a lawsuit against the Duke of Norfolk over the duke's wardship of Dacre's children. He had fortified his castle at Naworth, and raised 3,000 men, purportedly in defence of Queen Elizabeth *against* the northern earls. When he realised his cover was blown, he summoned the Scottish borderers to his aid, and Hunsdon knew he must act. He summoned an army of 1,500 men and set out from Hexham on a very cold February night – 19 February 1570.

Hunsdon and his army knew they were marching through enemy territory. Beacons flared on every high hill, and through every darkened valley that they marched they could hear the noise of horsemen gathering. They reached Dacre's fortified castle at Naworth at dawn. Dacre was waiting with an army twice the size of Hunsdon's. It was not the moment to give battle. Hunsdon marched onwards to Carlisle, and Dacre, with his wild army, who knew the country much better, pursued Hunsdon's men to a precipitous cliff overlooking the little River Gelt. Here the whooping borderers could have massacred Hunsdon's forces, but the Queen's cousin stood firm. The infantry resisted the charge of the border horsemen. Then Hunsdon's cavalry came round to their flank. Dacre panicked and fled to Liddesdale, and the thousands he had assembled were scattered like so many mountain goats. If Hunsdon had not shown such resolution, and if his tired, cold army who had been marching all night had not been so courageous, the Northern Rebellion could have flared up again. As it was, it was now decisively over. The victory over the rebels was so overwhelming that there was no need for heavy reprisals. Elizabeth, however, felt that punishment was in order, and asked that 600 northerners should be hanged, *pour encourager les autres*. Hunsdon, luckily, and the local magistrates saw to it that far fewer were in fact executed.

In her own elegant hand, Elizabeth wrote as a postscript to Cecil's official commendation:

> I doubt not, my Harry, whether that the victory given me more joyed me, or that you were by God appointed the instrument of my glory. And I assure you that for my country's sake the first might suffice; but for my heart's contention, the second more pleased me. It likes me not a little that, with a good testimony of your faith, there is seen a stout courage of your mind, that trusted more to the goodness of your quarrel than to the weakness of your numbers.'[22]

She had the gift of intimacy. 'My Harry' – such a good vocative. He had been named after another Harry, her father, and in her response to the Northern Rebellion she showed herself, not unfrighteningly, a chip off the old block.

Part Two

1570s

9
St Bartholomew's Day Massacre

Pius V had been elected Pope in January 1566. His election was a victory for the most uncompromising champions of the Counter-Reformation. Michele Ghislieri had been born in poverty at Bosco, near Alessandria. He was a shepherd before he joined the Dominican Order (Order of Preachers). When he became Pope he did not modify in any particular the extreme asceticism of his life. In Rome, and in the Papal States, he did his utmost to expunge public immorality and blasphemy. He enforced the holiness of the Sabbath and of holy days. Romans complained he was making their city into a monastery. Financial considerations compelled him to retain some Jews in the ghettos of Rome and Ancona, but the others he expelled. He enforced the Inquisition, building a special palace to house its officers and earnestly attending the trials of heretics. A flavour of his spirituality can be caught in his Bull setting out appropriate punishments for the violation of the Sabbath and for blasphemy. For the rich, there should be fines. The common man, who was unable to pay, should be made to stand before the church door for a whole day, with his hands tied behind his back, for the first offence. 'For the second he should be whipped through the city; for the third, his tongue should be bored through and he should be sent to the galleys.' For comparable authoritarian violence among religious leaders in modern times it would be necessary to think of the theocratic leaders of Islamic brigand states.[1] Pius V was determined to put into practice every decree of the Council of Trent. In accordance with that Council's wishes, he issued a uniform breviary (the prayer book of monasteries and priests) and a uniform missal (prayers for the celebration of the Eucharist) so that for the first time in history loyal Catholics everywhere would pray in exactly the same format without local variations. This is the rite nowadays called Tridentine.

As part of his programme of reform, this pope was especially eager to attack those secular powers who took it upon themselves to control ecclesiastical affairs. On Maundy Thursday 1568 he promulgated a new Bull, *In cena Domini* (At the Lord's Supper . . .) in which he especially had within his sights the King of Spain and the doges of Venice. It was symptomatic of the 'need' for such a Bull, from the Pope's point of view, that the Spanish bishops would not publish it until they had permission from the King of Spain.[2] (Pius V was frightened by the rumours that

Philip's son, Don Carlos, was a Protestant who supported the rebels in the Low Countries. It probably was not true, but even if it had been, Philip II had his own reason for getting rid of his son: Don Carlos was mad, and after his father had him arrested, he died in prison on 24 July 1568.)

If the King of Spain or the Doge of Venice were guilty of Caesaropapism, what of the Queen of England who was, if the accounts reaching Rome were to be believed, an unrepentant heretic, who had declared herself the Supreme Governor of her Church; who had authorised a vernacular liturgy, appointed her own bishops and had now put down with the utmost severity a rebellion against her by those who wanted the return of Latin Mass to English churches and the return of England to papal obedience?

The Roman Catholic enthusiasts who had supported the Northern Rebellion included those who called for Elizabeth to be excommunicated by the Pope. If this were to happen, they believed that all those who missed the old Mass in Latin, all those who wanted the rift with Rome to end, all those who deplored the narrowness and the vandalism of the Puritans, would rise up and, in a great populist conservative movement, return England to the Faith. Nothing could have been more short-sighted. However much Catholics (whether recusant Roman Catholics or 'church papists') might dislike the Church of England, this was not a reason for wanting to have Mary Stuart as Queen – Mary Stuart who had murdered her husband and exacerbated Scotland's internecine religious divisions. The will of Henry VIII had been enacted in law, and Mary was quite simply not legally entitled to the throne. For the Pope to excommunicate Elizabeth and dispense his English followers from loyalty to their sovereign was to place English Catholics in an intolerable position. They must choose between their religious scruples and their civic duty. Merely to be a Roman Catholic in the traditional sense would automatically become potentially treasonable.

This is what the fanatical Pope Pius V proceeded to do. On the Feast of Corpus Christi (2 June) 1570 he issued his Bull *Regnans in excelsis*. It called not merely for Elizabeth's excommunication, but her deposition. No wonder the Elizabethan Prayer Book had attached to it the *39 Articles of Religion*, a sort of manifesto for the National Church, the thirty-seventh of which declares, 'The Bishop of Rome hath no jurisdiction in this realm of England.' During one night a copy of the Bull was secretly affixed to the door of the Bishop of London. It was the first copy of the Bull seen in England.

The perpetrator was named John Felton, a barrister of Lincoln's Inn, and the nailing to the door was a witty parody, presumably, of Luther nailing his celebrated Treatises to the door of the church at Wittenberg. Felton's wife had been a maid of honour to Mary Tudor, and a childhood playmate of Queen Elizabeth, but this jape was meant in deadly earnest. Felton had received two copies of the Pope's Bull at Calais, and he gave one copy to another barrister of Lincoln's Inn, one William Mellowes. (The Inns of Court were full of Catholic recusants.) Felton and friends were calling for the overthrow of the English Crown and constitution. The government intelligence service, with Cecil at the centre of its web and Sir Francis Walsingham as its proficient spy-master, quickly found Felton out. (Mellowes had been arrested and tortured on the rack at the Tower of London.) Felton was himself arrested, tortured and half-hanged. Before he was quite dead, the hangman took him down and tore out his heart. Felton's daughter claimed that while the heart was in the hangman's hand, Felton was uttering the Holy Name of Jesus.

It is difficult to know how much to believe of such gallows legends. (My own favourite such story is of the seventeenth-century regicide who, when he heard the hangman holding up his internal organ with the words 'Behold the heart of a traitor', is reputed to have replied, 'Thou liest.') Felton was duly beatified by the Roman Catholic Church in 1886 ('Blessed John Felton') and of his courage and piety there need be no doubt. He died for the 'old religion'. When his turn for martyrdom came, the Jesuit Edmund Campion told his judges that he was merely defending the religion of their ancestors.

But was the truth more complicated? Had the Reformation and the extreme Catholic reaction against it – the Counter-Reformation – in fact changed *both* sides in this painful argument? Was the religion of Pius V and Carlo Borromeo really the same as the religion of the Venerable Bede and Dame Julian of Norwich? Or had everyone moved on, and were the extremists in both camps the ones now forcing more moderate Christians into positions of hostility with which they did not feel comfortable? For England, with its new National Church (too Protestant in some eyes, too Catholic in others), where should it stand in relation to the great Catholic powers, France and Spain, or in relation to the Dutch resistance-war against the Habsburgs, or the powerful Huguenot faction in France?

Opinion at court and in the Council was divided between Puritans, who were isolationists, and those such as Cecil who felt the country's best interests were served by forging an alliance with one of the great European Catholic powers against the other. In some senses it did not matter which power was chosen, as was seen by the fact that a royal marriage with either a Habsburg (the Archduke Charles of Austria) or a member of the French royal family was considered. After the crisis of the Northern Rebellion, however, the alliance with France was clearly one that it was in English interests to cultivate. If, as Cecil hoped, the Queen could be persuaded to marry one of the French principals, a double advantage would be served: England would have an ally against Spain in the Low Countries, and would undermine Mary Stuart's machinations. (The Scottish queen could hardly expect help from the Valois in deposing one of their own sons from the English throne.) Moreover there was still a chance, if Elizabeth were to marry (she was thirty-seven in 1570), that the longed-for heir could be born, and the succession question settled.

It was to further this political aim that Francis Walsingham was prepared to subsume his Puritan sympathies in religion when he became English Ambassador in Paris in succession to Sir Henry Norris. He had been much more moderate in his religious views than Walsingham, and moreover his wife was one of Elizabeth's favourite attendants, so that he had a hotline[3] to the Queen which cut out the influential Mr Secretary Cecil. Walsingham went to Paris not merely as an ambassador to the Queen, but as a spy-master for the Cecil faction.

The Queen could not marry the King of France, Charles IX – he was already married to Elizabeth of Austria. There remained his two younger brothers, Henri, Duc d'Anjou (born 1551) and François, Duc d'Alençon (born 1555). They were both young enough to be Elizabeth's sons, but since all three boys lived under the formidable dominance of their mother, Catherine de' Medici, this would not necessarily have constituted a problem for either of them. Negotiations began for a marriage with the elder boy, d'Anjou, but he was adamant that he would not accept Elizabeth's (to him) incomprehensible religious position, and the negotiations foundered. Attention now turned to the third son, the diminutive pockmarked teenager, François.

Cecil urged Walsingham upon his arrival in Paris to obtain a portrait of the youth to send back to London. No one could pretend that the Queen was contracting a love match, but they did not want a repetition of what happened when Elizabeth's father, Henry VIII, had taken one look at his fourth bride, Anne of Cleves, and brutally concluded that she was a Flanders mare. The portrait in paint not being found, Walsingham resorted to mere words, and they were the grovelling, circumlocutory words of a man who queasily knew that if his grotesque mission were successful, the tiny duke would become the King of England. 'In structure,' wrote Walsingham, 'by judgment of others that viewed us together, he was esteemed three fingers higher than myself.' As for the deep pockmarks of the duke's acned face, 'in complexion somewhat sallow, his body of very good shape, his leg long and small, but reasonably well-proportioned'.[4] It would have been a strange match indeed, had it come to anything. Preposterous as it seems with hindsight that the two should have married, it remained a possibility, on and off, throughout the decade, and even when events appeared to scupper the chances of a French match for ever in 1572, the marriage with François became something that clearly excited Elizabeth herself in 1579.

Yet it was far from being a matter of personal fulfilment, still less of love. The Alençon match, if it took place at all, would have been a matter of politics, a diplomatic alliance played out against the volatile religio-political climate of Europe in the 1570s. The diplomatic preliminary to an Anglo-French marriage was painstakingly worked out in the Treaty of Blois (April 1572): the English tried to make the French accept the Earl of Mar as rightful regent of Scotland and to drop their support for the restoration of Mary Stuart; both sides agreed to supply as much as 6,000 troops and eight ships in defence of the other, in the event of their being attacked by Spain. England and France were now at least notionally allied against Spain. But the treaty had scarcely been signed before the flaw was shown in the alliance: the lack of religious sympathy between the ruling French dynasty and England. The Duke of Alva put down a Protestant rebellion with the utmost severity in the Netherlands, and Elizabeth offered covert help to the Dutch Protestants. It is not as if the Dutch Protestants had no allies in France; but, rather, that the obvious preference of Elizabeth, Cecil and the great weight of opinion in the Council were with these Huguenots – and completely at odds with the family of her suitor.

Admiral Gaspard de Coligny, a prominent Huguenot, urged his government to make war against the Spaniards in the Low Countries. It would have been a brilliant tactic as far as France was concerned – witness the anxiety occasioned by the very idea in England. In June 1572 Cecil wrote to Walsingham warning that French control of Flemish ports would mean severe restrictions on English trade. The next month Queen Elizabeth sent Sir Humphrey Gilbert with more than 1,000 volunteer soldiers to occupy the Zeeland towns of Flushing and Sluys against the Spanish, to prevent their occupation by the French. It was a typical example of Elizabeth not wishing her left hand to know what was being done by her right, since the expedition was unofficial and, if it failed, Gilbert knew that the Queen would disown him.

Meanwhile in France, Catherine de' Medici had cold feet about the war, and worried about the influence that the Huguenots were having on French foreign policy. (Clearly, to defeat Spain in the Low Countries would be to strengthen Dutch Protestants and was in the interests of their prince, William of Orange.) The King of France married his daughter, Marguerite of Valois, to the Protestant Prince of Navarre, an alliance that was deeply unpopular with Catholics. (A generation would pass before the young man, as Henri IV, would convert to Catholicism with the cynical observation that Paris is worth a Mass.)

Four days after the wedding, on 22 August 1572, Coligny was walking along the rue de Béthisy after meeting the Duc d'Anjou at the Louvre. He bent to adjust an overshoe that he wore as protection against the filth of the Parisian street, and the action saved his life. At that very moment a bullet from an arquebus was fired at the admiral from the iron grille of a window in the house of Canon Pierre de Pille, former preceptor to the Duc de Guise. The would-be assassin escaped through the cloister of the nearby church, and Coligny, who had been hit, was carried home with a shattered left elbow, bleeding profusely.

Playing tennis in the Louvre, the King had heard the gunshot. When he heard of the assassination attempt he feigned anger and sent his physician, Ambrose Paré, to tend to the wounded man. But the King knew what was planned for the capital's Protestant population, of whom Coligny was a figurehead.

At dawn on the feast of St Bartholomew, 24 August, the tocsin was rung and the well-primed mob were set to their task. Coligny was the first to die, stabbed in the chest as he lay in a bedroom supposedly guarded by royal troops. His murderer was a Bohemian follower of the Ducs de Guise, known as Dianovitz or Besme. Coligny's body was thrown out of the window into the street. The Duc de Guise himself and the bastard brother of the King, the Duc d'Angoulême, watched as Coligny's head was hacked from its body, which was hung from chains on a public gibbet at Montfaucon. A dozen other Huguenot leaders were murdered in swift succession. François, Comte de La Rochefoucauld, who had been chatting and joking only hours before with the King, was stabbed. The Seigneur de la Force and one of his sons had their throats slashed.

By now the mob was busily at work, looting Huguenot houses and killing Protestants. No accurate tally has ever been made of the exact count of those slaughtered. It seems as though at least 3,000 were killed in Paris alone. As the carnage, lasting two or three months, spread to other parts of France – to Toulouse, to Bordeaux, to Lyons, Rouen and Orléans – some say that 10,000 were killed.[5] A recent history places the death count as high as 70,000.[6] Certainly, France had never seen such an orgy of violence, and it would wait until the Terror of 1793–4 until it saw such a thing again. (Thereafter periodic internecine massacres have been a bloody feature of French life, as in the Paris Commune of 1870 and the retributory epidemic of murder after the Liberation in 1944.) The massacre lived in the French collective psyche, a terrible smoking crater, never quite extinct, ever likely to erupt with hate-filled destruction. (Three years before the Terror itself began, there was a massacre of Protestants by Catholics in Montauban, prompting the pamphleteers to see it as 'la nouvelle Saint-Barthélemy',[7] but it was Robespierre's full-blown Terror that truly reminded the French of the terrible legacy of St Bartholomew's Day, 1572.)

'But yet, O man, rage not beyond thy needs.' This was the advice to kings and tyrants given by Philisides in Philip Sidney's *Old Arcadia*:

> Deem it no gloire to swell in tyranny
> Thou art of blood; joy not to make things bleed.[8]

Sidney knew what he was talking about. As a young man just down from Oxford and about to start his Grand Tour of the continent, he was staying with Walsingham (as it happens, his future father-in-law) in the English Ambassador's residence on the quai de Bernadins in Faubourg Saint-Germain. Walsingham eventually managed to smuggle his wife and infant daughter Frances, then aged about five, out of the city, but not before they had witnessed scenes of blood in which friends were killed. The Huguenot general François de Beauvais, Sieur de Briquemault, tried to take refuge with the Walsinghams, but was dragged out of the house by royal troops and later hanged.[9] A new friend of Sidney's, Pierre de la Ramée, a distinguished logician, tried to take refuge in a bookshop in the rue Saint-Jacques. After two days it seemed as if the coast was clear, but when he returned to his lodgings at the Collège de Presles, he was repeatedly stabbed as he knelt at prayer.[10] In the mayhem three Englishmen were killed. Others were forced by the mob to ride through the streets of Paris to admire the piles of corpses of their fellow Protestants, and to see them floating in the Seine.[11]

Timothy Bright was a young Englishman who was staying at the embassy at the same time as Sidney. Bright, then a medical student, was the first Englishman to invent a system of shorthand. Fourteen years after the Paris massacre, he was to publish a classic *Treatise on Melancholy*, as well as an abridgement of Foxe's *Book of Martyrs*. He was one of the many Englishmen who had reason to regard Foxe's book – ghoulish as it may seem to modern taste – to be no more than an accurate account of the Counter-Reformation, red in tooth and claw. He owed his life to Walsingham, to whom he wrote, 'Many of my countrymen, partly of acquaintance and partly of the noble houses of this realm . . . had all tasted of the rage of that furious tragedy, had not your honour shrouded them.'[12]

Walsingham, throughout his negotiations over the potential marriage of Queen Elizabeth to the Duc d'Alençon, had tried to convince himself that the King of France and Catherine de' Medici had been genuine in their protestations of friendship. Now, Paris and several other French towns were awash with blood. Englishmen had been killed. The reaction of the new Pope, Gregory XIII (Ugo Boncompagni, elected 14 May 1572), was to order a solemn *Te Deum* to be sung in St Peter's and a medal to be struck, depicting an angel holding a cross in one hand and a drawn sword in the other, with which he was massacring Protestants.[13] Of King Charles IX, Walsingham wrote to Burghley, 'I never knew so deep a dissembler.'[14]

Walsingham protested to the French court about the killings, and to the Council in London he reported back:

> Seeing the King persecuteth that religion with all extremity that her Majesty professes . . . seeing that they that now possess his ear are sworn enemies unto her Majesty . . . seeing that the King's own conscience . . . maketh him to repute all those of the religion, as well at home as abroad, his enemies . . . I leave it to your Honours now to judge what account you may make of the amity of this crown. If I may without presumption or offence say my opinion, considering how things presently stand, I think less peril to live with them as enemies than as friends.[15]

In the immediate aftermath of the massacre, the possibility of the Queen of England marrying the duc d'Alençon looked less than inviting. It dimmed Elizabeth's hopes for an Anglo-French alliance. English foreign policy now switched from a slightly false flirtation with the House of Guise to more or less open encouragement of any Huguenot rebellion against the French Crown.

More immediately unsettling than events abroad was the threat posed by the Counter-Reformation to English stability at home. 'Can we think,' Walsingham asked, 'that the fire kindled here in France will extend itself no further? . . . Let us not deceive ourselves but assuredly think that the two great monarchs of Europe together with the rest of the Papists do mean shortly to put in execution . . . the resolutions of the Council of Trent.'[16]

Since one Pope excommunicated Queen Elizabeth in 1570, and his successor celebrated the St Bartholomew's Day Massacre two years later with a *Te Deum*, there could be no doubt of the threat. This was felt especially warily in the North, so recently a scene of Roman Catholic insurgency. Sir Thomas Gargrave, Speaker of the House of Commons, was Vice President of the Council of the North, where he was considered 'a great stay for the good order of these parts' by the Earl of Huntingdon.[17] He wrote to Burghley from the North, a month after the Massacre of St Bartholomew, 'The people here are, as I think, like others in other parts of the realm; one sort is pleased with the late affront in France, another sort lament and are appalled at it; others would seem indifferent, and those be the greatest number; they are dissemblers, and yet many of them obedient subjects, and to be led by authority, and by their landlords and officers.' In a 'List of the principal gentlemen in the East, North and West Ridings of Yorkshire' Gargrave reckoned that '26 are Protestants, 15 doubtful or neuter, of more or less evil, and 11 of the worst sort'.[18]

It just was not possible to know, any more than the government of a Western nation today knows how many, among its potential terrorist population, are 'more or less evil' – that is, intent on murdering their fellow citizens for the sake of religion, and how many are 'obedient subjects'. The idea of the Elizabethan Settlement in religion was that Catholics and Protestants should be prepared to come together in one national Church, which was both Catholic and Reformed. By 1572 it was by no means easy to tell how successful the experiment had been, and how much religious conformity was really a cloak for a set of divisions that could at any moment turn into an English version of the St Bartholomew's Day Massacre.

No wonder even moderate men such as Matthew Parker wanted Mary, Queen of Scots beheaded. He was less outright in his demand for it than was the Bishop of London,[19] but in wanting this they were asking not for vengeance against Catholics so much as the lancing of a dangerous boil. An anonymous correspondent of Leicester's begged the Queen to remove Mary Stuart:

> For God's sake, my Lord, let not her Majesty in these great sorrows forget the greatest danger. Let her Highness be prayed to remember conscience and eternity. Let her not bring on England murders, rapes, robberies, violence, and barbarous slaughters, and the damnation of so many seduced souls by the advancement of papistry; and all for piteous pity and miserable mercy in sparing one horrible woman, who carries God's work wherever she goes.[20]

One of Burghley's correspondents at the end of that terrible year, 1572 ('Wrytten by Mr Carleton, sent by Tho. Cecil to me'), reckoned that 'the realm is divided into three parties, the Papist, the Atheist and the Protestant. All these are alike favoured; the first and second because, being many, we dare not displease them; the third because, having religion, we fear to displease God in them. All three are blamed, the Papist as traitor, the Atheist as godless, the Protestant as a precisian.' [It means a stickler for form, and was a synonym for Puritan.] The correspondent realised that the precarious balance which stopped these parties fighting hinged on one fact – the life of the Queen. She alone could hold it together. He argued that 'such Protestants as do not like the Queen's form of religion be encouraged to go to Ireland and settle in Ulster'. Meanwhile, those who did like the Queen's form of religion should arm themselves. He suggested a permanent stand-by force of armed horsemen in the twenty counties near London, and for the nobility to be in a state of constant readiness for the defence of 'the gospel, and preservation of the State, and the Queen's person'.[21]

The cruelty with which the recusants were treated by Walsingham's spy network and torture-chambers has never been forgotten, not least because so many of the victims were at a much later date declared to be saints of the Church. The martyrologists on both sides on the painful argument polarised opinion until our own day, and continue to do so. Opinions at the time must often have been nuanced, and heavily influenced by such untheological questions as personal liking, or disliking, and family kinship. Philip Sidney is a case in point. He was the nephew of Leicester – that 'captain general of the Puritans'[22] – and his work, in poetry and prose, is often seen as the quintessential expression of 'Protestant chivalry'.[23] He witnessed the Massacre of St Bartholomew's Day at first hand. Yet five years later when he found himself in Prague he renewed his acquaintance with Edmund Campion (1540–1581). They probably first met at Oxford in 1566 when Sidney, an eleven-year-old Shrewsbury schoolboy, had been taken out of school to witness the royal visit to the university in the company of the Chancellor, Leicester, and two other uncles – the Earl of Sussex and the Earl of Warwick.[24] A high point of the visit had been when Campion, a brilliant Fellow of St John's College in his mid-twenties, had welcomed the Queen on behalf of the university and taken part in a Latin disputation in the Queen's presence. Elizabeth had especially commended Campion's eloquence and he became something of a protégé of Leicester. Yet though persuaded to take deacon's orders in the Church of England by the most Catholic-minded of the bishops – Edward Cheyney of Gloucester – Campion could not shake off the conviction that, in severing itself from the papacy and the parent-stem of the Roman Catholic obedience, the Church of England had ceased to be the Church.

Sir Henry Sidney asked him to Dublin in 1569 to revive the idea of funding a university there. Campion was to have a major role to play, had it not been for his religious scruples. By the time Pius V had issued his denunciation of Elizabeth, Campion had cut loose. The trial in London in 1571 of Dr Storey,[25] who was executed in June, confirmed Campion in his desire to become a Roman Catholic priest, and it was as a Jesuit that he met Philip Sidney in Prague in 1577.

The two men – Sidney aged twenty-three, Campion aged thirty-seven – clearly liked one another. Sidney heard Campion preach before the Emperor and they had a number of meetings and conversations. Clearly, the Catholics felt that Sidney, not merely a brilliant 'Renaissance man' – poet, swordsman, linguist, soldier – but also a nephew of some of the most powerful men in England, would have been a useful convert. It is difficult to know how much to credit their belief that he was tempted. Robert Parsons, Campion's fellow Jesuit, certainly thought so, and Campion himself wrote to another recusant Fellow of St John's, Oxford, now in exile:

> a few months ago Philip Sidney came from England to Prague, magnificently provided. He had much conversation with me – I hope not in vain, for to all appearance he was most eager. I commend him to your sacrifices [that is, remember him at Mass] for he asked the prayers of all good men and at the same time put into my hands some alms to be distributed to the poor for him, which I have done. Tell this to Dr Nicholas Sanders, because if any one of our labourers sent into the vineyard from the Douai seminary has an opportunity of watering this plant, he may watch the occasion for helping a poor wavering soul. If this young man, so wonderfully beloved and admired by his countrymen, chances to be converted, he will astonish his noble father, the Deputy of Ireland, his uncles the Dudleys and all young courtiers, and Cecil himself. Let it be kept secret.[26]

The conversations show how seriously a young Protestant intellectual took Campion's arguments. How could any Westerner who believed in Christianity *not* take these arguments seriously? Apart from any heresy that might have been promoted in the Reformed churches, you had only to witness the dissensions, wars, quarrels and killings which had ensued since Luther nailed his Theses to the church door at Wittenberg to wish that Christians could unite under one shepherd. And anyone who witnessed the fervour and heroic courage of the Catholics who risked ruin, imprisonment, torture and death for their faith would have been insensitive indeed not to be impressed.

Likewise, however, viewed from a narrowly English, or narrowly British, point of view (as religion increasingly was with the unfolding century), the activities of the European Catholic powers were, to say the least, alarming. Walsingham and his spies and torture-instruments made life unpleasant for their few hundred victims. The Inquisition, the Pope, the Kings of France and Spain had slain their tens of thousands. And was it an evil that men and women could hear God's word read and preached in their own language, rather than mumbled incomprehensibly in dog-Latin?

The 1570s saw the arrival of thousands of Huguenot refugees in England. In Threadneedle Street in London, the Huguenot church was a bastion of Calvinism and greatly strengthened the hands of English Puritans who had been arguing for a generation that the work of the Reformation was only half-done. The arrival of the French refugees could provide their English hosts with the double pleasure of resenting their arrival and crowing at the barbarity that had led to it. So, as early as February 1567, 'there was a great watch in the City of London . . . for fear of an insurrection against the strangers which were in great number in and about the City'.[27] The Huguenots were blamed for the increase in London's population, and for inflating the value of property. 'They take up the fairest houses in the city, divide and fit them for their several uses and take into them several lodgers and dwellers.' At the same time, disagreeable as Londoners might say they found the French Protestants, there was an eager readership for horror stories about the abominations perpetrated by French Catholics. The publisher Henry Bynneman brought out five editions (three Latin, one French and one English) of *De Furoribus gallicis* in 1573. Its anonymous author was François Hofman, a jurisconsult then living in exile in Geneva because he 'detested both the Roman law and the Roman church'. He also wrote a highly popular biography of Coligny, *The Lyffe of the most godly valiant and noble Captaine . . . Colignie Shalilion*, published in 1576. Thomas Vautrollier was a Huguenot publisher who settled in London and was responsible for many massacre pamphlets and accounts of Roman Catholic abominations. Among the army of hack-translators on Vautrollier's books was a really distinguished one: Arthur Golding, who was the uncle of the Earl of Oxford. He dedicated his translations of Ovid's *Metamorphoses* and Calvin's *Offences* to Leicester, and translated a very hostile biography by Bullinger of Pius V. For a time, he actually lived in Burghley's house in the Strand.

The Queen raised Cecil to the peerage, as Baron Cecil of Burghley, on 25 February 1571 and the following year she appointed him Lord Treasurer in succession to the Marquess of Winchester. Walsingham succeeded Cecil as Secretary, but Burghley was always the Queen's right hand. He was never a favourite to be petted or given nicknames. He was no courtier. He never asked the Queen for a dance – and by now, with the onset of gout, that would not have been a possibility.[28] He was the spider at the centre of the government's web, the Argus who saw all, the patient administrator who ensured that everything ran efficiently. And now he was presiding as Treasurer over the Exchequer Court, as well as being master of the Court of Wards, two very lucrative as well as time-consuming offices. The money enabled him to acquire and extend Theobalds, the manor house in Hertfordshire that he converted into a palace worthy to receive his royal mistress.

To receive the Queen into one's own home was the highest possible accolade, but it was one that cost dear. Sir Nicholas Bacon was sharply told by his monarch, when she consented to step over the threshold of his substantial manor at St Albans Gorhambury, that his house was too small. 'Madam,' he replied, 'my house is well, but it is you that have made me too great for my house.'

William Sitsylt of Stamford, so lately descended from a modest family of minor Welsh gentry, could not afford to make the same mistake when he acquired Theobalds, a moated Hertfordshire manor house not far from Bacon's St Albans, and some fourteen miles from London. No expense was spared. Visitors crossed an imposing bridge, into a courtyard. There was a chapel and a great hall, extensive gardens, and a 'his' and 'hers' wing – for Cecil continued through the 1570s to hope that his monarch would marry. During the late 1560s Cecil was spending well in excess of £1,000 each year on his building projects at Theobald's. Cecil himself was the architect, and the architectural historian John Summerson wrote of Theobalds:

> As a piece of architecture Theobalds has been totally forgotten [this was because it was demolished and rebuilt by James I as a royal palace in the early seventeenth century], yet I do not think it too much to claim that it was, with the possible exception of Longleat and Wollaton, the most important architectural adventure of the whole of Elizabeth's reign. Certainly it was the most influential of all. Both Holdenby and Audley End directly derived from it. Castle Ashby, Hardwick, Apethorpe, Rushton and Hatfield seem to owe it much. Slight as our knowledge of the house must necessarily remain . . . I do not see that the history of Elizabethan architecture can be written without some consideration of the part played by William Cecil.[29]

As outstanding as the buildings at Theobalds were the gardens, with walks and fountains stretching for two miles. A German visitor recalled:

> From the place one goes into the garden encompassed with a moat full of water, large enough for me to have pleasure of going in a boat and rowing between the shrubs. Here are great variety of trees and plants, labyrinths made with a great deal of labour, a jet d'eau with

> a basin of white marble and a table of touch-stone. The upper part of it is set round with cisterns of lead into which the water is conveyed through pipes so that fish may be kept in them and in the summer time they are very convenient for bathing.[30]

The gardener was none other than John Gerard, who dedicated his celebrated *Herball* to his employer in the year before his death.[31]

From this paradise, the fourteen-mile road to London led almost directly to his other palace, Cecil House in the Strand, where there was more of the same – courtyards, a chapel, great offices of state and gardens stretching down to the River Thames. If these two stupendous architectural demonstrations were to have survived, we should perhaps have an even more vivid sense of what a powerful man Cecil was – how, indeed, the England of Elizabeth's reign could be described as Cecil's England as much as it was Elizabeth's. And the power and influence of the Cecils in English life is one of the symptoms of how forcefully Elizabethan England continued. We began this book by stating that the England of Elizabeth survived into living memory – a Church of England and a Parliament and a set of colonies, which were all the creation of Elizabeth and Cecil. At the heart of this England was the Cecil family themselves. The family that provided Queen Elizabeth I with her most powerful right hand gave birth to Queen Victoria's last great Prime Minister, the 3rd Marquess of Salisbury. After the debacle of the Suez crisis in 1956 there was nothing so undignified as an election for the new leader of the Conservative Party. The two possible contenders were Harold Macmillan and Rab Butler. 'Each member of the Cabinet was summoned singly and in turn to the room of the Lord Chancellor. Beside Kilmuir was seated the traditional kingmaker of the Conservative party, Lord Salisbury. One question only was put to the visitor – "Who is it to be, Rab or Harold?"'[32] As told orally, it is usually rendered 'Wab or Hawold'. This was England in 1956. Even half a century later, when the political complexion of Westminster has been altered out of all recognition, the aristocracy of Elizabeth's reign are still figures of wealth, owning much land and, in so far as money always wields power, still wielding power: Cavendishes in Derbyshire and Yorkshire and London as Dukes of Devonshire; Russells as Dukes of Bedford; and Cecils at Hatfield.

Cecil House in the Strand, like Theobalds in the country, was a parable in stone and horticulture of Cecil's power. Its tennis courts and bowling alleys (the tennis court had a huge red-and-white brick floor) and its extensive library, housing Cecil's collection of books, paintings and Roman coins (the envy of Archbishop Parker, the other great bibliophile at the centre of Elizabethan affairs), were not simply pleasure grounds.

The statues of Roman emperors that Cecil bought from Venice in 1561, and the copy of Cicero *On Duties*, which Cecil carried with him at all times, were symbols of his political belief. He was a monarchist in the sense that he recognised that power resided in his sovereign. He was the master of living with her caprice, her wavering moods, her tantrums. He knew when to tap into her high intelligence and her political perspicacity. He also knew how to neuter her occasional follies. She had the power to cut off his head, and his enemies at court and in the Council came close on occasion to getting him removed – at least imprisoned in the Tower. But she had enough political nous to recognise that she needed this man.

We find here, of course, the origins of what will be English republicanism in the next reign but one. Elizabeth was not an absolute monarch, in the sense that Charles I wished to become. She was reliant on Parliament for money, but also on her ministers for advice. The Elizabethan aristocracy exercised power through their monarch, but it was real power, and it was theirs. We find this fact reflected in Sidney's *Arcadia*, which as well as being a romance about love, and an adventure story in which knights tilt for honour, and a moral tale in which intelligent people express their belief in rational religion and morality, is also a barely coded political handbook. It is a manifesto of aristocratic political power. The two young men who are at the centre of the story, Pyrocles and Musidorus, are the son and nephew respectively of a good ruler – therefore named Good Rule or Euarchus in Greek. But Arcadia, into which they have strayed in pursuit of love, is ruled over by an irresponsible duke, with the Greek name for king – Basilius – who has to be saved from his own follies by the wise counsel of old Philanax. Sir Philip Sidney's great-uncle, Northumberland, had been Lord Protector of England. His aunt, Jane Grey, had been queen for a week. His uncle, the Earl of Leicester, lost no opportunities of perpetuating the power and influence of the Dudley family. Cecil, always disliked by the Dudleys, hoped to tap into their power-source by marrying one of his daughters to Philip Sidney. When Anne Cecil was twelve and Sidney was fourteen, Cecil and Sir Henry Sidney drew up a marriage contract between them.[33] Why this marriage never went ahead remains a mystery. In the event, Anne married the 17th Earl of Oxford, Edward de Vere.

It was a disastrous marriage. Oxford, as well as being a poet (some people absurdly believe him to have been the author of Shakespeare's plays), was a highly ambitious courtier. He had more or less grown up in Cecil's household. When he was twenty-three years old, in 1573, it was reported that the Queen 'delighteth more in his personage, and his dancing, and valiantness than any other'.[34] But he was not the stuff of which real courtiers are made. John Aubrey immortalised him as an essentially comic figure: 'This Earle of Oxford, making his low obeisance to Queen Elizabeth, happened to let a Fart, at which he was so abashed and ashamed that he went to Travell, 7 yeares. On his returne the Queen welcomed him home and sayd, My Lord, I had forgott the Fart.'[35] His absences from court were in fact caused by his unfaithfulness to Anne Cecil. Leaving court without permission and fathering illegitimate children caused him to be imprisoned more than once in the Tower. He monstrously accused Anne of having another lover, whom he claimed was the father of their daughter.

The Queen became involved in the terrible wranglings between the couple. Burghley, with considerable heaviness, insisted that Oxford accompany his wife to court and display 'that love that a loving and honest wife ought to have' – or supply evidence of her wrongdoing. No such evidence existed. As time went on, Oxford quarrelled with all his friends, including Philip Sidney, fathered a child by one of Elizabeth's ladies-in-waiting, Anne Vavasour, and his marriage to Anne Cecil existed only in name. It was a serious worry to Burghley that he might lose the royal favour because of it. In 1582, when he was grievously ill, Francis Walsingham came to his bedside to assure him that Elizabeth had commended the marriage of Burghley's other daughter, Elizabeth, to William Wentworth and 'used so gracious speeches of me, my wife, and my daughter in such effectual sort, as thereby she hath increased and stablised his liking, as could not by my purse be redeemed: and therefore Her Majesty therein hath increased my daughter's value above my hability'.[36] The marriage with Wentworth lasted just eight months. He sickened and died aged twenty-three, leaving Elizabeth Cecil a widow at eighteen.

Through all these painful scenes of domestic failure, Burghley continued to exercise his influence on events, and Cecil House was the power-house of Elizabeth's government. At his desk, Burghley read and wrote hundreds of letters each year. There was barely any public matter, however trivial, in which he did not take an interest – appointments to academic posts, appointments of JPs, matters of legislation coming before Parliament, there was little that escaped his attention. When one sees his spidery, forward-slanting hand, one senses his intelligent and unblinking eye on almost every aspect of life in the England of his day.

Yet it would be a mistake to think of Burghley as a purely political figure. The young William Cecil, who had imbibed the Reformation theology and skills in the Greek language, imparted at Cambridge by Sir John Cheke, was still there, beneath the wrinkled countenance and costly subfusc gown of the sexagenarian master-statesman in Cecil House. The Massacre of St Bartholomew's Day had confirmed everything Burghley had been taught at Cambridge to believe about the Church of Rome. As a statesman, he saw it as his primary duty to protect his sovereign, who was God's anointed servant. Her enemies abroad, and her enemies in England itself, had to be crushed. The great threats – such as that posed by the continued existence of the Scottish queen – were threats not merely to Elizabeth in her person, but to the survival of what Cecil deeply believed to be the true version of the Christian religion.

Elizabeth herself, with her Henry VIII-inspired Anglo-Catholic faith, was less interested in the Reformed theology than Cecil, but when it came to a choice – whether to support the Protestants or the Catholic powers in the Netherlands, for example, or how to treat Catholic rebels at home – she was always guided by Cecil. The Pope's Bull *Regnans in excelsis* was a fatwa that offered the English no choice but to resist or submit *politically*. The Massacre of St Bartholomew's Day showed what the Roman Catholics were capable of doing to their enemies. Whether Elizabeth liked it or not, she and her loyal subjects were now *ipso facto* the Pope's enemies. Burghley's policy was simply, and daily, to do anything that strengthened his queen and weakened her enemies. And he remained convinced, deep into the 1570s, that one way of strengthening her was for her to marry.

10

Elizabethan Women

When the Queen had passed child-bearing age, it could comfort her subjects to make her into a Virgin-Goddess. Until that point had been reached, the country could mythologise its sovereign and figurehead less neatly. It was hard to forget the most basic function of her gender, the fact that she could be, like the country itself in John of Gaunt's imagination, 'this teeming womb of royal kings'.[1]

Most of the celebrated historians of the Tudor Age, even into our own day, have been male. It is only fairly recently, in the last couple of generations, that we have become accustomed to imagine what life was like for the female population of Elizabethan England. Mention has already been made of Elizabeth's learning, and this was something she had in common with a privileged handful of Englishwomen – Mildred, the second wife of William Cecil, with her fondness for reading the early Greek Fathers of the Church in their original tongue; Margaret Parker, who could converse with her husband the archbishop in Latin. Though in the larger towns there were Dames' Schools at which girls might receive a basic education, they would not have been allowed to attend the newly founded grammar schools, which had sprung up all over England since the Reformation. Learning, for the great majority of women, would only have been seen as a useful accomplishment to make them more charming or useful wives, rather than being something worth pursuing for their own good alone. Frances Sidney, Countess of Sussex, might have endowed a Cambridge College (for men), but nearly four centuries would pass before that university allowed women to take degrees.

The Elizabethan woman was not necessarily uneducated. In his *Scolemoster* Mulcaster suggests that girls should study drawing, writing, logic, rhetoric, philosophy and languages, as well as housewifery. How many did so is another matter. More than fifty women between the years 1524 and 1640 were published authors, either separately or in anthologies and collections. Elizabeth Carew's *The Tragedie of Mariam*, Jane Anger's *Protection for Women*, Rachel Speght's *A Mouzell for Melastomas* (a spirited reply to the misogynist Joseph Swetnam) show that there were plenty of clever, educated women in England at this period, as would a recitation of such names as Mary Sidney (Philip's sister), Margaret How Aschman, Jane, Countess of Westmorland, Esther Inglis and Elizabeth

Legge.[2] But they were in a minority, as clever people (not to say clever women) always are.

The Queen, as a learned single woman in her thirties, would in no sense have appeared to her female subjects as a role model. Many Englishwomen of her age in the 1570s, when Elizabeth was between thirty-seven and forty-seven, would have been grandmothers. Shakespeare's Juliet is, as her nurse reminds us, 'not fourteen'.[3] For Westerners of the twentieth century this would make her a Lolita, far too young to be viewed as marriageable. But for Elizabethans, fourteen was an ideal age to be married. Sir Philip Sidney's sister Mary became Countess of Pembroke at that age. Compass says to Parson Pilate in Ben Jonson's *The Magnetick Lady* (1631) that a particular girl is one 'who strikes the fire of full fourteen, to-day ripe for a husband'.[4] The disadvantages of such early marriages were obvious even then. Alexander Niccholes in *A Discourse, or marriage and wiving: and of the greatest Mystery therein contained: How to choose a good wife from a bad* (1615) was worried by 'forward Virgins' being married at such an age: 'the effects that, for the most part, issue thereafter, are dangerous births, diminution of stature, brevity of life and such like, yet all these pains will they adventure for this pleasure'. There would still have been many who would have shared the view expressed in Sir Thomas Elyot's *The Defence of Good Women* (1545) when Zenobia says she married at twenty, and Candidus says she waited too long.

Modern marriage customs in twenty-first century Europe and America (taking 'marriage' here to cover all shared domestic lives, and especially those that involve the bringing up of children) presuppose that the principal protagonists in the household are grown-ups. In Tudor England this is not to be taken for granted. Little as our contemporary morality might like it, this surely explains why so many Elizabethan reflexions upon the married state – whether comic or serious, in plays, handbooks, jokes or sermons – speak of wives as if they were recalcitrant children who need to be kept under control. Very often, they *were* children. As the century progressed, however, the average age for marriage increased.

Modern research into marriage licences in the diocese of Canterbury in the seventeenth century – between 1619 and 1660 – found that the average age for women to marry was twenty-four, and for men twenty-eight. The Elizabethans inherited a tradition of child-marriages and adapted it to a different convention. Whereas medieval and early Tudor people accepted child-marriages, Elizabethans increasingly expected the married couple to take responsibility for their own households, to farm their own plot of land, to run their own business, to be independent. This meant that whereas the landed classes could afford to continue marrying very young, the yeoman, the baker, the shopkeeper, the craftsman would have to wait until he could afford to be master of a household, however modest.[5] Marriage, for the huge majority, meant marriage for life, and if life was in many cases shorter, it was not invariably so, and Elizabethans paid as much attention as other generations that married mistakes be kept to a minimum. Elizabethan marriages usually came about in two stages: the espousal or contract, in which the partners (and their families) would agree upon the match, and then the marriage itself.

Espousals could take two forms – *in verbis de futuro* ('I shall take thee to my wife') or *in verbis de praesenti*, when the two people would say 'I do take thee' or similar words. 'I N doe willingly promise to marrie thee N. If God will, and I live, whensoever our parents shall thinke good, & meet till which time, I take thee for my only betrothed wife, and thereto plight thee my troth. In the name of the Father, the Sonne, and the Holy Ghost: So be it' is how a contract *in verbis de praesenti* is set out by Robert Cleaver in his *A Godlie Forme of Household Government* (1598). Once such a formula has been undertaken, although the partners were not yet married in law, the couple could consummate their union. In *Twelfth Night*, Olivia apologises to Sebastian for hurrying along their union, but she wants to become informally espoused in the presence of a priest:

> Blame not this haste of mine. If you mean well,
> Now go with me, and with this holy man,
> Into the chantry by; there, before him,
> And underneath that consecrated roof
> Plight me the full assurance of your faith,
> That my most jealous and too doubtful soul
> May live at peace.[6]

In John Webster's *The Duchess of Malfi* (1623), the Duchess says to Antonio:

> I have heard lawyers say, a contract in a chamber
> Per verba de presenti is absolute marriage
> Bless, heaven, this sacred Gordian, which let violence
> Never untrue.

The vagueness during this period about what exactly constituted a legally valid contract between partners is one reason why we find a very low illegitimacy rate in Elizabethan England. There must have been many in the position of the eighteen-year-old William Shakespeare, who found his lover/future wife Anne Hathaway to be pregnant before a formal marriage was solemnised. Whether Shakespeare and Hathaway had undergone an informal espousal or *in verbis de presenti* we do not know. Customs varied in different quarters of the British archipelago, with far more illegitimate children in Gaelic society – either in the Highlands of Scotland or in Ireland.[7] Edmund Campion, in his *Two Bokes of the Histories of Ireland*, complained of the Irish 'strumpets' who were used by noblemen to increase the numbers of descendants carrying their name. 'He that can bring most of his name into the field, base or other, triumpheth exceedingly; for increase of which name they allow themselves not only whores, but also choice and store of whores. One I hear named which hath (as he called them) more than ten wives in twenty places.'[8] In general, Campion thought that the Irish 'much abased':

> the honourable state of marriage . . . either in contracts unlawful meeting the levitical and canonical degrees of prohibition, or in divorcements at pleasure, or in omitting sacramental solemnities, or in retaining either concubines or harlots for wives. Yea, even at this day, where the clergy is faint, they can be content to marry for a year and a day of probation, and at the year's end to return her home upon light quarrels, if the gentlewoman's friend be unable to avenge the injury. Never heard I of so many dispensations for marriage as these men show.[9]

In England marriage customs tended to be more tightly regulated – as was the life of women generally. A statute of the fifth year of Elizabeth's reign decreed that if a woman between twelve years old and forty was unmarried and out of work, she could be forced by two justices of the peace (in the country) or the head officer and two burgesses (in the city) to serve and be retained by the year, week or day in any work these officers thought proper.[10] This was a very strong incentive indeed to marry. Many a husband must have echoed Otter in Ben Jonson's *Epicoene*: 'Wife! There's no such thing in nature. I confess, gentlemen, I have a cook, a laundress, a house-drudge, that serves my necessary turns, and goes under that title; but he's an ass that will be so uxorious to tie his affections to one circle.'[11]

In the twelfth year of Henry VII's reign, a judge, Justice Broone, ruled that 'if a man beat an out-law, a traitor, a Pagan, his villain [peasant] or his wife it is dispunishable, because by the Law Common these persons can have no action'. The judgement was quoted in a book of 1632 entitled *The Lawes Resolutions of Women's Rights: or, The Laws Provision for*

Weemen. A Methodicall Collection of such Statutes and Customs, with the Cases, Opinions, Arguments and points of Learning in the Law, as doe properly concerne Women. The author concluded (since the law plainly *did* allow wife-beating), 'God send Gentle-women better sport, or better companie.'

Perhaps, for the Elizabethans, as for us, marriage was partly a matter of luck. There are plenty of examples, in the literature of the period (both fiction and plays on the one hand, and manuals of moral instruction on the other), where harmony and friendship within marriage are encouraged or celebrated. Edmund Tilney, in *A brief and pleasant discourse of duties in Marriage – called The Flower of Friendship* (1568), says that a man should love his wife, if for no other reason, out of self-interest; for 'the man that is not lyked and loued of his mate, holdeth his lyfe in continuall perill, his goodes in great jeopardie, his good name in suspect, and his whole house in vtter perdition'.[12] Robert Cleaver went further and in *A Godlie Forme of Household Government* believed that a man should love not only his wife, but also her relatives. There is no reason to suppose that any more, or fewer, married pairs were unhappy together in Elizabethan England than at any other period of history.

The wedding ceremony itself was generally held, if at all possible, in the summer. In the church register of Everton, Nottingham, is the rhyme:

Advent marriages don't deny;
But Hilary gives thee liberty –

That is, marriages were forbidden in the penitential season of Advent, before Christmas; it became possible by canon law to marry again after 13 January (Feast of St Hilary of Poitiers). There follows another season when marriages were outlawed – from seventy days before (Septuagesima) Easter to eight days afterwards. It was also forbidden to have weddings on Rogation Days when people were supposed to be in church in early summer praying for a good harvest later in the year, but any time after Trinity Sunday (end of May beginning of June) was suitable:

Septuagesima says thee nay
Eight days from Easter says you may,
Rogation bids thee to contain,
But Trinity sets thee free again.[13]

The celebration of a wedding would take all day. At dawn, the village girls would wake the bride and dress her. The 'marrying smock' would be white: 'home-spun cloath' for the poor, the finest silks for the rich.[14]

The bride and her flower-clad party would walk to the church. If possible the bride would have a bouquet of myrtle, a plant with shining leaves and white sweet-scented flowers, sacred to Venus.

In the Middle Ages the marriage itself took place in the church porch. Chaucer's Wife of Bath had five husbands 'at chirche dore'. Once married, the couple would then enter the church for a blessing by the priest or a nuptial Mass. After the Elizabethan Settlement, however, the new *Book of Common Prayer* solemnised marriages in the churches themselves. 'At the day and the time appointed for solemnisation of matrimony, the persons to be married shall come into the body of the Church with their friends and neighbours.' So began a tradition that persists to this day in England. The wedding ceremony (emended in 1928/9 to omit the bride's promise to obey her husband) is the one part of the Elizabethan Prayer Book to remain integral to the common culture. Fewer than a million English people in the twenty-first century regularly go to church. When they do so, no more than a tiny fraction of these follow the rites of the old Prayer Book. But a much, much larger number attend weddings. The prodigious success of Richard Curtis's film *Four Weddings and a Funeral* attests to the abiding appeal of a wedding in church, with some of the old folklore surrounding such matters as flowers and female attendants on the bride. And people go to these old-fashioned weddings at least in part because the words, alone of all the others in the now all-but-defunct *Book of Common Prayer*, remain part of the shared language. 'In sickness and in health; and forsaking all other . . . for better, for worse, for richer, for poorer . . . with this ring I thee wed, with my body I thee worship . . .'

The Elizabethan wedding celebration customarily took place at the house of the groom, where there would be as elaborate a feast as the family could afford, and, with any luck, as denounced by the Puritan clergy, 'publique incendiaries of all filthy lusts'[15] – in other words, a great deal of drinking, singing and dancing. Madam Haughty complains bitterly to Morose in Jonson's *Epicoene* that he has let his wedding celebration 'want all marks of solemnity'. 'We see no ensigns of a wedding here; no character of a bride-ale: where be our scarves and gloves? I pray you, give 'em us. Let's know your bride's colours, and yours at least . . . no gloves? No garters? No epithalamium? No masque?'

Masques and pageants would have attended the greatest marriage feasts, but for most couples their wedding day was an occasion of less showy rejoicing. We do not know anything, unfortunately, about the festivities in the spring of 1543, when the thirteen-year-old Robert Barlow of Barlow (sometimes spelt Barley) married his fifteen-year-old Derbyshire neighbour Elizabeth Hardwick, who had been born in her father's small manor farmhouse in Hardwick in 1527. What we do know is that this woman, known to posterity as Bess of Hardwick, made a spectacular career out of serial monogamy. Robert Barlow left her a widow when she was sixteen. Although he did not leave her much of a fortune, it was enough to begin her portfolio. She went to court to claim one-third of the revenue from her husband's estates – with '80 messuages [dwelling houses], 7 cottages, 880 acres of land, 260 acres of meadows, 550 acres of pasture, 320 acres of woods, 400 acres of furze and heath, and £8 10s. 0d. rent with the appurtenances for sundry properties in the villages of Barley, Barley Leeds, Dronfield and Holmfield'.[16]

Bess came from the gentry or squire class. Many of these families held the same manors, and looked after the same English acreage, from the time of the Norman Conquest. Others were new money in early Tudor times and acquired lands that had formerly belonged to monasteries. They continued, a stabilising force in English society, until the agricultural crises of the 1870s – falling food prices and land value – forced many to sell. Some continued until the twentieth century. From this class came the magistrates, the JPs who administered local justice. They housed, and employed, the rural population – which in Elizabethan England was the great majority of people in the kingdom. They provided much of the officer class in the army and navy, and many of the clergy. Some, the richer ones, or the more socially ambitious, were to be found bettering themselves by marriage and entering the aristocracy; but most of them were not ennobled. They remained Mr (or perhaps Captain) this or that – the squire in his manor house. They would mix with local aristocrats, however, and some of them would have noble cousins. The Hardwicks, for example, were distantly related to the Dukes of Suffolk, the Marquesses of Dorset and the Earls of Derby.[17]

Widowed at sixteen, Bess Hardwick next married a man twice her age: Sir William Cavendish, a privy councillor and Treasurer first to Henry VIII, to whom he owed his knighthood, and then to Edward VI. Cavendish was one who had done well out of the Dissolution of the monasteries, many of which he had taken a personal hand in closing down. The Manor of Northaw, part of the vast riches and lands of the Abbey of St Albans, had fallen into his hands in 1534, and he bought the nearby manors and lands of Cuffley and Childergate. A decade later he bought Chatsworth, an estate that would have been familiar to Bess Hardwick, and they built a vast house there of old-fashioned neo-medieval design, with battlements and turrets. (This was demolished to make way for the seventeenth-century palace at Chatsworth which stands there now.) By the time Sir William died, in 1557, his widow Bess, now thirty years of age, had become one of the greatest landowners.

In 1559 Bess married for the third time – to Sir William St Loe, a widower and a soldier who was captain of Elizabeth's personal bodyguard during the reign of her sister Mary I. In the panelled and plastered parlour at Sutton Court, Somersetshire, Sir William's country seat, was an arras, or wall hanging, that depicted in heraldic form the accumulation of privileges and property brought about by the marriage – here were the arms of Hardwick and Cavendish, quartered with those of Sir William's own heritage, St Loe, Poynz, Fitznichols, Rivers, Fitzpayne and Arundell. These heraldic devices are also to be seen in stained glass in a window in the north aisle of the parish church at St Andrew's, Chew Magna.[18]

It is possible that Sir William was murdered by his brother Edward, with whom he had been at loggerheads for many years. After seven years of happy marriage, Bess buried him at St Helen's Bishopsgate in the City of London. She was now a woman of prodigious wealth, and a courtier of influence, attending the Queen's bedchamber with her friends Blanche Parry, Frances Cobham and Lady Dorothy Stafford. Inventories of Chatsworth in 1565 (incomplete as they are) indicate the rich stuffs, the pictures and jewels of which she was the owner, not to mention her lands and rents.

She married her fourth husband, George Talbot, 6th Earl of Shrewsbury, in 1568. Since there was by then only one duke in England – that of Norfolk – the Earl was all but the premier peer, a privy councillor, a Knight of the Garter, and eventually (1572) to become Earl Marshal when Norfolk forfeited the title, as well as Lord Lieutenant of the counties of Yorkshire, Derbyshire and Nottinghamshire. He was immensely rich, owning land all over Derbyshire, Nottinghamshire, Shropshire, Staffordshire and Yorkshire. He owned a great house at Sheffield, as well as Wingfield Market, Worksop Manor, Buxton Hall, Welbeck Abbey and Rufford Abbey. As Countess of Shrewsbury, Bess was a figure of great power, wealth and influence. She was also, after her Cavendish marriage, the mother of great dynasties. Her daughter Frances married Sir Henry Pierrepoint and was the mother of Viscount Fenton, the Earl of Kingston and Grace Manners, mother of future earls, later Dukes of Rutland. Her son William became first Earl of Devonshire (and ancestor of the Dukes of Newcastle and of Portland). Her daughter Mary married the 7th Earl of Shrewsbury, who begat future Earls of Pembroke, Earls of Kent and, in the restored line, Dukes of Norfolk. Her daughter Elizabeth married Charles Stuart, 5th Earl of Lennox, the father of Arbella Stuart (1575–1615), who became Marchioness of Hertford. Arbella stood to inherit the throne of England, should James VI of Scotland not live to do so. (She it was that the Gunpowder Plotters of 1605 intended to make the English queen if they succeeded in blowing up King, nobility and Parliament.)

This was a considerable lineage to proceed, via the womb of a highly ambitious and very determined woman, from a comparatively modest manor house in Derbyshire. Bess's marriage to the Earl of Shrewsbury began happily, but it went sour. In 1569 the Queen entrusted the earl with the appallingly delicate task of holding Mary, Queen of Scots in custody. The earl was to treat his prisoner, 'being a Queen of our blood, with the reverence and honour mete for a person of his state and calling, and for her degree'. She was to be accorded all the ceremony due to her position, 'not by this removing [to Tutbury Castle in Staffordshire] have her state amended'.[19]

It is not entirely clear why Queen Elizabeth considered Lord Shrewsbury's Staffordshire hunting lodge an apt prison for the Scottish queen. When they viewed it, both Bess and the earl considered it entirely unsuitable. It had not been inhabited for years. It was cold, dank and all but unfurnished. They sent some of the better tapestries and furniture from Sheffield and Chatsworth, but Mary Stuart herself found it a dismal place:

> I am in a walled enclosure, on the top of a hill, exposed to all the winds and inclemencies of heaven. Within the said enclosure, resembling that of a wood of Vincennes, there is a very old hunting-lodge, built of timber and plaster. Cracked in all parts, the plaster – adhering nowhere to the woodwork . . . [is] broken in numerous places . . . It is so damp that you cannot put any piece of furniture in that part without its being, in three or four days, covered with mould.[20]

So wrote a plaintive Scottish queen to Bertrand de la Mothe Fénelon, the French Ambassador. The garden was no more than a 'potato patch . . . fitter to keep pigs in the house, having no drains to the privies, is subject to a continual stench'.[21]

Bess was forty-one when the Scottish queen moved to Tutbury, Mary was twenty-six. Initially, they spent much of each day together. When it was deemed safe to take exercise – and there was constant fear that Mary would be kidnapped by her Roman Catholic supporters – Bess and she could ride together. (The expenses of the Queen's horses and those of her entourage were borne by the earl. The forty-five shillings a week sent by Queen Elizabeth to feed her cousin could not buy the foods demanded by Mary.)

An inventory of the Scottish queen's belongings six months before her death included many items of unfinished embroidery: bed hangings and chair covers, and the like. Mary liked to incorporate her own heraldic devices and anagrams of her name into her exquisite stitching. Into her cloth of state, which Shrewsbury allowed to hang in her room as if she were still a reigning monarch, was embroidered the ominous motto: 'In my end is my beginning'[22] – *En ma fin git mon commencement* – the motto of her mother, Mary of Lorraine, embroidered around her impresa, a phoenix rising from the flames.[23]

Much of the day was spent sewing in Bess's comfortable quarters; Bess was a good needlewoman, and the Scottish queen was an excellent one. Together with the ladies-in-waiting – Mary Seton and Agnes, Lady Livingstone – they would pore over pattern books, design gowns, discuss hairstyles. Inevitably, too, they gossiped, and this got Bess into trouble.

When gossip is repeated to third, fourth, fifth parties, it inevitably becomes difficult to establish who really said what to whom. Mary mischievously put it about that Bess Shrewsbury had been disloyal about Queen Elizabeth, that she had repeated tittle-tattle about the Queen's indiscretions with Leicester; more dangerously, that she had offered to plant Charles Cavendish, her son, at court as a spy for Mary; that she smuggled Mary's secret letters in cipher; even that she supported Mary in her political aims. How much Bess really said such things, and whether she said them because she meant them or because she wanted to please, who can know?

Mary was subject to frequent illnesses, to outbursts of hysterical weeping and to stomach pains. They moved her to another of Lord Shrewsbury's residences, Wingfield Manor. They allowed her to take the waters at Buxton. But these were major security operations, requiring an ever-increasing entourage. All the earl's entreaties to Queen Elizabeth for a corresponding increase in the forty-five-shilling weekly allowance were – highly characteristically – ignored. At some points there was a crowd of as many as eighty visiting Queen Mary, and all the extra bodyguards and security arrangements entailed by this had to be paid for out of the earl's pocket.[24]

One biographer of Shrewsbury estimated that he was spending £30 *a day* on looking after Queen Mary, and that he was therefore a staggering £10,000 per annum out of pocket. They were paying for such figures as Sir John Morton (whom everyone knew to be a Catholic priest, but to whom Shrewsbury turned a blind eye); John Beaton, Mary's master of the house; her physician; her cup-bearer; pages; secretaries; a master cook: it was hardly solitary confinement.

Bess believed that her husband had fallen under Queen Mary's spell, that his affections had been alienated. There is no evidence that she believed, or repeated, the rumour that Queen Mary had borne a child to Shrewsbury,[25] but it would not be surprising if daily contact with this famously enchanting, much younger imprisoned royal beauty, had not in some way bewitched Shrewsbury. Nor, though the very idea was loyally denied by Lady Antonia Fraser in her biography of Mary, would it have been entirely surprising if the Scottish queen had not exploited such a situation for all it was worth. Mary wrote an indignant letter to Queen Elizabeth denying the rumours and taking the opportunity to land Bess in trouble by repeating the allegedly satirical, scandalous and disloyal things about Queen Elizabeth that she had supposedly said over the embroidery sessions. Bess lived down these scurrilous and embarrassing revelations, but Mary succeeded in causing discomfiture to '*la bonne Comptesse*', as she maliciously termed her former friend.

Bess and her husband, of necessity, spent longer and longer periods apart. Bess was at court. Lord Shrewsbury was guarding – and not merely guarding, but becoming infatuated with – Queen Mary. If Mary did not actually cause the break-up of Bess's marriage, the situation did nothing to alleviate it.

Bess, as well as her life as a courtier, was a triumphantly successful manager of money and estates, and an inspired builder. At one point, in the early 1570s, her brother James got into money difficulties and it looked as if he would have to sell her childhood home, Hardwick Hall. By now Bess was settled at Chatsworth, which was entailed to her son Henry after her death. She had no obvious need of Hardwick, owning as she did so much former St Loe property in the West Country, and being, as Countess of Shrewsbury, the chatelaine, at least in name and title, of her husband's many houses. But she had always loved Hardwick and, either because she saw it as a house for her old age or for her two younger sons, she bailed James out of his difficulties. She settled a mortgage on the house and leased his coal and ore mines, which she proceeded to make profitable. This was the era when the coal industry in England – a key factor in its prodigious wealth and global domination before the Industrial Revolution in the eighteenth century – began. There were more than 100 collieries in Derbyshire between 1550 and 1615, most of them newly started. The Trent was an easily navigable river and that was of great advantage to such landowners as Sir Francis Willoughby, who was a pioneer of the Nottinghamshire coal industry at Wollaton and Strelley. (He also, like Bess, made money from iron-making.) In Northumberland and Durham the richest coal fields were found. In one manor alone, Whickham, leased from the Bishop of Durham, 100,000 tons of coal per annum were being produced in the seventeenth century.[26]

Bess was enabled, from her large rents and her judicious investments in industry, to be rich enough, when the time came, to build a new house at Hardwick, which became a byword for all that was splendid, all that was beautiful, all that was ethereal and strange about that age of architectural glory.

Never before, and never since, has there been an era in England of such stupendous domestic architecture. Just as there was no professional army, but there were many military heroes; a navy built by privateers; no civil service – just Lord Burghley and a spider's web of administrators; so there was no concept at that time of the professional architect in England. Robert Smythson (*c.*1535–1614) was one of the most inspired of all English architects. He trained as a stonemason, rising in the 1560s to become a master mason, travelling the country with a gang of highly skilled masons working under him. In 1568 he was summoned by Sir John Thynne to assist with the rebuilding of Longleat House in Wiltshire, the first of the great houses in England to bear no trace of fortification. Smythson worked at Longleat for eighteen years, in the interval designing or beautifying such great houses as Caversham House, near Reading (for Sir Francis Knollys), Wardour Castle in Wiltshire (for Sir Matthew Arundell), Wollaton Hall (for Sir Francis Willoughby), Worksop Manor and Welbeck Abbey in Nottinghamshire, and Burton Agnes in Yorkshire. Partly because more of Smythson's drawings and designs survive than of other Elizabethan master masons and builders, and partly because of the sheer magnitude of his achievement, Smythson stands out as the most innovative, the most prodigious of them all. His drawings show an instinctually intelligent consciousness of the English Gothic tradition, but he matched this to a classical sense of symmetry and proportion, and a use of light that was entirely innovatory and distinctly of its age. Symmetry applied to domestic architecture what was 'essentially a Tudor innovation'.[27] It is seen at its most luminous, most palatial, most inspired at Hardwick.

Since Smythson had reworked Worksop Manor in Nottinghamshire for the earl of Shrewsbury, it is possible, after the Earl and Bess had in effect split up, that Smythson held back from working for the countess until his lordship died. Once Shrewsbury was dead, he was able, in all likelihood,[28] to provide designs for Bess's new house at Hardwick, that air-filled, tall Derbyshire palace. 'Hardwick Hall, more glass than wall.' Glass, being very costly, was a status symbol. 'You shall have sometimes fair houses so full of glass, that one cannot tell where to become to be out of the sun or cold.' It must have been perishingly cold, as Mark Girouard, best of scholars in the field of Elizabethan architecture, who grew up there, attests.[29] The impracticality of life there was also, on one level, an absurdity. There were no servants' quarters in the house itself, as in a Victorian country house. Servants, who had to be at the beck and call of the occupants, slept all over the place – on landings, or at the end of masters' or mistresses' beds. The huge distances between the kitchens and the High Great Chamber, where ceremonial meals were served, guaranteed that food would always arrive at the table tepid or cold. Lighting was entirely by candles. Water was pumped from a well. Sanitation, of course, was non-existent, in modern terms. 'Bess,' wrote Mark Girouard, 'had her personal close stool in a little room off her bedchamber; it was "covered with blewe cloth stitch with white, with red and black silk fringe", but there were no backstairs and no amount of silk fringe can have offset the squalor of carrying the contents of the emptied close stools down the two great staircases.'[30]

Stinking as they must sometimes have been, the Elizabethan great houses, of which Hardwick Hall was one of the most splendid, were the settings of human magnificence, little theatres where aristocrats could hold what amounted to small versions of a royal court. (And many of the great houses were designed in part to provide hospitality for the Queen herself and her entourage during a progress.) And one of the things that give the Elizabethan great houses their distinction is that none of them were entirely designed by one person. They reflected the personalities of their owners and of those who worked there. The huge glass façades of Hardwick Hall could well have been designed by Smythson, but to Bess Shrewsbury's specifications. The 'style' of Hardwick is what we should immediately label 'Elizabethan', but this itself is an eclectic blend of Perpendicular Gothic, with its huge grids of glass, like the windows of some great cathedral or college, set into Mannerist styles based on contemporary Antwerp or Delft. A distinctively 'Flemish' feature of Hardwick is its abundance of obelisks and strapwork, modelled in stone, plaster or alabaster, as overmantels inside; crowning its outline on towers, walls and lodges outside. Then again, one of the most remarkable features of Hardwick is its embroideries – used as wall hangings, bed hangings, door curtains – the largest such collection of any private house in Europe.[31] Every detail of these phenomenal productions gives delight, whether in such huge symbolic images as Arthemesia flanked by Constans and Pietan, and those that depict Astrology or Perspective or Logic, or in the much smaller works, panels that bear the heraldic devices of Bess and the various men she married. The Talbot heraldic dog, for example, built up on a piece of crimson velvet with a linen base and teased-out wool, and then sewn over with twists of silver purl and gold filé. Cushions depict the Elements, interwoven with the Cavendish snake. Here are silken white roses picked out on green velvet, or crimson velvet cushions bordered with mistletoe. Needlework is a strong, vividly flavoured and intensely personal art-form. Looking at the Hardwick embroideries, we do not merely revere the craftsmanship, we feel the presence of the many prodigious seamstresses who worked them. We have almost certainly arrived at Hardwick in an ugly car and we stand before the embroideries in our mass-produced clothes. Light streams from those tall windows onto our sweatshirts and sneakers, challenging us to imagine a world where there was no ugliness, where no factory manufactured clothes or furniture, where life was a ceremony of beautiful clothes, beautiful objects and considered shapes and shades.

The infinite variety of Elizabethan architecture refreshes our eyes, delights and amuses us with its playfulness and complexity, as much as a polyphonic part song by Byrd or an intricate rhyme by Philip Sidney. Look up at the chimneystacks of brick and terracotta and stone on their palaces and country houses. All are recognisable as Elizabethan, yet how varied they are, whether we are looking at the zigzags of the chimneys at Penshurst Place in Kent, or the hexagonal brick stacks, crowned like a classical pillar, at Horham Hall in Essex, or the twisted terracotta barley-sugar of Hengrave Hall in Sussex. In all the details of Elizabethan buildings we find variety and ingenuity: in the chimneypieces, in the plastered ceilings, in lanterned columns at Montacute House in Somerset, in the pilasters and entablatures at Longleat, in porches and gateways, in gables and gatehouses. Their architecture was eclectic, and native, while absorbing the principles and classical inspirations of the European Renaissance. Their houses and colleges look like the dwellings of men and women who had revived the ability to read Greek, who could speak Italian, who ordered their expensive clothes from Paris, who wrote everything from prayers to shopping lists in Latin and who were yet deeply, and self-consciously, rooted in their native English soil, loving the English landscape, the English country sports, hunting, fishing and riding.

The 1570s were a decade of particular architectural creativity. Longleat was gutted by fire in 1567, but Smythson had no sooner finished his rebuilding than his patron, Sir John Thynne, commissioned him to wrap the existing house with an extraordinary classical encasement of Doric, Ionic and Corinthian pilasters. Vast amounts of stone were required for the embellishments. Thynne bought a whole quarry for the purpose at Haselbury, near Box.[32] Wheelless drags pulled by oxen were used to bring the stone through the steep Somersetshire combes and were transformed by Smythson into the crested parapets, the glorious lights, the soaring classical frontages that still awe and delight the visitor to Longleat today.

It is inevitable, when we are telling the story of the Elizabethans, that we should dwell upon their great houses, for these were the places that bore witness to so much of their political, and of their cultural, history as well. Mary Sidney married the 2nd Earl of Pembroke in 1577 and became the chatelaine of Wilton House. 'In her time,' wrote John Aubrey, 'Wilton House was like a college, there were so many learned and ingeniose persons.'[33] The house saw Ben Jonson, Edmund Spenser, Christopher Marlowe – perhaps even Shakespeare went there with Burbage's theatrical company – but few, even of these illustrious visitors, were as learned or as 'ingeniose' as Mary Sidney herself, or as her brother Philip, who probably wrote much of his poetry and of his prose-romance the *Arcadia* at Wilton.

It would be a mistake, however, only to remember the huge houses, and the great palaces of the upper aristocracy, when we try to get our panorama of Elizabethan life into focus. The aristocracy ruled England from Elizabethan to Victorian times (as they had done in the Middle Ages). The Elizabethan aristocracy, however, sprang very largely from the gentry class beneath them. The Cecils, the Bacons, the Russells, the Cavendishes, the Sackvilles were all gentry families who rose to become high aristocratic families.

An essential factor of Elizabethan society was its mobility. At the same time it aspired to a much more rigidly hierarchical social structure than had obtained in the Middle Ages. In medieval England, merchants – the unlanded rich – could have influence not just in the City of London, but in politics: they could serve as JPs or sit in Parliament. No merchant in Essex became a JP after 1564.[34] In the great cloth-producing county of Wiltshire not a single clothier was returned as an MP during the reign of Elizabeth. As Richard Mulcaster (Old Etonian and Member of Parliament, as well as headmaster of the Merchant Taylors' School) could write, 'All the people which be in our contrie be either gentlemen or of the commonalty. The common is devided into merchauntes and manuaries generally, what partition soever is the subsidivent.'[35] Or, as a contemporary put it, even more bluntly, 'All sortes of people created from the beginning are devided into 2: Noble and Ignoble.' And in reply to the old question about who was the gentleman 'when Adam delved and Eve span', there was a simple answer: 'As Adam had sonnes of honour, soe had hee Caine destined to dishonour.'[36]

This meant that all new wealth, if it was to be converted into power, had to be invested in land. This was particularly true of the successful lawyers. Sir Edward Coke (1552–1634), a close friend of the Cecil family and Attorney General in the last years of Elizabeth's reign, owned at least 105 properties by 1600 – manors, farms, rectories, advowsons and mills, dotted around Norfolk and Suffolk, as well as two huge houses. He had risen from very minor gentry at Mileham in Norfolk, himself the son of a lawyer.[37] In Devon the Prideaux, Pophams, Heles, Pollards, Periams, Rowes, Harrises, Glanvilles, Whiddons and Williamses were all families who acquired or solidified gentry status by buying land with money made from the practice of the legal profession.[38]

Merchants, too, were not content to remain as rich merchants, as they had in the Middle Ages. They bought themselves into the landed classes. William Offley was a case in point, a burgess of Stafford. He sent his sons to London to be educated at St Paul's. One, Sir Thomas, became Lord Mayor, and bought the manors of Mucklestone and Madeley, becoming an ancestor of the Earls of Crewe.[39]

In such a climate it was not surprising that those responsible for drawing up coats of arms for would-be, or new, gentlefolk, were kept prosperously busy. The heralds at the College of Arms were always occupied in the Elizabethan Age. In Lincolnshire, between 1562 and 1634, seventy-eight new names were added to the armigerous gentry. In Wiltshire, between 1565 and 1623, 109 names were added to the original total of 203. In Yorkshire, where there was an especially large number of recusant gentry, some of whom went abroad, 218 out of 641 gentry names in a comparable period were new gentry.[40] They were able, if they were lucky in that mineral-rich county, to extract more than just rents from their land. Since only landowners could mine, only gentry in the Elizabethan Age could be industrialists. In 1598 the Privy Council was informed that Hewett Osborne's mines in Wales Wood, Yorkshire, produced '2,000 lodes of coles' a year – about 2,000 tons. The iron industry in Yorkshire, very lucrative, was exclusively in the hands of the gentry and nobility, with ironworks at Kirkstall, Attercliffe, Wadsey, Lascells Hall, Colne Bridge, Honley, Cawthorne, Rockley, Wortley, Hunshelf, Midgley Bank and West Bretton.[41] The coat of arms and the ownership of land were passports not simply to status, but to power.

Nor was it permitted in that far-from-free society to pass yourself off as gentry if you were not. It was forbidden by law for common people to play bowls or tennis, for example. They were games for gentlemen.[42] Norroy King of Arms was empowered to confine the wearing of a hood and tippet to esquires and seniors. In 1562 there was a detailed search of women's clothes to make sure they were not getting above themselves (though Elizabeth I never went so far as Charles I, who in 1636 forbade the wearing of imitation jewellery).[43] It was Burghley, as Chancellor of Cambridge University, who distinguished the noblemen by ornamenting their academic dress with gold lace in 1578 – a custom that continued until the nineteenth century. These were the so-called 'tufts'. Snobs who sought out their company were 'tuft hunters'.

The Elizabethan heralds made assiduous visitations to all the English counties to make sure that no one was claiming gentility without entitlement. Robert Cooke, Clarenceux Herald in 1567–93, visited all the English counties of the southern province to this end.[44]

Visitations involved punctilious searches through family pedigrees. The Queen, and Burghley, took with intense seriousness the role of the heralds 'as a buttress for the stability of society', in Lawrence Stone's words.[45] The heralds were put in charge of public funerals for aristocrats, and so seriously did the Queen believe in such displays of hierarchy that, parsimonious as she was, she footed the bill for the obsequies of the Marchioness of Northampton in 1565, of Lady Knollys in 1569, of the Countess of Lennox (whom she hated) in 1577, and of her cousin Harry, Lord Hunsdon, in 1596 – though when the Earl of Huntingdon died in the same year she jibbed at paying for his funeral.[46]

The heralds might well have been buttresses of social conservatism in their symbolic role. In person they were sometimes difficult company. Those who choreograph great ceremonies are often prone to choler, but Sir William Dethick, Garter King of Arms in the latter part of Elizabeth's reign, was a man of exceptional irascibility. He struck his own father with his fist, and wounded his brother with a dagger at Windsor Castle. During Sir Henry Sidney's funeral in Westminster Abbey he struck a man with his dagger and wounded him and was detained in Newgate Prison. Perhaps the most extreme example of his peppery temper is found in a deposition made by Mary, wife of Dethick's colleague John Hart, Chester Herald, which she made to Burghley himself:

> May yt please your Honor I beinge alone in my chamber he put me in feare of my life, and almost took my breath from me, in most vyle sort: his cozin Richard Dethicke of Polstide in Suffolk hearing his doings came in and toke him by the middle and prayed him to be contente, I feared Yorke [Herald] wold have killed me els he spurned me downe with his foote so ofte (my hedde was verie neare the fire and my heare like to be burned) as yt maye appear by my cappe, which I had next to my heare. He put a depe cole baskette lined with lether on my hedde with some coles and dust in yt and kept it so longe aboute my hedde and shoulders that my breth was almost gone. Savynge the reverence of your Lordshippe, my chamber pott of urine he poured on my bare hedde and thereafter rubbed hot ashes into my heare and dipt a basen into a stand of newe drincke and flashed so much full on my face that I cold not see for a time. As sone as I came to myself I gotte down even as I was and wold have gone fourth to have showed myself to the gentlemen of the Arches, but my ladie Garter kept the gate, and kept me in by force and there I laide to his charge, how he had misused me and called me (saving your Honores reverence) pockie whore. He saide before Richmonde and Somerset heraltes that I hid like a pockie drable (or a queane) and wold have runed over me agayne with his foote but his mother held him backe . . .[47]

The sudden revelation that Dethick's mother was present during this appalling scene adds, for the reader (though not for the unfortunate Mary Hart), to its grotesque comedy.

It is strange to think of the aristocratic decorum of the realm being in the hands of such lunatics, but those who desired to establish their gentility did not mind too much about the characters of the heralds who granted them arms. Dethick and his father granted more than 500 coats of arms to aspirant gentlemen. Cook, Clarenceux King of Arms, granted another 500. Brook, when York Herald for ten years, granted 120. The heralds guarded their right to dispense arms with royally sanctioned vigour. When one William Dawkins compiled fake pedigrees for hundreds of families in East Anglia, he was imprisoned and lost an ear.

The Dethicks? They were an ancient Derbyshire family, and Sir William Dethick used their arms. In fact he was the grandson of one Robert Derrick, a yeoman armourer from Greenwich who died in 1525. He had been brought to the Royal Armoury from Germany by Erasmus Kyrkener. Although Sir William Dethick persisted in claiming kinship with the Derbyshire Dethicks, his fellow heralds enjoyed putting it about that he was really a Dutchman.[48]

11

Histories

In the church of St Andrew Undershaft in London is the tomb of John Stow (1525–1605), whose *Survey of London* remains one of the great histories of England's capital. The tomb is surmounted with an effigy of the historian, a remarkable funerary monument of Derbyshire marble and alabaster, being one of the very few Jacobean tombs that depicts a writer in the act of writing.[1] Every two years the Merchant Taylors' Company, who pay for the lavish upkeep of the tomb, assemble in the church for a ceremony in which Stow is given a new quill pen. Among other resonances, the ritual seems to say that history never ceases to be written. Most writers' tombs of the period suggest that the work is done. Stow, like Shakespeare over the grave in Stratford-upon-Avon, is still holding onto his pen.

I began this book about the Elizabethans with a reflection on our difficulty, in the generation that has put behind us in Britain the nationalist and colonialist mindset, of keeping them in a focus that is fair, truthful and just. Clearly, it is impossible for us to have unmixed feelings of approval of the Elizabethans' wish to colonise Ireland or to make money from selling West African slaves to the Portuguese, any more than it is possible wholeheartedly to endorse their inflicting torture on an albeit small number of Roman Catholic recusants. Yet equally it is hard to banish the thought that those historians of comparatively recent vintage, such as James Anthony Froude or Mandell Creighton in the nineteenth century, or A.L. Rowse in the twentieth century, who did broadly endorse the Elizabethan historical programme, painted them in colours that were clearer than those, more recent, who wish to arraign them for their crimes.

The Stow monument, with its repeatedly renewed and renewable quill pen, reminds us that the task of reinterpreting the past is never-ending, and that the Elizabethans themselves were adepts at the historical art, creators in chronicle, in mythology, in pageants and tournaments, in drama and poems – a history that explained themselves, to themselves, and themselves to posterity. Historians of our age have witnessed the dismantling of the nationalist and colonialist England/Britain, which was largely an Elizabethan inspiration. Ireland runs its own affairs. Colonialism as a political concept is dead – at any rate, British colonialism, and American 'colonialism' is something rather different. The Church of

England exists only in name and is no longer really the natural national Church. In the Elizabethan historians, myth-makers and poets, however, we see the written justifications for an emergent nationalism taking shape.

Stow was in some ways untypical of the Elizabethan historians. He was not a gentleman (his father was a tallow-chandler). He never studied at a university or an inn of court, though he had good Latin and wrote an excellent, fluent English. A member of the Merchant Taylors' Company, he had a rather humdrum job, as a surveyor of ale-houses. But, just as much as the gentleman-antiquaries such as Dr Dee or Archbishop Parker, Stow had an obsessive passion for presenting and chronicling the past. He had a large collection of manuscripts and books. He was suspected of Catholic sympathies, and when the Bishop of London – Grindal – ordered a search of Stow's house, they confiscated a number of suspect titles: Edmund Bonner's *An Exposition of the Creed, Ten Commandments, Pater Noster, Ave Maria* and other Romanist volumes. Whatever his private sympathies, Stow conformed to the church, however, and it was inevitable that so inveterate a hoarder and collector should have possessed religious books that offended the ultra-Puritan Grindal.

Stow's *Survey of London*, which was published in 1598, went through many versions. During the earliest years of Elizabeth's reign Stow's published work was less localised. He established a canon of English literature, with an edition of Chaucer in 1561; in 1568 he edited thirty-three poems of John Skelton. He also published *The Chronicles of England* (1580) and the *Annales of England* (1592).

An author who was much more obviously a creative historian, and who, as C.S. Lewis wrote, 'long retained almost Scriptural authority',[2] was John Foxe (1516–87). A more recent writer than Lewis calls Foxe's *Acts and Monuments* (first English edition 1563, followed by many revised editions, and known popularly as *Foxe's Book of Martyrs*) 'perhaps the single most influential work of historical writing throughout Britain and Ireland.'[3] Lewis, himself of Ulster Protestant origins, though in later life an Anglo-Catholic, makes the fair points that Foxe was an honest man who never knowingly wrote falsehoods, and whose horrifying accounts of the treatment of Protestants in the reign of Queen Mary I were true. His earlier original work, the *De Non Plectendis Morte Adulteris* (1548), is a plea for mercy; he confesses that he could never pass a slaughterhouse without discomposure; and when his own party was on top, he interceded (vainly of course) to save Anabaptists from the stake in 1575 and Jesuits from the gallows in 1581.[4]

Foxe was powerful as an historian (or, if you prefer, a propagandist for Protestant nationalism) precisely because the atrocities he itemised did in fact take place. Foxe provided the English with documentary evidence of what happened when the Counter-Reformation was allowed to influence governments. It is against the tortures and burnings of hundreds of Protestants in Foxe's book that the modern person must set many of the Elizabethan outrages: Walsingham's spy-networks and torture methods; Drake's simple theft of Spanish gold; the torture and killing of virtuous men such as the Jesuit Edmund Campion. The *Acts and Monuments* of Foxe entered the national psyche, so that almost any policy or action that ensured England's Protestant independence was seen to be justified. This mindset continued long after the actual religious controversies that preoccupied Foxe had faded from memory. Since Foxe taught his readers not simply to be anti-Catholic, but to be independent as an island-race. The huge folios of Foxe's *Acts and Monuments* did indeed suggest a unique destiny for the English and their Church. This was discernible not only in the text, but in the vivid woodcuts with which the work is illustrated. In the 1570 edition, volume one has a massive (larger than three folio pages) fold-out woodcut of the 'Heathen Tyrrannes of Rome' who persecuted the early Christians before the conversion of Constantine. There is at the end of this volume an illustration of the 'proud primacie of Popes paynted out in Tables, in order of their rising up by litle and litle, from faithfull Byshops and Martyrs'. But this was far from being the end of history. After the period of the popes there arose, in Foxe's vision of things, the re-emergence of the True Church with the arrival of Henry VIII. With the crowning of Elizabeth, and the continuation of the Tudor dynasty, Foxe could envisage the glad consummation of an historical process that would see the fulfilment of the Bible prophecy (in the eighteenth chapter of Revelations) and the downfall of the papacy.[5]

If Foxe saw the Tudor Age as a time when true Christianity eventually emerged from a superstitious past, Raphael Holinshed (died *c.*1580), whose *Chronicles* were first published in 1577, looked back to the anarchy of civil war in the fifteenth century and beyond and found further reason for celebrating now. It was a self-consciously political elevation of the present against the past, and of English national identity against outsiders. Hindsight sees Holinshed as a 'source' for Shakespeare's history plays, but it would be truer to say that Holinshed (from the 1570s onwards) and Shakespeare (from the 1590s onwards) were both drawing upon, and giving eloquent voice to, a sense of collective national identity.

Holinshed's *Chronicles* are in any event a compilation. They were originally planned as a huge 'universall cosmographie' with 'histories of every knowne nation' by a canny publisher (printer to Queen Elizabeth) named Reyne or Reginald Wolfe, who died in 1573 before the work got off the ground. The collaborators in 'Holinshed' included, as well as

Holinshed himself, Richard Stanyhurst, John Hoover (alias Vowell), Francis Thynne and William Harrison, and they in turn drew upon and simply copied earlier histories. As Lewis put it, 'the "English story" is a sort of national stock-pot permanently simmering to which each new cook adds flavouring at his discretion'.[6] Or, as a more recent scholar has put it, 'Holinshed's *Chronicle* was itself, or can now be seen, as a giant inter-disciplinary project. It was offered to the late Elizabethan reader, in two editions a decade apart, as the work of a group, a collaboration (the term "syndicate" can be loosely used) between freelance antiquarians, lesser clergymen, members of Parliament with legal training, minor poets, publishers.'[7] Like Elizabethan architecture – which, even if it followed the drawings of a great master-mason such as Smythson, was never the work of one mind – Elizabethan history was a collaborative enterprise, a palimpsest of different testimonies shaped into a common sense of the past.

When Wolfe the stationer/bookseller died, much of the contents of his shop was purchased by Stow, and the team of writers mentioned above moved into action to produce 'Holinshed'. The joint effort, the 'national stock-pot permanently simmering', should not, however, be considered a neutral chronicle merely because it was not personal and did not emanate from a single author. It did emanate from a particular place – London – and a particularly volatile political situation. Queen Elizabeth's failure, or refusal, to marry, and her occasional illnesses, put the regime in a particularly vulnerable position, the more vulnerable as the 1570s advanced and the likelihood of the Queen producing an heir dwindled (by 1580 she would be forty-seven). Not only was the regime vulnerable to attack from abroad, from France or Spain. It had, perpetually, to hold at bay the threats of discontent within: from Catholics (actual recusants who secretly used the services of Roman Catholic priests, and the much larger number who conformed to the National Church) who perhaps had believed that the Reformation was only half-complete. Both sides had a tendency to set their freedom to tell the truth above the need to conform to what the government wanted them to think.

The writing and rewriting of national history in the 1570s and 1580s was not happening in a political vacuum, still less in an atmosphere of easy tolerance, in which one person's viewpoint was considered just as deserving of hearing as another. In the year after the Pope's Bull of Excommunication, a new Treason Act was passed making it treason to affirm *by writing* that the Queen should not be queen, or that she was an infidel, tyrant or usurper.

The chronicles – all or nearly all London-based, and coming from the area and class that in a couple of generations would provide the power-base for Protestant republican resistance to Charles I – were as aware as the censors that history could be used as a code by which to make comments about the present. The Puritan *Admonitions to Parliament* of 1572 was highly critical of the bishops and of the government. On 7 July 1573 John Field and Thomas Wilcox, the joint authors of the attack, were imprisoned. Anyone found printing the work, 'all and every printer, stationer, bookbinder, merchant and all other men . . . who hath in their custody any of the said books [were] to bring in the same to the bishop of the diocese, or to one of her highness' Privy Council . . . upon pain of imprisonment and her highness' further displeasure'. The Queen's displeasure was not merely expressed in words. When John Stubbs, in 1579, published a pamphlet advising the Queen against marriage with the Duc d'Alençon, he was convicted of seditious libel. He, his printer and his bookseller had their right hands chopped off.[8]

These facts hardly justify an older[9] way of reading 'Holinshed's' *Chronicles* as being written simply to legitimise the Tudor régime. In the apparent muddle of the *Chronicles* much more is going on. Abraham Fleming, the editor of the 1587 edition, was a supporter of the Elizabethan Settlement, the merger of Church and state; but his late inclusion in Holinshed's earlier *Chronicles* of recent acts of defiance and nonconformity only emphasised the fact that the new régime, in its persecution of Puritans and other Protestant 'heretics' (as well as their persecution of Catholics), sat strangely beside some of Holinshed's original material. By lumping together stories of very recent repression of free opinion with Holinshed's stories of heresy-hunting in the old days, Fleming (who probably *intended* to make the reader more conformist, more afraid of stepping out of line) must have made some readers find in the older stories collected by Holinshed a case for believing in freedom of conscience. Thus, far from 'legitimising' the Elizabethan regime, the *Chronicles*, together with *Foxe's Book of Martyrs*, became part of the Puritan or Nonconformist library that would in a later generation be packed on the *Mayflower*, America-bound, or would sustain those supporters of the Good Old Cause that marched with Cromwell's Ironsides.

Fleming, for example, included an account for 13 April 1579 of how:

> Matthew Manon, by his trade a ploughwrite of Hetharset three miles from Norwich, was convented before the bishop of Norwich, for that he denied Christ our saviour. At the time of his appearance, it was objected that he had published these heresies following. That the new testament and gospel of Christ are but mere foolishnesse, a storie of man, or rather a mere fable . . . that the Holie ghost is not God . . . that baptisme is not necessarie in the church of God, neither the use

of the sacrament of the bodie and blood of Christ. For the which heresies he was condemned in the consistorie, and sentence was pronounced against him . . . And because he spake words of blasphemie (not to be recited) against the queen's majestie and others of hir councell, he was by the recorder, master sergeant Windham, and the maior Sir Robert Wood of Norwich condemned to lose both his eares, which were cut off on the thirteenth of Maie in the market place of Norwich, and afterwards, to wit on the twentieth of Maie, he was burned in the castell ditch of Norwich.[10]

When Fleming recounted the deaths of Catholics – and in fact he thoroughly *approved* of supporting nonconformity, Catholic or Protestant – against the Elizabethan Church and state, he found *himself* being censored. Queen Elizabeth herself insisted, for example, that he remove a sentence about Edmund Campion, the Jesuit who was tortured and executed for treason in 1581: 'he died not for treason but for Religion'. The *Chronicles*, which had begun, in part, as an illustration of the intolerance of earlier, Catholic regimes, found themselves taking up the story of Elizabethan intolerance and themselves became a victim of extreme religio-political censorship.

One can trace an amusing and bizarre vision of the historiography of religious persecution in the figure of Shakespeare's Falstaff.

Sir John Oldcastle (Baron Cobham) was a Lollard, a member of that late-medieval religious group whose beliefs and writings were seen by the sixteenth-century reformers as foreshadowing the Reformation. *The First English Life of Henry V*, and the other Catholic chroniclers of the late fifteenth and early sixteenth centuries, tell us that Oldcastle was buried alive while hanging in chains in 1417. He had helped to fight Owain Glyndŵr in his rising against Henry IV and was a friend of Henry V's youth; but when that king came to power, he was persuaded by Archbishop Arundel to continue the policies of his father in persecuting heretics. Oldcastle's 'rebellion' against Henry V, if it took place at all, appears to have been a hare-brained scheme to kidnap the King and his brothers with a band of some hundreds of Lollard supporters. Royalist propaganda translated this into a rebel army of 20,000. And by the time, for example, that Thomas Walsingham wrote his chronicle in the reign of Henry VIII, Oldcastle had become a sort of demon who needed to be exorcised before the English king could be blessed by God with victory over the French army at Agincourt.[11]

For the Protestant historian John Bale (1495–1565), however, Oldcastle was not a villain, but a proto-Protestant hero. In *A Brief chronicle concerning . . . Sir John Oldcastle, Lord Cobham*, Bale instructs his reader, 'Now pluck from your eyes the corrupted spectacles of carnal or popish judgements, and do upon them that clear sight which ye have by the Spirit of Christ; and that faithfully done, tell me which of these two [Cobham or Thomas Beckett] seemeth rather to be the martyr of Christ, and which the pope's martyr?'[12]

Bale, who became Bishop of Ossory in Edward VI's reign, was appointed to a canonry in Elizabeth's (having gone into exile in Marian times). Queen Elizabeth took an interest in him. She ordered that those who had taken, or come into possession of, Bale's papers and books during his exile should be made to return them. She wanted him to have research materials 'for the illustration and setting forth of the storye of this our realme, by him the said Bale'.[13] He died before he had a chance to continue his historical work. Elizabeth probably recognised in John Bale, as have modern scholars, the first English historian to acknowledge the profound historical significance of England's break from the papacy, which 'meant the ending of a whole historical tradition'.[14] It meant a reinvention of history, and to this extent Bale was the father of modern English history. Bale used 'enemy' documents and inverted their meaning. Chronicles designed to show that a figure such as Oldcastle was a dangerous heretic were plundered to show him to be a hero. Whereas Catholic chronicles mock Oldcastle's lack of Latin, Bale salutes the fact that he wrote in that good, patriotic, Protestant language, English.

Bale stresses Oldcastle's literacy (he 'toke paper & penne in hand, & so wrote a Christen confession or rekening of his faith'.) His Oldcastle not only addresses the people, warning them of the duplicity of Catholic priests ('Good Christen people for Gods love be wel ware of these men. For they will else begyle you and lead you blindelynge into hell with themselves'), but also 'admonished the Kinges, as Richard the second, Henry the fourth, and Henfy the fyft, of the clergies manifold abuses, and put into the parliament house certain bokes concerning their just reformacion . . .'[15]

So the Reformation transformed Oldcastle a century and more after his death, from an heretical troublemaker to a Protestant hero. Yet by 1596, when William Shakespeare wrote *Henry IV Part I*, Sir John Oldcastle the Lollard martyr had become the hero of the 'Puritan left'. The editor of the Arden Shakespeare *King Henry IV Part I*, David Scott Kastan, sees Falstaff as a parodic representation of a 'puritan'. Certainly there are traces of the Protestant ranter in Falstaff's language – he speaks in scriptural allusions. 'If to be fat is to be hated, then Pharaoh's lean kine are to be loved' (*Henry IV*, II.iv.345) . . . 'Thou knowest in the state of innocency, Adam fell, and what should poor Jack Falstaff do in the days of villainy?' (*Henry IV*, III. iii.120). He exclaims, 'I would I were a weaver;

I could sing psalms or anything.' (*Henry IV*,II.iv.127). Shakespeare originally called Falstaff Sir John Oldcastle, an amazingly tactless thing to have done, given the fact that William Brooke, 10th Lord Cobham, was Lord Chamberlain from 8 August 1596 to 5 March 1597, and responsible for censoring plays. Since the original Oldcastle had also been called Lord Cobham, it was a risky bit of cheek. Traces of the joke remain even after Shakespeare changed the name to Falstaff; as when Prince Hal refers to the fat knight as 'my old lad of the castle' (*Henry IV*, I. ii.29).

Whatever the origin of the joke – making a Puritan hero into the most dissolute comic character in the Shakespearean canon – it is clear that 'Falstaff' took on a reality of his own, which turned Oldcastle into a mere shadow. The relationship of the fat, boozy older man trying to corrupt a young man of much higher birth is a theme repeated in the Sonnets, and Fall-Staff/Shake-Spear must have had a strong element of autobiography in his composition. He erupted into the English chronicle-plays that had helped to make Shakespeare's name and had a greater reality than any of the 'historical' figures with whom he was surrounded on the stage. This was one way of extending the national mythology which was first enacted in the theatre in Shoreditch some time in 1597.[16]

The work of antiquarianism, and the reworking of mythological history, could be enlisted to justify contemporary political standpoints. In Spenser's by-now-notorious dialogue, for example, *A View of the Present State of Ireland*, one of the speakers wonders at the legitimacy of using the 'moste fabulous and forged' dross of Irish chronicles to justify the English policy in Ireland during the 1580s and 1590s. But Irenius, the more right-wing and in many ways more like Spenser of the conversationalists, defends the custom:

> Trevely I muste Confesse I do soe, but yeat not so absolutelye as ye doe suppose do I hearin relye upon those Bardes or Irishe Cronicles, thoughe the Irish themselves throughe theire Ignorance in matters of Learninge and deper judgement doe moste Constantlye believe and Avouch rheym. But unto them besides I add myne owne readinge and out of them bothe together with comparison of times likenes of manners and Customes Affinytie of words and names properties of natures and uses resemblances of rightes and Ceremonies moniments of Churches and Tombes and manie other like circumstances I doe gather a likelyhode of truethe, not certainlye affirming anye thinge but by Conferringe of times nacions languages monimentes and such like. I doe hunte out a probabilitye of things which I due leave unto your Judgement to beleeve or refuse.[17]

Like those British in India who fell in love with the architecture, antiquities, languages and culture which they threatened by their very presence on Indian soil, Spenser was to become a passionate devotee of the folklore and literature of Ireland, as well as a celebrant of its landscape. He was also a populariser of the Elizabethan falsehood, culled from medieval chroniclers and fantasists, that Ireland always had belonged to England.

Giraldus Cambrensis, the wonderfully entertaining and gossipy Archdeacon of Brecon, had invented, in his history (in order to bolster the claims of King Henry II to occupy Ireland) the myth of the 'Bayonne title'. This was the story that the sons of Mil, or Milesians, were granted permission to settle in Ireland by one Gurguntins, 'King of the Britons'. 'From this it is clear,' Giraldus wrote, 'that Ireland can with some right be claimed by the kings of Britain even though the claim be from olden times.' Giraldus's story, freely garbled, was reproduced in Holinshed's account of Ireland's 'First Inhabitants'. Spenser, both in the *Faerie Queene* and in his *View of the Present State of Ireland* asserts that 'it appearthe by good recorde yeat extante that Kinge Arthur and before him Gurgunt had all that Ilande in his Allegiance and Subieccion'. This 'goode recorde' was Giraldus's wild claim that Ireland owed tribute to King Arthur in the days of 'Giolla Már', a figure who had the convenient attribute of not having existed in the prosaic realm of fact.[18]

Spenser's historiography of Ireland was entirely consistent with other Elizabethan antiquaries, such as William Hakewill, who wrote of the Romans needing to subjugate a Celtic people 'by nature disobedient'. Comparing the benefits brought to the British mainland by the Saxon invasions with the conquest of Ireland by the Elizabethan English, Hakewill concluded that 'nothing is more of conquerors desired, and more usually put in practise; so indeed is there nothing of more honor and security in ages to come, if once it may be thoroughly performed.'

Hakewill (baptised 1574, died 1655) was of a later generation – serving as a Cornish MP in the reign of James I. But he was a serious historian, still valued today as an historian of Parliament, and a good indicator of how the English mindset vis-à-vis Ireland took for granted the rightness of the Elizabethan colonisers. 'Modern writers have praised Hakewill for his painstaking research and historical integrity.'[19]

Yet while modern academic historians might praise Hakewill, or more notably Stow, for their primary research, the Elizabethans themselves (perhaps they had this more in common with the journalists and general readers of the twenty-first century) looked to the past for lessons and patterns. Philip Sidney's *A Defence of Poetry* (perhaps written 1579–80) mocks the old bore antiquary:

> laden with old mouse-eaten records, authorising himself (for the most part) upon other histories, whose greatest authorities are built upon the notable foundation of hearsay; having much ado to accord differing writers and to pick truth out of their partiality, better acquainted with a thousand years ago than with the present age, and yet better knowing how this world goes than how his own wit runneth; curious for antiquities and inquisitive of novelties, a wonder to young folks, and a tyrant in table talk . . .'[20]

This sounds like a portrait of an actual pompous historian/antiquary who had bored young Sidney. The 'poetry' which the young writer defends is the truth that can be conveyed in fiction. Sidney amasses some impressive poets in his *Defence* of a fictive way to truth – Dante, Virgil, King David and Jesus are among those who tell fictitious stories to frame moral truths.

'Who readeth Aeneas carrying old Anchises on his back, that wisheth not it were his fortune to perform so excellent an act?'[21] Naturally Sidney, who was well versed in European literature, ancient and modern, defends the ingenuity and beauty of poetic *form*, as well as fictional content. The *Defence* was not published in Sidney's lifetime. Like most of what he wrote, it was meant for a tiny coterie. But he must have been aware that, in the 1570s, he himself and Edmund Spenser were bright new stars in the sky, the brightest in England since Chaucer. 'Homer, a Greek, flourished before Greece flourished.'[22]

Edmund Spenser, whom we last met as a poor schoolboy at Mulcaster's Merchant Taylors' School, is a triumphant example of the socially egalitarian effect of grammar-school education, which existed in England from the accession of the first Queen Elizabeth until the first or second decade of Elizabeth II. Whereas Sidney was born to near princely privilege, Spenser had no such advantages. The poor scholar of Merchant Taylors' School became the sizar of Pembroke College, Cambridge, obliged to work as a servant to the other students while pursuing his life of learning. Yet even before he went to the university, Spenser had been engaged by a London publisher to translate some sonnets of Petrarch and Joachim du Bellay's 'Visions'. Through the kindly influence of Mulcaster, his old headmaster, and with help from Gabriel Harvey, a Fellow of Pembroke, Spenser obtained work for powerful patrons: Sir Henry Norris, Ambassador to France and Norris's sons, John and Thomas, for whom Spenser worked in Ireland. Through the 1570s Spenser was at work on *The Shepheardes Calendar*, among other works. It was probably in the late 1570s that he came to know Philip Sidney.

Sidney and, rather later, Walter Raleigh were among the early supporters of Spenser in his great enterprise, *The Faerie Queene*, which was destined never to be finished. It is probably the most difficult of all long English poems fully to appreciate in this age of hurry. This is not because it is incomprehensible. Very far from it. You can best appreciate it as if you had gone back to childhood and were indeed reading a series of fairy stories, or adventure stories, all interwoven with one another.

When the schools of Eng. Lit. were set up in the universities, it was perhaps inevitable that *The Faerie Queene* should have been on the syllabus, and that an explanation of this vastly imaginative and extraordinary work should have provided useful and enjoyable employment for the academics. For here was an *Englishman*, writing a poem that was in some senses based upon the Italian epic of Ariosto. Plenty of material here for the Comparative Literature brigade. Then, too, the work is an 'allegory'. The Redcrosse Knight who rides across page one is an 'allegory' of holiness, or of the human quest for holiness. And then again, he is clearly a Protestant knight, so there is plenty of material here for academic minds, looking for the exact position that Spenser adopted towards the controversies of the Reformation.

As an eager reader of Spenser, I record my debt to all the Spenser scholars whose work has helped me. Yet I do not think there is any experience where I have felt more strongly the discrepancy between the achievements of the scholars and the work itself. It is useful to know everything that they have to tell us. (And Frances Yates's exposition of Spenser's interest in numerology, in magic, in the occult philosophy of Giordano Bruno is of especial interest.) And yet, when I think of the books that I have read about the Faerie Queene, or the helpful notes in learned editions, the mind supplies a parallel text. On one side of the page is all the learned stuff, necessary perhaps for the exposition of a learned poet. On the other side of the page is the poem itself, and the effect it produces on the mind if read for long stretches. I should strongly recommend any reader of this book to get hold of a copy of *The Faerie Queene* that does *not* have explanatory notes. Just give yourself up to the story and to the rather hypnotic and trance-like narrative. At some points you will get lost, as do all the characters in his many-stranded polyphonic theme:

> Like as a ship, that through the Ocean wyde
> Directs her course vnto one certain cost,

Is met of many a counter winde and tyde,
With which her winged speed is let and crost,
And she herself in stormie surges tost;
Yet making many a borde and many a bay,
Still winneth way, ne hath her compasse lost:
Right so it fares with me in this long way,
Whose course is often stayd, yet neuer is astray.[23]

You will find the monsters and witches frightening, the virtuous characters half-comic, half-uplifting, the variety of tone and mood unlike any other writer.

Possibly the best place to start is in the Third Book, the Book of Love. Stop worrying about whether you have 'caught' the meaning of any particular allegory. Spenser is a great artist, and he will do your work for you. When you come into the House of Busyrane, for example, you do not need to be told by a commentary that the 'Kings, Queenes, Lords, Ladies, Knyghts and Damsels gent' who are here 'heap'd together with the vulgar sort' are in the grips of insane, uncontrollable erotic love: they are in Venusberg, they are Anna Karenina and Vronsky, they are Tristan und Isolde. (If you have to find a parallel to reading the poetry of Spenser, it is closer to attending a Wagner opera than it is to reading a textbook.) The dreadful storms, the thunder and the lightning, as the chaste Britomart rescues Amoret from the griefs and deceptions of such love, come as a beautiful relief, on one level. But Britomart herself is as much confused as the girl she rescues by the end. The narrative does not end. It goes on into further complexities, just as the emotional-moral life does. And it is the inner adventures of the emotional-moral life that form one of Spenser's themes. No one who has been there ever forgets his Garden of Adonis or his Temple of Venus. But nor is there any work of literature known to me that makes it seem so positively romantic to be what we should call a Low Churchman.

Spenser places the theme in the archaic setting of pseudo-history, freely drawing upon the new Elizabethan mythologies and upon such pageantry as the Accession Day tilts.

Lovers of Spenser come to read him more and more slowly. You come to enjoy the exactitude with which he paints each scene, the inventiveness with which he takes over and rewrites old legends and mythologies, and the whole Spenser idiom, this 'olde tyme' language, drawing on Chaucer, but which is in fact completely contemporary. Spenser is the classic example of the radical conservatism of the Renaissance, its belief that in order to achieve a just society, or to be wise, it is necessary to go back and rediscover the wisdom of the ancients: 'O goodly usage of those antique times!'[24]

The paradox of his constant harping back to the olde tyme is that he is also celebrating the Now. When Britomart in Book Three is shown by Merlin a genealogical table, she springs from Arthur, and from Arthur's loins come the Welsh Tudors:

> Then shall a royal virgin raine, which shall
> Stretch her wide rod over the Belgicke shore
> That the great Castle smite so sore withal,
> That it shall make him shake, and shortly learn to fall.[25]

After a certain point, we shall probably turn to the scholars and discover that what we have been reading in this multifaceted story is in part the most glorious of all contributions to political and historical reconstructed propaganda. We will find out that the wicked Duessa is in some senses the Scottish Queene. We will find unmistakable references to Ireland and to the Low Countries, especially in Book Five, the Book of Justice, and in the story of Timias and Belphoebe we shall trace the relationship between the Queen and Sir Walter Raleigh. But that is not all that we shall find in the poem. If it were, the book would have no life. It would be as dead as an old newspaper. As it is, *The Faerie Queene* pulsates with a unique emotional energy. Spenser was artist enough never to make the allegory bear only one meaning, still less to write pure propaganda or pure satire. Rather, his observant, luxuriant, abundantly creative unfinished masterwork is a monument to the inner life. Once you are taken by it, you will not want to live in a room that does not contain a copy of Spenser's poem.

12

Kenilworth

On 30 September 1562 Henry Machyn, the old parish clerk of Holy Trinity the Less in the City of London, looked out of his window and saw an ugly street fight. Machyn's diary, as befitted a parish clerk, began as a record of heraldic funerals, and extended to bring a compendium of news, crimes, executions and gossip, as well as such city ceremonies as the Lord Mayor's Show. But this street fight, which he witnessed in the penultimate year of his life, was remarkable not least because both the participants were gentlefolk, and one of them was a (in his day) celebrated poet: 'The sam day at nyght be-twyn viii and ix was a grett fray in Redcrosse stret between ii gentyllmen and ther men, for they dyd mare [i.e. marry] one woman, and dyvers were hurt; thes wher ther names, master Boysse and master Gaskyn gentyllmen.'[1]

The accident-prone George Gascoigne was, when this affray took place, a member of Gray's Inn, though he appears to have spent as much time there involved in his own personal litigation, some of it with his own father, as he did in legal work on others' behalf. Gascoigne was the son of minor but prosperous gentry[2] in Bedfordshire and Buckinghamshire, MP for Bedfordshire (1542, 1553 and 1558), commissioner of the musters, justice of the peace and almoner at the coronations of both Edward VI and Mary I. At the time of Elizabeth's coronation Sir John was ill, and George, then about twenty, deputised for him. Gascoigne's mother was a northerner – Margaret, daughter of Sir Robert Scargill of Thorpe Hall, Richmond, Yorkshire: perhaps a kinswoman of Arthur Scargill, the leader of the National Union of Mineworkers at the time of Margaret Thatcher. It seems as if George Gascoigne spent some of his childhood in the North. He attended both Oxford and Cambridge, or so he says, though no college in either university has record of his attendance. He arrived at Gray's Inn in 1555, and it was his obsessed aim, as a young man, to become a courtier. He wrote later that he had ruined himself financially in the attempt.

It was, presumably, with the aim of mending his fortunes that Gascoigne married a rich widow, Elizabeth Bacon Breton, on 23 November 1561 at Christ Church, Newgate. She was a remote cousin of Sir Nicholas Bacon, Lord Keeper of the Great Seal, and marriage to her would have helped to advance his career at court, had it not been for Gascoigne's innate tendency to bad luck. (As he wrote in 'Gascoigne's wodmanship', he shot away at everything.) Elizabeth had five children, one of whom was the poet Nicholas Breton. Upon the death of her husband in 1559 she had married Edward Boyes of Nonington, Kent, but this was not a success and after lengthy and, for Elizabethan times, most unusual legal proceedings, she was divorced from Boyes. Unfortunately, the divorce was not finalised when she married Gascoigne, who thereby became implicated in a bigamy.

In May 1562 Gascoigne and his wife leased a farm at Willington in Bedfordshire, but the two years they spent there were far from being a bucolic idyll. He involved himself in a legal dispute with the Earl of Bedford from whom he leased his land, and with his brother John over the lease of a parsonage left to John by their father in his will. George Gascoigne claimed that his brother stole his sheep; John countered that he was merely recovering lambs stolen from his own mother, Margaret Scargill. By 1569 George Gascoigne was in Bedford gaol (ninety-one years later it would host John Bunyan, so it has a distinguished literary heritage) for debt. Somehow, in spite of the outrageous irregularity of his financial affairs, George Gascoigne followed in his father's footsteps and served as a Member of Parliament. When his right to do so, as a debtor, was questioned, there was yet more legal argy-bargy. A letter to the Privy Council complained that 'he is indebted to a great number of personnes for the which cause he hathe absented himself from the citie by a longe time and now beinge returned for a burgesse of Midehurste in the countie of Sussex, doethe shewe his face openlie in the despite of all his creditors'.[3] Gascoigne's name was accordingly struck off the list of MPs drawn up on 8 May 1572.

It was a good moment to cut loose. Gascoigne joined Sir Humphrey Gilbert's ill-starred expeditionary force in the Netherlands. It was very much an independent operation, with Queen Elizabeth always insisting to the Spanish that she did not sanction English support for the Dutch rebels, while privately hoping that they would drive the French out of Flushing and overthrow Spanish hegemony in Holland. Gascoigne served as a soldier in the Netherlands, probably from July 1572 until the second siege of Leiden in May 1574. He returned to England from time to time – he attended the funeral of Reginald Grey, 5th Earl of Kent, at St Giles, Cripplegate on 17 April 1573 – but was able to observe the war at close hand. Being Gascoigne, he had plenty of complaints and quarrels. He was shocked by the incompetence of Gilbert and the other leaders and by the ineffectualness and downright cowardice of the English and Scottish mercenary troops. After the naval battle of Flushing (26–7 August 1573) Gascoigne quarrelled with his colonel about the lack of discipline in the regiment and resigned his captain's commission. There was then another highly characteristic dispute as he waited to get paid at Strijen. But

Gascoigne, who quarrelled freely with his incompetent English commanders, impressed the Prince of Orange with his soldierly qualities. Although he took a break at Christmas to return to England on leave, Gascoigne rejoined Prince William to lend his support during the siege of Delft. The Prince paid Gascoigne 300 gulden above his pay for his part in the Spanish surrender of Middelburg. Gascoigne's last spell of active service was his participation in the siege of Leiden in early 1574. The Dutch edgily feared that the English were colluding with the Spanish, and Gascoigne himself was accused of treacherously surrendering to the Spanish; 400 English mercenaries were taken prisoner and led to Haarlem. It seems as if Elizabeth did a deal with Philip II. In exchange for sparing the lives of these prisoners, she allowed the Spanish fleet to revictual in England. Among the released prisoners was George Gascoigne.

> How so it were, at last we were dispatcht,
> And home we came as children come from schoole,
> As gladde, as fishe which were but lately cacht,
> And straight againe were cast into the poole:
> For by my fay I coumpt him but a foole,
> Which would not rather poorely live at large,
> Than rest in pryson fedde with costly charge,

as he wrote in his rather deft verse account of the expedition, 'The fruites of warre' or '*Dulce Bellum Inexpertis*', a Latin motto all too apposite to politicians of our own day as well as to the warmongers of the sixteenth century: that war seems a good idea to people who do not know anything about it.

Gascoigne skilfully represented himself as one such, who has returned from the battlefields of the Netherlands disgusted by war. Brave as 'our English bloudes' have been in the fighting (and Gascoigne writes the poem partly to repair his own reputation and to rebut the rumours of his treachery), he left his readers in no doubt that war is a bloody business. He ended the poem with a 'Peroratio' to Queen Elizabeth, urging her (she hardly needed urging, all her instincts were those of the sensible peacemaker) not to get involved in unnecessary war:

> Your skilfulle minde (O Queene without compare)
> Can some conceive that cause constraynes me so,
> Since wicked warres have bredde such cruell care,
> In Flanders, Fraunce, in Spaine and many mo,
> Which reape thereby none other worth but wo . . .

The Peroration contains apostrophes not merely to Queen Elizabeth, but also to the Earl of Bedford, the Earl of Oxford, the Earl of Kent, the Archbishop of Canterbury, the Law Lords ('You gemmes of Justice, chiefe of either bench') and the merchants of London. Clearly, it was a penitent Gascoigne who returned from the Netherlands, resolved to make friends with many of his former enemies, and desperate for advancement. And in 1575 his luck turned. He published a revised version of his war and other poems, this time under his own name (*A Hundreth Sundrie Flowres*, the anonymous volume of 1572/3, became *The Posies of George Gascoigne Esquire* of 1575). He revised and republished his amusing novel, *Master F.J.* He advertised his own reformed character by translating and publishing a version of a Dutch play based upon the parable of the Prodigal Son (*The Glasse of Government*) and put together a collection of prose and poetry on a subject, which he knew to be close not only to his own heart, but to the heart of the Queen: *The Noble Arte of Venerie or Hunting . . . Translated and collected for the pleasure of all Noblemen and Gentlemen*. The source of Gascoigne's work was a French book, Jacques du Fouilloux's *La Vénérie*, and it reflects the delight in the hunt, which has been the passion of countrymen and women in France and England since the Middle Ages. The new, moralistic Gascoigne cannot resist pointing out that the real devious foxes were not Mr Reynard who was chased over the fields, but human beings who are as cunning and devious as a fox!

But shall I say my minde? I never yet saw day,
But every town had two or three which Rainard's part could play,
So that men vaunt in vaine, which say they hunt the Foxe
To kepe their neighbours poultry free, & to defend their flockes.
When they them selves can spoyle, more profit in an houre,
Then Raynard rifles in a year, when he doth most devoure.

Although Gascoigne dwells on fox-hunting and badger-hunting ('I have lent a Foxe or Badgerd ere nowe, a piece of my hose, and the skyn and fleshe for companie, which he never restored agayne'), his chief concern in *The Noble Arte of Venerie* was with hunting the deer: the Queen's great passion. He showed himself an adept, even of such tricky situations as hunting a hart 'at bay' in a stream when the animal will not come out of the water. If a huntsman finds himself in this situation: 'let him get a boate, or if he can swymme, let him put off his clothes, and swymme to him with a Dagger readie drawne to kyll him . . . It hath beene my happe oftentimes to kyll in this sorte verie great Hartes, and that in sight and presence of divers witnesses, and afterwardes I have guided their deade bodyes to the banke swymming.'[4]

There is some comedy in the fact that Gascoigne should have described himself as 'friend to al Parkes, Forress and Chases' when most of his experience of 'venery' had been as a poacher. He illustrated the work himself with woodcuts, which boldly showed him kneeling before no less a hunting enthusiast than the Queen herself. One of the woodcuts shows a shooting picnic. Another shows a dead hart at the foot of Queen Elizabeth, and the kneeling Gascoigne about to 'breake' it up with a knife. (Did Landseer know this woodcut when he painted a remarkably similar scene of a Highland ghillie presenting a slain deer to Queen Victoria?) Another delightful woodcut demonstrates 'How to slee the Hearon', with a heron falling out of an English sky towards the Queen and a group of noblemen.

These woodcuts are probably intended to be illustrations of the Earl of Leicester's lavish summer entertainments for the Queen at Kenilworth in 1575. That summer's royal progress had been the most extravagant of the reign, and Leicester was determined that Elizabeth's sojourn with him should be longer and more splendid than her visits anywhere else.

Burghley spent in the region of £3,000 each time the Queen visited Theobalds, and the sum was nearly ruinous – in his private capacity. In 1588, in his public capacity as Lord Treasurer, between £8,000 and £9,000 paid the wages of every mariner in the Royal Navy.[5]

By 1563, Leicester had spent £60,000 on extensions and improvements to the castle and by the time of the Queen's 1575 visit – her third to Kenilworth – it was spoken of as one of the three most splendid estates in the country. In addition to all the new buildings and the newly planted parks Leicester had created, in readiness for Elizabeth's arrival, there was an Italianate garden, with a (fake) jewelled aviary and a (real) marble fountain. The garden was like a theatrical set designed especially for the Queen and her court. Yet although it was spoken of for centuries afterwards as one of the most splendid extravaganzas ever to occur on English soil, there was something lacking in the entertainments. She stayed for a shorter time than Leicester had hoped. Nineteen days were long enough to be ruinously expensive for him and she did not actually insult him by leaving earlier. But neither of them could hide from the other that there was now something a little sad about their relationship, and she never visited Kenilworth again.

A number of factors dampened the hoped-for exuberance. One was that Elizabeth's digestion, never very strong, was upset even before she arrived. She had stopped on her way through Oxfordshire at Grafton, where she had a house of her own. It was a hot July, and when she arrived at Grafton 'there was not a drop of good drink for her'. The local beer was too strong for her. She liked a very weak 'small beer' and, upon being presented with the stronger stuff, threw one of her tantrums.

Leicester's entertainment of the Queen at Kenilworth was intended to be momentous. Was there even the hope, or the thought, in the minds of the host (or of the royal guest) that they might revive their old love of fifteen years earlier? Or if this thought is too sentimental, was there the hope in Leicester's mind that it was not too late, even now, for the Dudleys to resume their all-but-regal status by his marriage to Elizabeth? In so doing he would not only advance himself, but also put an end to her capricious suggestion that she might after all marry François, Duc d'Alençon. This prospect – of Elizabeth marrying into the family that had initiated the St Bartholomew's Day Massacre – was a nightmare of the forward Protestant party in government, of which Leicester was the figurehead, the 'captain-general of the Puritans'.[6]

Kenilworth marked for many a turning point in their perceptions of Elizabeth. And perhaps for Elizabeth and Leicester it marked a turning-point in their perceptions of one another. Their relationship was, and remains, a puzzle. The likeliest explanation of the puzzle is that it was never quite clear, even to Elizabeth and Leicester themselves, exactly what they wanted or needed from one another. In July 1575 they were both forty-two years old. He had begun to go bald, and florid in complexion. Relatively tall, he was able to carry off the increase in his weight, and he was never – as was claimed in libellous Catholic pamphlets, such as 'Leicester's Commonwealth' – gluttonous or obese. But health problems dogged him throughout this decade and in the later 1570s he had swellings in his legs, for which he paid visits to Buxton and Harrogate. He prided himself upon his active life, as a sportsman and a countryman, and in 1573 had lectured the Queen, 'So good a medycyne I have alway found exercise with the open good ayre as yt hath ever byn my best remedye ageynst those dellycate deceases gotton about your deynty city of London'. When she was in the right mood (an important conditional), she was able to allow herself to be lectured by him in this way. And she, the stingiest of monarchs and patrons, was always generous to her beloved Robin.

Throughout the 1570s she lavished him with large estates, adding to his holdings in 1572 with the lordships of Arwystili and Cyfeiliog, and the lordship of Denbigh. She let him have a ten-year lease on the farm of the customs on sweet (Mediterranean) wines – he collected the tax on wines such as Marsala and pocketed it. Thousands of tons of wine were imported yearly. Over the previous two centuries England (thanks to global cooling) had ceased to be a wine-producing country, and the English had become especially fond of Bordeaux wines, which they called claret, and of sherry sack from Spain. (The wine of Jerez, sack, was an Anglicisation of *sec* = dry, but by modern tastes all these wines would have tasted sweet.) They loved all sweet alcoholic drinks: mead, which had gone out of fashion in the late-medieval period, became popular again, and hippocras – sweet mulled wine with spices and hot pear or apple cider.[7] So having the tax on sweet wine was a huge concession to Leicester. She also lent him £15,000. Leicester was not a notably extravagant man except in the matter of clothes. He would appear to have spent most of his money on patronage, ensuring that he had a finger in every pie. He was high steward of ten boroughs (Bristol, Great Yarmouth, King's Lynn, Abingdon, Windsor, Reading, Wallingford, Tewkesbury, St Albans and Evesham). He was an active, and popular, Chancellor of Oxford University. At least ninety-eight books were dedicated to him, which made him one of the most active literary patrons of the reign. He was a keen backer of explorations and voyages, from which, obviously, he hoped to profit – investing in Frobisher's voyage of 1576, Hawkins's second voyage and Drake's circumnavigation of the globe. From the Drake voyage he would have profited, but he also sank money in losers, such as the voyage of Fenton in 1582.

And another drain on his pocket was Kenilworth.

We who are used to reliably fresh water to drink, and who have tea and coffee whenever we like it, need to make a mental adjustment when we travel in our imaginations to sixteenth-century England, reminding ourselves that it was not safe to drink the water and, even if you were the Queen, there were some occasions when there was nothing to drink but beer. The crisis passed; 'God be thanked, she is now perfect well and merry,'[8] said Leicester on the day that he was due to bring her to Kenilworth. But it was not a good start. At the 'ambrosial banquet' prepared for her, Leicester had ordered more than 300 dishes. 'Her majesty eat smally or nothing; which understood, the coorsez wear not so orderly served and sizely set doun, but wear by and by az disorderly wasted and coorsly consumed, more courtly the thought then courteously,' said one observer. The next sweltering day, the Queen spent the entire time in the castle, 'for coolness'.[9]

Most of the food at an 'ambrosial banquet' such as this would have been sweet. The 300 dishes would have been chiefly sweetmeats of a kind that have now disappeared altogether from the English table, or would only be served with fruit and nuts for a 'dessert' at a formal dinner in, say, an Oxford college or a city Livery Company. Even savouries, if they formed part of the banquet, would have had sweet admixtures. Their herring pies were made with currants, raisins and minced dates;[10] capons would come roasted with orange peel, sugar and prunes;[11] a chicken pie would contain brown sugar and raisins.[12] All disgusting to a modern palate. Vegetables, if served at all, would be overcooked and, yet again, sweetened. Their artichoke pie was made with sherry, sugar, orange peel and raisins. The English critic Walter Pater thought all art aspired to the condition of music. All Elizabethan cooking aspired to the condition of marmalade.

The splendour of pageantry, and the jangling lack of harmony between the two great protagonists at Kenilworth – Elizabeth and Leicester – are perhaps both recalled in Shakespeare's *A Midsummer Night's Dream*. The gunfire and fireworks that greeted the Queen's arrival at the castle were seen and heard more then twenty miles away,[13] so they would surely have been seen and heard five miles away in Stratford-upon-Avon. Only ten miles north-east of Stratford, at Long Itchington, Leicester put on a stupendous hunting picnic for the Queen, and she spent much of her time at Kenilworth, in the cool of the late summer afternoons and early evenings, pursuing the deer. She loved hunting. (She personally killed six deer during this visit, as the surviving game-books show.[14])

A modern visitor might have found the Kenilworth pageants and games spectacular, even the deer-hunting. The one activity that would surely not appeal even to the most thick-skinned time-traveller would have been the bear-baiting in the outer wood of the castle. It is good to know that even in Elizabethan times there were those who abominated this gratuitous cruelty. Philip Stubbes, in his *Anatomy of Abuses* (1583) asked, 'What Christian heart can take pleasure to see one poor beast to rend, tear and kill another, and all for his foolish pleasure?' The answer to this rhetorical question must be: the Earl of Leicester and his guests, including – we must presume – Queen Elizabeth herself, for he would surely not have had his hounds slavering at the prospect of fighting and tormenting the bears if he had not thought this would be diverting for his monarch?[15]

Even the hunting parties were punctuated with pageantry. As she came riding home one evening, she was met by Gascoigne dressed as the Savage Man. On another evening he was Sylvanus, god of the woods, who told her that all the forest-dwellers, the fauns, dryads, hamadryads and wood-nymphs were in tears at the rumour that she might be about to leave. In one of his entertainments it would seem that Gascoigne blundered. Most of his verses and entertainments at Kenilworth seem to have been written spontaneously, but the masque of *Zabeta* had been commissioned long in advance. The reason given for the Queen's refusal to see this masque was that the weather had broken and the banquet in a temporary partition had to be called off. But it could have been rescheduled for another night. Clearly the Queen had cast her eye, at least once, over an argument of the masque and had censored it. The show was to have been acted by James Burbage and Leicester's own players, and Diana the Virgin-Goddess was to have lamented the loss of [Eli]zabeta her famous nymph, seventeen years ago – that is, the exact length of time [Eli]zabeta had been on the throne. But Gascoigne's clumsy text reminded the nymph of her captivity under Queen Mary, attributed her preservation to the Dudley family and told her:

> A world of wealth at wil
> You henceforth shall enjoy
> In wedded state, and there with all
> Holde up from great annoy
> The staffe of your estate.[16]

The 'staff' is the heraldic device of the Dudleys. The masque was offering Elizabeth one last chance to marry her Robin. No wonder she did not wish to cringe her way through this appalling 'entertainment', and moved the royal progress on from Kenilworth only a week later.

Like many with a strong love of ceremony, Elizabeth also possessed a keen sense of the absurd. One evening at Kenilworth the Queen stood on the bridge by Mortimer's Tower and watched a pageant on the lake where a mermaid swam, drawing her tail through the water, and Harry Goldingham (a Bottom-like comic actor) was performing the role of Arion astride a splendidly constructed dolphin. After a melodious six-part song emanated from the belly of the dolphin, Harry/Arion took off his mask and declared that 'he was none of Arion not he, but honest Harry Goldingham'. The Queen broke into peals of laughter and afterwards said this had been the best part of the show.[17]

In *A Midsummer Night's Dream*, Oberon says to Puck:

> thou rememb'rest
> Since once I sat upon a promontory,
> And heard a mermaid on a dolphin's back
> Uttering such dulcet and harmonious breath
> That the rude sea grew civil at her song,
> And certain stars shot madly from their spheres
> To hear the sea-maid's music.

Yet Oberon's memory of the pageantry was of Cupid's arrow-shot misfiring:

> That very time, I saw but thou couldst not
> Flying between the cold moon and the earth
> Cupid all armed; a certain aim he took

At a fair vestal thronèd by the west
And loosed his love shaft smartly from his bow
As it should pierce a hundred thousand hearts . . .
Yet marked I where the bolt of Cupid fell.
It fell upon a little western flower,
Before milk-white, now purple with love's wound
And maidens call it love-in-Idleness.[18]

As well as admiring the fireworks, the floating islands, the jousting, the bear-baiting, the feasting and all the other spectacles at Kenilworth, the Warwickshire locals (including the Shakespeare family) would have gossiped freely about the Queen and Leicester and his other *amours*. What great ones do the lesser prattle of. It has long been acknowledged that Oberon's words contain some memory of the Kenilworth pageant and its prodigious floating islands, mermaids and musical dolphins. It is not too fanciful to go further and see in the contentious, playful, spiteful and sexually frustrated relationship between Oberon and Titania the flavour of what common gossip had to say concerning Elizabeth and Leicester.

But with Leicester, as with his new protégé Gascoigne, Elizabeth was prepared to be indulgent. She did not banish either of them. They accompanied her on her progress when the court left Kenilworth and moved on to the Earl of Essex's house at Chartley in Staffordshire. Essex (Walter Devereux[19]) was in Ireland. Leicester had probably by now begun an affair with Lady Essex – an earlier affair, with Douglas Sheffield, having seemingly petered out in this or the previous year. The affair with Douglas Sheffield began in 1570–1 when she would have been about thirty. She was the daughter of William Howard, first Baron Howard of Effingham (1510–73), a cousin of the Dukes of Norfolk and widow of a Lincolnshire nobleman, Lord Sheffield. She had two legitimate children. With Leicester she certainly had one, Sir Robert Dudley, who was born on 7 August 1574. Gossip at court that suggested there had also been a daughter born stillborn was something Lady Sheffield vigorously denied. Her sister Frances was also said to be 'very far in love' with Leicester. Douglas Sheffield married Sir Edward Stafford in 1579. He was a friend of Leicester's, but there is no evidence that Leicester 'arranged' the marriage. The evidence would suggest that both Howard sisters were free-and-easy girls who could be expected to have colourful and varied love lives. No one knows why Leicester did not marry her. Perhaps he was still holding back in the hope of marrying the Queen, or perhaps the relationship with Douglas Sheffield was simply too volatile to turn into a marriage. In the only surviving personal letter among Leicester's correspondence, he advised her, before 1574, to break off relations with him and find someone else:

> For you must think hit ys some marvellous cause . . . that forceth me thus to be cause almost of the reigne of my none [own] hovse; for ther ys no likelyhoode that any of our boddyes of menkind like to have ayres; my brother you se long maryed and not lykke to have Children, yet resteth so now in myself, and yet such occasions ys ther . . . as yf I should marry I am seure never to have favour of them that I had rather yet never have wife than lose them, yet ys ther nothing in the world next than favour that I wold not gyve to be in hope of leaving some children behind me, being nowe the last of our howse.[20]

The Queen, if she knew of Leicester's affair with Lady Sheffield, chose to turn a blind eye. She was so close to her 'sweet Robin' that she must have guessed that something was 'up' and this had probably been one of the factors in her sudden and capricious adoption of a new favourite, when the Leicester–Douglas Sheffield *amour* was at its hottest. She had lighted upon the rather comical figure of Sir Christopher Hatton (1540–91).

He was an excellent dancer, and he appeared to be without irony when it came to his ability to flatter. These are two useful qualities in a courtier. 'Everyone likes flattery; and when you come to royalty, you should lay it on with a trowel,' said the canny Victorian.[21] Hatton did not need such counsel. He naturally worshipped Elizabeth. He spoke of himself as an everlastingly frustrated suitor in love with an unattainable goddess. 'This the twelfth day', he wrote to her, 'since I saw the brightness of the sun that giveth light unto my sense and soul I wax an amazed creature.'[22]

He was her 'happy bondman'. She called him 'sheep'. Tall, thick-bearded, unmarried – one imagines 'very unmarried' in Betjeman's useful phrase – Hatton was a perfect distraction for the Queen and she would go on basking in his adoration for two decades. The court first noticed that Hatton had gratified her vanity in 1572 when Leicester's affair with Lady Sheffield was at its most involved. At the annual exchange of New Year gifts between courtiers and sovereign, Hatton, who had already been made Keeper of the Parks of Eltham and Home and had been given the keepership of Wellingborough, received 400 ounces of silver plate from the Queen, about twice what others of his rank received. By July 1572 he was a Gentleman of the Privy Chamber and captain of the Yeomen of the Guard. He sat as MP for Higham Ferrers. Amazingly, this lightweight lawyer of the Inner Temple would end up in 1587 being made Lord Chancellor of England: it was an appointment greeted with outrage[23] by the legal establishment. He lived in enormous grandeur that he could ill afford, building himself a never-finished palace in his ancestral manor of Holdenby, Northamptonshire, as well as buying nearby Kirby Hall. When in town he occupied the former palace of the Bishops of Ely. He said he would never visit the rebuilt Holdenby until his royal saint – that is, Elizabeth – had set foot in it. There were two great courts, one 128 feet by 104 feet, covering two acres. It was the size of Hampton Court. The saint never did visit, probably aware that she would ultimately have paid for the privilege. When Hatton died aged fifty-one he owed her £18,071 – a colossal sum by any standards, but stratospheric by those of the cheeseparing Elizabeth. She who jibbed at paying her army in Ireland, and who was so unwilling to equip the navy against the Armada, was prepared to spend the price of several fighting ships in order to cosset the vanity of a fawning flatterer.

Elizabeth had known of Leicester's interest in his next lover for a long time. Lettice Devereux, the Countess of Essex who entertained the Queen when she progressed from Kenilworth in the summer of 1575, was a Boleyn cousin – a great-niece of Anne Boleyn. Her mother, Katherine Knollys, was good friends with her cousin Elizabeth. Lettice Knollys was appointed Gentlewoman of the Privy Chamber at the very beginning of the reign when she was only eighteen or nineteen. She was one of the beauties of the age, with thick curling auburn hair, mischievous dark eyes and full, sensuous lips. In her portrait she looks like Big Trouble, the sort of Trouble men yearn for. She married Walter Devereux, 1st Earl of Essex, in 1560 and withdrew from court in order to have five children in as many years. This did not stop her flirting, and when in 1565 the Queen heard of Leicester's fascination with Lettice, she flew into a major rage.

The fascination was an abiding one. Ten years later, when the grand entertainments at Kenilworth were performed and her husband was in Ireland, Lettice was more or less installed in Warwickshire as Leicester's resident mistress. The rumours were very public, but, astonishingly, they had not yet reached the ears of the Queen. And although the matter was 'publicly talked of in the streets', it was not safe to be known as a party to the gossip. Leicester was a powerful, ruthless man whom it was unsafe to cross. For the Kenilworth entertainments he asked the local gentry to array themselves in his livery, the blue coat with a silver badge of a bear and ragged staff. One neighbour refused. This was Edward Arden of Park Hall, Warwickshire, who had been High Sheriff of the county the previous year. Moreover, Arden unwisely made comments touching the Earl's private access to the Countess of Essex, and called Leicester 'a whore-master'. These remarks were not forgotten. Eight years later a spy handed Arden over to the authorities. He was a Catholic. His son-in-law, who lived with him, was a simpleton called John Somerville. The 'gardener' at Park Hall was a disguised priest called Hall. Somerville had apparently bragged that he would go to London and shoot the Queen and put her head on a pole because she was a 'serpent and a viper'. Although neither Hall nor Arden were violent men, all three were arrested. It seems as if Hall was a double agent, for he was spared at Leicester's intercession. Arden was put to death for treason. His lands were escheated to the Crown and some of them were immediately given to Leicester. No one who spoke slightingly of the great earl could expect to do so with impunity.

Then the court moved on to Woodstock where the host was the Queen's Champion, Sir Henry Lee.[24] The Kenilworth entertainments had been an extravagant but ultimately incoherent business. Leicester had been determined that his show should be the showiest and the most expensive to date, but his complicated amatory situation, his driving political interest and his fundamental coarseness could not stop the Kenilworth display spilling over into meaningless vulgarity. Lee, however, was a man who raised royal ceremonial into an art-form. And, indeed, was strongly influential on the art-forms of others – notably portraiture and literature. He had a high forehead, curly hair, dark laughing eyes, a long nose and a mouth that looked as if it had just closed having made an elaborate compliment, but might open at any moment to make an equally elaborate joke. His portrait of 1568 by Anthonis Mor shows a playful obsessive, a humorist, but one who was a true *homo ludens*, a man who took masques, tilts, tableaux and displays as seriously as Burghley took the economy or the wars in the Netherlands. In that age of display, Lee was a figure of immense significance, helping the Elizabethans towards a definition of themselves, which was appropriate in a man who could legitimately claim kinship with so many key figures of the age: Burghley, Leicester, the Earl of Essex, even the Queen herself. Her mythic status owed much to his creative pageantry.

As she approached Woodstock, the Queen and her entourage encountered two knights, Contarenus and Loricus, engaged in combat. The hermit Hemetes (played by our old friend Gascoigne) came forward and dissuaded the knights from fighting. The hermit's somewhat rambling speech went down extremely well with the Queen – she asked for a copy of it. Hemetes said he had once been a famous knight beloved of ladies. He told of how Loricus loved a lady of high degree, but, as was the courtly-love convention, he had hidden his love and pretended devotion to another. A sibyl had foretold that Loricus (one of the knights – it was a name used more than once by Lee for himself) would come at last after many sad wanderings to the best country in the world, governed by the best of rulers, 'best Ladie and most beawtyfull'.[25]

When the tale was over, the hermit conducted the Queen and her suite to a banqueting house built especially on a hill in the wood, roofed with turf, bedecked with flowers and 'spanges of gold plate', which glimmered magically. Above them soared a great oak. The two tables, one round and one a half-moon, were turfed with grass, and then, as the food was served, music struck up in the summerhouse and there appeared, probably for the first time in Elizabethan literature, the Fairy Queen. It is generally recognised that the elaborate tilts in the revised edition of the *Arcadia* are an allusion to actual tournaments in which Philip Sidney and Henry Lee took part. In the Woodstock entertainment of the Fairy Queen we can see an inspiration for Spenser's great epic. Sidney, who had been present at the Kenilworth entertainments, would have been all but certain to have followed the court to Woodstock on the royal progress. Certainly his twelve-year-old sister Mary was there, the future Countess of Pembroke, the one for whom he wrote the *Arcadia*. She was handed a posy from the oak above the banqueting hall in the wood during the masque in which the Faerie Queene made her arrival.[26] This was almost certainly the first appearance of the 'Faerie Queene' in Elizabethan literature.

Richard Corbet (1582–1635), poet Bishop of Oxford in the reign of James I – High Church, boozy, whimsical, and later Bishop of Norwich – is chiefly known for one lyric, the first line of which Rudyard Kipling appropriated for one of his volumes of Puck stories: 'Farewell rewards and fairies . . .'

Corbet identifies the fairies with the Roman Catholics. In Queen Mary's time, they had footed 'rings and roundelays':

> But since of late, *Elizabeth*,
>   And later James came in,
> They never danc'd on any heath
>   As when the time hath bin
>
> By which we note the Fairies
>   Were of the old profession,
> Their songs were Ave Maryes,
>   Their dances were procession.
> But now, alas! They all are dead
>   Or gone beyond the Seas
> Or farther for Religion fled,
>   Or else they take their ease.[27]

Pace Corbet's charming and well-known ballad, however, the two greatest works of fairy literature – *The Faerie Queene* and *A Midsummer Night's Dream* – belong to that heyday, the late Elizabethan Age. It is central to the fairy-mythos that they are a threatened species who either just have departed or are just about to do so: Tolkien's Grey Elves enforce this tradition when they disembark with Frodo at Grey Havens.

The cult of the Faerie Queene, both in pageant and in the great epic of the age by Spenser, the Elizabethan Virgil, was yet another example of the reinvigorated archaism of the collective Elizabethan collective imagination. Just as they revived the cult of St George, in all the Garter ceremonies, at the Queen's insistence, so Spenser made St George, his Redcrosse Knight, an emblem of Protestant virtue. The tourneys and tilts, in Spenser's poetry, as in Sidney's revised polyphonic narrative of his *Arcadia*, are a deliberate throwback to the age of chivalry. Yet all this was not done to deny the fundamental breaks with the past that the Elizabethan Age represented – a new National Church cut loose from the parent-stem of Rome; a new aristocracy composed of families such as the Herberts and the Cecils, who had been little more than minor Welsh squires during the Wars of the Roses; new learning; new fashions; new geographical horizons; a new politics. Even in the cult of the Virgin Queen, the Fairie Queene, the National Saviour, there was an element of the new taking over a novel form and subverting it. Obviously one element of this was the religious one. The language used is so exalted that the modern reader is half-shocked, half-amused. It takes a while to get eye and ear adjusted to the tone. 'The Kingdom of Saturn and the Golden world is come again, and the Virgin Astraea is descended from heaven to build her seat in this your most happy country of England,' said Jan van der Noor, a Dutch refugee from Spanish persecution in his book translated as *A Theatre for Worldlings* (1569).[28] A song in John Dowland's *Second Book of Airs* says:

> When others sing *Venite exultemus*!
> Stand by and turn to *Noli emulari*!
> For *Quare fremuerant* use *Oremus*!
> *Vivat Eliza*! For an *Ave Mari*![29]

You could not find a more specific substitution than this. There is an engraving of Elizabeth with her device of the phoenix, below which is written, 'This Maiden-Queen Elizabeth came into this world, the Eve of the Nativity of the Blessed Virgin Mary; and died on the Eve of the Annunciation of the Virgin Mary, 1602.'

> She was, she is (what can there more be said?)
> In earth the first, in heaven the second Maid.[30]

In life she had taken precedence even over Mary in the worship of the faithful; in death she was second only to the Blessed Virgin herself. Even the cults of personality of the most megalomaniac twentieth-century dictators never went as far as this. We are here almost in the territory of the idolatrous worship of divine Roman emperors. Or so it would seem.

But here is another case of imagery being subverted. Spenser's Redcrosse Knight is not the St George of medieval devotion. He is a new, Neoplatonic symbol of Protestant virtue. The Virgin Elizabeth is not a mere 'substitute' for the Virgin Mary, still less does the cult of the quasi-divine Elizabeth imply that the Queen enjoyed absolute power.

13

Ireland

In the 1570s the confused and violent condition of Ireland continued to be confused and violent. The Irish lords continued to feud among themselves for dominion over patches of land. The English increasingly came to regard Ireland as a colonial problem, which it was their job to solve. And even though these confusions and resentments long antedated the Reformation (Mary Tudor was, if anything, more interventionist in Ireland than Elizabeth in the early years of the reign, and Mary's settlement of Maryborough and Philipstown in Leix and Offaly were 'plantations' every bit as invasive as anything devised by later Protestants), the Counter-Reformation gave everyone the excuse to be more belligerent, and less compromising. (By the end of the decade in Munster, for example, it was the boast of the Earl of Desmond that he would defend the Catholic faith and oppose Englishmen who 'go about to overrun our country and make it their own'.) Having abandoned his castles, Desmond (Gerald Fitzjames Fitzgerald) took to the woods and became an outlaw, to the discomfiture of the English military governor of Munster, Sir Thomas Malby. But was Desmond's action motivated by Catholic piety, or by age-old anxiety to get his hands on the lands and properties of those ancient enemies of the Fitzgeralds, the Butlers?

It was not easy to say. The Pope's Bull of 1570, which both excommunicated and deposed the Queen of England, could only delight Irish malcontents, even those who had hitherto been prepared to accept the Reformation and help themselves to former monastic properties. Such Irish lords as James Fitzmaurice Fitzgerald wrote to Maurice Fitzgibbon, the papally recognized Archbishop of Cashel, and between them, in 1570, they sought to include King Philip in making Don John of Austria the King of Ireland: 'If we had a king like other nations none would venture to attack us.' Quite how it was in the gift of the Fitzgeralds, or the archbishop, to bestow crowns upon an Austrian prince (or indeed whether Ireland possessed, legally, an independent monarchy) was not likely to be a question that held them back from joining with other Irish lords, not in a struggle against 'the legitimate sceptre and honourable throne of England' – that is, an imagined English power – but against the actual government, 'Elizabeth, the pretensed queen of England', a 'she-tyrant' who had 'deservedly lost her royal power by refusing to listen to Christ in the person of his vicar', the Pope.[1]

'In spite of their relationship to Leicester, the Queen does not seem to have much liked the Sidneys.'[2] If proof were needed of these words of Dr A.L. Rowse, look no further than the fact that Elizabeth made Sir Henry Sidney the Lord Deputy of Ireland not once, but twice – 1566–71 and 1575–8 – even though Ireland was a country that, in his own words, he 'cursed, hated and detested'.[3] She did not send Sidney as a punishment, but rather because he had shown himself to be so able an administrator. Such was the intractable problem of Ireland, however, that it could be said that the more able the English administrator, the less the Irish were prepared to accept his administration. Whereas the Irish had one set of visions about how their country should be governed, or not governed, the English had another, so much at variance, that it could never succeed. By the end of the 1570s the English aim was 'the Anglicisation of that island, namely the full acceptance, at least by the Irish elite, of English institutions, social, political and legal'.[4]

As we noted in the opening chapter of this book, it is difficult for modern readers, who have lived through thirty and more years of 'troubles' in Ireland, and who no doubt have their own perspectives, to see any of the participants in the sixteenth-century Irish calamity with unbiased eyes. Most non-English readers will see the story as a disastrous example of the colonial mindset. Ireland, it would be clear to the huge preponderance of human beings at present thinking about the issue, should have been left to the Irish to work out. (Quite who 'the Irish' in this sentence are – whether, for example, they include the old Norman families the Desmonds and the Butlers – is a matter of taste.) Those who read with a sympathetic eye those English historians of Ireland, from Froude to Rowse, who cheer on the colonisers are in a distinct minority. This minority might still ask, 'What else could the Elizabethan administrators have done?' They might have behaved with less violence; that is for sure. When Francis Drake did a brief spell of duty in Ireland, he served under John Norreys and took part in the wholesale massacre of the inhabitants of Rathlin Island in July 1575. Not only did they kill the small army of Gaelic mercenaries – the so-called Redshanks who came from the Hebrides to fight for any Irish warlord who would hire them – but they killed everyone: women and children included. As late as 1972 an English biographer of Drake could describe this as 'an unpleasant episode' . . . A glowing picture of this cruel event was conveyed to the Queen by the Earl of Essex, a nobleman to whom she had farmed out the task and profits of the Irish 'purification'. In the end, the Irish business broke her heart.[5]

Henry Sidney's idea was to plant colonies of Englishmen all over the island of Ireland. He saw the possibility of Spain using the dissatisfaction of the Irish lords in Munster, for instance, 'to restore them to their ancient tytells of honner, lybertie and papistrye'.[6] Sidney's colonies were to consist of 3,000 people made up of three distinct elements: 1,500 men between twenty-five and thirty-five years 'brought up as servants in husbandry'; after three years' service in Ireland these English agricultural workers could claim copyhold of sixty acres of land. The second group would be 750 married men who were yeomen, would-be gentlefolk, 'having no freeholdes in England and being mete to have husbandry holdes of iiii ploughlands' – or 360 acres. The third group would be wage-earners, tradesmen, ploughwrights, fishermen. They would be leased enough ground to feed three cattle and two horses and to sow a garden.[7] For their own protection these colonies would always be established near military garrisons.

Sidney's colonial policies were resented, naturally enough, by many strands of Irish life. They were also more expensive than any plausible system of taxation could maintain. Elizabeth herself, always parsimonious, was self-destructively mean in Ireland. Sidney believed, surely correctly, that his scheme depended upon the establishment of local presidencies, *gauleiters* who would in the fullness of time be paid for by local taxes, but who in the meantime needed to be paid by the Crown. Elizabeth reluctantly agreed[8] to this, but she was in general unwilling to fund sufficient troops, transport and supplies, let alone administrative cash, to fund the Irish enterprise.

Hardly a year passed in which there was not fighting of some kind in Ireland. In 1576, Walter Devereux, 1st Earl of Essex (1541?–76), was appointed Earl Marshal of Ireland. (Was Elizabeth being kind to the Earl of Leicester and sending Essex abroad while his wife and Leicester conducted their by now rather public affair?) Essex, nicely described by Penry Williams as 'a nobleman with modest estates and high ambitions', had no choice but to accept the marshal post, but he plaintively asked his monarch, 'Why should I, wear out my youth in an obscure place without the assurance of your good opinion?'[9]

When he set out for Ireland in July 1576, aged thirty-something, Essex was accompanied by the twenty-one-year-old Philip Sidney, and later in the month they joined Sidney's father Sir Henry on one of his tours of duty. After a period of rebellions in the west, matters were becoming quiet again and the Privy Council had written to Sir Henry sending their 'most hearty thanks . . . for his diligence and execution of justice in all places'. Walsingham perhaps went implausibly far when he wrote to Sir Henry, 'your very Enemyes can not but commend you'. Sidney senior reported back to the Council optimistically that the whole of Ireland could now be considered pacified.[10]

It was during this spell of peace that the Sidneys, together with Essex, went to Galway. Their visit coincided with the arrival on the shore of that celebrated Amazon of the Ocean, Grania O'Malley. Did she so impress Philip that she suggested in his mind the men who dressed up as women in the Arcadia in order to pass themselves off as Amazons?

One of the more hilariously improbable explanations given by young Pyrocles – in *The Old Arcadia* – for his having invaded that confused scene in 'drag' was:

> a journey two years ago I made among the Amazons, where having sought to try my unfortunate valour, I met not one in all the country but was too hard for me; till, in the end, in the presence of their queen Senecia, I (hoping to prevail against her) challenged an old woman of fourscore years to fight on horseback to the uttermost with me: who, having overthrown me, for saving of my life made me swear I should go like an unarmed Amazon till the coming of my beard did with the discharge of my oath deliver me of that bondage.[11]

Grania O'Malley, like her husband, commanded a ship, and sometimes more than one, and became a celebrated smuggler and privateer. Sir Henry Sidney recalled:

> There came to me also a most famous feminine sea-captain, called Granny O'Malley, and offered her services unto me, wheresoever I would command her, with three galleys and two hundred fighting men, either in Ireland or Scotland. She brought with her her husband, for she was as well by sea as by land more than master's mate with him. This was a notorious woman in all the coast of Ireland. This woman did Sir Philip Sidney see and speak with. He can more at large inform you of her.

Back in Dublin, the Earl of Essex succumbed to dysentery. The archbishop, Adam Loftus, wrote graphically to Walsingham that the earl was 'sorely vexed with the flux . . . having every day and night no less than twenty, thirty or sometimes forty stools through which being sore weakened and natural strength diminished'. Essex died on 22 September.[12]

14
Sir Francis Drake's Circumnavigation

Francis Drake, some kind of cousin of John Hawkins, had taken part in Hawkins's ill-fated slaving voyage from West Africa to the Caribbean, and had escaped from the battle of Ulua rather than fall into the hands of Spain. That experience, in 1568, was an object lesson, as far as Drake was concerned, in Spanish duplicity and cruelty. Don Martin Enriquez, the Viceroy of New Spain, had promised the English sailors friendship and assistance as they sailed their leaky slavers into Spanish waters. He had then attacked the old *Jesus of Lübeck*, Henry VIII's purchase from the Hanseatic League, which had been abandoned. Many English sailors were either killed or tortured, or compelled into galley-slavery. Years later, Drake told a Spaniard that if he ever met Martin Enriquez he would teach him how a gentleman should keep his word.

The unhappy experience confirmed all the fiercest prejudices of Drake, the Devon man, against Roman Catholics. He was born – perhaps in 1543, it is not certain – in Crowndale, near Tavistock. His father, who had also been a sailor, had settled as a yeoman farmer on land belonging to Francis Russell – afterwards Earl of Bedford. Drake was named after Francis Russell. Edmund Drake, his father, belonged to the first generation of Englishmen to hear the new doctrines of Protestantism, and he absorbed them greedily, ardently. When the conservative Catholics of the West Country rose in protest, in 1549, against the introduction of Edward VI's first Prayer Book, the mob hated the Drakes for their Protestantism. The Drakes had their farm trashed, and they escaped to Gillingham in Kent, where Edmund Drake housed his family in an old ship. Edmund, who later took Holy Orders and from 1560 was the vicar of Upchurch, Kent, appears to have been a freelance preacher to the sailors and shipwrights in the new dockyards that the Admiralty of Edward VI was creating on the Medway. This was the origin of the great Chatham yard which played so big a role in British naval history – it is also, as it happens, where Charles Dickens was born and, anachronistic as it may sound, there is something Dickensian about Drake's childhood in the decayed old ship at Gillingham. It presaged the life that was to come, the life of one of the greatest mariners the world ever saw, and an Englishman who changed the destiny of his country. The 'great man' or 'great woman' theory of history is regularly dismissed, whether by Tolstoy, who sought to diminish Napoleon by an assertion of a sort of Hegelian inevitability to his defeat in Russia; or by Marx, another Hegelian (albeit an Hegelian heretic), who explained the movement of history in terms of economic necessity and dialectical materialism; or by more recent historians who wish us to take account of the social and economic conditions in which so-called geniuses or 'great' human beings functioned. The thrilling thing about the history of Elizabethan England is that the technicoloured personalities of the chief participants really compel us to think again. If Mary Tudor's younger sister had been a silly, weak-charactered girl like Lady Catherine Grey, do we really think that sixteenth-century English history would have been no different from the way it was with the wise, courageous and often ruthless Elizabeth as Queen? If she had appointed a fool or a sycophant, rather than Cecil, as Secretary, would things have been no different? Likewise, Francis Drake was one of those rare individuals who influenced events, who changed things radically.

After his experience on 'the third troublesome voyage of Master John Hawkins', Drake returned to England. He married, in 1569, a Mary Newman at St Budeaux, but he did not stay at home for long. Late in 1570 he sailed from Plymouth in a 25-ton ship, the *Swan*, which was probably paid for by Hawkins and his partner Sir William Winter.[1] He was accompanied by another ship from Plymouth, the 70-ton *Pasco*. All the crews were young – there was only one man of them over the age of thirty. Drake's aim was an adventure of the utmost boldness. The Spanish, who mined the gold and other treasures of Peru, conveyed it by the Pacific coast to the Panama Isthmus (no Panama Canal until 1914). Drake's plan was to dock at the Atlantic sea-port of the Panama Isthmus, Nombre de Dios (Name of God). There were actually very few Spaniards in the city. In the wooded hills of the Isthmus there were several thousand escaped African slaves, known as Cimarrones, who were, with their wives and children, in the process of making themselves into a nation. Drake's idea was to make common cause with the Cimarrones, cross the fifty miles or so of the isthmus and waylay the Peruvian gold, share it out with his Cimarrone allies and sail for home one of the richest men in England. Needless to say, the Queen, who was technically not at war with her brother-in-law the King of Spain, could not openly encourage the venture, but she knew of it, and as she said to Drake on another occasion, 'The gentleman careth not if I disavow him.'

Drake had studied maps of Nombre de Dios and, although he had never been there in his life, by the time he had crossed the Atlantic he knew the whole layout of it; he knew the depths of the harbour, he knew every street and battery. As they entered the Spanish Main they captured and plundered a number of Spanish vessels, and Drake pumped captured Spaniards and their African slaves for information. The one vital piece of information which he had not gleaned was that the town was empty of treasure. It had sailed some time before. The hope that Drake might simply lift the Peruvian gold – or silver ingots – from Nombre de Dios was dashed upon arrival.[2] Drake, moreover, was shot during his unsuccessful raid upon the port. With great resourcefulness, he decided to sail down to Cartagena, let his wounds heal and wait for the next treasure train to arrive at Panama in January 1573. With a party of Cimarrones, Drake made his way across the isthmus with the intention of intercepting a fourteen-mule load of gold. The plot was uncovered and he was compelled to return to base camp, where he joined forces with a French pirate, one Guillaume Le Testu. The next raid was luckier, and they were able to intercept the mule train and overpower the Spanish guards. Le Testu was killed. Drake was able to sail home a rich man, with booty of £20,000. They reached Plymouth harbour at sermon time on Sunday, 9 August 1573. The parson watched his church empty as word spread through the pews and the people ran down to the quay to praise 'the evidence of God's love and blessing towards our gracious Queen and country, by the fruit of our captain's labour and success'. There stood Drake on his quarterdeck, sturdy,[3] of slightly stocky build, with red hair, beard and curly moustaches, a high colour, bright, intelligent green eyes. The crowds cheered him as a hero. Modern prudery can denounce what he did as an act of simple piracy, but the next great maritime achievement cannot be so lightly dismissed.

After a spell in Ireland, in which Drake fought for the Earl of Essex, he made friends with Essex's retainer Thomas Doughty. Through Doughty, or possibly through Essex himself, Drake met Sir Francis Walsingham, who was by now the Queen's Secretary. (Cecil, no less close to her, had become officially her Lord Treasurer.) Between them, they hatched a scheme for Drake to sail with a small fleet into the Pacific and raid Spanish settlements there. The whole plan was to be kept secret, but the joint aim of the enterprise was to weaken the Spanish Empire and collect further loot by acts of piracy. Investors backing the scheme included Walsingham himself, Christopher Hatton, John Hawkins, William and George Wynter and the Queen herself. Perhaps the vital clue to the vibrancy of the Elizabethan Age is to be seen in this episode. The population of this archipelago was tiny, and the majority of that population were engaged in the busyness of life – ploughing, begetting, making, selling, eating. A few, a very few, were making the dynamic decisions that made Elizabethan England so distinctive. Politics was carried on not by a huge cumbrous parliament and an even huger and more cumbrous civil service, but by a small Council. Parliament was only summoned when the Queen needed money. The Church, the entire settlement of the religious future of England, was not settled by a great synod. After the initial debates in Parliament and Westminster Hall about such matters as the nature of the Sacrament, the Church of England, its structure, hierarchy, rites and doctrines, was defined by the Queen herself with a few pet Cambridge dons. And here in the matter of Drake and his great voyage, which turned out to be the circumnavigation of the Earth, the Queen was personally involved, and with piratical boldness, having a flutter on the success of his enterprise. Back in the early 1570s when Drake had sailed to Panama, the Queen had been reluctant to annoy Philip II. By 1577 Philip had begun to extricate himself from his Mediterranean war against the Turks and concentrate his fire on the Protestants in the Netherlands. Elizabeth was now much more ready to listen to the 'hawks' in her Council – Leicester and Walsingham – and to realise that fighting the Spanish overtly would eventually become unavoidable. They appear to have kept the much more cautious Burghley (William Cecil) in the dark about the expedition. The outline of the scheme is contained in a document that was partly burned in the Cotton fire and is therefore charred round the edges (BL Cotton MS, Otho, E.viii). It has had to be reconstructed by modern scholars. It appears that the plan required Drake to enter the Straits of Magellan, lying 52 degrees north of the Pole, and having passed therefrom into the South Sea, 'then he is to sail northwards seeking along the coast aforenamed . . . to find our places meet to have traffic for the renting of commodities of these her Majesty's realms'. They anticipated 'great hope of gold, silver, spices, drugs, cochineal and divers other special commodities, such as may enrich her Majesty's dominions and also put shipping a-work greatly'.[4]

Before he left, the Queen summoned Drake for a private interview. The two redheads at last met and instantaneously liked one another. 'Drake,' she said, 'I would gladly be revenged on the King of Spain for divers injuries that I have received.' There were just three of them present: Walsingham, Elizabeth, Drake.

It was essential to keep the expedition a secret. 'Of all men my Lord Treasurer [Burghley] is not to know it,' Elizabeth said. And it was of even greater importance that the Spanish should not know of it. They sailed from Plymouth, with Drake in the *Pelican*, which was later to become one of the most famous ships in the history of the world when it changed its name to the *Golden Hind* (in deference to his patron, Sir Christopher Hatton, whose coat of arms included a hind); the *Elizabeth*, commanded by John Winter; a pinnacle named the *Benedict* and a store-ship named the *Swan*. There was a setback almost immediately when the little squadron sailed into a gale, which forced it back into Falmouth harbour with loss of masts and spars. They had to return to Plymouth for repairs. Meanwhile John Oxenham, Drake's old comrade from the Panama expedition, had sailed back to the isthmus with the aim of intercepting more treasure ships coming from Peru. This expedition had come to grief.

It was publicly announced that Drake was to sail to the Mediterranean to open a spice trade at Alexandria. Meanwhile he set off across the Atlantic. Part of the plan was piratical. It was also hoped, however, that they might find a new continent. Sir Richard Grenville and friends maintained that somewhere in the South Pacific there was a great continent – *Terra Australis Incognita* they called it – that could become an English colony.

In the South Atlantic the squadron captured a Portuguese vessel, and Drake put Thomas Doughty in charge of it. But things were not going well. Thomas Drake – one of the three brothers Drake took on the voyage – warned Francis that Doughty was disloyal. They began to suspect that he was somehow in touch with Burghley or that he had come on the voyage as Burghley's spy. By the summer of 1578 Drake had Doughty taken prisoner and bound to the mast. When untied, Doughty was forbidden pen or paper or any books that were not in English (for Doughty was a learned man). One of the many curious facts about the two men is that Doughty and Drake remained friends, even after Drake had put Doughty on 'trial' for treason. At the end of the trial, they dined and received the Sacrament together. Perhaps there were no hard feelings, even the next morning, when Drake had Doughty beheaded.

By now the crews of the various ships were demoralised and restless. What was the purpose of this arduous journey? They had begun it with the hope of gold. Now there was talk merely of discovering some fantasy Australia, and their commanders had fallen out among themselves. Conditions on a sixteenth-century sailing ship were cramped. Food was rationed, as was water. It was safer to drink beer than water, and each crew member was entitled to a gallon a day. Not surprisingly, there was much drunkenness. With no fresh fruit or vegetables available on the voyage, disease was rife, both among the human population of the ships and among the rats that travelled with them in great numbers.

A month or so after Doughty's beheading, Drake ordered all hands on shore for the Sunday service. He told the ship's chaplain, Fletcher, that he himself would deliver the sermon. The sailors were by now half-mutinous, drunken, unruly, insolent and refusing to do their share of the work.

'My masters!' exclaimed Drake in his resonant voice as he surveyed the boozy, piratical, unshaven rabble on the Argentinian sands, 'I must have it left. I must have the gentlemen to haul and draw with the mariner, and the mariner with the gentleman. I would know him that would refuse to set his hand to a rope.' He had grabbed their attention, and made them frightened. Was he going to name the idlers? Keel-haul them after the Prayer-Book Matins? Finish reading the Collect for the Day and administer the cat? His men knew that Drake was a captain who was capable of worse harshness than this. But, no. With a rhetorical flourish, having said he 'would know' such an idler, he added, 'I know there is not any such here.'

Next, he turned to the captains and masters of the ships and dismissed every one from his post. He said that when he thought of the overwhelming difficulty of the task he had undertaken, it 'bereaved him of his wits'. But he must have loyal obedience. No man from now on was obliged to stay with him. If any wished to leave now, they were to declare it.

No human voice was heard; only the cry of gulls, the crash of the waves on the sand, the movement of the winds. Drake had his men in the palm of his hand.

'You come then,' he said, 'of your own free will: on you it depends to make the voyage renowned or to end as a reproach to our country and a laughing-stock to the enemy.'

There was no further dissension after that. Drake now reduced the squadron to three ships: the *Pelican*, which was at this juncture renamed the *Golden Hind*, the *Elizabeth* and the *Marigold*. The auxiliary ships were emptied of their stores and destroyed. On 21 August 1678 these three English fighting ships entered the Straits of Magellan. The Portuguese explorer and navigator Ferdinand Magellan (*c.*1480–1521), after whom the Straits are named, was the first man to circumnavigate the world, but although he rounded the Cape from the Atlantic to the Pacific Ocean, Magellan never made it home, being killed in the Philippines having accomplished about half the journey. Some of Magellan's crew made the journey home in his ship the *Victoria*, but Francis Drake was the first commander to sail round the world. To sail through the Straits of Magellan is a hazardous undertaking. Most sailing ships since then have gone round Cape Horn to the southward, but Drake – in common with all his contemporaries who had thought about it – supposed that Tierra del Fuego, to the south of the straits, was part of a great continent stretching all the way to the South Pole and that the Straits were the only way through. The normal time for navigating the Straits was seven weeks, during which it was necessary to brave powerful currents, jagged rocks and gale-force winds. Drake broke all records and sailed through the Straits in sixteen days.

But once he was in the Pacific his luck did not last, and a gale drove him southwards. He found open water. Thus it was discovered that there was no need to have sailed through the Straits in the first place, and the world map could be redrawn. (But not yet: Drake kept the secret of the meeting place of the Atlantic and Pacific Oceans from the Spaniards.) The other two ships were blown far apart. John Winter, commanding the *Elizabeth*, went back to the Straits and sailed home to England; His men simply refused to go on. The *Marigold* was lost. John Oxenham, in his ship, landed at Panama. So the *Golden Hind* alone of the three was in the Pacific Ocean. Drake sailed up the coast of Chile, making sporadic raids, which were to make his fortune. There was still no news of Oxenham in Panama, but when he had captured some Spanish prisoners, Drake began to piece together a narrative of the disaster: Oxenham and three of his officers were prisoners in Lima; the Spanish troops were ruthlessly subduing Drake's old comrades in arms, the Cimarrones. The Spaniards expected Drake to return to Panama, but with only one ship he would have had no hope of success. Besides, he had another aim, which was to continue his voyage across the Pacific Ocean to the East Indies and open up English trade for the spices which were at that date the richest merchandise in the world.[5] Drake meanwhile sailed on northwards, up the western coast of South America. Not one Spanish ship on this coast had a gun on board.[6] Why should they need one? The idea of enemy vessels entering the Pacific did not enter their calculations. When he captured a Spanish ship that he nicknamed the *Cacafuego*, Drake knew his fortune was made. It was laden with eighty pounds of gold, twenty-six tons of silver, thirteen chests of money and 'a certain quantity of jewels and precious stones', valued in all at £150,000–200,000. There was so much treasure that they 'believed that they took out of her twelve score tons of plate; insomuch that they were forced to heave much of it overboard because their ship could not carry it all'.[7]

Drake realised that if he told his aim to the Spaniards on this vessel – whom he released when he had robbed them – they would take his words back to their military, naval and political leaders. So he told them the truth, gambling correctly that they would not believe him capable of his intention: sailing the *Golden Hind* across the Pacific Ocean.

By now the ship was quite literally groaning with silver and gold, and it was leaking badly. The north-west winds prevailed as he sailed far out to the ocean, but when he reached a point between 42° and 48°N he coasted southwards and found a haven. It is said that he set up a metal plate claiming the territory for the Queen. In 1936 a motorist near San Francisco found a brass plate inscribed in Elizabethan English. Recent scientific tests dated it 'sometime between the eighteenth and twentieth centuries, most probably the late nineteenth or early twentieth century.[8] In any event, the sunny Californian coast was a good place for Drake and his men to pull in to shore and overhaul the *Golden Hind* before the next stage of the adventure.

As they set out, it is perhaps worth reminding ourselves of how little equipment Drake had at his disposal to assist his prodigious navigational skill. He possessed, obviously, a compass. It was probably in the twelfth century that Europeans discovered that a lodestone – that is, a mineral composed of an iron oxide – aligns itself in a north–south direction, as will a piece of iron that has been magnetised by contact with a lodestone. By the sixteenth century compasses were quite sophisticated. At London's National Maritime Museum is exhibited Drake's Dial, a brass instrument made by Humphrey Cole in 1569 (it was once believed to belong to Drake, but now they are not so sure). It consists of a compass along with lunar and solar dials, which enable the user to calculate the time. Engraved on the casing are the latitudes of many of the important ports in the world.

The other instrument Drake had at his disposal would have been a cross-staff. This was used to calculate a ship's latitude (north–south position) at night by observing the angle between the horizon and the North (or Pole) Star, and by taking a reading off the scale. This could then be coupled with a compass reading. (It was not until the eighteenth century that an English clock-maker named John Harrison devised an instrument for calculating longitude, or the east–west position.)

So, with the stars to guide them, and instruments that most modern navigators would deem inadequate for an afternoon's recreational sailing, Drake and his mariners set off from the coast of California to cross the Pacific Ocean.

His first stop would seem to have been one of the Palau Islands, where his attempts to trade with the natives led to a fracas. Twenty islanders were killed, when Drake realised that they wanted to steal his merchandise. It was brutal treatment, but no one has ever pretended Drake was other than brutal. Next, he made for the Spice Islands, which came into sight in early November. His negotiations with the Sultan of Ternate, lasting less than a week, enabled Drake to build up a prodigious cargo: six tons of cloves. Drake began negotiations with the Sultan for the establishment of a trading post in the Spice Islands; certainly the East India Company regarded the verbal agreement between Drake and the Sultan as one to be taken seriously, and Drake's week in Ternate was seen by imperialist historians from the seventeenth to the twentieth centuries as 'an example once again of Drake being wished into the role of a founding father of the British Empire'.[9] Equally, post-imperialist historians have dwelt on Drake's moral shortcomings and shown remarkably little admiration for this man's achievement: namely, the circumnavigation of

All portraits of Queen Elizabeth told a story. This one was a present from her Champion Sir Henry Lee, and shows Elizabeth dominating her kingdom, with her toe on his own estate at Ditchley Park.

The Tudor dynasty – Henry VIII is depicted with his heirs :
Mary Tudor and her husband Philip II of Spain. Edward VI and Elizabeth I.

(Facing Page)
The rigid control of the Elizabethan state was in the hands of (*above*) Sir Francis Walsingham and (*below*) Elizabeth's long-term Secretary and adviser, William Cecil, first Lord Burleigh.

William Shakespeare, and the grammar school at Stratford-upon-Avon where he went 'unwillingly to school'. The grammar school system of the Elizabethans was a key ingredient of their great national Renaissance.

The Queen's childhood friend and great love was Robert Dudley. Kenilworth, his Warwickshire seat, was the scene of one of the most spectacular of Elizabethan pageants.

Edmund Spenser, whose unfinished *Faerie Queene*, infused with Protestantism, numerology and adventure, defined the Elizabethans to themselves in stupendously elaborate verse.

Mary Herbert, Countess of Pembroke, and Sir Philip Sidney's sister, was herself a poet and patron of the arts.

Sir Francis Drake (*left*) and his cousin Sir John Hawkins (*right*) were navigators of genius. Drake circumnavigated the globe. Both men instigated the challenge to Hispanic world-dominance, and their defeat of the Spanish Armada (*below*) changed world history

Sir Philip Sidney, soldier, scholar, poet and novelist, was the archetypical Renaissance man. At Penshurst Place (*below*) he was the patron of many other poets. His death in the Low Countries, as a result of a wound in battle, was followed by one of the largest funerals ever witnessed in Elizabethan London.

the globe in a small wooden sailing ship with a drunken, semi-mutinous crew and next to no navigational instruments.

Examples of Drake's cruelty are again rehearsed as he is called to the bar of modern liberal-minded history for having been the hero of old-fashioned history of a different tradition. When they reached Crab Island, they marooned a black woman who was heavily pregnant, with two black male slaves. No doubt William Camden, the semi-official national historian, was right to say that Drake behaved 'most inhumanly' in this matter. How the woman became pregnant – she was 'gotten with child between the captain and his men pirates' – does not indeed reflect well upon Drake, if you choose to judge a sixteenth-century privateer who was at sea for nearly three years by the enlightened standards of a land-bound modern historian. And Drake's treatment of his chaplain, which is seen as quasi-comic by Victorian and early twentieth-century writers, is (perhaps understandably) offensive to modern sensibilities. The *Golden Hind*, the first English ship in the Pacific Ocean, was also the first in the Indian Ocean. When, during gales of 9 January 1580 she struck a submerged rock, it looked for a while as if all was lost.[10] It was necessary to ditch precious cargo – three tons of the cloves, two cannon, some precious metal, and beans. Fletcher, the hapless chaplain, preached a sermon to the terrified men suggesting that they were being punished for the judicial murder of Thomas Doughty.

Drake was not a captain to take such talk on his ship. Morale was low, nerves were taut and he was determined to get back to England with his treasure ship. He simply could not afford at this stage of his voyage to allow the Reverend Francis Fletcher to upset the men even more than they were already disturbed. He needed to make an example of him. The chaplain was clapped in irons and nailed fast to one of the hatches, while Drake, his judge, sat opposite him, cross-legged on a sea-chair. The clergyman had claimed to speak for God. Drake would match this by establishing that he, and not the priest, had the ultimate authority on his ship. No one questioned Drake's physical or legal authority over his men. He now, in a sort of maritime parody of Henry VIII claiming to himself supreme governorship of the English Church, asserted his spiritual authority too. There was no trial, and no preamble. He merely bellowed at the chaplain, making sure that every man aboard heard the words: 'Francis Fletcher, I do here excommunicate thee out of the church of God and from all benefits and graces thereof and I denounce thee to the devil and all his angels.'[11]

The cleric – or ex-cleric, if you believe in Drake's power to defrock the clergy – was obliged to remain below deck and, upon pain of death, to wear upon his arm a label that read, 'Francis Fletcher the falsest knave that liveth'.

And so they went on their way rejoicing. On 8 February they reached Baratina, where they could take in much-needed food supplies. The next port of call was Java. They took on board plantains, coconuts, sugar-cane, chicken, cassava and beef. Drake paid an astounding £4,000 for this revictualling. By 26 March the *Golden Hind* was sailing west-south-west for the Cape of Good Hope, and by July they had sailed up the west coast of Africa as far as the Guinea coast.

Drake had a clear run home, but three political or legal hazards threatened his ultimate triumph. They were all summed up by the famous question that he asked, of a fisherman bobbing about in those Devonian waters, on 26 September, when he finally dropped anchor in Plymouth harbour: *Does the Queen still live?*

If, in his absence, England had been conquered by France or Spain, or reverted to Roman Catholicism under Mary Stuart, Drake's position would have been uncertain indeed. Already, dispatches from the Viceroy of Peru and the President of the Court of Panama and the Viceroy of New Spain had reached Europe. Philip II knew of Drake's piratical antics in Panama and South America, and the Spanish Ambassador in London, Mendoza, had demanded restitution. So the first hazard was that Elizabeth might be dead. The second was the possibility that, dreading a war with Spain, Elizabeth might disown Drake and his adventure. A third danger was that John Doughty, brother of the unfortunate Thomas, would demand full legal retribution for what was an illegal killing.

Luck, as so often, was on Drake's side. Queen Elizabeth was a mercurial and far from dependable patroness, but there was in her nature something of the pirate queen. She took a gamble. Although Spain was still England's chief trading partner – with many merchants and ships and perhaps as many as 2,500 sailors around the Iberian peninsula – and although Philip II sent 800 mercenaries to fight in Ireland, Elizabeth gambled that he would not declare outright war because of Drake's adventure. As for the grievances of John Doughty, who attempted to get Drake prosecuted for murder in the Earl Marshal's court, he looked as if he would be successful. Once again, Drake was lucky. Drake contested Doughty's claim at the Queen's Bench, submitting that the Earl Marshal could not exercise jurisdiction in the case. The Lord Chief Justice ruled against him. Conveniently the Queen delayed appointing a Lord High Constable when the position became vacant. He would have been the judge responsible for the offences committed outside the realm. John Doughty meanwhile, driven half-mad by the delay, conspired with a Spanish spy to have Drake murdered. He was arrested – his drunken conversation having been overheard – and died in prison.

Queen Elizabeth loved a rogue, and she loved treasure. On New Year's

Day 1581 she appeared at court wearing a crown of emeralds and a diamond cross that Drake had presented to her. The Spanish Ambassador, who knew that she was dripping with loot from the Spanish Main, priced the cross at 50,000 ducats.[12]

The precise details of how much of the stolen treasure was presented to Elizabeth, and how much remained at Drake's disposal, were left deliberately vague. Those who had invested in his voyage of circumnavigation were rewarded handsomely. In 1638 Lewis Roberts claimed to have seen a paper written in Drake's hand certifying that all his backers had received a dividend of £57 for every £1 invested. Since the expedition had cost £5,000 to furbish, the yield (if Roberts's figures were right) would have been £285,000, more than the Queen's entire annual revenue. Mendoza thought Drake had plundered £450,000, while other Spanish sources placed it at 950,000 pesos or £332,000. Whatever the exact figures, the gains were prodigious, the equivalent not of the personal fortunes of individuals, but of entire nations.[13] Drake bought Buckland Abbey, a former Cistercian monastery near Plymouth, which had been converted into a private estate when Henry VIII suppressed the religious houses. By April 1581 – when the people of the Netherlands had decided to depose their Spanish ruler, Philip II, and nominate François Hercule, Duc d'Alençon, as their 'prince and lord' – Elizabeth was prepared to revive the ridiculous idea of her marriage, and as a further act of defiance to Spain she conferred a knighthood on Francis Drake.

At her request, the *Golden Hind* was taken to Deptford. She accepted Drake's invitation to dine on board. £10,000 of looted Spanish silver was spent on the feast. The ship had been repainted and revarnished. A huge crowd gathered. A gilded sword was produced, and the Queen joked as she took it in her hands that she was going to use it to cut off Drake's head. She was sparing with honours. This knighthood, and the arms and privileges that went with it, were of the utmost significance. The message given to Spain, and to the world, was that Elizabeth herself endorsed Drake's (and by extension the other privateers') adventures on the high seas. England was a pirate kingdom, prepared to enrich herself at the expense of the rest of the world. If, by stealing silver and gold and jewels, mined by slaves for Catholic colonists of abominable cruelty, these buccaneers implied a gesture of defiance to the Pope and the Inquisition, so much the better. And if there was the implication, in the declaration of trade agreements with far-away potentates in the Indian Ocean, that England was now a world trader, a colonial power in the making, then better still – better and better.

When the Italian poet Ariosto, in his chivalric epic *Orlando Furioso*, included a prophecy of the Emperor Charles V, he called to mind Charles's famous heraldic device, the two columns and the words *Plus oultre*. The columns were the Pillars of Hercules. The motto, 'more – even further' was presumably at the back of A.C. Benson's mind when he wrote 'Land of Hope and Glory': 'Wider still and wider shall thy bounds be set'. When Sir John Harington (Queen Elizabeth's godson) translated Ariosto, he rendered the prophecy in these words:

> Yet I foresee, ere many ages passe,
> New mariners and masters new shall rise,
> That shall find out that erst so hidden war,
> And shall discover where the passage lies
> And all the men that went before surpasse
> To find new lands, new starres, new seas, new skies,
> And passe about the earth as doth the sunne,
> To search what with Antipodes is done.

A marginal note by Harington speaks of Drake's circumnavigation of the world. Harington transfers to Drake those maritime exploits which the prophetess in Ariosto had seen as the portent of a coming universal Empire.[14] Drake's exploit was thereby seen to be something much more than a stupendous exploit by an individual. It made a significant contribution to the National Myth.

15

A Frog He Would A-wooing Go

By the late 1570s the Cold War that existed in Europe – between France and the Habsburgs, between England and the Habsburgs, between Catholics and Protestants – began to look as if it would turn into a real war. And the theatre of that war was to be found in the Low Countries: modern-day Belgium and Holland. All Queen Elizabeth's instincts were for peace, and for saving money: both were reasons, from her point of view, not to be involved with the troubles in the Low Countries.

Fighting had continued there intermittently throughout the 1570s, with terrible loss of life. William of Orange, the Protestant champion, a convinced Calvinist, had successfully led the Northern Provinces in rebellion against the Spaniards. But victories were followed by reversals (12,000 lives had been lost in the siege of Haarlem in the winter of 1572–3). The Pacification of Ghent in 1578 looked like a victory for Dutch independence. In conceding that the Spanish king was *de jure* their absentee sovereign, the states united under William of Orange, and it was agreed that there should be religious toleration. Everyone knew, however, that the peace was fragile, and the resentments of the Catholic Belgians in the south against the (largely) Protestant Dutch in the north was only one factor in a volatile situation that could at any minute plunge not merely the Low Countries, but Europe as a whole, into war.

Among those foreign powers willing, and even eager, to become involved, were John Casimir, the brother of the Elector Palatine, who led an army of German mercenaries to protect the Protestants into Mons at the beginning of 1578, and the Duc d'Anjou – formerly the Duc d'Alençon, who, though a Catholic, was anxious to exercise power in some sphere, and was happy if this could be combined with causing agitation to the Spanish. (The great nineteenth-century American historian of the Dutch Republic, Motley, said of the duke that he was 'ferocious without courage, ambitious without talent, and bigoted without opinions'.[1])

When Don John of Austria, Habsburg Governor General, died in 1578, his successor Alexander Furnese, Duke of Parma, began a campaign of reconquest of the Low Countries.

Queen Elizabeth was in a perpetual state of uncertainty about the Netherlands. Very unwillingly she donated money to John Casimir for his army, but as far as he was concerned, it was not enough. 'It is better,' said

Thomas Wilson, Walsingham's fellow Secretary of State, 'to annoy by offence than to stand at defence, and to begin war than to withstand war.'[2]

Elizabeth was not so sure. For one thing, she never shared the 'forward Protestants'' love of the Dutch Calvinist religion. In fact, she hated it. For this reason alone, apart from her innate distaste for war, she tried to avert her gaze from the obvious: namely, that Europe was poised for a great religious war. In fact it was not fought until a generation later – the Thirty Years War – but the war in the Netherlands was in some sense a dress rehearsal for it. The new Pope had repeated his predecessor's condemnation of Elizabeth. Gregory XIII was determined to give the Counter-Reformation a yet more militant slant. Don John of Austria had been in favour of an invasion of England on purely religious grounds. William Davison, Elizabeth's envoy in the Low Countries, warned her in 1578 of the 'holy league of Catholic princes . . . long since projected, often reformed, and now like to be put in execution . . .' to secure the ruin of 'the reformed religion'. England was the strongest of the Protestant powers. Davison told the Queen that the Catholic powers held 'it for a maxim that if she, being the chief protectrice of our religion, were once supplanted, they should the more easily prevail over the rest'.[3]

If this were true, there could be no standing back from the fighting in the Netherlands. In the government of Elizabeth there were, broadly speaking, two views. The forward Protestants – of whom Walsingham and Leicester were the chieftains – saw no need or possibility of compromise. The Protestants of the Low Countries, the Huguenots of France and the English should all stand together against a common foe. The Roman Church had shown its hand – in the torture and enslavement of Hawkins's sailors in the Caribbean, as in the fires of Smithfield and the slaughter initiated on St Bartholomew's Day 1572. So their sentence was for open war.

Another, more politic view, was adopted by Lord Burghley and – much of the time – by the ever-vacillating Elizabeth. This was to ally themselves with the young Duc d'Anjou. The advantage of this plan was that it would drive a wedge between 'the league of Catholic princes'. By playing upon the French hatred of the Habsburgs and encouraging the self-interest of the Valois in the Low Countries, was there not a possibility of playing the game of European power-broker? As Gascoigne had reminded readers, the war was an ugly, horrible affair. If it could be averted by politics, or even better by the combination of politics and a royal matrimonial alliance, would not this be the best possible outcome?

So it was the situation in the Netherlands that prompted the Queen, in 1578, to revive the idea of marrying François, Duc d'Alençon/Anjou (he had become Duc d'Anjou when his brother, previous holder of the title, became King Henry III of France in 1574). The larger plan, congenial to William of Orange, was that Anjou would be offered the sovereignty of the Netherlands, and that the good Protestants of the Low Countries, protected by France and England, could at last see off their Habsburg oppressors. That was how it might have seemed in the big European power-game that Elizabeth and Cecil were perhaps playing. But the truth is, historians remain puzzled to this day by Elizabeth's behaviour over the match: both by her return to the notion in 1578 and by her apparently capricious abandonment of it in 1580–1.

Clearly one element in the bizarre episode was the fact that Elizabeth would, on 7 September 1579, celebrate her forty-sixth birthday. Even if she had no intention of marrying Leicester, her old love, his marriage to the dowager Countess of Essex on 21 September, while the court was returning from the progress in East Anglia, must have played its part in her decision to promote the Anjou courtship for all it was worth.

It was indeed the duke's Master of the Wardrobe, who had been sent to England to woo Elizabeth on Anjou's behalf, who broke the news to her that Leicester had remarried. Jean de Simier, a fawning courtly Osric, whom the Queen nicknamed her 'monkey', misplayed his hand. True, the disclosure of the Leicester–Lettice Knollys marriage gave him a moment of power over Elizabeth. She was wounded both by the news and by the fact that Leicester had not given it to her himself. In her highly predictable fury she temporarily transferred her favours and affections to the monkey, who was wheedling and flirtatious. The monkey, however, did not have as many cards to play as Leicester. He did not reckon on the strength of the Protestant cause in England, that party of which Leicester was the chieftain. Simier did not realise how profoundly his master's religion was hated, how keenly his part in the St Bartholomew's Day Massacre was remembered, and how ludicrous both he and the Queen appeared in the eyes of the court while the flirtation between them was at its embarrassing height.

Simier crept into the Queen's bedroom and stole one of her nightcaps so that his master could sleep with it. The gesture charmed her and caused irritation and alarm to the court. Simier, as his luck apparently held, confided in a French friend, 'I have every good hope, but will wait to say more till the curtain is drawn, the candle is out, and Monsieur in bed. Then I will speak with good assurance.'[4] He claimed, perhaps accurately, that whenever 'Monsieur' was mentioned, her face lit up. '*Elle est plus belle, plus gaillarde, qu'il y a quinze ans*,' exclaimed the French Ambassador. 'Not a woman or a physician who knows her, who does not hold that there is no lady in the realm more fit for bearing children than she is.'[5]

This optimistic diagnosis is not borne out by a study of the obstetric statistics. Lady Anne Somerset, in her biography of Queen Elizabeth[6], points out that the Queen's grandmother, Elizabeth of York, two of her stepmothers (Jane Seymour and Catherine Parr) and all three of the Duke of Norfolk's wives had died in childbirth. Although the Queen was still menstruating – as Burghley had made it his business to find out from her ladies – there was the greatest possible danger for a woman of her age giving birth. The number of rich or upper-class children who died in childbirth, and the number of women who died giving birth to them, was much higher than among the poor – principally because the poor were spared the attention of Elizabethan doctors.[7] The poor did not have to endure such quack treatments as having their bellies wrapped in the fleece of a freshly skinned sheep or the skin of a hare flayed alive. 'Poor women, hirelings, rustics and others used to hard labours, also viragoes and whores, who are clandestinely delivered, bring forth without great difficulty, and in a short time after rising from their bed return to their wonted labours.' The Elizabethan poor, in other words, had natural childbirth. The richer women had midwives whose standard practice was to stretch and dilate the genital parts, cutting or tearing the membranes with their fingers where this was deemed necessary. Deaths from sepsis and puerperal fever followed with unsurprising frequency.

Perhaps the Queen, mindful of these things, had no intention at a deeper level of going through with the marriage. If so, she certainly succeeded in concealing any such reluctance during the summer of 1579, both from her French wooer and from his English detractors. On 16 August the duke himself arrived from France, very early in the morning. The twenty-year-old was no beauty. Tiny, puny and pockmarked, he had a nose 'so large it amounted to deformity', in Elizabeth Jenkins's vivid phrase.[8] The Queen did not appear to notice his defects. Did this give some of her courtiers grounds for hope that she was merely play-acting as she threw herself into cringe-making displays of affection for her 'frog'. At a court ball on 23 August Anjou was posted behind an arras while the forty-six-year-old Queen danced, making supposedly 'secret' amorous gestures to her concealed lover. As he pushed his spotty face round the edge of the tapestry, the courtiers pretended not to see, while the Queen went into raptures.

Four days later he went back to France, writing her letters as he went. Their ardour, said Maurissière, the French Ambassador, would have set fire to the water. What the public thought was conveyed by the revival and adaptation of an old folk-song:

A frog he would a-wooing go
Hey-ho! says Rowley.
A frog he would a-wooing go
Whether his mother would let him or no
With a rowley-powley-gammon and spinach
Hey-ho! says Anthony Rowley.

The mother in question was the woman Philip Sidney called 'the Jezebel of our age',[9] the formidable Catherine de' Medici, mastermind behind the St Bartholomew's Day Massacre, who had given Elizabeth a superb diamond for her betrothal ring.

The Council, which met daily, did not mince their words. 'The doubt that her Majesty may not have children or that she may be endangered in childbirth' was how Burghley's polite memo summarised fears that one old councillor, Sir Ralph Sadler, expressed more bluntly: 'Few old maids escape.'

The extreme unpopularity of the French match with the public was reflected in a pamphlet by John Stubbs, an ardent Puritan, who entitled his warning *A Gaping Gulphe wherein England is like to be swallowed by another French marriage*. The Queen's response was her usual one to publications to which she took exception – writer, printer and publisher were arrested and had their right hands chopped off. Even the barrister who had had the temerity to take on Stubbs's case and defend him in court was imprisoned. The sentences were carried out 'in the market-place at Westminster'. William Page, a gentleman-servant to the ultra-Protestant Earl of Bedford, who was an MP and who lost his hand for distributing fifty of the offending pamphlets, cried out to the crowd, 'I have left there a true Englishman's hand.' Stubbs himself, when his turn came, exclaimed, 'God save Queen Elizabeth!' and suggested to the crowd that the blood pouring from his veins was unstaunchable. In any event, the effect of his words could not be easily staunched, and the French terms were extremely unlikely ever to have found favour with the English Council, or the nobility of the realm, or with Parliament and people: (1) Monsieur to be crowned King of England immediately after the marriage; (2) to share jointly with the Queen the authority to grant all benefices, offices and lands; (3) to have an annual income of £60,000 during the marriage and during the minority of any child being heir to the throne.[10]

It is interesting that when it was all over, and the little duke was casting all the blame on Simier for the failure of the match, he singled out for particular censure the monkey's having antagonised the Earl of Leicester.[11] The duke had enough experience in the Netherlands of Leicester's power and influence to know that the monkey's trick, of infuriating the Queen with the news of Leicester's marriage, had been a fatal mistake. By antagonising Leicester, said Anjou, 'the greatest and most powerful friend he had', Simier had 'prevented him from influencing the Queen as he desired'.

There were many complicated strands woven into the somewhat grotesque tapestry of the Alençon match. Had she married him, and established a dynastic alliance with France, the whole position of Spain, England and the Netherlands would have been very different, and Elizabeth would have been in a stronger position vis-à-vis the Scottish queen. But there was no doubt that she encouraged his wooing, in part as a salve for the hurt caused her by Leicester and Lettice Knollys. She had given Leicester her heart in youth, and he was the great love of her life. The possibility that she would marry Leicester had always been there, since the death of Amy Robsart. Now it was removed.

Hindsight makes it obvious that the Anjou match was a farcical idea. Some of the less percipient courtiers and privy councillors were surprised by the Queen's tears when it all unravelled. But it was obvious why she wept. Her woman's body wept. However remote the possibility, that body had held out the hope of the physical embrace of a man and the birth of a child. She had passed her forty-sixth birthday. The chance would not come again. From now onwards the Virgin Queen would come into her own. The decade that was about to begin was the glory age of the reign. But she knew more acutely than anyone that a price had been paid.

Part Three

1580s

16

Religious Dissent

On Easter Day 1575 there was a police raid on a house in Aldgate, East London. About thirty Dutch Anabaptists had assembled there to commemorate the Passion and Triumph of Christ. The point of the name, or nickname, 'Anabaptist' was that the adherents to this brave Protestant group did not believe in baptising babies. Baptism for them (as it had been for all Christians in the first 300 or 400 years of the religion's existence) was something to set a seal upon a mature person's decision to dedicate a life to Christ. They always rejected the 'Anabaptist' label. They had begun in Germany, and had spread across most of those European countries where Protestantism had taken root. They did not believe that any of the visible institutions on Earth corresponded to the ideal Church of Jesus Christ, of which pious and hopeful glimpses illuminate the New Testament. These idealistic dreamers, dubbed fanatics by all who disagreed with them, were vigorously persecuted wherever they testified. The thirty Dutch Anabaptists in London's Aldgate were not doing any obvious harm. Unlike those Catholics who supported the Pope's call for the deposition of the Queen, they were not plotting anyone's death, still less the overthrow of the state. They were not even English. In so far as they were Dutch Protestants who had fled the Low Countries, and Spanish persecution, they could be said to have been on the same side as the Elizabethan government, which more and more overtly funded the war of resistance by the Dutch against imperial Spain.

Yet these thirty Dutch Anabaptists, by their refusal to attend the services of the Church of England on Easter Day, had undermined the whole idea of the Elizabethan Settlement: namely that the National Church was comprehensive. Its rites and formularies had been painstakingly worked out to satisfy the consciences of as many Christians as possible, both those who inclined to a Catholic position and those who were convinced Protestants. To refuse to go along with this, for whatever reason, undermined the whole system.

The Dutch Anabaptists were asked four questions:

1 Whether Christ did not assume this flesh from the body of Mary.

The Dutch replied that 'He is the son of the living God.' This implied that they did not literally believe in the Virgin birth.

> 2 Whether infants should not be baptised.

Their reply was, 'We cannot understand matters so, for we read nothing of it in the Scripture.' Then came an exposure of their essential anarchism – again, an attitude and set of beliefs that they shared with the huge majority of early Christians:

> 3 Whether it was lawful for a Christian to attend or discharge the duties of a magistrate's officer.

They replied that their conscience would not suffer them to do so, but they considered the magistracy as a minister of God for the protection of the servants of God.

Last, they were asked:

> 4 Whether a Christian was allowed to take an oath.

They replied, quite truthfully, that the taking of oaths was forbidden by Christ in the Gospel of St Matthew.

The Bishop of London, Edwin Sandys, told them that they must choose between recanting these opinions and being burned at the stake.[1] Five chose to return to prison, where they were given fifty days, until the Feast of Pentecost, to make up their minds. Some recanted, and the rest were banished. Of the five in prison, one died and two, having been tortured, were allowed to go free. Jan Pieters and Hendrick Terwoot were burned at the stake. John Foxe, the martyrologist, wrote to the Queen to plead for them:

> As to these fanatical sects . . . it is certain they are by no means to be countenanced in a commonwealth, but, in my opinion ought to be suppressed by proper correction. But to roast alive the bodies of poor wretches that offend rather through blindness of judgment than perverseness of will, in fire and flames, raging with pitch and brimstone, is a hard-hearted thing, and more agreeable to the practice of Romanists than the customs of the Gospeller.[2]

The Queen and the bishop were both adamant. She who preferred to watch the abominable sport of bear-baiting to stage plays,[3] and who was prepared to profit from John Hawkins's slave trading, was not the sort of Christian who would be swayed by appeals for clemency. Throughout her reign, she displayed an unremitting intolerance towards Protestant dissent. Prison or exile were the choices for those whose Protestant sensibilities made it impossible to attend the services of the Established Church.

The number of Protestants burned by Elizabeth was tiny compared with the number burned by her sister Mary. The persecution was nonetheless fierce. And if Elizabethan England is compared with the rest of Europe, it was just as intolerant as the other countries in its laws and attitudes. The difference, perhaps, was that by virtue of its very nature the Church of England, and its early apologists, were obliged to indulge in much saving 'double-think'. Though the laws were draconian, and toleration was theoretically non-existent, there were many nods and winks, and much of the 'persecution' took the form of fines, which appealed to the parsimonious monarch.

William Byrd (1543–1623), for example, was an Elizabethan whose work endures, continuing to delight and uplift all who are not tone deaf. He lived to the age of eighty. We remember the anthems and songs, the keyboard works and the madrigals that survive as such exuberant witnesses to his fertile, imaginative life. But his greatest work is liturgical. His *Nunc Dimittis* from his setting of Evensong has been described as 'probably the finest and the most beautiful ever written for the English use'.[4] No one who has ever heard it will forget the end of the Canticle in G, and then the switch of chord to F for the *Gloria*, the phrase 'and ever shall be' passed contrapuntally from voice to voice while the bass sings the same phrase in augmentation. A similar 'trick' occurs in his setting of the Creed, where he switches from the main key of the work, C major, to B-flat major for the phrase 'And was crucified.'

Byrd wrote two complete 'Services' – *Venite*, *Te Deum*, *Benedicite*, *Magnificat* and *Nunc Dimittis* – several settings of the Prayer Book Eucharist and many settings of the Latin texts of the Mass. Queen Elizabeth was lucky enough to have him as the organist of the Chapel Royal, where he worked in tandem with Thomas Tallis (*c*.1505–85). Tallis was one of the most sublime of all English composers, and his motet for forty voices, *Spem in alium*, must be one of the greatest pieces in the English repertoire. Almost certainly he was a Roman Catholic, or Catholic sympathiser, but he was able to function as a court musician. Byrd was in the same position. When Tallis retired, Byrd took over as organist of the Chapel Royal. To compensate Byrd for loss of potential income as a teacher (he was obliged to attend daily at court) the Queen allowed him and Tallis the exclusive right to print 'any songe or songes in partes, either in English, Latine, Frenche, Italian or other tongues that may serve for musicke either in Church or chamber, or otherwise be either plaid or soonge' for a period of twenty-one years (the licence was given in 1575). This was tantamount to an official recognition that Byrd's settings of the Mass in Latin would be used in the private chapels of Roman Catholics. Byrd was always short of money. This was partly because of his commitment to the badly paid post of organist at the Chapel Royal, where he supplied the Anglo-Catholic Queen with glorious settings of the liturgy, largely in Latin. It was also partly because he and his wife, Julian Birley, sympathised with the Roman Catholic position. When not in London, they lived with their children in the village of Harlington in Middlesex. It would seem as if Julian was more obdurate than her husband in her refusal to attend services in Harlington parish church, and they paid stiff fines. Nevertheless, in spite of his open sympathy for Roman Catholic recusants, Byrd continued to be organist in the Chapel Royal until 1595, and even after he moved to Stondon Massey in Essex, he continued to have some part in the music of the court. He attended the Queen's funeral, and the coronation of James I, and sang 'melodious songs' with the likes of Orlando Gibbons, Elway Bevin, William Lawes and other gentlemen when James I dined at the Merchant Taylors' Hall in 1607.[5] His career was obviously a special case – the Queen liked his music. But his long life touched many others, and his friends included open dissidents, as well as conformists of one kind or another, many of whose experience reflected what an historian of the English Reformation called 'legislative severity and administrative moderation'.[6]

Nor should we imagine that even those recusants who suffered imprisonment were all confined in vile dungeons. Francis Mills, one of Walsingham's secretaries, describes a priest in the Marshalsea prison:

> C was with me last night and tells me that he was yesterday invited for his farewell to a banquet in the chamber of Lister, the priest in the Marshalsea, where among other guests were three gentlewomen very brave in their attire, two of them daughters to Sir John Arundel, the third the daughter or wife of one Mr Becker. There were also one Browne, a citizen, and one Mr Moore, with others. It was Magdalen Day and the priest catechised the company with the doctrine of Popish repentance, taking for his theme the story of Magdalen, absurdly applying the same to his purpose. You see how these kind of prisoners be by their keepers looked unto.[7]

And there was a very practical reason why in so many cases the severe laws were not severely enforced: a high proportion of judges and lawyers were themselves either recusants or secret Catholic sympathisers. John Milton (1608–74) in his pamphlet *Of Reformation Touching Church*

Discipline in England and the causes that hitherto have hindered it (1641) listed among the reasons why 'Religion attain'd not a perfect reducement in the beginning of [Elizabeth's] Reigne' the fact that 'the Judges, the lawyers, the Justices of Peace' were 'for the most part Popish'. Milton, though a famous Puritan, came from a popish family and his brother was both popish and a judge. So he knew whereof he spoke.

Archbishop Parker and Sir Francis Walsingham were both worried by the number of Catholic lawyers. In October 1577, when the Council insisted upon the bishops all making returns of all the recusants in their dioceses, they realised they had overlooked the Inns of Court, which were 'greatlie infected with Poperie'. The Lord Chancellor was told to make a similar investigation into the Inns of Chancery. As you would expect from clever lawyers, the evidence is conflicting and confusing, but the certificate for Lincoln's Inn listed forty recusants, or 25 per cent of all members of the Inn.[8] Of the Inner Temple, 33 per cent of members were 'Popish' – sixty-two members out of 189. But those who had been expelled from their inns for religious reasons are not included in these statistics, and by definition many of the Catholics were secretive about their allegiance. So the proportions must have been much higher than these statistics suggest. In 1583 in the Inner Temple there was a row about a bencher called Ridgeley being given a particular set of rooms. Those who were against Ridgeley alleged that he had made 'persuasion to . . . fellows that now are or have been of this house either to draw them to popery or confirm them in the same'.[9] In other words, the Inner Temple was perfectly prepared to accept Catholic lawyers so long as they kept quiet about it and did not attempt to proselytise.

This is the background to the story of the persecution of the Roman Catholics in Elizabeth's reign, and the attempted extirpation of all dissent, whether Protestant or Catholic. At times it was intrusive. At times it caused great hardship and suffering, but they *were* hard times. The great majority were not truly hurt or inconvenienced by the laws forbidding dissent; and with a few pathetic exceptions, the Catholics who were actually killed by the Elizabethan state were deemed, in most cases rightly, to be actively engaged in treason. It is difficult to think of any political system, any state, that could tolerate in its midst those who plotted the murder of the head of state and the overthrow of the system. Comparable cases today, in which Islamists have been involved in terrorist plots or attempts to bring about a pan-Islamic world order, are rooted out as thoroughly as governments are able. Likewise, the government of Elizabeth, Burghley and Walsingham would have deemed itself irresponsible not to repress Jesuit missionaries and others who could not accept Elizabeth as Queen and who tried to persuade others to take part in plots for her overthrow. Government fears were well placed, as was shown in 1586–7 when the Pope offered the King of Spain two million gold ducats if he would invade England, and in 1588 the English who lived on the south coast would watch the magnificent sails of the Armada speed past Plymouth and the Isle of Wight towards London.

Obviously, on one level, the Elizabethan Settlement in religion had not worked. There was a significant number of Protestants for whom the Reformation had not gone far enough. For them, the solution was to flood the land with preachers. Elizabeth, who knew how rare was the gift of effective preaching, thought that three or four preachers for a shire were sufficient. This shocked the puritanical Archbishop Grindal,[10] who wanted 13,000 preachers loosed upon the unresponsive population.

Examples multiply, wherever you go in England, of the sheer inefficacy of evangelical propaganda. Richard Greenham was the rector of Dry Drayton in Cambridgeshire for more than twenty years, from 1570 to 1591. Filled with the new learning and the desire to convert his village flock to the exciting new ideas of Luther, Zwingli or Calvin, he preached six sermons a week – some 6,000 in all. But when he left for London he felt disgust at the 'untractableness and unreachableness of that people among whom he had taken exceeding great pains'. In 1602 Josias Nichols, a comparably serious clergyman, had a parish in Kent:

> I have been in a parish of 400 or so communicants, and marvelling that my preaching was so little regarded I took upon me to confer with every man and woman before they received the communion. And I asked them of Christ, what he was in his person; what his office; how sin came into the world; what punishment for sin; what becomes of our bodies being rotten in the graves; and lastly whether it was possible for a man to live so uprightly that by well-doing he might win heaven. In all the former questions I scarce found ten in the hundred to have any knowledge, but in the last question, scarce one, but did affirm that a man might be saved by his own well-doing, and that he trusted he did so live, and that by God's grace he should obtain everlasting life by serving of God and good prayers.

Had they absorbed the tenets of European Protestantism these agricultural workers in Kent would have known that, to satisfy their vicar's definition of true faith, they should have said that no amount of upright living could save a person: only faith in Christ could do that.

Protestant enthusiasts could look at the fledgling Church of England and think it a poor thing because it was so un-Lutheran, un-Calvinist or un-Zwinglian. Catholic enthusiasts, and Catholic revisionist historians, could make a comparable mistake, by imagining that widespread conservatism and attachment to Catholic habits of mind and, indeed, sympathy for the heroism of the Catholic recusants when they suffered for their faith, constituted a wish to return to the Pope's obedience at any price. And that certainly was not true.

Of course the Church of England, as it was evolving or failing to evolve in the first quarter-century of Elizabeth's reign, could not satisfy purists. It was a compromise, designed to appeal to the largest number; or, if that was impossible, to offend as few as possible. Even those at the very top, as we have seen, were divided: many of Elizabeth's bishops wanted a Church on the German Lutheran pattern. Elizabeth herself wanted to revert to her father's religion in his latter days: Catholicism without the Pope. The clergy at the beginning of the reign had nearly all been ordained in Catholic times, and had begun their careers saying the old Latin Mass. No wonder that in parishes all over England throughout the first three decades of the reign were found priests who still said the old Mass, or who muttered the new Mass as if it were the old, who raised the bread and wine in elevation; who used Communion wafers – 'singing cakes' – rather than ordinary bread as laid down in the rubrics. In Berkshire in 1584 and Hampshire in 1607 we find parishes that refused to communicate except with 'singing cakes'. In Oakham in 1583 a preacher called Thomas Gibson was displeased to find the congregation 'hold still their papistical transubstantiation'. But of course the most common complaint was not that the congregations were too papistical; rather, that they were irreligious, bored by religion, that they were people 'that love a pot of ale better than a pulpit and a corn-rick better than a church door', as the poet Nicholas Breton said in *A Merrie Dialogue betwixt the Taker and Mistaker* of 1603.[11]

The Protestant-minded rector Francis Trigge found a congregation in 1598 'weeping and bewailing of the simple sort. Who going into the churches and seeing the bare walls, and lacking their golden images, their costly copes, their pleasant organs, their sweet frankincense, their golden chalices, their goodly streamers, they lament in themselves and fetch many deep sighs and bewail this spoiling and laying waste of the church as they think.' But this did not mean that any of these women would, the previous year, have wished that the King of Spain had sailed victoriously up the Thames to be crowned King of England in Westminster Abbey. And that is the difference between the large Catholic-minded church-going population and the tiny minority who believed it was necessary to their salvation to be in communion with the Pope.

During the first decade of the reign the government had been very lenient towards Catholic dissent. Puritans in particular were scandalised that bishops who in the reign of Queen Mary, had licensed the burnings of so many of their fellow countrymen should still be at large – 'which sticketh much in the hearts of many, the suffering of those bloody Bishops and known murderers of God's people and your dear brethren, to live, upon whom God had expressly pronounced the sentence of death, for the execution whereof he hath committed the sword into your hands, who are now placed in authority,'[12] as Christopher Goodman wrote to the Queen.

The House of Commons was much more bloodthirsty than the Queen. Cecil wrote to Sir Thomas Smith that 'a law is passed for sharpening laws agaynst Papists, wherein some difficulties hath bene because they be made very penal; but such be the huymours of the commons house, as they thynk nothing sharp ynough agaynst Papists'. This was in 1563, when Cecil and Smith were united in their distaste for penal laws against people's religious faith *per se*.[13] But the northern rising, the papal Bull of 1570 and the changing situation abroad – worsening relations with Spain, the torture of Hawkins's shipmates in the Caribbean, the sufferings of Protestants in the Low Countries at the hands of Spain and of Huguenots at the hands of the Catholic monarch – hardened the attitudes of the political classes.

In 1574 missionary priests began to be infiltrated into England from the continent in a concerted attempt to reconvert the population. Cuthbert Mayne, a secular priest living in the house of Francis Tregian of Golden, was arrested. He was hanged, drawn and quartered at Launceston. In 1580 Edmund Campion and Robert Parsons, Oxford men who had converted and joined the Pope's *Sturmabteilung* – the Jesuits – came back to England. Evelyn Waugh, in a pious biography of Campion published in 1935, described the setting up of the English seminary at Douai to supply priests for the population who could not in conscience attend their parish churches. The book was much impugned for its inaccuracy, but one assumes Waugh was right to assert that 'Martyrdom was in the air of Douai. It was spoken of, and in secret prayed for, as the supreme privilege of which only divine grace could make them worthy.'[14] Again, the parallels between the sixteenth-century Jesuits and modern suicide bombers comes unmistakably to mind. Clever, educated men such as Parsons and Campion were not blowing themselves up in crowds, but, by persuading young university students, or members of the Inns of Court to risk prosecution in these dangerous times, they were preparing to take others with them as they readied themselves for their martyrs' deaths.

One of the most dramatic stories told of the recusant martyrs was that of a young Yorkshire woman, Margaret Clitherow, who was converted by missionary priests in her very early twenties in 1574. She had been married, aged eighteen, to a prosperous butcher in York (John Clitherow), who gamely paid the fines – after her conversion – for her failure to attend church, and for harbouring priests. In 1585, with the worsening political situation, it became a capital felony to harbour Roman Catholic clergy. On 10 March 1586 the Clitherow premises were searched (her husband was a Protestant) and one of her frightened children revealed a secret room, and the unmistakable signs of a priest's presence: the chalice and paten for saying Mass, vestments, and so on. The priest himself was hiding next door and was not found. Margaret Clitherow refused trial by jury, to preserve her servants or children from the necessity of testifying against her. The Mayor of York, Henry May, accused her of committing suicide, so willingly did she go to her death: 'I pray God His will may be done, and I [may] have that which He seeth most fit for me. But I see not in myself any worthiness of martyrdom; yet, if it be His will, I pray Him that I may be constant and persevere to the end . . .' Her missionary-priest biographer, Mr John Mush, wrote of how she openly yearned for martyrdom – 'to His glory and her own felicity and the just punishment of many'.[15]

They devised a sadistic punishment for her. She was to be stripped naked and pressed to death under seven or eight hundredweight. They took her to the toll-booth on the Ouse Bridge to suffer this fate on Lady Day. In the event, they relented about the nakedness and allowed her to put on a linen shift, before tying her hands to two posts in a cross shape. A door was then laid on top of her. The first weight was a stone about the size of a man's fist. They continued to pile weights on the door until she was dead. It took about quarter of an hour.[16]

It is a horrible story, from which no one emerges well. Obviously, the authorities who inflicted this punishment upon a young woman fill us with horror. But so, too, does the martyr herself: her neighbours in York thought her mad.[17] A son – Henry Clitherow – whom she had educated in Reims and Rome and who joined first the Capuchin and then the Dominican Order, died insane.[18] In 1970 Margaret Clitherow was canonised as one of the Forty English Martyrs.

These terrible deaths entered the collective minds of the recusants. Roman Catholicism all but died out in England during the eighteenth century, but in Victorian times there was a revival, in part fuelled by the conversion of the popular Oxford don, John Henry Newman, in part by mass immigration from Ireland. The cult of the English martyrs really took off at this juncture in history, nearly 300 years after their deaths. The triumphalist hymn, written by the high camp convert F. W. Faber, became an anthem of English Roman Catholics:

Faith of our fathers, living still
In spite of dungeon, fire and sword.

The Roman Catholic convert son of an Archbishop of Canterbury, Monsignor Hugh Benson, wrote popular best-sellers with titles such as *Come Rack! ComeRope!* With the changes that came upon the Western Church after the Second Vatican Council, the cult of the English martyrs became less popular and was largely confined to Catholics on the conservative wing of the Church, or to those living in the North, where recusancy had been most popular. This was partly because many English Catholics were shy of upsetting their friends in the Church of England; but at a more serious level, it was because the cult of the Catholic martyrs was perceived as historically something of an anachronism. It was a way of marking out the identity of what was in effect a new Church – the Victorian Catholic Church, with its new dioceses in the industrial cities, Salford, Leeds, Birmingham – as much as it was a revisiting of the sixteenth century.

This is not to diminish the suffering caused to many English families during the reign of Elizabeth by the persecutions. John Donne, the great poet-priest who died as the much-revered Dean of St Paul's, was brought up by recusant parents. He was, as he said, 'deriued from such a stocke and race, as, I believe, no family, (which is not of farre larger extent, and greater branches) hath endured and suffered more in their persons and fortunes, for obeying the Teachers of Romane Doctrine, than it hath done'.[19] Donne's mother was descended directly from the sister of Thomas More, Henry VIII's Lord Chancellor and the noblest of Catholic martyrs. Donne's grandfather, John Heywood, had fled with his wife to Louvain in 1564 for religious reasons. John Heywood's brother Thomas (Donne's uncle) was a monk who was executed in 1574 for saying Mass. Donne's own brother Henry harboured a seminary priest – a Yorkshireman named William Harrington – in his chambers. Harrington denied he was a priest, but under cross-examination Henry Donne broke down, admitting that 'he was a priest and did shrive him'. Harrington was – Stow tells us – 'drawne from Newgate to Tyborne; and there hanged, cut downe alive, struggled with the hang-man, but was bowelled and quartered'. Before this gruesome end for the priest, Henry Donne had himself died of plague in Newgate gaol.

Although Donne was right to suggest that his family knew more painfully than most the experience of growing up as a Catholic in Elizabethan England, the threat of persecution affected many; the existence of the persecution was a stench in the atmosphere. Inevitably, the martyrologists liked to dwell on the quasi-pornography of torture. For most recusants, however, it was a matter of putting up with poverty, fines and painful inconvenience, rather than active physical nastiness. For instance, we find Michael Tempest attainted for taking part in the Northern Rebellion of 1570. He escaped to France, leaving behind a wife, Dorothy, and five children. On 17 October 1581 William Byrd brought the plight of these northern gentlefolk to the Queen, and Elizabeth arranged for an annuity of £20 to be paid to Mrs Tempest.[20] This isn't the monster-queen of Catholic martyrology. She was always insistent that Catholics should have freedom of conscience so long as they did not ally themselves *politically* with traitors. The one question she allowed to be included in the terrible interrogations of suspected infiltrators was the 'bloody question', which, during the 1580s and 1590s, had become a matter of urgency: 'If England were attacked, would these priests support Elizabeth or a foreign army bearing the Pope's approbation?'[21]

The tragedy was that the distinction attempted by those who framed the laws, and perhaps above all by the Queen herself – the distinction between religion and politics – was in this situation impossible to draw. Short of the Queen's conversion to Roman Catholicism (a political as well as a psychological impossibility) there was no way round the difficulty that the Pope's Encyclical of 1570 had set up, and the Jesuit missionaries compounded. Slowly but inexorably a gulf widened between those 'church-papists' who were prepared to go along with the Elizabethan Settlement, however much, in religion, they loved the old ways, and those who were for the Pope, with all the seditious implications that position brought with it. Walsingham with his spy-networks and low torturers, and the fervent missionary priests and their converts, saw the same truth here, and inhabited the same stark world of uncompromising metaphysical choices. And it was a starker choice than the mere political one: Pope or Queen. On one side, there were those who believed that Christ himself came down to altars at which a Roman Catholic priest presided, but deserted the altar where the words of Archbishop Cranmer were used. For these Catholics, England had become a place of Apocalypse. God had deserted the altars of its church and His glory was to be manifested in the torture chambers and gallows where His martyrs suffered. On the other side, serious Protestants did not merely dread England being ruled by foreigners. They deeply and seriously believed that Christ's Gospel was distorted and corrupted by the Pope's Church, that salvation was by Faith in Christ alone, and could not be found either in a personal attempt at virtue or by sacramental allegiance. It was these deep religious divides, and these profoundly held convictions, which made the espionage so intense, the political legislation so fierce, the confrontations and trials – when the victims were apprehended – so electrifying.

The more eloquent and virtuous the martyr, the more agonising the confrontation – as was demonstrated by the arrest and death of Edmund Campion. The young scholar of St John's who had welcomed the Queen to Oxford, the friend of Sir Philip Sidney and the 'well-polished man . . . of a sweet disposition' had returned to England in the summer of 1580 in an ineffectual disguise and was arrested as soon as he landed at Dover. The Mayor of Dover, however, released him and for eight or nine months Campion travelled about England. At Easter 1581 he had finished writing a polemical work, *Decem Rationes* – Ten Reasons (for becoming a Roman Catholic). Robert Parsons of Balliol, also a Jesuit, had a printing press and they printed Campion's pamphlet and strewed the benches of the university church with it just before the Commemoration Sermon in June.

Campion was arrested, through the treachery of a servant, in July, at a manor house at Lyford in Berkshire, not far from Oxford. He was taken to the Tower of London and imprisoned in the narrow dungeon known as 'Little Ease'. Then, after four days, the guards took him from the Tower to the Earl of Leicester's house. Here he was questioned, not merely by Leicester, but by the Earl of Bedford and by two Secretaries of State; but not, as was once supposed, by the Queen. It made such a good story – Elizabeth slipping secretly into Leicester's house and confronting Campion's eager, tortured faced with the question: did he think she was the Queen of England? It implies that she doubted it herself! Alas, the tale is 'no more than a figment of the imaginations of Campion's biographers'.

No one questioned Campion's virtue, or his impressiveness. His demeanour throughout the inquiry converted Philip Howard, Earl of Arundel, to Roman Catholicism. Howard was canonised in October 1970. He died in the Tower of London. The Queen had offered him restitution of all his estates and entitlement to the Dukedom of Norfolk, if he would only conform to the Church of England, and he bravely refused. His imprisonment seems harsh, but then he had been in cahoots with the exiled Cardinal Allen, and a fellow prisoner in the Tower, a priest named William Bennett, did admit that Arundel had asked him to say a votive Mass for the success of the Spanish Armada. His wife lived on until 1630, and the Queen gave her a pension of £8 per year.[22]

Howard died mysteriously – some said he was poisoned. Campion's end was gruesome: he died repeating his claim that his faith was not treasonable and that he and his fellow Catholics were loyal to the Queen. Many must have regarded with disgust the attempts to assassinate Campion's character during his trial, and deplored the disgusting manner of his death – hanged, drawn and quartered at Tyburn. Among them, it has convincingly been argued,[23] was Sir Philip Sidney, who almost certainly modelled the brutal cross-examination of Pyrocles in the *Arcadia* by Philanax on the cruel interrogation of Campion by Edmund Anderson, QC.

Although Campion's mission as a Jesuit was based on a belief that it was possible to convert the people of England to Roman Catholicism by prayer, by argument and by example, this optimistic attribution was abandoned by his fellow Jesuit missionary Robert Parsons and by the exiled Cardinal Allen.

Parsons, a Balliol man, was the son of the village blacksmith from Nether Stowey in Somerset. A great bruiser of a man, he was tireless in the writing and printing of seditious pamphlets. Campion's death was one of the factors which persuaded this fanatic that war alone could solve the Catholic dilemma. From 1581 onwards Parsons looked to Spain, and a Spanish invasion of England, as the only viable option. Shakespeare encapsulated the recusant position, their willingness to support treason and war and Gunpowder Plots on the one hand, and their personal heroism on the other:

> To this I witness call the fools of time
> Which die for goodness, who have lived for crime.[24]

17

Sir Philip Sidney

The birth of the nation known (somewhat oddly) in English as Holland was one of the most prodigious political consequences of the Protestant Reformation. When the Emperor Charles V abdicated in 1556 he was the last dynast with plausible aspirations to rule over a pan-European dominion. He divided his empire between his brother, Ferdinand I – who inherited the title of Holy Roman Emperor and the broad land-mass of the Palatinate (roughly, the area covered by modern-day Germany, Austria, northern Italy and Hungary) – and his son, Philip II, who was given Spain and the Low Countries – modern-day Belgium, the Netherlands and Luxembourg.

Holding his arm as he took this momentous step of renunciation was the remarkable man known to history as William the Silent (1533–84) – or *le Taciturne*. (The soubriquet did not mean that this eloquent figure never spoke, but that he kept his own counsel.) William of Nassau-Dillenburg, or William of Orange as he could also be known, was one of the richest noblemen in Europe. In essence a German, he was the child of two generations of dynastic marriages, which made him the heir to the sovereign principality of Orange, on the left bank of the Rhône, just north of Avignon; of Nassau, a duchy on the banks of the Rhine; and of large tracts of northern Brabant. He was also heir to the defunct kingdom of Arles. Though his father was Lutheran, William was brought up by a Catholic at the imperial court. It was only when Philip II took over control of the Netherlands from his imperial father, and made it clear that he was intending to place the Dutch under Spanish rule, that the stirrings of independence among the states radicalised William the Silent. He became the champion of the movement for Netherlandish independence. There were seventeen provinces of the Low Countries, all with their own local laws, aristocracy and privileges. The seven northern provinces, backed by William, declared for independence – demanding religious toleration for their largely (not exclusively) Calvinist population. This was the origin of the modern Netherlands, of which Holland is one state or county. It would not enjoy full political independence until the seventeenth century, but from the moment these states were destined to make an extraordinary impact on the world they would become a great maritime power. Their pioneering republicanism was ground-breaking. They were to become a cradle of science and philosophy and they invented modern capitalism. Spinoza and Rembrandt were the sons of this political wonder.

Philip II was determined to strangle the infant states at birth, and the struggles of William the Silent and the Dutch against their Spanish oppressors became the great ideological battle of late sixteenth-century Europe, comparable in the twentieth century to the much shorter and bloodier civil war in Spain. In the war between General Franco and the Republic, Europeans saw a titanic struggle for their soul, between Left and Right. In the fight in the Low Countries the question was partly a matter of local sovereignty versus Habsburg bullying. And there were plenty of Dutch Catholics who resisted Philip II. But as attitudes hardened and the fight became bloodier, it became an emblematic struggle between the Counter-Reformation, represented by Spain, and the Protestant aspiration. It was a struggle between a vast machine and a collection of individuals: between a papalist system that insisted upon obedience as a condition of salvation, and a new attitude to life, expressed by men and women who placed their consciences above a system. Deep things, therefore, were at stake, which is why so many English enthusiasts for the Reformation went to fight for the independence of the Dutch States.

The Catholic powers plotted constantly for a military and political defeat of the independent or hierarchical states, preceded by the assassination of the key figure in each drama. The Earl of Moray in Scotland had been assassinated. Admiral Coligny in France was killed at the behest of his own queen. The Pope urged the English to assassinate Queen Elizabeth. And in July 1584 William the Silent was shot at Delft, by a marksman called Balthasar Gérard. His sister, the Countess of Schwarzenburg, held his hand and asked him, 'Do you die reconciled to your Saviour Jesus Christ?' He was able to answer 'Yes' before he died.[1]

William had been the one man with the intelligence and the unflappability to hold together the quarrelsome states. There had always been many exasperating moments. When the burghers of Antwerp had refused him the means to save Maastricht from the Prince of Parma, William had sat with his head in his hands.[2] But he knew how to lead them. Without William, the people of the Netherlands desperately needed help, and they looked to the Queen of England to supply it.

English involvement in the Low Countries was something about which Queen Elizabeth nursed ambivalent feelings. In the years 1585–6 the English soldiers serving there, and the people of the Netherlands, suffered acutely from an excess display of all her worst character traits – vacillation, tight-fistedness, hysterical rages. Presumably the ill-fated campaigns in which thousands of Englishmen, including Sir Philip Sidney, perished coincided with her menopause. That being said, events were moving in such a way that any English monarch in the circumstances would have been jittery.

The case for maintaining peaceable relations with Spain was a strong one. Philip II was the most powerful monarch in Europe. He was Elizabeth's brother-in-law, and it was no secret that he believed that if anyone succeeded Elizabeth, it should be himself rather than Mary, Queen of Scots – too much under the influence of her French relations – or her son James, who was being brought up in Scotland as a heretic. Philip had no wish to antagonise the English people, whose king he aspired to become. Therefore he wanted peace with them, peace with their queen. He insisted to Pope Sixtus V, for example, that Elizabeth posed no real threat to the Catholic faith and that she could be talked out of her heresies. Everyone was playing an ambivalent game, however. The Pope promised Philip two million gold ducats – *Dos millones de oro* – if he invaded England and brought it back to the faith. Philip, for his part, disturbed the Pope with his pro-French bias. (Sixtus excommunicated Henry of Navarre in 1585, but when Henry converted to Catholicism on the celebratedly pragmatic grounds that 'Paris is worth a Mass', the Pope refused to ride with Philip in his attempts to limit French power.)

Moreover Elizabeth, as well as being unwilling to risk an expensive, bloody war with Spain on Dutch soil, was temperamentally unattracted to their cause. The Dutch sought her protection against the religious intolerance of Spain; but she herself did not practise religious tolerance in her own country and she intensely disliked the Calvinist creed of the Dutch States.

Walsingham and the advanced Protestants in the Queen's entourage took a different view. The Protestant struggle was *their* struggle, whether in Antwerp or in London. Moreover, however much Elizabeth wanted a peaceful life, the Spanish (who had spies everywhere, including in the Queen's own Council) had to be resisted. To conquer them in the States would be to put a check on their power and hugely reduce the chance of a Spanish invasion of England. The united fleets of England and the States would make a formidable navy and would secure the English Channel for the Protestant allies.

While the Queen dithered between the two opinions, and while the States openly asked her to become their governor, the Spanish took matters out of Elizabeth's hands. On 29 May 1585 a decree went forth from Madrid that any English vessel found near the Spanish coast should be arrested and appropriated: the crew imprisoned; the guns commandeered for the Armada that was being assembled at Cadiz. Hundreds, certainly, and perhaps as many as thousands[3] of English sailors and merchants found themselves heaving oars as galley-slaves or languishing in the prisons of Seville. One Englishman wrote, 'Our countrymen are still in prison and in great misery; except there be better order taken, better for men to stay at home than raise the price of corn in our country to bring it hither to so ungrateful a nation.'[4]

Elizabeth's reaction to this was highly characteristic. She allowed Walsingham, and her friends in the Low Countries, to remain in suspense. She said she would undertake to pay for 4,000–5,000 men in the Low Countries until the end of the war, but when this army had been dispatched, reinforced by 2,000 volunteers, they awaited her instructions and received mixed signals. Antwerp fell to the Spanish in August. It was time for a big military operation, and for an English figurehead who could match the legendarily successful general Alexander Farnese, Prince of Parma. The all-but-universal view in England was that the Earl of Leicester was that man. One of the only important figures to dissent from this view was the Queen herself. When Lettice, Leicester's wife, came down to London to join her husband, the Queen threw a tantrum and said that she would send someone in Leicester's place to the Low Countries; or send no one. On 26 September Walsingham wrote to Leicester, 'Unless God give her Majesty another mind, it will work her and her subjects' ruin.'[5] Already the Dutch States were in anarchy. The troops who had been sent out there were without pay, food or equipment. The companies who had been intended to garrison the town of Flushing had no commanding officer. They were kept in open boats exposed to the October rains and storms, and hundreds died before a bedraggled remainder marched into Flushing to replace the Flemish soldiers who had earlier defended the town.

One reason for Elizabeth permitting this deplorable state of affairs was her indecisiveness. Another was that she had a secret up her sleeve, which she did not wish to disclose to Burghley, Walsingham or any of the respectable members of her government. Whereas one side of her mercurial nature wished to make peace with Spain, and even to suggest – through the backstairs emissaries who moved between the two powers, London and Madrid – that she would contemplate conversion to Catholicism and make Philip II her heir, another aspect of her nature wanted adventure. Elizabeth the Pirate Queen wanted revenge for her imprisoned merchants and sailors. She secretly licensed Francis Drake, who was the dread of the Spanish, to wreak havoc on the Spanish coast. Elizabeth loved this sort of adventure. If it went wrong, she could disclaim responsibility. If it worked, and Drake came home with a shipload of loot, she could bag her share. The great Spanish admiral, the Marquis of Santa Cruz, spoke for his country when he said that 'England had many teeth', and that the man who with a single barque and a handful of men could take a million and a half of gold from under the eyes of the Viceroy of Peru might go anywhere and everywhere with such a squadron as he now had at his back.[6] By 14 September Drake and his fleet were in Vigo Bay – to offer freedom to the English merchants marooned there, and to loot the place. In the churches Drake's soldiers took pleasure not merely in stealing anything valuable, but in stripping the statue of the Virgin of her clothes and treating her with indignity. Chalices, copes, patens and an enormous cross were collected by Drake's pirates as so much plunder. He met with almost no resistance in Spain before sailing off to the West Indies. En route he sacked the towns of Santiago and Porto Praya in the Cape Verde Islands. By the middle of December they had reached the Antilles. In San Domingo he took the Spaniards completely by surprise and extracted money from the inhabitants by hanging two friars *per diem* until they surrendered 25,000 ducats. Drake – this was typical of his humour – asked the Spaniards to translate for him the Latin inscription over Philip II's royal arms carved over the grand staircase: *Non sufficit orbis* – the world is not big enough for him. After calling at a plague-ridden Cartagena, he sailed home via the infant colony of Virginia and reached Plymouth harbour on 28 July 1586. In one voyage he had demonstrated what an English land army in the Low Countries could not do: that Spain was vulnerable.

One man who had tried to sail with Drake's voyage was Leicester's nephew, the thirty-one-year-old Philip Sidney.

For some years Sidney had longed for the New World. In the revised version of his *Arcadia* there is a characteristic account of the two princes putting out to sea, which is both a 'poetic' description of the process of a sail catching the wind and a vivid expression of wonder that such a process could actually work!

> They recommended themselves to the sea, leaving the shore of Thessalia full of tears and vows, and were received thereon with so smooth and smiling a face, as if Neptune had as then learned falsely to fawn on princes. The wind was like a servant, waiting behind them so just, that they might fill the sails as they lifted; and the best sailors showing themselves less covetous of his liberality, so tempered it that they all kept together like a beautiful flock, which so well could obey their master's pipe: without sometimes, to delight the princes' eyes, some two or three of them would strive, who could, either by the cunning of well-spending the wind's breath, or by the advantageous building of their moving houses, leave their fellows behind in the honour of speed: while the two princes had leisure to see the practice of that which before they had learned by books: to consider the art of catching

the wind prisoner, to no other end, but to run away with it; to see how beauty and use can so well agree together, that of all the trinkets, wherewith they are attired, there is not one but serves to some necessary purpose.[7]

It is a beautiful passage, as elaborately spun as a polyphonic part song by Byrd, as encrusted with jokes, clever thoughts, allusions and visual delight as might an Elizabethan dress on a great lady gleam with a variety of fabrics, jewels, facets and surfaces. But it is landlubber's prose, which believes it possible for two young men, if sufficiently well born and well educated, to master navigation from what 'before they had learned by books'. This alone would have been enough to make Drake shudder. But Drake, lately promoted from pirate ruffian to admiral in the Royal Navy, did not want to incur Royal displeasure; and anxious letters from court, forbidding the admiral to take Sidney aboard, could not be gainsaid. Walsingham, Sidney's father-in-law, attributed the young man's yearning for America to pique at not being made governor of Flushing.

Sir Philip Sidney hath taken a very hard resolution to accompany Sir Francis Drake in this voyage, moved hereunto for that he saw Her Majesty disposed to commit the charge of Flushing unto some other; which he repeated would fall out greatly to his disgrace, to see another preferred before him, both for birth and judgement inferior unto him. This resolution is greatly to the grief of Sir Philip's friends, but to none more than to myself. I know Her Majesty would easily have been induced to have placed him in Flushing, but he despaired hereof, and the disgrace that he doubted he should receive hath carried him into a desperate course . . .[8]

It appears that the Queen was going to give the governorship of Flushing to Thomas Cecil – 'Burghley's talentless eldest son',[9] as Katherine Duncan-Jones calls him. If so, the dig in Walsingham's letter about Sidney's superiority of birth has a distinctly acid flavour. Sidney was, as it happened, eventually sworn in as the governor of Flushing on 22 November 1585. He had ten months left to live and they were all spent in the Low Countries. He missed the baptism of his daughter Elizabeth (at St Olave, Hart Street, on 20 November – the Queen attended in person as a godmother), his father's death on 5 May 1586 (the Queen refused Philip leave to come back to the deathbed), his mother's death on 9 August and the illness of his beloved sister, the Countess of Pembroke.

Sidney was confronted in the United Provinces by chaos, caused by lack of organisation and exacerbated by the Queen's parsimony. The troops stationed there were sick, many of them starving. It was a period when Protestant refugees were flooding from the southern Netherlands into Holland and Zeeland, rents and food prices were high, shortages acute; it was obvious that in such circumstances starving English and Welsh soldiers would turn into marauders. One of the English members of the Council of State (*Raad van State*), Thomas Wilkes, admitted, 'So great is the lack of discipline among the garrisons, especially of our nation, that I am ashamed to hear the continual complaints which come to the councell-bord against them . . . We beginne to grow as hatefull to the people as the Spaniard himself who governeth the townes of conquest with a milder hand than we doe our frends and allyes.'[10]

Leicester's remit was an impossible one: it was to defeat, or hold at bay, the Spanish in the Low Countries; and it was to 'bring the rebel provinces under the benign protection and control of a foreign ruler'[11] himself. The disadvantages with which he contended included: a recalcitrant population who disagreed among themselves; a formidably powerful Spanish army under a superb general, Parma; a capricious queen, who was not prepared to spend money on the campaign and was prepared secretly to negotiate for the destruction of the Dutch. She wanted to make peace, and her ever-volatile relationship with Leicester was going through one of its volcanic phases. The fact that he had brought his still-loved second wife to London to see him off scarcely improved Elizabeth's mood. When the States offered Leicester the governorship of the new republic, and he accepted it, this was a sure sign that her creature was getting above himself. He was 'one of her own raising', she stormed. Rumours that Lady Leicester was setting out for the Low Countries in fine clothes and carriages, as a Dutch First Lady, exacerbated Elizabeth's fury: 'The Earl and the States had treated the Queen with contempt' . . . either the world would 'refuse to believe that a creature of her own would have presumed to accept the government contrary to her command, without her secret asset' or it would be thought that she could not rule her own subjects.[12]

While Elizabeth played out these comic operatic tantrums at home, to the flinching of courtiers and the cowering of ambassadors, the campaign limped on. Sidney was not enjoying cordial relations with his uncle; Leicester, in his turn, did not think highly of his nephew's capabilities, 'despising his youth for a counsellor, but withal bearing a hand upon him as a forward young man'.[13] Sidney, who was made colonel of a Zeeland regiment, tried to shift the role of English forces from defence to offence. He took part – with his brother Robert and Count Holenlohe – in attacks on the Spanish army around Breda; with Prince Maurice, he successfully besieged Axel. He narrowly escaped Spanish capture during a miserable little battle at Gravelines, and as summer ended he took part in another successful siege: of Doesburg, this time fighting alongside his uncle, Leicester. Then, on 14 September 1586, the English army moved off towards Zutphen, having heard that Parma and the Spaniards were on their way there. It was on 22 September, a thickly misty day, that Sidney rode out against the Spanish army outside Zutphen. The enemy were more numerous than, in the mist, the 200 English and Dutch horsemen and 300 or 400 foot-soldiers had realised – numbering 2,200 musketeers and 800 foot-soldiers.[14] Sidney was not wearing thigh armour and was hit by a musket-shot just above the knee. The skirmish failed to stop the Spanish relief of Zutphen. Sidney, accomplished in the tilts, kept his saddle – 'The foe shall miss the glory of my wound.'[15] The seriousness of his wound was hard to assess. Leicester was now impressed by his nephew's courage. Sidney was taken by barge down the River Issel to Arnhem, where he lay at the house of Mademoiselle Gruithuissens. He lay there for twenty-five days. His mind was lucid and, we are told, he wrote a large epistle to Belerius, the learned divine, in very pure and eloquent Latin – alas, it is now lost and scholars do not know who Belerius was. But Sidney, in death, as in life, like the twentieth-century poet, could 'teach the free man how to praise'. As in later examples of squalid wars, nothing is remembered of Leicester's disgraceful and unsuccessful Netherland's campaign – nothing but the death of a poet. Sidney's wound developed gangrene, and on 17 October he died.

He left unfinished his great book, the revised *Arcadia*. It is a much richer, more complicated, more satisfying reading experience than the simpler version (known as the *Old Arcadia*). He purged the story of improprieties – Pyrocles does not, as in the old version, sleep with Philoclea, nor is Musidorus tempted to rape Pamela. The comedy is still there: the inherent absurdity of the older characters, Basilius and his wife Gynecia, both being in love with Pyrocles in drag is exquisitely worked out. And the scene in which Basilius thinks he is sleeping with 'Zelmane', but in fact makes love to his own wife in the dark, is both hilarious and deeply touching. The device, taken up and imitated by Shakespeare in his comedies, of Zelmane, disguised as a pageboy and loving Pyrocles, is extremely affecting: her death one of the finest things in English literature. To the old version is added a much sharper sense of menace, especially in the character of wicked Cecropia. Then there are all the exciting fights and tournaments, with their extraordinary pageantry – 'Argalus was armed in a white armour, which was all gilded over with knots of woman's hair, which came down from the crest of his head-piece and spread itself in rich quantity over all his armour . . .'[16]

You never feel the emotions in the *Arcadia* are fake. These are real young people with real passions, real sexual frustrations, and real anguish in a grown-up world not of their making. It is a sexy world – think of the extraordinary pageant with six bare-chested maids – 'their breasts liberal to the eye; the face of the foremost of them in excellency fair and of the rest lovely, if not beautiful'.[17] It is shot through with visual and moral realism. It is a world in which fighting, in however elegant an armour, ends with the eye seeing the truth and 'all universally defiled with dust, blood, broken armours, mangled bodies, took away the mask, and set forth horror in his own horrible manner'.[18] It is a book aware of the realities of the sordid political world: spies are 'the necessary evil servants to a King'.[19] It mingles high rhetoric with homely and humorous idiom – 'You shall see (if it come to the push' – and the multifaceted and variegated prose is interrupted at regular intervals with verse of dazzling proficiency and glittering variety, and with images that are often both homely and devastating in their accuracy – as when Sidney sees the God of Love as:

> Though thousands old, a boy entitled still
> Thus children do the silly birds they find,
> With stroking hurt, and too much cramming kill.

Sidney's funeral did not take place for four months. The body was brought back to England in November and lay in the Minories while Walsingham tried to sort out his son-in-law's chaotic finances. It is said to have cost him £6,000.[20] Eventually, on 16 February 1587, the mourners processed from the Minories to St Paul's Cathedral for the burial. There were 700 people in the procession.

It is usual to think of great funerals as endings and a time of looking back. No doubt there was that element to this extraordinary pageant, recorded for us in Theodore de Bry's thirty-two plates in which the mourners, haltered and robed, walked; the knights, the aristocrats and the hooded heralds in their tabards preceded the coffin, emblazoned with the arms of this young embodiment of a Renaissance Man; followed by Sidney's Dutch and English comrades in arms; by Members of Parliament, muffled drummers and halberdiers with trailing pikes. The panorama stretches to thirty-five feet in length.

Yet Sidney's funeral did not spell the end of an age. Rather, it reminded many, and especially the poets, of what he and his sister had initiated. The quite prodigious change in English literature that occurred in the third decade of Queen Elizabeth's reign was not an accident. During the reign of Richard II the King and certain cultivated aristocrats gave patronage to poets. The result was a brief glory-phase in literary history:

The Canterbury Tales, *Piers Plowman's Vision*, *Sir Gawayne and the Green Knight*. During the fifteenth century, while the aristocracy all but destroyed England with their internecine wars – the Wars of the Roses – patronage, and poetry, went dead. The first half of the sixteenth century saw, likewise, relatively little literary interest on the part of patrons. One of the Latin poet Martial's epigrams explains it: '*Sint Maecenates, non derunt, Flacce, Marones.*' If you have patrons (like Maecenas) you will get good writers (like Virgil).

Literature, just as much as music and architecture, is created by demand; and not simply by a market, important as it is that poets, composers and architects should be able to eat and feed their children while they work. Had the market alone determined Elizabethan literary output, the poets would all have written for the stage and there would have been no Daniel, no Drayton, no Gascoigne, no Campion, no Churchyard, no Barnfield, no Spenser, no Donne, no Dyer, no Wotton, no Chapman. There were more than 230 Elizabethan poets, pouring out a prodigious quantity of songs, narrative poems, pastorals, satires and epigrams. No other period of literature in the English language matches it, and the reason is simple: the Elizabethan aristocracy, tiny and for the most part cultivated as it was, patronised literature. In the mock-heroic, but semi-serious dedication of his hilarious novel *The Unfortunate Traveller* to the Earl of Southampton (Henry Wriothesley), Thomas Nashe wrote, 'unreprievably perisheth that book whatsoever to waste paper, which on the diamond rock of your judgement disasterly chaneth to be shipwrecked. A dear lover and cherisher you are, as well as of the lovers of poets themselves . . .' A cheeky, camp joke referring to Southampton's obvious delight at being fancied by male poets such as Shakespeare. But when Nashe wrote his dedication he also meant it: 'a new brain, a new wit, a new style, a new soul will I get me to canonise your name to posterity . . .'[21] The taste of the patrons determined the quality of the literature. Sidney and his aristocratic contemporaries were well read in the classics and in the Italian poets, which they esteemed almost as highly. They were conscious of England acquiring a new glory under Elizabeth. Such a new civilisation needed a new style and a new soul: an English Virgil to create an epic that would match the Latin poet's glorification of the new Augustan republic; an English Ariosto who could provide discerning readers with a great narrative in which their queen, the Protestantism, their patriotism, their love of pageant, were fashioned in a new *Orlando Furioso*.

Chief among the patrons – chief because brightest, cleverest and themselves distinguished practitioners – were Mary, Countess of Pembroke, and her brother Philip Sidney. But as is shown by the life of the greatest (non-dramatic) poet of the age, Edmund Spenser, a literary life was nurtured by many. Spenser, a 'poor scholler' of the Merchant Taylors' School, was the beneficiary of the will of a rich Lincolnshire-born London lawyer, Robert Nowell (brother of the Dean of St Paul's), which paid for the poor to go to university. At Cambridge, Spenser's brilliance was recognised by that peculiar, quarrelsome don, Gabriel Harvey, who put him forward and enabled him to get employment – for example, in the household of Dr John Young, Bishop of Rochester. By the late 1570s Spenser had attracted the attention of the poetry-crazed Leicester circle and had befriended Sidney, and it was through Sidney that Spenser, who had been writing verse in ever greater quantity throughout the decade, was taken on by Lord Grey de Wilton as his confidential secretary in Ireland. 'We cannot imagine Spenser as a publisher's hack, writing pamphlets to order, like Nashe, and living a hand-to-mouth existence in the back streets near St Paul's. Sidney knew that something better than this must be found for the poet who was to write the great English heroic poem.'[22]

At the beginning of this book we faced up to the fact that the Elizabethan policy in Ireland, and Edmund Spenser's *View* of the Irish question, were, to put it mildly, problematic for the modern reader. It would, however, be a distortion of the truth if all we remembered of Spenser in Ireland was his career as an administrator, seen through the Fenian lens of a later age's sensibilities. True, Spenser was one of those Englishmen who made himself the enemy of the Irish people. He took possession of the castle of Renny in County Cork, for £200, as well as Buttevant Abbey. He was made Sheriff of Cork by the Privy Council for his 'good and commendable parts (being a man endowed with good knowledge in learning and not unskilful or without experience in the service of the wars)'.[23] On 15 October 1598 his castle at Kilcolman was sacked and burned by a marauding army of 2,000 Irish – 'rebels' or 'patriots', depending upon your viewpoint. Years later, Ben Jonson, gossiping to Drummond of Hawthornden, said that 'the Irish having robbed Spenser's goods and burnt his house and a little child new born, he and his wife escaped, and after he died for lack of bread in King Street'.[24] This melodramatic foreshortening is probably a distortion. Spenser did have a small pension. But the fire is true, the violent expulsion from Ireland is true, and Spenser died aged less than fifty (probably forty-seven) in London, with his great epic unfinished.

Great, however, it is, not least in its evocation of Ireland, a place whose languages, traditions, landscapes, rivers and coastlines he paints more beautifully than any other poet – as with his passage about the Irish rivers in Book IV, Canto XI:

There was the Liffy, rolling downe the lea
The sandy Slane, the stony Aubrian,
The spacious Shenan spreading like a sea,
The pleasant Boyne, the fishy fruitfull Ban.
Swift Awniduff which of the English man
Is cal'de Blacke water, and the Liffar deep,
Sad Trowis, that once his people overran,
Strong Allo tombling from Slewlogher steep,
And Mulla mine, whose waues I whilom taught to weep.

Spenser's premature death left the great Elizabethan epic poem unfinished. In its reflections on Ireland, the poem, and all it represents, left unfinished a tale of woe that reverberates to this day.

18
Hakluyt and Empire

Is England, or what is now called Britain, at one with the rest of Planet Earth, or is it pursuing a parallel life of its own, with its own Church, its own weights and measures, its own monarchy, its own arcane sense of comedy? This is a question that sets up puzzles in many non-English minds, and in the writings of our contemporary historians and political commentators. Conversations about, for example, modern Britain's relationship to Europe or to the United States might begin with very specific concerns: the economic advisability of joining a single European currency, the need (or otherwise) to send troops alongside American forces to one of the world's troublespots. Sooner or later, however, when the pros and cons of such a strategy have been rehearsed, we find ourselves in the realm of metaphysics; we find that our view of contemporary events – in Afghanistan, in Ireland, in the Church – is determined by some vision of a Platonic England. And the origins of these concepts took shape in the sixteenth century during the reign of Queen Elizabeth, when England – here the word means the land-mass containing the English counties and Wales – shaped an entirely new relationship with the rest of the world. On the one hand, because of its decision to reject the Pope, England cut itself off from the European mainstream; it became a beleaguered little island doughtily maintaining its difference from the rest of Europe, and prepared, ultimately, to ward off an invasion threat from the greatest military and naval power in the world. In this respect, Elizabethan England's attitude to Philip II and the Spanish Armada prepared generations of English people for the belligerently insular mindset that served it so well when resisting Napoleon and Hitler, but which, viewed from another perspective, seemed embarrassingly anachronistic when contemplating the new world order and the European Union. Another part of the story, however, is of an Elizabethan England which, because of the skills of its navigators and its pioneer geographers, had a truly global sense of itself. The two most portentous examples of this are from the English advances into India in the 1570s, with the subsequent founding of the East India Company, to compete with Dutch merchants; and, second, the establishment of English colonies in America, and the efforts, between 1583 and 1588, by Walter Raleigh, to found what became, in turn, the states of Virginia and North Carolina. From these two outgoing ventures stemmed the growth of the British Empire (the phrase first coined by Dr John Dee) and the existence, on the western side of the Atlantic, of an English-speaking people.

From this it can be clearly seen that modern history began with the Elizabethans: not simply modern English history, but the modern world as we know it today, with the English-speaking United States, with the post-colonial East. And these two great enterprises, as we have already hinted when considering Sir Francis Drake's circumnavigation of the Earth, are only two of the Elizabethan expansions into the greater world. Humphrey and Adrian Gilbert had laid claim to Greenland for the Queen and discovered the North-West Passage. Anthony Jenkinson had voyaged to Siberia, China, Japan, Canada, the coasts of Africa – there was no part of the *known* world unvisited by English voyagers at this date. Humphrey Gilbert, who had made an abortive attempt to land Englishmen in America in 1578, was inspired to try again because of the experience of Davy Ingram, a common sailor from Barking (a town just east of London) whose story was winkled out of him partly by Gilbert, partly by Walsingham himself: for, if even a part of it were true, it showed what marvels, what riches, existed on the other side of the Atlantic, ripe for the picking.

Ingram, about forty years of age when interviewed by Gilbert, had been one of the unlucky sailors on John Hawkins's slave-trading mission of 1567, when Hawkins had that disastrous battle with the Spanish and abandoned half his men on the shores of Mexico. Having heard that English fishing vessels regularly visited Newfoundland, and having no notion of the distances involved, Ingram and two friends decided to risk the hike. Twelve months later they turned up in Nova Scotia, and were able to secure a passage on a French ship to Le Havre. Ingram had vivid stories to tell – of 'brutish' Native American tribesmen whose heads were 'shaven in sundry spots'. ('When any of them is sicke and like to die [the] nexte of his kinne doe cut his throte and all his kinne must drinke up his bloude.') He had seen 'savages' feast on raw human flesh. Adulterers he had seen pinned to a stone slat, 'flat on their backs, and their hands and legges being holde or tyed, the executioner commeth and kneeleth on their breastes, and with a crooked knife cutteth both their throats'. He had escaped the beasts of the forest. He had seen – and this was of especial interest to Gilbert and Walsingham – tribesmen carrying buckets made of 'massie silver', lumps of gold 'as bigge as his fyst' and stark-naked women wearing 'plates of gold over their body'. The adventures of Othello in his youth, which melted the heart of Desdemona, were culled by Shakespeare from contemporary travel-writers, and the London audiences who heard these experiences filtered through what has been called the Othello-music would have realised what a large and extraordinary world they inhabited compared with their late medieval grandparents:

> Wherein I spake of most disastrous chances,
> Of moving accidents by flood and field,
> Of hair-breadth scapes i' th'imminent deadly breach.
> Of being taken by the insolent foe
> And sold to slavery, of my redemption thence,
> And portance in my traveller's history;
> Wherein of antres vast and deserts idle,
> Rough quarries, rocks, hills whose heads touch heaven,
> It was my hint to speak: such was my process.
> And of the cannibals that each other eat,
> The Anthropophagi, and men whose heads
> Do grow beneath their shoulders . . .[1]

At one and the same time, then, Elizabethan England was more insular and more outward-looking than it had been in the past, more open to the world, but more insistent that the world must accept it on its own terms.

The last sentence perhaps asks to be rephrased. 'At one and the same time' as the rest of Europe the England of Elizabeth refused to be. Few things are more eloquently emblematic of Elizabethan England's difference from the world than its ignoring the change in the European calendar, which took place in 1582.

The solar year is 365 days and the lunar year is only 354 days, and this has always presented the human race with a challenge when devising calendars. The ancient calendar of the Christian Church had been founded on two mistakes. One was that a year consisted of 365.25 days and the other was that 235 lunations were exactly equal to seventy-nine solar years.[2] In 730 the Venerable Bede had noted that the equinoxes took place about three days earlier than they must have done when the calendar was fixed at the Council of Nicaea (AD 345). By the time of the later Middle Ages the divergence was seven or eight days. Pope Sixtus IV in 1474 had commissioned the foremost astronomer of the time to superintend a revised calendar, but he – Regiomontanus – had died before the scheme got under way. The Reformation and other little local difficulties had distracted subsequent popes from attending to the matter.

Gregory XIII was determined to set his mark on history by commissioning Luigi Lilio Ghiraldi, an astronomer from the University of Naples (Latin name Aloysius Lilius), and the mathematician Clavius to do the necessary calculations. The lunar cycle contained 6,939 days 18 hours, whereas the exact time of 235 lunations is 6,939 days 16 hours and 31 minutes. This amounts to an error of one day every 308 years. By the time of the sixteenth century the error had accumulated to four days, so that new moons marked on the calendar as happening on the fifth of the month were actually happening on the first.

It was decided, in order to get the calendar back into kilter with the actual movements of the planets, that the feast of St Francis of Assisi, 1582 – that is, 5 October, – should become 15 October. This meant that the next vernal equinox, instead of occurring on the eleventh, would take place when it should, on 21 March. The difference between the old, or Julian, Calendar remained ten days from 1582 to 1700; because 1700 was a leap year, and a common year in the new Gregorian Calendar, the difference in styles then became eleven days. The Protestant states of Germany held out against the Pope's astronomical innovation until Frederick the Great brought them into line in 1774. Great Britain had caved in rather earlier, with the passage of the Calendar (New Style) Act of 1750. This was also the moment when England adopted the Scottish habit of regarding 1 January as the first day of the year. Until then in England the year began on Lady Day (25 March), the day in the calendar when Almighty God became incarnate in the womb of the Virgin Mother and brought new life to the world.

From 1582 onwards, therefore, the Elizabethans were on a different time-scale from Spain, Portugal, Italy and France. For us, who have adopted *both* the Gregorian method of regarding the solar calendar and the Scottish division of the calendar months, the Elizabethans were doubly out of sync. For instance, Sir Philip Sidney's funeral happened on what we call 16 February 1587, which for those who were present was 1586. It makes dating any event in the later Elizabeth period a fiddly and confusing business and adds to our sense of their otherness. But one should not be distracted by this small thing from seeing their bigger thing, and above all their imaginative enlargement through the pioneering study of geography.

The figure who stands out as the greatest English geographer of the age is also the man who in his monumental multi-volume book brought to life the Voyagers. Richard Hakluyt's *The Principall Navigations, Voyages, Traffiques and Discoveries of the English Nation* did for explorers and navigators what John Foxe did for the Protestant martyrs. There is no better book in which to browse if what you want is armchair-travel, excitement, wonder and human oddity. But Hakluyt (*c.*1552–1616) – his name is pronounced Hackle-wit – was much more than just an anecdotalist. He was one of those Englishmen (note the title of his book: the achievements are those of the English *Nation*) who saw the almost limitless political possibilities of the new geography and who radically redefined the position of England in the world. 'Give me a map,' says Marlowe's Tamburlaine, 'then let me see how much is left for me to conquer all the world.'[3]

Fear of Spain, and fear of the perils of ocean travel, were two very good reasons for English mariners not to venture upon the expansions that Hakluyt urged forward. As long ago as 1494, Henry VII had given letters patent to John Cabot of Bristol and his three sons 'for the discovering of newe and unknown lands'. Hakluyt printed them in his *Divers Voyages* of 1582 as an incentive to try to follow the Cabots' lead. Ninety years had passed, and fishing fleets had sailed out from Bristol almost every year into the Atlantic since then. They had gone, however, to catch cod, and not – as had the Spanish, the Portuguese and even the French – to establish colonies. Apart from the fact that this put England at a political and economic disadvantage, it worried Hakluyt that the Roman Catholic colonisers were spreading error as they collected gold, pearls and spices. It was time that Native Americans heard the words of Cranmer's Prayer Book and the English Bible, for Hakluyt, like so many notable Elizabethans, was a clergyman – from 1583 to 1588 he was Preacher Hakluyt in Paris, chaplain to Sir Edward Stafford, the English Ambassador there, and in later life he was the rector of Wetheringsett, Suffolk.

The Hakluyts were an old Herefordshire family and it is possible that Richard, as a boy, saw the *Mappa Mundi* in Hereford Cathedral Library, a magnificent late-medieval thirteenth-century depiction of the world, with Jerusalem at its centre. (The word *mappa* means cloth. The medievals had no word for map, and the modern concept of the map is a sixteenth-century phenomenon.) As late as 1520 English sailors possessed no sea-charts 'except a very few drawn by foreigners'.[4] It was a world in which the western hemisphere was unknown, and whose southern hemisphere must, for theological reasons, have been uninhabited. (Since Christ redeemed mankind, divine providence could only have planted human souls within the catchment area, so to say, of the Roman Empire.) God could scarcely have come to Earth and left it again without everyone on the face of the planet having the possibility of knowing about these saving events. This they could only do by living in the northern hemisphere. Whether or not Hakluyt went to Hereford during his boyhood, he grew up in London and was educated at Westminster School. It was in 1568, when he was sixteen, that he went to see his elder cousin, also called Richard Hakluyt, who was a lawyer of the Middle Temple. Lawyer Hakluyt kept a close eye on his often papist legal colleagues, reporting any suspicious goings-on to the government; he was also keenly interested in the new science, in maps and in that system of universal knowledge which they called cosmology: a study of geography, history, political systems, flora and fauna, and anthropology.

When young Hakluyt called on his lawyer cousin he found 'lying open upon his boord [table] certain books of Cosmographie, with an universall Mappe'. The boy was gripped as his cousin showed him maps of the New World. He would have seen a world not unlike the Hereford *Mappa Mundi* in one sense: Jerusalem was still at its centre, but now there was this difference – there was America. If he was looking at Sebastian Münster's *Cosmographia*, he would have seen Americas that had an eastern seaboard, but no Pacific coast. Sea monsters would have gambolled in the Atlantic. Lawyer Hakluyt waved his hand over his collection of maps and told of 'all the knowen Seas, Gulfs, Bayes, Straights, Capes, Rivers, Empires, Kingdomes, Dukedomes and Territories of each part'. He spoke of the riches to be had in these parts, if only merchants would visit them. And then he opened the Bible and pointed to Psalm 107: 'He directed mee to the 23 and 24 verses, where I read, that they which go downe to the sea in ships and occupy by the great waters, they see the works of the Lord, and his wonders in the deepe.'

For the boy Hakluyt, it was an epiphany. He resolved, 'If ever I were preferred to the University, where better time, and more convenient place might be ministred for these studies, I would by God's assistance prosecute that knowledge and kinde of literature, the doores whereof (after a sort) were so happily opened before me.'[5]

Hakluyt went up to Christ Church in 1570, where he would have overlapped with Philip Sidney.[6] William Camden, destined to become a fine antiquary and headmaster of Westminster, was a poor scholar of the college. Richard Carew – who would one day collaborate with Camden on *The Survey of Cornwall* – was up at the same time. Walter Raleigh was at Oriel, Richard Hooker was at Corpus, all at the same time.[7] Unlike Sidney, who went out into the great world, Hakluyt was an archetypal don, destined (apart from his embassy work in Paris, and later withdrawal to married life and a country living) to spend much of his life in the university. To the Greek and Latin that he learned at school he added a mastery of Italian, Spanish, Portuguese and French, and he read *everything* relevant to his obsession, all travel books, works of cosmology, works of geographical discovery.[8]

Hakluyt was one of those influential intellectuals in Elizabethan England who saw that possession of power at sea truly was open to those with the skill and the *panache* to seize it. When Columbus had crossed the Atlantic, the Borgia pope Alexander VI had simply drawn a line down the map of the known world and decreed that it should be divided between Spain and Portugal. Although the Cabots had sailed the Atlantic too, for half a century, the English had been supine in their acceptance of the fact that the ocean, and the lands beyond the Atlantic, were the possession of the superpowers. But unlike the military domination of great land-masses, which requires huge armies, to command the sea needed few ships and much skill.

At the funeral of Charles V in Brussels in 1558 – which must have been one of the most stupendous funerals of all time – there were between 2,500 and 3,000 candles burning around the hearse; all the religious orders were represented; there were fifteen abbots, four bishops and an uncountable procession of European princes and aristocrats. But almost the most impressive item in the entire funeral pageant was a great ship, twenty-four feet in length, twenty tons in weight, encrusted with gilt. There were men inside this gilded ship, who simulated its movement on the high seas. And, noted the awestruck English observer, who wrote back to London to describe it:

> there stood in the sea before the ship two strange monsters, who had either a collar or a bridle about their necks, whereunto was made fast a cord of silk being fast unto the ship and unto them, and so it seemed as if they pulled the ship forwards. Upon the ship from the water to the shrouds were painted all the voyages and victories that the Emperor had done by water. The sea wherein the ship went was stuck full of banners of the Turks and Moors fallen down and lying in the water . . .[9]

Hakluyt's multi-volume account of English travellers and voyagers, and his celebration of English maritime skills, are the literary equivalent of that great ship in the Emperor's funeral. They are an advertisement to the world that England had awakened; that while it had cut itself off from membership of a Europewide Church and declared an independent island-identity, it had also reached out to the great world, to explore and to conquer.

By the 1570s the Elizabethan urge to cross the Atlantic and to establish commercial footholds – in defiance of Spain – had grown stronger than ever. Sir Martin Frobisher made three voyages (in 1576, 1577 and 1578) in quest of the North-West Passage, journeys deflected by the prodigious discovery of gold, and 'everyone' – from the Queen to Sidney and his sister Mary, to Dr Dee – investing money in the venture. The late 1570s had also seen the rise of the fervently ambitious Walter Raleigh.

Unusually tall – six foot or more – handsome, clever and with a broad Devon accent, Raleigh (1552–1618) came from an old West Country family that had come down in the world. The Raleighs who fought at Agincourt, or supplied a thirteenth-century Bishop of Winchester, had now become decayed gentry. Walter Raleigh went up to Oriel College, Oxford, then served abroad in the Huguenot armies of France. In 1578 he was back in England, taking a close interest in the ventures of his half-brother, Sir Humphrey Gilbert, who was fitting out a small fleet to explore America. Gilbert obtained from the Queen the first English colony in North America. There were several voyages, all more or less abortive, with Gilbert aiming to establish a base in Newfoundland.

While these journeys into the American unknown were in progress, Raleigh was making his way into the no-less-dangerous terrain of court politics, and of Ireland. Having fallen in with Leicester and become one of his protégés, Raleigh then fell foul of Burghley's horrible son-in-law, the Earl of Oxford, who somehow persuaded Raleigh to carry a challenge to Philip Sidney. Sir Philip accepted it and was prepared to fight the duel, but Oxford withdrew, and then attempted to embroil Raleigh in a murder plot against Sidney. When Raleigh would have none of it, he found he had made a bitter enemy of Oxford. Perhaps to escape all this unpleasantness, Raleigh went as captain over 100 soldiers to Ireland in 1580, and took part in the bloody engagement at Smerwick, where some Spanish and Italian adventurers were walled up in the Fort del Oro. Some 600 of them were slaughtered by Raleigh and his men. When the Queen heard of it, her only criticism was that Raleigh had spared the officers. Edmund Spenser was also present at Smerwick, and it was probably then that the two poets became friends.

Much of 1580–1 was spent by Raleigh in Ireland: at Cork, and then at Lismore, where he accepted a temporary commission for the governorship of Munster. He was very nearly killed when making his way from Lismore to Cork with a troop of 800 men who were set upon by the Irish, who stabbed the horses of the Englishmen with their knives.[10]

It was in December 1581 that Raleigh came back to London and it was then that he appeared at court in Greenwich and first attracted the notice of the Queen. The story told by Thomas Fuller in his *Worthies* was printed years after Raleigh died, and its authenticity has been doubted. Nevertheless, it is easy to see why it passed into legend: '[He] found the Queen walking still, meeting with a plashy place, she seemed to scruple going therein. Presently Raleigh cast and spread his new plush cloak on the ground; whereon the queen trod gently, rewarding him afterwards with many suits, for his so free and seasonable tender of so fair a foot cloth.'

Whether or not Raleigh put his cloak in a puddle, he certainly attracted the devoted attention of Elizabeth. It was now some years since Leicester had committed the cardinal sin of matrimony, as well as becoming paunchy, white-haired and middle-aged. Hotspur had turned into Falstaff. She needed someone to love extravagantly, capriciously and to the point of enraging the rest of the court. Raleigh, an outrageous flirt, a man of colossal intelligence and enterprise and very deep reserves of humour, was the worthy object of her new-found love. 'Fain would I climb, yet fear I to fall,' he scratched – prophetically – on a windowpane with his diamond ring. She reportedly added, 'If thy heart fail thee, climb not at all.' But if the story is true, she did not mean it. She wanted him to climb.

His half-brother, Sir Humphrey Gilbert, died, and six months later Raleigh was granted Gilbert's patent – the right to colonise America, authorising him to occupy 'countries and territories not actually possessed of any Christian prince'.

The Queen had given him a crumbling palace in which to live, none other than Durham House, the London residence of the Bishops of Durham, overlooking the Thames. This now became his centre of operations to plan the colonisation of America. He enlisted one of his most accomplished Oxford contemporaries, Thomas Harriot, a scientist and mathematician, who was determined that Raleigh's expedition should have what Gilbert's had so lamentably lacked: adequate navigation. Harriot conducted classes in navigation with Raleigh's captains, pilots and masters. Meanwhile, Raleigh got in touch with the younger Richard Hakluyt, who was now 'Preacher Hakluyt', the English chaplain at the embassy in Paris. Hakluyt was engaged to present to the Queen what amounted to a manifesto for a full-scale colonial planting in America: the *Discourse of Western Planting*. Hakluyt presented a number of cogent reasons why America should be invented.

First, it was to prevent the possible calamity of Native Americans being converted to Roman Catholicism. A modern sensibility might smile (or, depending upon temperament, be offended) at this belief, but if one considers the Enlightenment and the American Revolution of 1776 to be the natural prerequisite, it is not so absurd.

Hakluyt's most powerful arguments were economic. Trade with Spain and trade with Russia were sources of Elizabethan wealth. But trade with America could become much, much more lucrative. In Paris he had seen the vast quantities of furs coming from Newfoundland. The resources of America – minerals, spices, and other commodities – were limitless. The passage across the Atlantic was easy, involving no cut across other countries. English colonisation could, he maintained, be humane, by contrast with the Spanish and Portuguese subjugations of the West Indies and South America. In 1580 Philip II was the ruler of all the European settlements so far established in the New World. It was time for a change, and Hakluyt, the geographer of brilliance – geography taking in demography, anthropology and what we should call sociology – saw that Spain's population was falling; England's was rising, and England's time had come. He knew (as did everyone) that getting money out of Queen Elizabeth was like getting blood from a stone, except in the case of a favourite. As a man who had dreamed since adolescence of colonial expansionism, Hakluyt could see that Raleigh, who had captured the Queen's heart, was the ideal man to open her purse-strings.

By April 1584 Raleigh was able to send out an exploratory party, with two ships, captained by Philip Amadas and Arthur Barlowe. They came back from the coast of what is now North Carolina, and from the island of Roanoke, enraptured. English peas planted in the soil had grown fourteen inches in ten days. The Native Americans were 'most gentle, loving and faithful, void of all guile and treason'. To prove it, Barlowe brought two of them with him to London: Manteo and Wanchese. Thomas Harriot set to work with them to see if he could write a grammar of the Algonquin language which they spoke. In order to transliterate their speech, Harriot devised a complicated thirty-six-digit alphabet. He was able to discover, from Manteo, that Roanoke Island was ruled by competing tribal chieftains. The most powerful of these, Wingina, had lately been wounded, which was why Barlowe had not met him on his reconnaissance. Most of Manteo's talk appears to have been of the weapons and tactics of the other tribesmen, but Harriot was able to reconstruct from his conversations with the two Algonquin that Roanoke Island contained no suitable building materials. Hakluyt therefore urged upon the Queen that if they planned to construct a colonial settlement, they would need to transport 'brickmakers, tilemakers, lymemakers, bricklayers, tillers, thackers (with reede, rushes, broome or strawe), sinkers of welles and finders of springs, quarrellers to digge, tile, rough masons, carpinters and lathmakers'. They would also need blacksmiths to 'forge the irons of shovels' and spade-makers that 'may, out of the woods there, make spades like those of Devonshire'. Health would also be a major consideration. The whole enterprise could be destroyed by an epidemic of some as-yet-unknown disease, so it would be necessary to take doctors and what medical supplies then existed. (As always, when reading of medical preparations in history, the modern reader makes the mental note that they would have been more likely to survive without the quackery of the medical men.)

Raleigh flatteringly deemed that 'Virginia', in honour of the Virgin Queen, would be an appropriate name for the first English colony in the New World. He was rewarded with a knighthood for this pretty idea and she named him 'Lord and Governor of Virginia'. Elizabeth could not spare him to make the voyage himself, so that expedition to colonise Roanoke Island was commanded by Raleigh's cousin, the hot-tempered Sir Richard Grenville. ('He was of so hard a complection,' wrote one contemporary, '[that] he would carouse three or foure glasses of wine, and in a braverie take the glasses between his teeth and crash them in peeces and swallow them downe, so that oftentimes the blood ran out of his mouth.')

The other commander, with more responsibility for the actual establishment of the colony, was Ralph Lane. In addition there was Thomas Cavendish, the second Englishman to circumnavigate the world, Thomas Harriot and John White, one of the best cartographers and illustrators of the age. When he came back to London, White was introduced by Hakluyt to Theodore DeBry, who made twenty-three engravings of White's drawings, which one can now see in the British Museum. It is therefore possible for a wider readership to see what the Native American inhabitants of Roanoke looked like. There are pictures of the English arrival. We see the women and children. We see the men making boats, broiling fish, praying and dancing. We see their winter clothes, their hunting clothes, their religious regalia. We see a conjuror, a great lady and a great lord. Raleigh was not what a modern age calls a racist. After Manteo had been baptised, Raleigh appointed him – rather than one of the Europeans on the expedition – Lord of Roanoke, subject only to the *Weroanza*, or chieftain, Queen Elizabeth.[11]

The attempt to settle Roanoke was not a success. When Drake came up the coast in 1586, he found that the surviving English settlers wanted to leave *en masse*. As they departed, 'the weather was so boisterous, and the pinnaces so often on ground, that the most of all we had, with all our Cardes, Bookes and writings, were by the Saylers cast over boord, the greater number of the Fleete being much aggrieved with their long and dangerous abode in that miserable road,' as Lane put it in Hakluyt's *Principall Voyages*.

But the historian A.L. Rowse was right – in his Trevelyan Lectures at Cambridge in 1958, entitled *The Elizabethans and America* – to stress the importance of the Roanoke expedition in the larger history. The colonists made many mistakes, but they learned from them. They came back to England with an enriched knowledge of the flora, fauna and weather conditions; and they learned of the Algonqin way of life. 'We can see the influence of that first experience, as well as some lessons that should have been learned and were not, through all the subsequent attempts until at last permanent settlement was effected at Jamestown in 1607, and even beyond.'[12]

Raleigh's career was marked by triumph and disaster. In the reign of James I he was falsely accused of treason and condemned to death – a sentence that was commuted to long imprisonment in the Tower, where he wrote his patchy, but inspired *History of the World*. Upon his release he was allowed by the King to lead the voyage to Orinoco, which had obsessed him for half a lifetime. During the voyage he lost his son, and his fleet, but he broke the terms by which he had been released by attacking a Spanish town, and he perished on the block – beheaded at Whitehall on the insistence of the Spanish Ambassador in 1618.

Many an adventure had taken place before then. His imprisonment in the Tower by James I was not his first visit. In 1592 the beloved courtier of Elizabeth committed the great sin of falling in love with Elizabeth Throckmorton, one of the Queen's ladies-in-waiting. Just before he died, twenty-six years later, Raleigh said to Bess his wife, 'I chose you, and I loved you in my happiest times.'

19

The Scottish Queen

That summer, of 1586, while Philip Sidney was yet alive and trying to control his angry, sick, unpaid troops garrisoned in Flushing; and while the dome of St Peter's in Rome was at last completed, and the new Pope Sixtus V was offering Sidney's godfather, King Philip II, two million gold ducats to invade England; and while London audiences were being thrilled by Thomas Kyd's *Spanish Tragedy*; and while the thirty-four-year-old Walter Raleigh was returning to England with the first cargo of tobacco, and Sir Thomas Harriot was bringing Europe's first potatoes across the Atlantic; while Camden published his *Britannia* and the religious martyr Margaret Clitherow was being crushed to death in York; while El Greco was dying at Badajoz – the park at Chartley Manor, in the county of Stafford, was as peaceful in appearance as any corner of rural England when the trees are in full leaf and the deer have finished breeding.

Chartley is a beautiful place in the understated mode of Staffordshire. The manor house, which burned down in 1847, must have been of some splendour. It was there in 1575, after the extravagances of Leicester's entertainments at Kenilworth, that the Queen and her court had moved on to enjoy the hospitality of the beautiful Lettice, Countess of Essex. Elizabeth had not, during that visit, realised perhaps, that Lettice and Leicester were lovers. And it was at Chartley that Philip Sidney had first glimpsed Essex's thirteen-year-old sister Penelope Devereux, the Stella of his sonnet-sequence. Much had happened since then. Lettice and Leicester had married. Chartley had been inherited by her son, the young Earl of Essex.

In the high summer of 1586, however, Chartley saw no house-parties, no sonneteers, no pageants, no young lovers. It had become in effect a prison for the Scottish queen. Her custodian was no longer the sympathetic Earl of Shrewsbury, but a former English Ambassador to Paris, Sir Amyas Paulet. He was in all senses a Puritan. (In the chapel at Chartley he held Protestant Bible services rather than use the authorised liturgy of the Church.[1]) He made no secret of his contempt for Mary Stuart, whose custody he undertook at the hated Tutbury in January 1585. Under instruction from Walsingham, he was a much stricter guardian than Shrewsbury had been. None of the Queen's entourage were allowed to leave Tutbury Castle without military escort. He refused to allow her to hang the royal cloth of state over her chair. He wore his hat in her presence and refused to treat her as a royal personage. Her outdoor exercise was severely curtailed and she became ill. Paulet tried to burn a packet sent to Mary from London full of 'abominable trash' – rosaries and pictures marked in silk with the words *Agnus Dei*. He objected to her giving alms to the poor of Tutbury on Maundy Thursday.

The move to Chartley was inspired by considerations of security. The house was moated. Once immured there, Queen Mary was even more restricted than she had been at Tutbury, but at least the house was not malodorous and the prospects were beautiful. And as that high summer ripened, the uncongenial Sir Amyas Paulet allowed her exercise. Someone had sent her a greyhound from Scotland, and it was added to the lapdog entourage of that dog-loving lady. Perhaps it was with a thought of giving this creature some exercise that Sir Amyas permitted the Scottish queen to ride out with him through the park at Chartley on 11 August. They were going to join a buck-hunt at the nearby estate of Tixall on the banks of the Trent. The tall queen was arrayed in a new suit of riding clothes and her mood, which had been fretful most of the summer, was light. She rode faster than Paulet, but paused on her horse to allow him to catch her up. At this point they saw horsemen galloping towards them.

Their arrival perhaps explained the gaiety of Queen Mary's demeanour. Throughout her long life of imprisonment Mary had known of plots to place her on the throne of England, to assassinate Elizabeth and bring the English Church once more into communion with the Bishop of Rome. In the previous months she had been privy to the latest such hare-brained scheme in which Anthony Babington, a rich young gentleman from Dethick in Derbyshire (he had been the Earl of Shrewsbury's page when Queen Mary first arrived in Sheffield), offered to kill Queen Elizabeth and, with six other associates, murder Cecil, Walsingham, Hunsdon and Sir Francis Knollys. With Leicester and a substantial representation of Protestants now in the Low Countries, it was deemed by the conspirators a propitious moment to bring about the longed-for Catholic counter-revolution. And hence Queen Mary's smiles as she waited for Sir Amyas Paulet to catch her up on their ride. The strangers who galloped towards them had not, however, ridden hard from London to tell Mary that she had been proclaimed Queen of England by popular acclamation. Sir Amyas knew their business. The leader of the troop was Sir Thomas Gorges. In his splendid bright-green serge, luminously embroidered,[2] Sir Thomas could have been playing a symbol of summer in a pageant. But he was one of Queen Elizabeth's trusted courtiers. (Trusted, that is, except when he went through that dangerous, familiar courtier's obstacle-course, marriage without the Queen's knowledge or consent. His bride, also a courtier, was the immensely wealthy and beautiful young Marchioness of Northampton, a Swedish noblewoman born Helena Henriksson. Sir Thomas Gorges – one of the richest men in Wiltshire and buried in Salisbury Cathedral when full of years – was briefly English ambassador to the Swedish court.[3]) As soon as Queen Mary saw Gorges, she must have known that here was no romantic Catholic recusant come to pay homage. Gorges, now aged fifty was an incarnation of the court and the Protestant establishment. In a loud voice he said, 'Madame, the Queen my mistress finds it very strange that you, contrary to the pact and engagement made between you, should have conspired against her and her State, a thing which she could not have believed had she not seen proofs of it with her own eyes and known it for certain.'

Mary turned aside and, flustered, began to protest her innocence, but Sir Thomas was explaining that her servants were now to be taken away from her and she would be conducted at once to Tixall.

The Babington Plot was a real one, but what none of the conspirators realised was that Walsingham had known about it from the beginning, and that the consummate spy-master had decided to use it as a way of finally entrapping the Scottish queen. Letters had come in and out of Chartley concealed in beer barrels. They now had written proof that Mary was colluding with the would-be murderers of the Queen of England.

The conspirators were publically executed in the manner that gave the greatest delight to the crowds. As Camden recorded, 'They were all cut down, their privities were cut off, bowelled alive and seeing and quartered.' No wonder Anthony Babington groaned, '*Parce mihi, domine Jesu* (Spare me, Lord Jesus)'[4] as these barbarities were perpetrated.

The fate of the Scottish queen, who lay at the heart of the conspirators' aspirations, was in some senses more delicate. As far as Walsingham, Cecil and Parliament were concerned, the matter was simple: she must die. But she was the deposed sovereign of a foreign state, not an English subject. Her execution would have far-reaching international consequences. It could be seen as justifying the foreign invasion that the Pope had already urged; as providing an incentive for the Armada that Philip II was already trying to assemble. And there was the deep complexity of Queen Elizabeth's attitude.

'Amyas,' she wrote:

> my most faithful and careful servant, God reward thee treblefold in three double for thy most troublesome charge so well discharged. If you knew, my Amyas, how kindly, besides dutifully, my grateful heart accepteth and praiseth your spotless actions, your wise orders and safe regards, performed in so dangerous and crafty a charge, it would ease your travails and rejoice your heart. In which I charge you to carry

this most just thought, that I cannot balance in any weight of my judgement the values that I prize you at, and suppose no treasure to countervail such a faith; and shall condemn myself in that fault, which yet I never committed, if I reward not such deserts. Yea, let me lack what I most need. If I acknowledge not such a merit with a reward *Non omnibus est datum*. Let your wicked murderess know, how with hearty sorrow her vile deserts compelleth these orders; and bid her from me ask God forgiveness for her treacherous dealing towards the saviour of her life many a year, to the intolerable peril of her own; and yet not contented with so many forgivenesses, must fall again so horribly, for passing a woman's thought, much less a prince's; and instead of excusing, whereof not one can serve, it being so plainly confessed by the authors of my guiltless death, let repentance take place; and let not the fiend possess her, so as her better part be lost, which I pray, with hands lifted up to Him that may both save and spill.

With my most loving adieu, and prayers for thy long life, your most assured and loving Sovereign, as thereto by good deserts induced, E.R.[5]

This missive, so characteristic of its sender, is full of drama. It has no doubt that Mary is 'treacherous', and a 'wicked murderess'. The injunction that she should pray for delivery from the fiend implies that Elizabeth meant Mary to die – but how? As she moved, over the next few months, through agonies of indecision, she wanted Mary's death, but 'she wished it could be done in some way that would not throw the blame on her'. Through Walsingham, she let Paulet know that she would be grateful if he would simply murder the Scottish queen. Paulet's reply was – unlike anything the Queen thought, did or said at this juncture – unambiguous: 'It was an unhappy day for him when he was required by his Sovereign to do an act which God and the law forbade. His goods and life were at her Majesty's disposal, but he would not make shipwreck of his conscience, or leave so great a blot to his posterity as shed blood without law or warrant.'[6] But that was all a long way in the future, after Mary Stuart had been tried and condemned to death.

The trial took place at Fotheringhay Castle in Northamptonshire. It was a strong, capacious castle. It was the property of the Crown. It was a compromise. The Council wanted Mary brought to the Tower of London, but Elizabeth, 'variable as the weather' as Burghley complained,[7] would not hear of it. She needed her left hand to be in ignorance of the activities of her right. She who was an anointed queen could not, with a large part of herself, countenance the trial (let alone the execution) of another so anointed. She who had known the horror of imprisonment in the Tower could not bring herself to inflict such a punishment on her cousin, 'wicked murderess' though she was. Though Mary had abdicated when she escaped from Lochleven in 1567, English law had never recognised the abdication. As far as the law of England was concerned, Mary was still the regnant Queen of Scots.

Now, the world waited to see what her fate was to be. Among Mary's letters and papers at Chartley had been found her will, disinheriting her son James for his heresy. This was forwarded to Scotland. It was now a *fait accompli* that James VI would become Elizabeth's Protestant heir, and the Council felt it was imperative to assure James that this was the case. M. D'Esneval, the French Ambassador at Holyrood in Edinburgh, had been doing his best to persuade James that, if his mother were executed, he would be dishonoured throughout Europe and would lose the honour of his English inheritance. Philip II, poised now to invade England, was preparing to be King himself and to govern as the successor.

Meanwhile, the papers discovered at Chartley, and used in evidence at the trials of Babington and his friends, had made public the nature of England's enemies. These young Catholic men revealed how carefully they had been groomed (or radicalised, as we should say) by the priests of their Church. The Jesuits at Reims openly taught the legitimacy, and indeed the merit, of murder. Babington told the court that the murder of Queen Elizabeth had been represented to him as 'a deed lawful and meritorious'. The King of Spain would have agreed. He had said to Mendoza that to kill his sister-in-law would be an enterprise so saintly ('*tan santa empresa*') that it would be of great service to Almighty God.[8]

A number of the Council members themselves would have been embarrassed to discover, among the papers at Chartley, the now-public knowledge that the Scottish queen, the French Ambassador and the King of Spain regarded them – the Earls of Rutland and Cumberland, Lord Montague, Lord Lumley and St John of Bletsoe – as likely to be Catholic sympathisers who would join forces with them in the event of the counter-revolution. It was all the more necessary for *these* Council members to demonstrate their loyalty to Elizabeth and distance themselves from any seditious murder plots.

So it was that the entire Council made the journey to Fotheringhay in mid-October 1586. The castle was built on the hillside over the River Nen, surrounded by trees in their autumn gold. It was not a large castle and it was already filled to the attics by Paulet's soldiers and Mary's entourage. Members of the Council had to find accommodation in village cottages or in the surrounding farms. The peers did not come alone. All these great lords had an entourage, and they were all armed to the teeth; 2,000 horses crowded into the little village.[9]

As had been expected, Mary refused to acknowledge the authority of the court. The Lord Chancellor and Burghley went and remonstrated with her. Burghley said that if she had been imprisoned without cause, there would be justification in her refusal to appear before the court; but Elizabeth had shown a forbearance to her that was without historical precedent. If she refused to attend, 'we will proceed tomorrow in the cause, though you be absent and continue contumacious'.[10] Two clever people confronted one another in their exchange: 'Search your conscience. Look to your honour,' she had rejoined; but Burghley was the cleverer. He knew that Mary's exhibitionism would triumph over caution and that after her years of incarceration in which she had charmed only Lord Shrewsbury and a succession of underlings, she would be unable to resist making an 'impression' on the peerage of England. Nor did she disappoint. From now on, until her death, she was magnificent. But shifty and, as always, transparently dishonest.

When examined next day by Gawdy, a judge of the Queen's Bench, Mary denied knowledge of Babington and his letters. She even denied having written a letter in her own hand to Babington. 'Do not believe that I have consented to the Queen's destruction.' Then she burst into tears. 'I would never make a shipwreck of my soul by conspiring the destruction of my dearest sister.' (The same phrase that Paulet was to use when refusing to murder *her* – it had sunk into *his* soul.) On the second day she pulled rank and said that the words of 'Princes anointed' were not 'evidence' that could be challenged. She also issued a threat: 'The Princes her kinsmen' in Europe might prove too strong for the Reformation. Burghley challenged her. He recapitulated the confessions of Babington and the others. He proved that Cardinal Allen and the Jesuit parsons were even at that moment in Rome petitioning the Pope to persuade the King of Spain to go to war against England. She did not reply directly, but when he had finished she demanded to be heard by Parliament or to speak directly to Queen Elizabeth. Paulet noticed that, now that the proceedings had begun, she seemed fearless. She was enjoying the discomfiture of her judges and she probably knew enough of Elizabeth's character to realise how difficult the Queen of England would find it to decide the fate of the Queen of Scotland.

The commission had no difficulty in finding her guilty, though they prorogued their assembly for ten days and did not pronounce the verdict until they had met in the Star Chamber. What next? Parliament had been summoned for 15 October, but it was prorogued, opening on 29 October (8 November, new style) with Elizabeth not appearing. Her absence was for reasons of decorum. She could not be seen to take part in proceedings against a queen.[11] The Commons had already twice petitioned for the Scottish queen to be beheaded. Now a joint committee of Lords and

Commons made a statement. The Queen of Scots regarded the Crown of England as belonging to herself. Ever since coming to England she had been a canker at its heart, corrupting its people. Mercy shown to her would be a cruelty to all loyal subjects. Sir Christopher Hatton made an impassioned speech. He described Mary as 'the hope of all idolatry', conceived by 'a number of subjects terming themselves Catholics . . . to be a present possessor of the crown of England'. Her manner of life had from earliest years been 'most filthy and detestable'; 'her ambitious mind, grounded in Papistry' had 'thirsted after this crown . . . and our overthrow'. He called for her death. Otherwise 'the Queen's Majesty's most royal person cannot be continued with safety. *Ne pereat Israel, pereat Absalom* – Absalom must perish, lest Israel perish.'[12] Parliament unanimously agreed, and formally demanded that Mary Stuart be executed.

Ever since news of the Babington conspiracy had begun to trickle out in August, England had been in suspense. When the sentence of Parliament was agreed – verbally – by Queen Elizabeth, it was received with rapture by the populace. Not only in the capital, but all over the country, bonfires blazed and bells rang. The bells of London rang for a full twenty-four hours in celebration.

Crowds become ghoulish when there is war-fever in the air. They were not whooping with joy and lighting bonfires because a woman had been condemned to have her head chopped off, so much as exultant that a great threat to their collective nation had been checked.

Elizabeth, as a rule, was intuitively in touch with her people, but not on this occasion. Her feelings were complicated, her emotions were tortured. Still, everyone waited for her to do the final, the legally necessary, thing and issue a death-warrant to enable the execution to take place. And still she continued to receive deputations from abroad: M. de Belièvre, the French Finance Minister, to entreat Elizabeth for mercy. If mercy were not offered, he was commissioned to pass on the fact that the King of France was in warlike mood; so was the Papal Nuncio in Paris, so was Mendoza. If the Scottish queen were executed, not only would the King resent it, but he would see it as a special affront to himself.

'M. Belièvre,' said the Queen, 'does the King your Master bid you use these words to me?'

'Yes, madam. It is his express command.'

But England had spoken – the Council, the Parliament, the people. There could be no doubt what they all wanted. Walsingham had news of other conspiracies hatching, and the longer the Scottish queen lived, the more chance there was of such schemes gathering momentum. Walsingham became ill, an illness exacerbated by the strain; but perhaps there was an element of self-protection here. He was a cunning enough man. He knew Queen Elizabeth well. He knew the danger of being the man who actually put Mary, Queen of Scots's death-warrant under Elizabeth's nose and asking her to sign it.

This task fell to Walsingham's deputy, Mr William Davison. As they entered the month of February (Wednesday, 1 February, old style; 11 February, new style) he went down to Greenwich, that pleasantest of all the Queen's palaces, where, from the windows of her apartments, she could watch the ships sailing down the Thames and out to sea. Davison decided not to deceive Her Majesty, but to numb the sharpness of what was needed by sandwiching the appalling document in a pile of trivial papers that required her signature. It appeared at first as if she knew his game, and wished to play it this way. She made small talk, and remarked upon the brightness of the morning. She signed the papers, all of them, including the death-warrant, casting them to the floor as she did so. Davison must have thought that he was going to get away without having to discuss the matter any further.

But this was not Elizabeth's way. Of course she could not allow the significance of what she had done to pass without notice. She told him to take the warrant at once to the Lord Chancellor and to have it sealed. Only when the Royal Seal was attached to it would it become a fully legal document. She specified the hall, rather than the lawn at Fotheringhay, as a more seemly place for the dreadful deed to happen. Then, with a bitter joke, she told Davison to call on Walsingham with the news, adding that the grief would probably kill him outright.

As Davison withdraw, walking backwards, she called him back. It was then that she raised the possibility of an assassination rather than a formal execution. It would disarm the resentment of Scotland and France; it would remove any necessity that James VI or King Henri III might have for quarrelling with her. She asked him to approach Paulet or Walsingham. Davison was brave enough to tell her that he was sure they would refuse. Nevertheless she insisted that he should do so. As soon as Davison had taken the death-warrant to the Chancellor, a seal was attached to it. The Chancellor did not even bother to read it. The next day Davison received a note from the Queen telling him *not* to go to the Chancellor until she had spoken to him again. Davison hurried back to Greenwich and told the Queen that the document was already sealed and dispatched to Fotheringhay. After a spell of impatiently pacing the room, Elizabeth suddenly walked out on him and left him alone.

Secretary Robert Beale, clerk to the Privy Council, was entrusted with the task of taking the death-warrant to Fotheringhay. He rode hard out of London, broke the journey at Wrest in Bedfordshire and reached

Fotheringhay Castle on the Sunday evening. He then went in search of the Queen's erstwhile guardian, Lord Shrewsbury, and on Monday evening Shrewsbury and the Earl of Kent assembled. A message was sent to the Sheriff of Northamptonshire to be in attendance on Wednesday morning.

Shrewsbury had not been in London for some time. He had taken no part in the Parliament that insisted upon Mary Stuart's death. Nor had he seen her since Amyas Paulet had taken charge of her. It was his task to break to her the awful news. With Kent at his side, on Tuesday, 7 February (17th), he told Mary that she must die in the morning. Perhaps in part because the bearer of these tidings was a man of whom she was fond, and who patently loved her, the emotion of the scene was too much for her. In Paulet's presence she was able to keep up a cool disdain. At the trial she had maintained a lofty swagger. But now, as Shrewsbury told her that she was to be executed, and so soon, she found it impossible to believe. With much tossing of the head she called for her physician. When Shrewsbury and Kent made their awkward withdrawal from her presence, she had broken down altogether and both men were haunted by the spectre of her committing suicide in the night; or, when morning came, of the painful possibility of her having to be dragged to the block.

They need not have feared. When morning came, Mary had composed herself and was ready to put on one last spectacular show.

On that freezing day, 8 February (18th), the hall at Fotheringhay had been arranged as for a drama, with a miniature stage, three feet high and some twelve feet by eight, placed at its upper end; as if the company were expecting a troupe of travelling players. The new wood of the platform had been swathed in black velvet, and there, centre stage, was what they had all come to see: the block. At 7 a.m. nearly 300 spectators took their places: soldiers, local gentry. Outside the castle walls there was a crowd of thousands. At eight, the provost marshal knocked on the outer door of Mary's apartments. There was no answer. Fearing the worst, he hurried to fetch the sheriff. By the time they had returned the doors were open and Mary Stuart stood there in a robe of black satin, with a black satin jacket, looped and slashed and trimmed with velvet. She must have had this costume in readiness. One of her greatest admirers, who witnessed her end, was to compare her demeanour on her last morning to that of a great actress (*'Si le plus parfait tragique qui fust jamais venoit à present avec un desire et soing indicible de représenter sa contenance, paroles et gestes et façon de faire sur un theatre, il pourrut mériter quelques louanges, mais on le trouveroit court'.*[13]). 'If the most perfect tragedian, with indescribable desire and care had tried to represent her face and words and gestures on the stage, he might have won some praise, but he would still have fallen short [from her performance].' She was dressed for her finest role. The cruel, but accurate, Victorian historian James Anthony Froude summed it up by saying, 'she was a bad woman, disguised in the livery of a martyr'.[14]

After some haggling about whether she should be permitted to take her attendants with her, she was allowed six: her physician Burgoyne, Andrew Melville, the apothecary Govian, and her surgeon, with two ladies-in-waiting, Elizabeth Kennedy and Barbara Mowbray (the wife of her secretary Gilbert Curle, whose baby Mary had herself baptised). Speaking in her first language, she said, '*Allons donc*' – 'Let us go' – and, accompanied by the Earls of Shrewsbury and Kent, the procession set off.

When it entered the hall, by a small side door, everyone remarked on Mary's composure. Not a muscle of her face quivered. Round her neck she wore a gold crucifix, and another, made of ivory, was clutched in her ivory-white hands. Beale then mounted the platform and read the death-warrant. Lord Shrewsbury then said, 'Madam, you hear what we are commanded to do.'

'You will do your duty,' she said.

It was now the turn of the Church to speak its bootless lines. In full canonicals, Dr Richard Fletcher stepped forward. This jobsworth parson is chiefly known to history as the father of the dramatist Giles Fletcher, of Beaumont and Fletcher fame. He was to rise through the ecclesiastical ranks, becoming Bishop of Worcester and then of London. When attending to that dignity in 1595, he very nearly lost it again – infuriating the Queen by marrying a widow. (How often she was made angry by marriages!) His must be one of the first recorded smoking mortalities. It occurred a year after he became Bishop of London, when he was fifty-one years old: puffing away, he removed his pipe from his lips to remark to his servant, 'Boy. I die', which he did.

When he attended upon the execution of Mary, Queen of Scots, he was merely the Dean of Peterborough. Clearing his throat and making a low bow, he began, 'Madam, the Queen's most excellent Majesty . . .' Fletcher had no notes to help him if he stumbled and, although he had preached at her trial, he was now lost for words. 'Madam,' he began again, and again words failed him. He was only two or three years her junior – she was forty-three – and the inherent shockingness of what was about to happen was surely increased by the fact that she was a beautiful woman, with coils of auburn hair under her coif-caps, and with gold glinting on her white throat. 'Madam, the Queen's most excellent Majesty.'

Again, Fletcher failed. Though nothing could have been further from the truth, it was as if this sturdily Protestant figure was deliberately giving her a cue.

'Mr Dean', she supplied with pious courtesy. 'I am a Catholic, and must die a Catholic. It is useless to attempt to move me, and your prayers will avail me but a little.'

Suddenly Fletcher found his voice and he bellowed, 'Change your opinion, Madam! Repent of your sins, settle your faith in Christ. By him be saved.'

'Trouble not yourself further, Mr Dean', she replied. 'I am settled in my own faith, for which I mean to shed my blood.'

'I am sorry, Madam,' Shrewsbury interjected, 'to see you so addicted to Popery.'

And the Earl of Kent added, 'That image of Christ you hold there will not profit you if he be not engraved in your heart.'

She did not reply. This was a moment when such disputations were entirely inappropriate. The dean began to pray, and we are told that the crowd joined in, so it must have been some familiar form such as 'Our Father'. The Queen of Scots, however, raised her voice above his and recited the penitential Psalms in Latin, translating them into English as she did so. Then, in English, she prayed aloud for her holy father the Pope, and for the Church, and for the Queen of England in whose murder both Mary and the Pope had conspired. She called on King Philip not to forget her in death and, kissing her crucifix, she cried, 'Even as thy arms, O Jesus, were spread upon the cross, so receive me into Thy mercy and forgive my sins.'

Now she was ready for the final scene of the melodrama. All eyes were on the stage. Shrewsbury's were streaming with tears. The ladies helped her, with conspicuous care, to remove her lawn veil without disturbing the magnificent auburn tresses. Then began a spectacular striptease. Off came the black robe and the black jacket, to reveal Mary to be dressed in crimson satin, blood-red from head to toe. Hers was the only splash of colour on that black stage surrounded by ink-black-clad figures. Barbara Mowbray bound Mary's eyes with a handkerchief. With a smile, Mary waved to her ladies: *Adieu, au revoir!* Then she sank to her knees and recited in Latin the psalm *In te, Domine, confide* – 'In Thee, O Lord, have I put my trust.' Finally, feeling blindly for the block, she declared the words of the Compline psalm that Christ Himself is said to have repeated as He died on the Cross. *In manus tuas, Domine, tuas, commendo animam meam* – 'Into Thy hands, O Lord, I commend my spirit.'

The axe fell, but the practised headsman sent specifically from the Tower of London, like the Dean of Peterborough, was disconcerted by Mary. He wavered. The axe hit the knot in her handkerchief, scarcely breaking her skin. When Louis XIV was cut for the stone, without any anaesthesia, one of his attendant lords who held his hand was merely aware of a very faint tightening of the royal grip as the surgeon's knife penetrated the royal innards. Mary Stuart showed comparable royal courage on the scaffold. She uttered not a squeak, she moved not a millimetre. The axeman tried again and this time he was successful. He moved to the next stage in the tradition of these gruesome procedures. Reaching for the luxuriant auburn hair, he intended to hold up the victim's head. But the hair, like so much about her, was fake. He found himself ridiculously holding up a red wig. What rolled away from him on the platform was not what the audience had believed themselves to have seen only seconds before – not the head of a still-young beauty, but the grizzled, close-cropped grey head of a prematurely aged crone. With what seemed paranormal grotesqueness, its lips were still moving for a few seconds, as if determined to have the last word. From her skirts there escaped the Skye terrier that had been her companion to the end. It clung whimperingly to the corpse and had to be dragged away.

For the joint perpetrators of this melancholy deed were determined that Mary should not be allowed her wish to be regarded as a Catholic martyr. The gauze veil that she had worn to be beheaded was preserved by one of her ladies and eventually passed to her descendant, the last of her doomed Stuart line, Henry, Cardinal of York. The prayer book and rosary that she had with her on the scaffold were bequeathed to Anne, wife of Philip, Earl of Arundel, and they may be seen to this day at Arundel Castle, the Duke of Norfolk's seat in Sussex. These survive as what Catholics term 'secondary relics'. Not a speck of her actual blood, flesh or bone was allowed to survive for the veneration of the faithful. The castle gates were kept firmly locked to prevent the intrusion of the mob. The blood-stained block was burned. All items of clothes and all personal belongings were burned or scoured. The executioners were tipped with cash to compensate them for loss of the victim's jewels, a normal prerequisite of the job. The little dog, its fur matted with Mary's blood, was washed and washed again. It pined away for sorrow and starved itself to death, refusing all inducements to eat.

Mary's body was stripped and swabbed and embalmed. The heart and other organs were secretly buried somewhere in the castle – no one knows where. The body, on Walsingham's specific order, was wrapped in a wax winding sheet and enclosed in a heavy lead coffin. It was not buried for more than five months – on 30 July – at Peterborough Cathedral. The ceremony was conducted according to the rites of the English Church. She was accompanied by a procession of a hundred mourning widows, five heralds, hooded and tabarded – and a seemly proportion of the nobility. In Peterborough Cathedral, near that other unfortunate queen, Catherine of Aragon, Mary lay until her son, James VI of Scotland, became James

I of England. In 1612 she was moved in state to Westminster Abbey and commemorated by a splendid white-marble tomb. When Dean Stanley, a keen antiquarian, opened up the Stuart vaults in Westminster Abbey in 1867, he found Mary's coffin against the north wall of the vault. He did not open it. Mary in death was surrounded by the coffins of her descendants: her grandson, Henry, Prince of Wales, who died prematurely; her granddaughter, Elizabeth of Bohemia, the Winter Queen; Rupert of the Rhine, her great-grandson, who was such a gallant cavalry officer in the Civil Wars; and dozens of tiny coffins – the first ten children of James II and the heart-rending eighteen dead babies of Queen Anne. The whole vault is yet another reminder of the extraordinary misfortune that hovered over the Stuart dynasty. Mary's son, James I, eluded the search of the Victorian dean until he was eventually found in the tomb of Henry VII.[15]

So much for Mary Stuart, resplendent in her death. As a political act, her execution was self-justificatory. 'The entire Catholic organisation as directed against England was smitten with paralysis; and the Queen found herself, when the invader arrived at last, supported by the loyal enthusiasm of an undivided nation.' Froude's jingo-analysis is true.[16]

But it is not the whole truth. The beheading of the Scottish queen was a tragic, as well as a grisly, act, and it showed Queen Elizabeth in an eerie light. Seen as a chess-game between Walsingham on the one hand and the King of Spain on the other, the removal of the Scottish queen from the board is a masterstroke. In the more nuanced psychological rivalry between Mary Stuart and Elizabeth Tudor, the drama of Fotheringhay was a very hard act to follow. And in all her roles in the play, Elizabeth writhed with mixed feelings, nearly all of them painful: in her role as childless old maid upstaged by the three-times-married, ten years younger woman who left behind her a male heir; in her role as crowned head, deeply shocked that another monarch could be so easily removed; in her role of quasi-Catholic who hated the Protestantism of Fletcher or Walsingham much more than she hated the Romish ways of her cousin; in her role as a woman who, in spite of her imperiousness, her temper and her bursts of cruelty, could not but recoil at the thought of that castle hall, full of men, gathered for the ritual judicial killing of her younger, female cousin.

Lord Talbot, the younger son of the grief-stricken Earl of Shrewsbury, was entrusted with the task of taking the news to London. He accomplished the journey down the muddy winter roads from Fotheringhay in an impressive twenty-four hours. The Queen was herself mounting her horse – she was going out hunting – when Talbot arrived at Greenwich Palace. Elizabeth did not see the young man, who was therefore able to find Burghley before confronting his monarch. By the time the Queen came back from hunting the whole palace was abuzz with the news, and it had spread round London before she was officially told. By three o'clock in the afternoon, as she came back from her ride, she could hear all the bells of London joyfully clanging across the Thames, so she knew. Those who were with her remarked on the fact that her composure was quite undisturbed.

The absurd Sir Christopher Hatton, in his speech to the Commons demanding Mary's death, had likened her sacrifice to the necessary death of King David's perfidious son Absalom. And Elizabeth, having received the news of Mary's death with an apparent absence of emotion, decided to pull out all the *vox humana* stops and stage a lamentation worthy of David's *Absalom, Absalom, O my son Absalom*.

20

The Armada

Nothing illustrates more vividly than the story of the Spanish Armada how radically Elizabethan history has changed in the last fifty years. From the time of the crisis itself, right down into the mid-twentieth century, it was axiomatic that this was one of the key events of English history – ultimately of world history. Had the Spanish plans succeeded, what would have happened? Queen Elizabeth would have been killed. The Reformation in England would have been reversed, the Church of England abolished and the English returned to Roman Catholicism. English colonial adventures in the Americas would have been curtailed, or allowed to continue only in collaboration with their Spanish masters. The land now called the United States, if it existed at all, would be even more largely Spanish-speaking than it is today. Spanish would be its official language. It is highly improbable that a Spanish tradition would have produced anything remotely resembling the American Declaration of Independence or the Constitution of the United States, which so visibly derive from John Locke and the Protestant-rationalist traditions of late seventeenth-century England. For the greatest of all English historians of the sixteenth century, James Anthony, John Locke and James Froude, it was obvious that the Armada was a stupendous event in European history, the pivotal battle between an independent fledgling nation-state and a pan-European Habsburg autocracy; between Protestantism and Catholicism. Froude wrote when the British Empire was reaching its zenith, and even those readers (a distinct minority in those days) who questioned the merits of Britain, Protestantism or Empire would have seen the Armada in the same terms that he did.

What was noticeable about the quatercentenary of the Armada in 1988 was how radically all this had changed. True, there was a splendid exhibition at the National Maritime Museum at Greenwich, with contemporary maps, portraits, gold medals – as well as haunting recoveries from the wrecks of Armada ships: shoes, buckles, beads, a boatswain's pipe, spoons, beakers, talismans, pendants, a brazil nut. We could find, among this multiplicity of detail, an empathy with the men and boys on their fighting ships, but the bigger picture was something that, if we saw it at all, embarrassed us. Four hundred years rolled away and allowed us to imagine the young hands, clutching the daggers, swords, pikes and halberds on display. But for many visiting the exhibition, the thought of

'The great Globe itself' (*The Tempest* Act IV.ii) – when a carpenter named Burbage built the first theatre in London he made possible the prodigious renaissance in the drama which produced Marlowe and Shakespeare.

Hunting and outdoor sports were a passion for Elizabethans, most of whom lived in the country.

Sir Henry Lee, the Queen's Champion, stage-managed nearly all the great Accession Day tilts and other examples of royalist pageantry.

Lettice Knollys, a mischievous beauty, was a Boleyn cousin of the Queen. She was by turns Countess of Essex (and mother of the Queen's last favourite) and second wife of the Earl of Leicester (the Queen's childhood friend and great love).

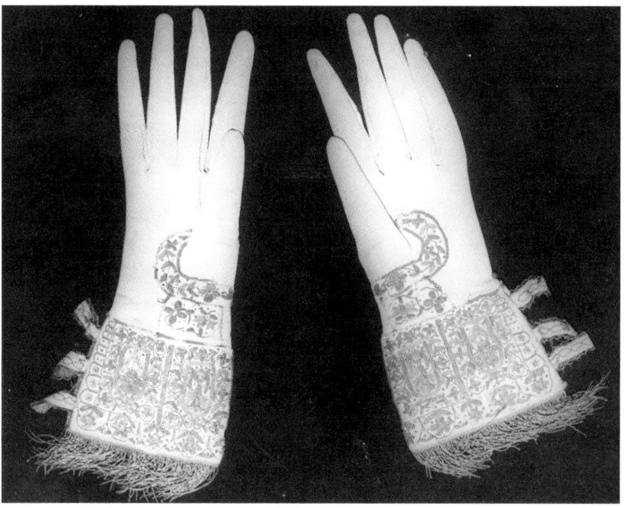

Queen Elizabeth's extensive and elaborate wardrobe was largely paid for by her admirers and courtiers. A pair of gloves would be the least she would expect as a New Year's present from a member of her court.

A satirical picture which depicts Spain losing control of the Low Countries. Philip II, by now an old man, is barely in control of the Cow (the Dutch) who is being surreptitiously fed by Elizabeth.

It was the great era of domestic building. Longleat was one of the first great houses not to be fortified, a sign that the civil wars of the past were over.

Hardwick Hall in Derbyshire was a sign of the enormous wealth of its proprietress, Bess of Hardwick. It is also a wholly original, modern piece of architecture, anticipating the modern movement in its dazzling use of glass.

The Middle Temple Hall was the scene not only of many legal dinners but also of plays. Shakespeare's *Twelfth Night* probably had its first performance here.

The 16th century religious legacy. (*Above*) Pope Pius V, whose tomb is shown, excommunicated Elizabeth and called Catholics to depose her, if necessary by violence. (*Right*) Mary Queen of Scots became the (willing) figurehead for Catholic rebellion. (*Below*) On her state visit in May 2011, Queen Elizabeth II, with bowed and silent head, acknowledged the disaster of English attitudes to Ireland since Queen Elizabeth I.

Two luminaries. (*Above*) Dr Dee, mathematician, mage, and book-collector, was one of the first to popularize the astronomical discoveries of Copernicus, and coined the phrase 'the British Empire'. (*Left*) Richard Hooker, whose statue dominates the close of Exeter Cathedral, was a great philosopher and theologue who in a sense invented what is today called Anglicanism.

In this portrait, the Queen, looking particularly Welsh, fingers pearls. She loved jewels, but the picture is full of symbolism. The pearls are loot from the Spanish Main, used as a symbol of her virgin purity.

the conflict in which the warriors were engaged will have only accentuated a modern sense of the futility of war. Most Christian opinion of the modern age would emphasise the closeness of Catholics and Protestants, rather than their fundamental opposition. As for the secularists who dominate academic discussion in modern Britain and Europe, there could be but small interest in a quarrel between two sides of an outworn creed. If the Armada's religious aspect made it arcane in 1988, its political importance seemed to have been swept away by history. Great Britain and Spain were not enemies, and had not been enemies for hundreds of years. They were now part of the European Union, which might one day transmogrify into a collection of federalist states. This was scarcely the moment to be banging the drum and celebrating the isolation of England from Europe, the successful defeat of a great European power by a small island race.

Perhaps the *ne plus ultra* of Armada revisionism in 1988 was achieved by Felipe Fernández-Armesto, whose *The Spanish Armada: The Experience of War in 1588* did not merely tell the story from the Spanish point of view. It attempted to belittle the incident altogether. Had it not been for the bad weather blowing the Armada off-course, Fernández-Armesto provocatively maintained, it would not have been seen as a 'defeat' at all. 'While the two hostile fleets confronted each other, the balance of success was evenly poised between them.' What survives, he claimed, is 'the shared experience of the muddle and misery of war that was common to the antagonists of both sides. The Armada, seen in this light, is less 'important' than our ancestors supposed.[1]

Though one assumes that Fernández-Armesto wrote his book partly as a tease – and he remains a wonderful historian – his book now reads, more than twenty years on, as a joke that slightly misfires, as an example of the difficulty felt by modern people in confronting the Elizabethan phenomenon. Yes, there must seem to us something grotesque about a question of narrow theology being settled by a great sea battle. Equally, we can not easily empathise either with the imperialism of Spain or with the chauvinism of the Little Englanders who resisted Spain. But distaste for Habsburg autocracy or Little Englandism, and bafflement at fighting a war over the Eucharist, is in danger of blinding us to the facts. This *was* a stupendous enterprise. Those who took part in it had no doubts about that. And, however unfashionable Protestantism and nationalism might have become, the defeat of the Spanish Armada was an event of supreme historical consequence. It was also, with the possible exception of the summer of 1940, one of the most exciting summers in English history.

Philip II had every reason to believe, when the enterprise was set in hand, that a display of gigantic naval strength by Spain would finally put a stop to the religious and political menace (as he saw it) of Protestantism both in Britain and in the Netherlands. We know precisely how he regarded himself vis-à-vis his sister-in-law's kingdom. One of the siege guns raised from the wreck of the *Trinidad Valencera* in Glenagivney Bay, County Donegal, in 1971 is a splendid cannon, cast by Rémy de Halut in 1556. It is emblazoned with his royal arms, the upper and lower quarters dexter of the coat being the arms of England. The legend – *Philippus Rex* – spoke of him as King of England, which (in his own eyes and that of his wife) he had been, and would be again. In his monkish apartments in the Escurial a frescoed mural depicted the huge Spanish fleet, commanded by Don Álvaro de Bazán, 1st Marquis of Santa Cruz, in his mighty victory of Terceira in 1582. Though greatly outnumbered, Santa Cruz beat a combined force of French, English and Portuguese ships and annexed the Azores for the Spanish Empire. It was a mid-Atlantic triumph to match Don John of Austria's Mediterranean victory in Lepanto in 1571. Don John, Philip II's illegitimate younger brother, overcame the Turkish fleet and checked the westward advancement of Islam for generations. (Santa Cruz commanded the reserve fleet at Lepanto – 100 ships, eighty of them galleys, and 21,000 fighting men.)

With a fighting force of this kind, Philip II had every reason to be optimistic that, to add to the triumphs of Lepanto and Terceira, he could achieve a victory in the English Channel, moor a Spanish fleet in the Thames and bring the Elizabethan Age to an ignominious conclusion.

But he did not have a fighting force of this kind. First, Philip himself, now aged sixty-one, was an *old* sixty-one. One of the more vivid exhibits in the Armada exhibition of 1988 – though actually it was a 'repro' from the Patrimonio Nacional, the Escurial museum – was an invalid chair in which the gout-ridden, prayer-obsessed Philip spent much of each day.[2] Santa Cruz was a year older than the King. For years he had been obsessed with schemes for invading England. He and his king spent more and more time planning. Santa Cruz wanted a navy of 556 ships, and 200 flat-bottomed barges for transporting soldiers – a total, when he had added in all the vessels, of 796; he wanted around 65,000 soldiers and 30,000 sailors. He calculated for a long haul (six to eight months at sea, with all the victuals carried on transport ships): 373,337 hundredweight of biscuits, 22,800 hundredweight of bacon, 46,800 pipes of wine, and so on. While Santa Cruz took charge of the operation at sea, the land troops would be commanded by the young Duke of Parma, who had proved himself to be such a successful strategist against the combined Dutch and English forces in the Netherlands.

As Parma, Santa Cruz and the King discussed the plan through 1587 and early 1588, it changed in its details, but the fundamental aim was clear. The Armada of fighting ships would keep the English navy at bay and escort Parma's army of 30,000 men across the Channel (probably from Dunkirk) in their barges. An advance party of ships and troops would, if possible, have secured Kent and London. A flying column of soldiers would have captured and killed the Queen and her council of ministers.

By the end of January 1588, Santa Cruz's plans were going badly. He had by then decided that fifty galleons were needed to beat the English. He had mustered only thirteen – some of the ships came from Spain and Portugal, some from the shipyards of Dubrovnik (known as Ragusa in those days). Many of the ships he had commandeered were in poor shape, and nearly all were armed merchant ships rather than purpose-built war ships. Philip was by now harrying Santa Cruz and insisting that the Armada set out from Lisbon harbour on 15 February, even if the fleet was much smaller than intended. Santa Cruz failed to meet the deadline. In fact, he died on 9 February at Lisbon.

This was a disaster for Spain. Santa Cruz had been a seaman all his life, and he would have been a match even for Drake, Hawkins and Howard, had he been in command of the fleet when it entered the English Channel. Philip's instinct, in the face of this calamity, was to turn to the next generation. The Duke of Medina Sidonia (Alonso Pérez de Guzmán) was one of the grandest, and richest, aristocrats in Spain. Had Philip appointed a commander from among the Spanish naval 'top brass' he might have excited the envy of rivals. Any Spaniard would serve under Medina Sidonia, but for the duke himself it was an unwelcome assignment. He was not a sailor, and he wrote to the King attempting to wriggle out of it: 'But, Sir, I have not health for the sea, for I know by the small experience that I have had afloat that I will soon become seasick and have many humours.' As for the Armada as a whole, 'I do not understand it, know nothing about it, have no health for the sea, and no money to spend upon it.'[3]

The last point was not really true. What the letter really meant was that Medina Sidonia did have money – one of the King's reasons for appointing him – but did not wish to waste it on a scheme that his native intelligence told him would be difficult, if not impossible. Yet in obedience to his royal master, and three months later than planned, the Armada sailed from Lisbon harbour on 9 May. It was a bright, choppy day, ideal sailing weather for the ships, which in the end numbered a mere 134: four quadroons of merchantmen, twenty-three freighters or supply ships. Four galleys – oared slave-ships that had seen action at Lepanto, seventeen years before – and then a motley fleet of *fregates* and *zabras* (small frigates). They must have made not only a splendid sight, but also a beautiful noise.

The Duke of Medina Sidonia was a religious man and he was ever mindful of the essentially religious purpose of this act of war. All but the smallest vessels had a priest aboard, but Spanish regulations strictly forbade the saying of Mass on board ship, for fear that a gust of wind could blow away the consecrated Host, or upset the chalice of Christ's blood. However, the Divine Office would be, and was, sung daily – that is, the recitation of the psalms in the seven monastic hours of the Church – Matins, the night-office, Lauds before and Prime at dawn, the day-offices of Terce, Sext and None, and the evening prayers of Vespers. By Spanish maritime tradition, these services would be sung by the ships' boys. In addition to the monastic offices, Medina Sidonia specified that they should sing to the Blessed Virgin, the Stella Maris, Star of the Sea: 'Every morning at daybreak the boys, according to custom, shall sing their Salve at the foot of the mainmast, and at sunset the Ave Maria. On some days, and every Saturday at least, they shall sing the Salve with the Litany' [of our Lady].[4] If we had come alongside the Armada, it would have been like chancing upon a floating cathedral or college choir, the boys' voices piercing the wind, the flapping ropes and sails, the crashing of waves on the prow, blending with the moan and wail of gulls.

A fair wind took them at a rate of about four knots to Finisterre, but then Medina Sidonia met his first major disaster. The supplies – casks of meat, fish, vegetables and water, some of them packed in February – were now rotten, and dysentery had broken out among the men. Medina Sidonia seriously questioned whether the expedition could continue. They spent a month regrouping in the large harbour at Corunna and revictualling from the rich surrounding farmland of Galicia. Although the duke still warned the King that he should 'deeply ponder . . . what you are undertaking', the royal command was absolute. The Armada was to go ahead. At the beginning of July a Spanish pinnace, commanded by Ensign Esquival, came into Corunna harbour having rounded up a dozen English ships off the Scilly Isles. He had taken prisoner some English sailors and two Irish priests. From them he learned that Drake (which for him was a synonym for the Royal Navy) had 180 ships in three squadrons, one in Plymouth and two to the east of Dover. This young Spanish ensign had sailed within sight of the coast of Cornwall and seen Land's End and St Michael's Mount. It seemed like a good omen. On 20 July Sidonia had a meeting of all the Spanish pilots. They assured him that the weather was favourable. By daybreak the wind had dropped, and by 26 July, having sailed out of harbour, they were becalmed. It was not a good look-out – after the calm came gales, which raged for two days, but by 29 July a somewhat scattered, seasick and shaken flotilla had assembled off the Scillies. In the *San Martin*, Medina Sidonia's flagship, the duke ordered a huge banner to be unfurled. It depicted Christ crucified with his Virgin Mother, on one side, and the Magdalen on the other. The banner had been blessed by the Pope itself, who had decreed that the expedition would be deemed a success if, and only if, it effected an invasion of England. There could be no ambiguity. If God wished England to abjure her heresy, this most Catholic of navies would surely succeed in its purpose.

On that Friday, 29 July 1588, Sir Francis Drake was in Plymouth with the High Admiral of the Fleet, Charles, Lord Howard of Effingham. The legend, one of the most charming in English history, is that the two men were playing bowls on Plymouth Hoe, with its clear views of the English Channel, when the news reached them. It was brought by Thomas Fleming, captain of the fifty-ton pinnace *Golden Hind* (*not* Drake's old ship, which sailed around the world, but another). He had sighted the advance squadron commanded by Don Pedro de Valdés. Drake is supposed to have remarked, 'We have time enough to finish the game and beat the Spaniards too.'[5]

The story first saw print in a pamphlet of 1624 – that is, within living memory of the event. Obviously there is no way of proving the truth of the story. In Victorian times, when it was most popular, it inspired the painting of the event by Seymour Lucas, in which the greatest mariners of the Elizabethan Age were assembled rather like a public-school cricket XI, effortlessly confident of beating Johnny Spaniard. Richard Grenville, Humphrey and Martin Frobisher, Francis Drake, Howard of Effingham, John and Richard Hawkins, Walter Raleigh and the rest might be wearing sixteenth-century costume, but they could be Flashman and pals about to run up a century for Rugby against Winchester.

But the fact that the story appealed to public-school adventurers of a later age does not necessarily mean that it is substantially false. As Garrett Mattingley remarked in his masterly, and unsurpassed, *The Defeat of the Spanish Armada* (1959): 'The words are like Drake; they have his touch of swagger and his flair for the homely jest to relieve a moment of tension. Also it would be quite like Drake to say the first word, even though his commander-in-chief stood at his elbow. And finally, it would be like Drake, too, to appreciate a second or two before any of the others and be amused by the fact that there was indeed time.'[6]

It had been Drake's idea that spring to attack the Armada when it still lay in Lisbon harbour. Excitedly, incoherently, ungrammatically, he had written to the Queen:

> Your Majesty shall stand assured, if the fleet come out of Lisbon, as long as we have victual to live upon that coast, with God's assistance, they shall be fought with . . . The advantage of time and place in all martial actions is half a victory, which being lost is irrecoverable . . . Wherefore, if your Majesty will command me away with those ships which are here already and the rest to follow with all possible expedition, I hold it, in my poor opinion, the sweet and best course.

Even had the weather made such an Elizabethan 'Pearl Harbor' possible, it was never logically feasible. As the Spanish had already discovered, the victualling of a vast navy – in those days before refrigeration, before aircraft-carriers, before credit banking – was a formidable challenge. The cheese-paring queen, before, during and after the Armada crisis, was extremely unwilling to supply her navy with adequate funds for ship-building, and the additional costs of wages and victuals were a constant pain to her. When Walsingham's intelligence suggested that Santa Cruz might be prepared to sail back from Lisbon at Christmas 1587, Elizabeth had grudgingly mobilised an army, but after the Spanish admiral's death she speedily demobilised it. She reduced the navy to a reserve fleet, well into the spring of 1588. Four galleons and a small number of pinnaces were all that were required to patrol the coast of Flanders, and she and Burghley gleefully contemplated that they were saving £2,433 18s. 4d. per month by keeping the navy confined to dock.

She did, however, allow land defences to be prepared. Burghley, by instinct rather than as a result of detailed secret intelligence, was exactly of Philip II's mind – that the key to the whole campaign lay in the Armada's ability to reach the mouth of the Thames. Philip imagined them reaching Margate and thereby holding the English fleet at bay or dividing it, as Parma's barges, with their thousands of Spanish boats, sailed up the Thames into London. Burghley had precisely the fear that the Spaniards would capture London and said he was unable to sleep for worry about the Thames defences. £1,470 was spent on a boom across the river, which collapsed under its own weight. It was the brainchild of an Italian engineer, Federigo Giambelli. Though his Thames barrier did not work, his mere presence on the English side was a major propaganda coup, rightly calculated to put terror into the Spanish. For Giambelli's most-celebrated contribution to the history of warfare were the 'hell-burners' of Antwerp, fire-ships that were in effect huge floating bombs, which would be used with deadly effect as the Armada crisis deepened.

But – at first – as Drake and Howard of Effingham and the others (whether or not playing bowls) looked out from the Devon coast, both sides remained in ignorance about the other's precise intentions. Would the Spanish ships try to put into an English harbour? At Plymouth? At Weymouth? Would they plan to engage, by grappling with the English ships at close hand, or pound them with heavy guns? Would the English fleet – this was one of the Queen's dreads – sail out to fight the Spanish and, deflected by wind or mist, sail past them, leaving the seas defenceless? The whole of southern England was on alert. Trenches were dug across fields. Forts were repaired. Beacons were constructed at strategic points all down the coast from the Lizard to Kent, and up from hillside to hillside throughout the island, to the Midlands, to Nottingham, to Durham, to York. On that night, 29 July, the fires were lit:

> From Eddystone to Berwick Bounds, from Lynn to Milford Bay,
> That time of slumber was as bright and busy as the day;
> For swift to east and swift to west the ghastly war-flames spread –
> High on St Michael's Mount it shone, it shone on Beachy Head.
> Far on the deep the Spaniards saw, along each southern shire,
> Cape beyond cape in endless range, those twinkling points of fire.[7]

But although the fires alerted the English to the Armada's arrival, and although as the fires blazed and the church bells rang, the English land army mustered at rallying points, led in each county by the Lord Lieutenant, there followed nearly a fortnight of absolute suspense. It was impossible for those on land – for the English who embraced themselves for invasion, or the Duke of Parma encamped in Dunkirk, or the Pope in Rome, or the Queen immured in St James's Palace – to know what was happening at sea. For eleven days the fate of the Elizabethans lay in the hands of Poseidon, god of the sea, though human beings had some part in reacting to his caprice. Notable among the heroes of the drama must be named John Hawkins.

It was through the mechanisms of Burghley that Hawkins, in 1577, had become Treasurer of the navy. It was an inspired choice. Hawkins had spent his young manhood as a privateer. He had a long, and sometimes painful, experience of life at sea. He was not alone in pioneering new designs of fighting ships for the Queen's navy,[8] but he was a pivotal figure. If Sir William Winter had streamlined ships, replacing demi-cannon with more accurate long-range culverin; if royal shipwrights Peter Pett, Matthew Baker and Richard Chapman[9] are now credited with the design of some of the new ships, it was Hawkins – the sailor, the entrepreneur, the navigator, the money-lover and the millionaire – who saw through the reform of the Elizabethan navy. He, who had left behind the cumbrous old *Jesus of Lübeck* in the Caribbean in 1569, had learned the hard way that the majestic old wooden castles, useful in close fighting, were cumbrous and slow when there was a need to pursue the enemy or escape his fire-power. By 1588 two-thirds of Elizabeth's navy comprised streamlined galleons, with greatly improved sail plans. It was this navy that was able to confront the Armada. Technology alone did not win the war, but it was a vital ingredient in the victory. Thanks to Hawkins, the English navy had made a fundamental psychological adjustment. It saw ships as gun-carriers, whereas the cumbrous old ships accumulated by Medina Sidonia were seen as troop-carriers. Victory, if the Spanish achieved it, was to be achieved by boarding tactics, which the new English vessels – with their speed of escape, longer-range fire-power and lower height – made all the less easy.

Nevertheless, when both fleets confronted one another, in the dawn of 30 July, they saw a formidable sight. The English saw that Medina Sidonia had drawn up his ships in the crescent battle-formation that had made the Spanish navy such an unbeatable force at Lepanto and Terceira. No one on the English side knew (as was obvious to the Spanish captains) that many of their ships would be useless in battle. It must have been the sheer size of the Spanish fleet, this huge crescent stretching across the sea from the Cornish coast, that sent a tremor into the hearts of the English sailors.

The first engagement took place off the Eddystone rock, with Howard's *Ark Royal* crossing the stern of the rearmost Spanish ship, de Leiva's *Rata Coronada*, and Drake in the *Revenge*, Hawkins in the *Victory* and Frobisher in the *Triumph* assailing the other side of the formation. The English did not come out of the exchange very well, and they had failed to check the stately advance of the Spaniards along the Channel. The English sailors were still uncertain of Spanish intentions. The two concerns uppermost in their minds were the possibility of the Spanish landing (they were beyond Plymouth now – but in Weymouth?) and the uncertainty of engagement at sea (when would the Spanish ships attack?). Sidonia's prime concern – as we know – was to reach Calais or Dunkirk and meet up with the forces of Parma.

By the time they had all reached Portland Bill the weather had turned squally and we must assume visibility was poor. Drake made an extraordinary blunder, detaching himself from the main fleet and challenging an innocent German merchant ship, which loomed up out of the mist. By the time he had realised his mistake and rejoined the Lord Admiral, they found themselves a cable-length away from the *Rosario*, Don Pedro de Valdés's flagship, which had been captured during the night by Captain John Fisher. The *Rosario* had already suffered damage by colliding with another Spanish ship. Although Drake had behaved foolishly during the night, Don Pedro apparently considered it something of an honour to surrender to the celebrated vice admiral. He himself enjoyed some hero-worship – among both sides – when he was imprisoned in England.

Just south of the Needles on 2 August, following a council of war, Howard divided the English navy into four squadrons, commanded respectively by Howard himself, Drake, John Hawkins and Martin Frobisher. In what was now a calm sea, Hawkins's squadron, followed by Howard's, attacked the Spanish ships. The battle intensified as they drew near the Solent, whose eastern entrance had been recommended by King Philip as a good place for emergency anchorage, a place possibly to await Parma's invasion force. Drake and Hawkins tried to push the Spanish ships towards the treacherous rocks called the Owers off Selsey Bill, but Sidonia was too quick for them. By dodging the rocks, however, the Spanish admiral narrowly missed capturing Frobisher in the *Triumph*, which would have done much for the morale of his squadron.

The Royal Navy, during this first week, had not achieved any notable victory, but it regarded the non-landing of the Spanish as an English achievement. For this reason, as if a victory had already been achieved, Howard knighted Hawkins and Frobisher on the deck of the *Ark Royal*. Hawkins's streamlining of English ships had ensured that they had always eluded the big, lumbering Spanish castles and evaded the grappling, boarding and hand-to-hand fighting, which they might well have lost. Frobisher had not been captured. Men have been given knighthoods for lesser achievements. Yet English victory – or perhaps it would be more accurate to say Spanish defeat – was still very far from being accomplished. In fact, there had been some heroism on both sides, some blunders and some unavoidable setbacks.

The crucial days were yet to come: 6 and 7 August, as the Spanish ships reached Calais. The weather was worsening all the time and there was a danger that the Armada would be driven on to the Flanders shoals or, worse, tossed into the North Sea, out of reach of the Duke of Parma.

The Duke of Parma, an accomplished soldier with no experience of naval warfare, was resolved not to imperil his invasion force of thousands of men. He was also hampered by scepticism. He never really believed that the Armada would beat the British navy or arrive in time to provide his troops with a safe passage across the English Channel. Parma had been understandably impressed by the 'flyboats', fast, shallow-draught little ships-o'-war, which had been pioneered in the early days of the Netherlands revolt by the Dutch admiral, Justin of Nassau. Parma convinced himself that it would not be safe to cross the Channel until the Spanish had constructed a fleet of such ships in the yards of Dunkirk. At Dunkirk and Nieuport he had assembled a huge 'fleet' of canal boats

– flat-bottomed open-ended barges, which, far from risking on the open sea, he would not even venture on a coast-hugging voyage the thirty miles or so to Calais.

On Sunday morning, Don Rodrigo Tello de Guzmán came aboard the *San Martin* in Calais harbour to break catastrophic news to Sidonia. Tello had been to Dunkirk and found no waiting Spanish army, merely a flotilla of unseaworthy canal barges. Parma was skulking in his headquarters at Bruges, forty miles away.

There was nothing for Sidonia to do but wait, but time was not, as it happened, on their side. Having successfully driven the Armada into a French harbour – this was how it seemed to Howard – they were now in a position to use Federigo Giambelli's deadly weapon of fire-ships. They had not been especially constructed. Drake gave one of his ships, the *Thomas of Plymouth*, of 200 tons. Hawkins gave a ship. They had eventually assembled eight big ships (150–200 tons each), which they loaded with explosives. At midnight on Sunday, 7 August these great infernal, blazing ships drifted destructively across the water of Calais Roads. They maintained a perfect straight line, as if manned by some unseen force; they were very close together. With phenomenal skill the Spanish used two pinnaces to swing round two of the fire-ships and drag them towards the shore in the choppy waters, but by now the six remaining fire-ships had borne down into the heart of the Armada. Their double-shotted guns were white-hot and were spraying shot at random. Exploding guns, a fountain of sparks, a roar of noise and fire broke upon the anchored Spanish ships, and there was panic. The *San Martin* raised anchor and sailed out to sea for a mile, but most of the Spanish captains lacked Sidonia's *sangfroid*. Many cut their cables. The fire-ships had not managed to set a single Spanish ship ablaze, but they had broken the order of battle that Sidonia had maintained unflinchingly all the way up the Channel. Without their primary anchors, these ships were going to suffer dearly in the weeks ahead. Many were now rudderless.

The Spanish ships were in disarray in choppy seas on that Monday morning, 8 August, in unknown seas, when they confronted the whole naval force of England, 150 sails. At Gravelines the disheartened and bedraggled Spanish fleet took a pounding. Ammunition on both sides was now low after ten days of Channel fighting, but the English had the advantage. For the first time since the Armada had been sighted off the Lizard, there was close-range fighting. The ships were about fifty yards apart, and the superiority of the English artillery began to tell. English rates of fire were of the order of one or one-and-a-half rounds *an hour* per gun; the Spanish about the same *per day*. At least one Spanish ship was sunk, but the exact progress of the battle is impossible to reconstruct.

The Spanish evidently managed, in spite of English fire and bad weather, to restore a fighting formation. They avoided being driven into the Zealand Banks, which would have exposed them to wreckage on the shoals and to being taken by the Dutch, who were waiting for them. But they chose between Scylla and Charybdis. The only way to avoid this fate was to head northwards, into the North Sea. No Spanish pilot was familiar with these waters, and not one chart of the North Sea was possessed by any ship in the Armada.[10] It had never been part of any Spanish plan to enter this turbulent and unknown area. With Howard's ships chasing behind them, they lurched into the heaving northern waves. Where were they heading? The English sailors feared they would attempt a northern landing. Or perhaps they were going to Hamburg, or to Norway? In any event, the worst of the danger was now over. And the worst English nightmare was over: that the Duke of Parma, with all his military expertise and his thousands of troops, might be landed on English soil. Drake wrote to Walsingham, 'God hath given us so good a day in forcing the enemy so far to leeward as I hope in God the Prince of Parma and the Duke of Medina Sidonia shall not shake hands this few days; and whensoever they meet, I believe neither of them will greatly rejoice of this day's service.'

Remember that, as yet, those on land knew nothing of the outcome of the naval battles over the previous long ten days. The rumour flew across Europe that Drake had been captured by the Spanish. As late as 20 August, the Spanish Ambassador in Paris, Don Bernadino de Mendoza, was writing to Philip II, 'as yet the story wants confirmation from the Duke himself, but it is widely believed and seems highly probable'. In Prague a solemn *Te Deum* was sung in thanksgiving for a Catholic victory. If Pope Sixtus failed to do the same in Rome it was only because he did not wish to pay out the first instalment of two million golden ducats, which he had promised as his contribution to the war effort if Parma set foot on English soil. Cardinal Allen nevertheless asked for his legatine Bulls at once, so that he could set out immediately from Italy to the Netherlands in order to expedite the conversion of England.[11]

It was in this atmosphere of total uncertainty that Elizabeth herself acted with decisive courage. Leicester, with his experience of fighting in the Low Countries, was convinced that the Spanish would sail up the Thames. The mustering of a land army, which was largely his responsibility, took much longer than he would have hoped. The everlasting shortage of money for victuals continued throughout the crisis. On 26 July Leicester had complained to Walsingham that he had an army of 'as gallant and willing men as ever were seen', but that, after a twenty-mile march, there was 'not a barrel of beer nor a loaf of bread' among them.[12] The Council had hoped to raise an army of 50,000 men, but nothing like this number had materialised. Leicester had only 4,000 men in the main army camp at Tilbury.

At this decisive hour, thirty years into her reign, Elizabeth was caught between the conflicting temperaments of Cecil and Dudley. Lord Burghley, the snow-haired old Polonius, was appalled when she declared that, if necessary, she would ride to the confines of her realm at the head of an army:

> Now for your person being the most dainty and sacred thing we have in this world to care for, a man must tremble when he thinks of it, specially finding your Majesty to have the princely courage to transport yourself to the utmost confines of your realm to meet your enemies and to defend your subjects. I cannot, most dear Queen, consent to that, for upon your well doing consists all the safety of your whole kingdom and therefore preserve that above all.

Always cautious, Burghley was also ever-mindful of the nightmare that would ensue, were Elizabeth to be removed from the scene. As the Armada made its fateful progress up the English Channel, with guns pounding and boys' voices singing the Litany of Our Lady, everything that Cecil had worked for politically over the previous thirty years hung in the balance: the Protestant-humanist life of the universities; the power of the Protestant axis at court and in the Council; the prodigious wealth and power of the Cecils, the Dudleys and the other members of the junta, who kept alive this particular way of governing England; the independence of England both from France and from Spain. All this and so much more was embodied in the fifty-five-year-old woman to whom Burghley had consecrated his existence. He trembled indeed at the thought of her riding out in an act of extravagant daring. Among the 4,000 men mustered at Tilbury, who was to know if there was not a Catholic with a pistol, yearning for the return of monasteries and papal rule?

But Elizabeth would never have captured the hearts and imaginations of her people if she had been the obedient slave of all Burghley's balance, caution and common sense. She was also the flamboyant woman who had deeply loved Robert Dudley, and probably – though he was now vermilion-faced, paunchy and grey-haired – she still did. It was Leicester who could see what a tremendous boost to national morale would be occasioned by her riding forth, rather than huddling immured under guard in Whitehall. He told her to go to her house at Havering, fourteen miles from the camp at Tilbury, where she should spend 'two or three days to see both the camp and the forts . . . I trust you will be pleased with your poor lieutenant's cabin and within a mile there is a gentleman's house, where your Majesty may also be. You shall comfort not only these thousands, but many more shall hear of it, and thus far, but no farther can I consent to adventure your person.'

By the time Elizabeth reached this gentleman's house – it belonged to a Mr Rich and was 'a proper, sweet, cleanly house' – Walsingham and Burghley were beginning to receive rumours that the Armada had been defeated. It would have been the perfect excuse for them to save money by disbanding the army, but Leicester longed for the great drama of her appearance before the troops. He could not know that it was the final pageant he would ever lay on for her, but he could know the significance of the hour. And he knew that her words and actions would more than rise to the occasion.

She travelled to the camp by river. A causeway was constructed, enabling her to ride from the boat to the assembled ranks of soldiers, who all fell to their knees as she trotted among them. She wept at the sight, and told them to rise. Then she dined with Leicester under canvas.

The next day they strapped plate-metal armour over her bodice. The breastplate shone 'like an angel bright' as the procession made its way among the troops, preceded by the Garter King of Arms and the Sergeant Trumpeter. Then followed Leicester and the Lord Marshal, and Leicester's stepson, the twenty-two-year-old Robert Devereux, 2nd Earl of Essex. 'The air and earth did sound like thunder,' recalled an eye-witness, presumably because of the tumultuous applause.

When Elizabeth addressed the army, her voice was too faint to be heard at the back of the ranks. That evening, therefore, Leicester told one of the chaplains, Dr Leonel Sharp, to redeliver the oration 'to all the army together to keep a Public Fast'. Sharp wrote out the words and had them copied as a pamphlet. When he gave a copy to the Duke of Buckingham twenty years later he said, 'I remember in '88 waiting upon the Earl of Leicester at Tilbury camp.' He recalled how the Queen 'rode through all the Squadrons of her army as Armed Pallas'. And, thanks to that military padre, we have her magnificent words:

> My loving people, we have been persuaded by some that are careful of our safety to take heed how we commit our self to armed multitudes for fear of treachery, but I assure you, I do not desire to live to distrust my faithful and loving people. Let tyrants fear, I have always so behaved myself that under God I have placed my chiefest strength and safeguard in the loyal hearts and good will of my subjects. And therefore I am come amongst you as you see at this time not for my recreation and disport, but being resolved in the midst and heat of battle to live or die

amongst you all to lay down for God and for my kingdom and for my people my honour and my blood even in the dust. I know I have the body of a weak and feeble woman, but I have the heart and stomach of a King, and of a King of England too, and think foul scorn that Parma or Spain or any Prince of Europe should dare invade the borders of my Realm to which rather than any dishonour shall grow by me, I myself will take up arms, I myself will be your General, Judge and rewarder of every one of your virtues in the field. I know already for your forwardness you have deserved rewards and crowns and we do assure you in the words of a Prince, they shall be duly paid you.

In the meantime my Lieutenant-General shall be in my stead, than whom never Prince commanded a more noble or worthy subject, not doubting but by your obedience to my General, by your Concord, in the Camp, and your valour in the field we shall shortly have a famous victory over those enemies of God, of my Kingdom and of my People.[13]

A cynic would say that Elizabeth and Leicester already knew, when the Tilbury display was orchestrated, that the Armada had in fact been defeated. An Elizabethan enthusiast might reply that whatever the truth of that (and we do not know for certain how fast the news of the Gravelines setback reached the Queen), she showed immense courage in riding among so many thousands of men at a time when many Catholics wished her dead. As so often, from the first spectacular theatre of her coronation procession, Elizabeth sensed the mood of her people and provided them with a display that strengthened national unity. England, from 1588 until the 1950s, would be shaped in its self-perception by the experience of the Armada, and by Elizabeth's eloquent vision of herself as holding out against 'any prince of Europe' who threatened the island kingdom. Churchill would draw on all this spirit for one last glorious display of collective insular courage in the summer of 1940. Froude the agnostic, hesitantly Church of England and vehemently anti-Catholic, concluded his essay on 'The Defeat of the Armada'[14] with the cruel but unforgettable sentence, 'Both sides had appealed to Heaven, and Heaven had spoken.' If so, it was the pitiless Heaven that overwhelmed the Egyptian chariots in the waters of the Red Sea, rather than the merciful Father of the New Testament who notes even the fall of a sparrow. No English ships were lost.[15] The Spanish fleet headed into the North Sea to avoid further confrontations with the English guns off the Essex or Kent coasts. Without hope of returning home via the Channel, they had no choice but to sail round the north coast of Scotland and back down the coast of Ireland. This was a navy that had scarcely collected enough provisions for the initial journey from Lisbon to England. Given this fact, and the appalling weather they had to endure, it is remarkable that any ships returned home. The Spanish lost between fifty and sixty-five ships, but the human losses were more devastating: of the 30,000 men who had left Lisbon, 20,000 died, more than half through sickness, starvation and disease, 6,000 in shipwreck, 1,000 by murder and 1,500 in battle. (Though the English gave out that only sixty-eight deaths had been suffered on their side as war casualties, it has been calculated that as many as 6,800 English sailors died as a result of the filthy conditions on the ships.) So the sailors on both sides had an horrific time, and those on the Spanish side had by far the worst of it because they were at sea for longer. The depredations were horrific and the death-figures speak for themselves. In order to preserve supplies of food and water, horses and mules were hurled into the sea. No one seems to know why they were not eaten.

For most of August, the Armada, or what was left of it, stayed together, but during September and October it drifted apart, many ships being wrecked off the Scottish and Irish coasts. Pedro Coco Calderon, the Paymaster General aboard the *San Salvador*, wrote, 'from 24 August to 4 September we sailed without knowing where we were, through constant fogs and storms'. Then they found themselves on the Irish coast. In many ships the men were starving, but for those who had cut off their anchors at Calais there was no chance of getting ashore – their only fate was to be wrecked.

Those who did come to land faced further horrors. Sir Richard Bingham, the Governor of Connaught, claimed to have killed 1,100 Spaniards taken prisoner on his watch. He sent armed search parties throughout Clare and Connemara to round up the bedraggled, half-starved boys and young men and to massacre them with axe, rope or sword. His son, George Bingham, went up to Mayo to do the same. And thus, wrote Sir Richard, 'having made a clean dispatch of them, both in town and country, we rested Sunday all day, giving praise and thanks to Almighty God for her Majesty's most happy success and deliverance from her dangerous enemies'.[16] Sir Geoffrey Fenton took a comparably religious view of the matter: 'God hath wrought for her Majesty against these idolatrous enemies, and suffered this nation to blood their hands upon them, whereby, it may be hoped, is drawn perpetual diffidence between the Spaniards and them, as long as this memory endureth.' The only Spaniards spared were those of sufficient wealth to have a ransom paid for them.

The cruelty seemed abominable at the time, but it was not gratuitous. The English in Ireland, even more than those who had watched the Armada make its sinister progress down the English Channel in early

August, felt extremely vulnerable. Even the hungry rabble cast ashore from the semi-wrecked Armada could have provided a formidable army against England, if they had reinforcements sent from Spain and had joined forces with Irish malcontents. Fenton was not alone in this belief when he wrote to the Privy Council in December:

> It may please your Lordships upon inquiry made of Don Alonso de Leva's casting away upon these coasts, I have learned that in his abode here he wrote several letters, sent away by special men into Spain, but whether directly from hence or through Scotland, I cannot find out. Only it may please you that if upon this letter, tending as may be thought to that end, there had been but 1,000 men with victuals and powder of both him and his 2,600 men, which now are all rid hence, I see not how but that before I could have given your Lordships advertisement Her Majesty might have been dispossessed of Ireland.[17]

21

London and Theatre

From our England, industrial and post-industrial, with its huge cities, its road networks and railways and airports, its unstoppably expansive suburbs and its population racing towards seventy million, it is difficult to recapture the overwhelmingly rural character of Elizabethan England. The huge majority of the population lived in the country, and worked on the land. Villages, cut off from the towns by primitive roads, were tiny. The larger towns were not, as in the nineteenth century and after, likely to be centres of manufacture; much more likely, they were market towns, such as Norwich, with a population of 17,000, or ports such as Bristol, rather smaller.

So, the places you think of now as the big English cities were often quite small in Elizabethan England. Manchester, where Dr John Dee became warden of the 'college' of priests in 1594, was described by John Leland in 1540 as 'the fairest, the best-builded, quickest and most populous town of all Lancashire'. By Elizabethan times, the population of Manchester was probably about 3,300 – with three big cullings caused by plague in the course of the reign.[1]

To be the most populous town in Lancashire was to have a population that later times would think of as a village. Cheshire was a more populous county than Lancashire at this period – an era when Totnes was much bigger than Liverpool, when Leeds, Halifax and Wakefield were tiny villages, when Sheffield was a small manor governed by a castle belonging to the Earl of Shrewsbury.[2]

In this England, the growth of London appeared all the more prodigious, and made the capital – even more than it had been in the Middle Ages – the hub of power and cultural interest. (York, the largest city in the North, had a population that is hard to estimate, but was probably around 10,000 in the mid-sixteenth century.)[3]

It is in this context that the population boom of London appears so prodigious – from 50,000 or 60,000 in the mid-1530s to perhaps 85,000 in 1565, and 155,000 in 1603 when the Queen died. (It was to continue rising with ever-greater rapidity during the first half of the seventeenth century, reaching half a million by the time of the Great Plague of 1665.)[4]

The population growth was not 'natural'. It was not caused by Londoners breeding at an unusual rate. In fact, so plague-ridden was sixteenth-century London that the population would have fallen without the migrants who entered the city in such numbers, from the English provinces, and from Europe. Protestant refugees from the Low Countries and France accounted for the larger proportion of foreign migrants – between 3 and 4 per cent in the course of the reign – some 4,700 in 1567 and 5,450 in 1593.[5]

English migrants to London fell into two broad categories. There were those who came driven by ambition, and there were those who came driven by hunger. 'In London we find rich wives, spruce mistresses, pleasant houses, good diet, rare wines, neat servants, fashionable furniture, pleasures and profits the best of all sort', as one such ambitious young man wrote.[6]

On the other hand, there were those who had been driven off the land for the simple Malthusian reason that existent crops could not sustain an increased workforce. Population growth in the country produced land shortage, reduced the size of smallholdings and led to a fivefold increase in food prices. In the course of the sixteenth century the real value of wages halved. The poor became poorer. Living-in servants, apprentices and day-labourers were the lucky ones. Many simply drifted towards London with the vague hope that it would provide them with some form of livelihood. The number of homeless beggars was vast.

In 1581 Elizabeth was riding by Aldersgate Bars towards the fields of Islington when she found herself surrounded by a crowd of beggars, 'which gave the queen much disturbance'. That evening, William Fleetwood, the Recorder, arrested seventy-four of them who had dispersed in the fields, where they lived in a kind of shanty-town. Eight years later, a mob of some 500 beggars threatened to disrupt Bartholomew Fair. They had formed their own collective and were trying to sell stolen goods at a fair of their own – Durrest Fair.[7]

Yet it was a fluid underclass, never a settled one. No state-sponsored social-welfare system existed. In the absence of religious houses, there was nowhere for the indigent or the starving to find charity. The beggars took what they could, and then found work or moved on. It all had a cruel effectiveness. The authorities, ever anxious about the double dangers of plague and insurrection, kept a merciless eye on the swarming hordes. In 1580 the Privy Council noted, 'the great number of dissolute, loose and insolent people harboured in such and like noisome and disorderly houses as namely poor cottages and habitants of beggars and people without trade, stables, inns, ale houses, taverns, garden houses, converted to dwellings, ordinaries, dicing houses, bowling alleys and brothel houses'. The instinct of civic authorities in the late nineteenth and twentieth centuries would be to house the poor, and where possible to keep them clean and disease-free. The instinct of the Elizabethan Lord Mayor and

Aldermen of the City of London was to discourage them from coming to London in such numbers – and their expedient was to forbid any building within three miles of the City. These decrees were ignored. The Privy Council itself in 1598 warned JPs about landlords letting out tenements in Shoreditch and Clerkenwell to 'base people and to lewd persons that do keep evil rule and harbour thieves, rogues and vagabonds'. They were unable to limit the population themselves. Plague did it for them. Without bubonic plague, the Elizabethans would have had real political and social problems on their hands. Plague killed rich and poor alike, but whereas the prosperous were sometimes able to get out of the City to escape the plague – and they had somewhere else to go – the waifs and strays of the Elizabethan shanty-town stayed to die, until the next wave of beggars came to town; 17,500 people (the size of the entire population of England's next-biggest city, Norwich) died in London in 1563; 23,000 in 1593; 30,000 in 1603, with many a more minor outbreak in between, and disease everlastingly rife in that filthy, overcrowded city with no drainage and no sanitation.[8]

That having been said, it would be a mistake to regard the Elizabethans as being without any charitable impulses. Compared with a modern welfare state, designed to cater for the social problems of a population numbering in the tens of millions, it was obviously haphazard. One reason for this was that the numbers of people living in Elizabethan England were, by modern standards, so tiny. Nevertheless, there did exist a kind of micro social-welfare system. Each parish was expected to organise 'poor relief'. Prosperous parishioners were specially taxed for the purpose. In many city parishes much care was given to foundling babies, to the old and to the sick; even, on occasion, to strangers and 'blackamoors'. In parishes that contained prisoners, local people would feed the prisoners through the bars and gratings. It was common for wealthier parishioners to adopt orphans, often seeing that they were taught a skill or a trade. Parish registers provide an abundance of evidence of such charitable activity.

There were also almshouses in many towns designed to house the poor. One thinks of Edward Alleyn's at Dulwich or of Archbishop Whitgift's at Croydon. Naturally there were many poor people who slipped through the net and who found themselves homeless, but so there are in any system. The Queen was regarded, among other things, as a source of bounty, and wherever she travelled, ladies-in-waiting took purses to distribute among suppliants. The aristocracy imitated this more-than-ritualised generosity. The household accounts of Lady Anne Clifford, or Lord Berkeley, to name but two, record frequent giving to the poor. Lord Berkeley not only entertained all his retainers and tenants in true feudal style each Christmas, but made sure that suppliants at his door were rewarded all through the year. There was a brutality about life in early modern times, when so few effective cures for disease or hunger had been discovered. But Lear's compassion for the 'poor naked wretches' was something felt by more than just one old king upon a stage. It was a society which, perhaps more self-consciously than others, since religious debate was so much to the forefront of contemporary discourse, was aware of its Christian obligations.[9]

Crime, nevertheless, was widespread. From the records of the courts, as from the drama, fiction, diaries and pamphlets, we find a city of filthy, narrow streets swarming with pickpockets, confidence tricksters (known as cony-catchers), whores, pimps and swindlers. We also find a world where authority criminalised the population as a method of draconian control. It has been estimated that 6,000 people were executed in the modern Greater London during the reign of Elizabeth. Translate that statistic into the population of modern London, and you are talking of the equivalent of thousands of people a year being killed. The 200 or 300 recusant spies or martyrs are lost in this ghoulish statistic, where to be indigent, or a thief, or a careless pamphleteer could earn you the most terrible punishments. As well as those killed, there must be remembered the thousands who endured whippings, mutilations, brandings or being placed in the stocks for quite trivial offences. Evelyn Waugh, in his life of Campion, likened the regime to the brigand states of the twentieth century. But surely here is a case where analogy is misleading. As when we attune our ears to Elizabethan poetry and sentence structure, so, when attempting to acclimatise ourselves to their socio-political realities, we must resist the laziness of parallel. Sir Francis Walsingham was not Dr Goebbels. None of the monster regimes of the twentieth century would have retained 'benefit of clergy' as a defence in law, not only for bishops and curates, but for the educated. When Ben Jonson killed a fellow actor in a duel in 1598 he pleaded guilty, but escaped hanging merely by demonstrating to the judge that he could recite the penitential Psalm *Miserere mei, Deus, secundum magnam misericordiam tuam* (50 in the Vulgate, 51 in the Hebrew Bible) in Latin. So the sixteenth century was another country.

You cannot draw a parallel between the early modern age and the mechanised dictatorships of the twentieth century. By proportion, Stalin and Mao and Hitler killed infinitely more of their own dissident population even than Mary Tudor did, or the Habsburg regime of Philip II in Spain and the Low Countries. Rather than draw modern parallels, we must continually re-enter the Elizabethan world to try to acclimatise ourselves to its atmosphere. The Catholic recusants have a surviving constituency in our own day, who continue to revere their struggles and their martyrdoms. But they were not alone in falling foul of a system that was completely repressive.

In any society that was changing as rapidly as the early-modern period in England, however, there were bound to be dissidents of all kinds: those who did not conform to the norm decreed by the all-powerful, all-centralising Council, dominated by the inner ring of Burghley, Walsingham and the Protestant junta, who both accepted the capricious absolutism of the Queen and judiciously manipulated it. That caprice could take off the head of a Duke of Norfolk. Burghley himself had come close to being sent to the Tower. If she had positively insisted upon a dynastic marriage with a European prince who disliked them, the position of the junta would have been precarious indeed. But, for the most part, the coalition between the Queen and the inner ring was mutually beneficial and this fed and strengthened the arm of Walsingham's spy-network. Anyone who threatened the state, anyone who threatened the prevailing orthodoxies, was in danger of losing ear or hand or tongue or life. Yet – and here was one of the great differences between Elizabethan England and the totalitarianisms of the twentieth century – there was a palpable sense in the country at large of rebirth, of creative energy, of newness and expansion. There was a new religion; or at any rate, a National Church which ratified the Reformation. Perhaps many disliked it, for not being the old Latin rite, or for not following the new Reformed paths. But it was itself new. There were new schools. Ships – English ships – sailed to new lands, and brought back not merely undreamed-of treasure, but the sense of an expanded world. In churches, halls, palaces and country houses, new music delighted the ear. You could not be alive in Elizabethan England and not feel that it was a young country, full of the capacity to reinvent itself.

And central to its stupendous flowering, its intense magnification and its Herculean self-discovery was the vastly expanding capital of London. In this teeming womb of new life, new disease, new squalor and new glory, we should expect strange things to emerge. Patrons, such as the Sidneys, or as the young Earls of Oxford or Southampton, might bring on poets and musicians, courtly writers who could embroider new verses as finely wrought as their tapestries. But the masque, the madrigal or the privately circulated sonnet-sequence would not be enough to contain all the loud, sharp, all-but-unutterable matters that this changing world was bringing to birth. Novels, pamphlets and, above all, plays began to emerge as fascinating expressions of their times, and as subversions of them.

Sidney's *Arcadia*, in its developed and unfinished revision, was by far the most interesting work of prose-fiction of the times, but it was never intended by its author for publication, as far as we know: his sister saw it through the presses in 1590 in a somewhat mangled form.

John Lyly (*c.*1554–1606), who was probably roughly of Sidney's age, was one of the so-called University Wits to emerge onto the literary scene, a figure of interest not merely for what he wrote, but for what he represented: namely, that first generation who emerged from what we should call higher education into an entirely Protestant world; where, if you were not lucky or clever enough to become a don, or to enter one of the professions, you needed a combination of a patron's help and your own wits to keep afloat. From figures in such circumstances was to emerge much of the most interesting literature of the time. The explorer among the Elizabethan bookshelves encounters Lyly in several modes – as proto-novelist, as playwright, as government lickspittle and as a Member of Parliament.

Lyly, like Sidney, was an Oxford man (Magdalen College), but from a far less-exalted family background. He was born in the Weald of Kent, and when he matriculated his university described him, with a no doubt accurate lack of mercy, as '*plebeii filius*', a son of a pleb. This would not have meant that he was the son of the lowest rank. It meant he was not a gentleman. Edmund Spenser, George Peele, Thomas Lodge, William Shakespeare, Christopher Marlowe, Thomas Nashe – they all came from the middle rank, from the class who made or sold things rather than living, as their sons would do, by their wits. Lyly was of slightly higher stock than this: the grandson of an Eton master and the nephew of two masters at St Paul's. This is the class that in later generations and other countries would produce the French revolutionaries, the Russian communist-anarchists. It is the class from which dissent and discontent and change comes, but it is also the class that in a creatively successful society wishes to 'better itself'. One of the measures of a society's health is what this class does to the greater group. In Weimar Germany, the discontented shopkeeper, the clever weaver or glover or tanner would help the 'extremes' of Right or Left to devour the Common Good like cancers. In Victorian England, the clever aspirant classes actually became the new order. Lord Salisbury, Burghley's Cecil descendant, could sneer at the *Daily Mail* as being written by and for office boys, but he ended his career wooing the political votes of office boys. In the pre-industrial world of Elizabethan England, those who were too clever to belong to the class in which they were born did not create a petty bourgeoisie, as in Joseph Chamberlain's Birmingham. But they were emerging all over the place, entering the professions, entering the universities, and when successful – as was the glover's son from Stratford-upon-Avon – wanting to make themselves into gentlefolk. To be able to write the letters MA (Master of Arts) after your name made you, in this world, '*generosus*', a gentleman.

That was Lyly's hope and aspiration, too; though it was not the path trodden by other 'University Wits'. He hoped for advancement. There was evidently some family connection that enabled him to approach Burghley for patronage. He tried to get a Fellowship at one of the universities, but it did not happen. He wrote a novel whose title was destined to become an epithet in literary history: *Euphues: The Anatomy of Wit*. It is a crib of a translation – North's rendering of Antonio de Guevara's *El Reloj de Principes* (*Diall of Princes*). It is not so much for the boring story that *Euphues* is remembered, as for its style – an excessive use of alliteration and antithesis, and constant allusion to classical literature and mythology. This alone, even if it were not for the crashing tedium of Euphues and his chum Philautus pursuing their romantic attachment to (in the first book) Greek and (in *Euphues and His England*) English girls. Yet the book, which almost no one outside English Literature courses in universities would today find so much as readable, was highly regarded. There was no such thing as mass literacy, but when we see that *Euphues: The Anatomy of Wit* went through four editions between 1578 and 1580, we could rank it as the equivalent of a best-seller. Lyly was able to attract the patronage of Lord Oxford, and the kindly notice of Oxford's father-in-law, Burghley. In 1584 Lyly's ambition to have a place at court advanced one stage when he was offered a prestigious writing job: plays to be performed by the child actors' companies of the Chapel Royal and St Paul's Cathedral.

The choristers of St Paul's had been performing plays since the Middle Ages, even before Colet founded the school in the reign of Henry VII. Plays, particularly at Christmas time, were a part of life in many schools – either the Latin comedies of Terence or Plautus, or morality plays, or plays based on the Bible – 'so always', as a cautious Henrician statute of 1543 made clear, 'the said songes playes or enterludes medle not with the interpretacions of scripture'.[10]

The huge population growth in London changed the place of theatre. Among the floating population who came into London to beg or to steal there were players. The Act for the Punishment of Vagabonds, of 1571/2, stipulated that 'all Comon Players in Enterludes Mynstrels Juglers . . . [who] wander abroade . . . [without] Lycense of two Justices of the Peace . . . shall bee taken adjudged and deemed Roges Vacaboundes and Sturdy Beggers'.

In the short term, the panic felt by the authorities when crowds gathered together necessitated a strict licensing code for theatres. And this had the effect of making the boys' theatres, one of the few sources of licensed entertainment in a populous capital city, increasingly popular. By 1584 Lyly had written a couple of well-wrought comedies for the joint boys' company of St Paul's and the Chapel Royal, and they had been performed at court. But although the City fathers by their draconian laws had hoped to exclude the vagabond players from London, the fluting-voiced company of boys from St Paul's had demonstrated to would-be professional grown-up actors the full extent of theatrical possibilities in London: not simply in summer, when 'enterludes', dances and other theatricals could be performed on open-air stages, but in purpose-built theatres.

It was the triumph of a joiner-cum-actor, James Burbage, to persuade the City to license the first purpose-built theatre in London. Burbage took a lease of land in Shoreditch, just outside the City walls, in 1576. The plays he staged were so popular that an imitation, known as the Curtain, was built nearby in the same year. This was the beginning for a new mirror on the world. A new literature could be born to supply the structures that Burbage built. Nine years after Burbage's 'The Theatre', the Rose was built on Bankside, just opposite St Paul's on the south side of the river, on the edge of some of the seediest brothels and taverns in London. In 1595 Francis Langley would build the Swan, also on Bankside. In 1598 came perhaps the most famous theatre ever built, the Globe, and in 1600, in Cripplegate, Henslowe and Alleyn built the Fortune.

The children who had in some senses precipitated the theatre-mania of adult Elizabethans were to remain part of its success story. No woman was permitted to appear on the Elizabethan stage. It was an all-male affair, which meant that female parts, as well as parts suitable for children such as fairies, angels and imps, were always played by boys.

In his elegy for Salathiel Pavy, a famous child actor who appeared with the St Paul's company, Ben Jonson gives us an exact account of the ages of these theatre-children:

> Yeeres he numbred scarse thirteen
>   When Fates turn'd cruell,
> Yet three fill'd *Zodiackes* had he beene
>   The stages jewell:
> And did act (what now we mone)
>   Old men so duely
> As, sooth, the *Parcae* thought him one . . .

So we know that boys were engaged into theatrical companies aged ten. Nathan Field, another famous boy actor, was thirteen when he was 'pressed' into service in a theatrical company. He continued to be an actor as a grown-up.

As with other trades, boys served an apprenticeship if they wanted to work in the theatre. The length of the apprenticeship would vary. Some court cases show that boys were apprenticed for as long as twelve years; for others, the apprenticeship was as little as three years. In an agreement between one Martin Slater and the Whitefriars Theatre in 1609, it was agreed that all children would be bound to Slater for three years. In his diary, Philip Henslowe, who died *c.*1610, the builder of the Rose theatre and a theatrical impresario, mentions two boy players who were apprenticed to Thomas Dowton: 'Delivered unto Thomas Dowton's boy Thomas Parsons to buy divers things for the play of the Spencers the 16 of April 1599 the sum of £5'. The next year Dowton himself borrowed £2 to enable him to buy the costume for his boy in a play about Cupid and Psyche.[11]

The apprentice boy actors would not have received wages, but they would have been clothed and fed, perhaps better than if at home with their families. They would have lived with their masters, and they would learn by taking part in plays from the start – first, as extras in a crowd, then in smaller roles as pages, fairies or children, and finally as women. Although there were no theatre schools, the training for actors would have been formal. They would have studied gesture, for example, from books such as Bulwer's *Chirologia or the Naturall Language of the Hand*. Although this was a seventeenth-century book, which described in precise detail the meaning of individual hand-gestures – and was prompted chiefly by medical interest, partly by social observation, for the purposes of teaching etiquette – we know that it was studied in the theatre, and that Elizabethan actors would have made similar studies.[12] Boys who were to grow up to play members of the nobility would have to learn to move like noblemen and women. They would learn swordsmanship, to make the fight scenes convincing. They would perfect their dancing:

> They bid us to the English dancing-schools
> And teach lavoltas high and swift corantoes

as Bourbon says of the English in *Henry V*. And they would have sung – hence the great importance of the boys' theatre companies attached to the cathedrals. Choir boys in England, then as now, were trained in a way that differed markedly from continental operatic styles. In the windows of the Beauchamp Chapel of St Mary's, Warwick may be seen angels opening their mouths laterally, with the natural jaw position adopted by sixteenth-century (and modern English) choir boys. The tongue is in contact with the lower teeth, and the jaw is brought forward, enabling a pure, high sound; a lightly flexible voice of the kind needed to sing sixteenth-century polyphonic music. A well-trained boy can produce a three-octave range from B-flat or D below middle C to the G above top C. These English traditions dated back to pre-Reformation times in England. The Venetian Ambassador, hearing the choir boys sing for Henry VIII, said they were 'more divine than human', and when we consider what William Cornish (who died in 1523) required of the boys in his *Eton Choirbook* – an astounding vocal agility by the trebles in his *Magnificat*, for example – you realise what a very distinctive level of prodigy could be found among boy voices. This talent was taken into the theatres, where song was so frequently used, and where trained verse-speaking was developed to a superbly high standard.

Nothing happens by accident. The theatre in London was made by a group of immensely talented boys and young men, fired up by theatrically minded entrepreneurs. At first they displayed their skills on the comedies of Lyly, but almost literally waiting in the wings were Marlowe and Shakespeare. They could not have existed, however, had not the likes James Burbage built the first public theatre, and had not the acting companies been of a superlative quality.

The boys, many of them, were choir boys or ex-choir boys. And many of the men of the Elizabethan theatre might easily, in a pre-Protestant age, have exercised their talents in the Church. Christopher Marley (baptised in Canterbury in 1564), whom we know as Marlowe, the son of a shoe-maker, went to King's School, Canterbury, and then on to Corpus Christi College, Cambridge, on a Parker Scholarship – money given by Archbishop Parker for a scholar at the King's School and intended for candidates for Holy Orders.[13] Lyly would surely, too, have taken orders if he had managed to obtain a Fellowship at Oxford or Cambridge.

Robert Greene, a sizar (a scholar who did the work of a servant to pay his way) of St John's College, Cambridge (1575), who died in wretched poverty in his very early thirties in 1592, was aptly described as 'in some sort the hero and spokesman of all the commercial writers'.[14] Greene, like other University Wits, considered himself 'too good' for the theatre. He published from fifteen to twenty works of fiction, and pamphlets, before he turned to the theatre because it was so profitable. Burbage and Henslowe and the other entrepreneurs could pack in, perhaps, 2,000 spectators to one performance. If they charged a penny a time, there was huge money to be made.[15] Henslowe paid his poets £6 for the completion of a play.[16] It was a lot of money. No wonder a figure like Greene, an impoverished intellectual who had failed to secure an academic post, was drawn to it. Yet, as his self-dramatising autobiographies show, he despised the coarse, stupid actors, and half-loathed himself for the dissipation into which theatrical life drew him. In *Francesco's Fortune* his self-image, Francesco, 'fell in amongst a company of players, who persuaded him to try his wit in writing of comedies, tragedies or pastorals, and if he could perform anything worthy of the stage, then they would largely reward him for his pains'. As so often in Greene's autobiographical fantasies, the work is stupendously successful. (Greene *was* a popular writer, but perhaps never as popular as his exaggerated stories suggest.) In *Greene's Groatsworth of Wit*, the Greene-figure, Roberto, has been swindled by a prostitute. He sits disconsolately beside a hedge, reciting Latin and English verses, and happens to meet a player who is a gentleman-scholar fallen on hard times. 'I was a country author passing at a moral, for it was I that penned the moral of man's wit, the Dialogue of Dives, and for seven years apace was absolute interpreter of the puppets. But now my almanac is out of date.' Roberto (Greene) is lured into the tempting world of the theatre and then, eaten up with self-hatred for the waste of talent that the life of the jobbing playwright entails, needs to drown his sorrows among criminals and debauchees. With luridly grovelling repentance, he warns those 'gentlemen his quondam acquaintance that spent their wit in making plays': obviously, he is thinking of such figures as Marlowe, Peele, Lodge and Thomas Nashe – the most ingenious of Elizabethan 'novelists' and an incomparably better writer than Greene.

But Greene's writings paint an indelible picture of the world into which the University Wits were lured. Theatre-history at this period exemplifies something comparable to the pop-culture of the 1960s. It began by attracting young people from the fringes of society, and it became mainstream. By modern standards, the restrictions upon the drama were adamantine. But there was more room in the theatre for the subversive than there was in pamphlet literature. The actors were alive, the plays brought to life an alternative world and an alternative set of values, or, in the most colourful case – that of Marlowe – of non-values.

Marlowe (1564–93), Greene's Cambridge contemporary, had a lurid, short life – he was twenty-nine when he was murdered. Hazlitt saw that there 'was a lust of power in his writings, a hunger and thirst after unrighteousness, a glow of the imagination, unhallowed by anything but its own energies'.[17] In his brittle abnegation of conventional morality, and in his swaggering espousal of violence, blasphemy and sexual deviancy, he seems to anticipate twentieth-century figures such as Jean Genet and Michel Foucault. We certainly feel in Marlowe's life that the

London theatre was an outlet for his genius, which no other medium could conceivably have supplied.

Absolutely no biographical evidence exists that could furnish psychological explanations for the Marlowe phenomenon – and perhaps such explanations are always inadequate, even when they have data upon which to feed. The records in Canterbury supply abundant evidence of the father's pugnacious, quarrelsome nature. Marlowe himself may, or may not, have been the precocious writer or pot-boy cited as a witness at a Canterbury 'victualling house' when one John Roydon committed a sexual assault on a serving girl, but this is the *sort* of boyhood we should expect for Marlowe, before his cleverness was trained at the King's School and got him to Cambridge.

As a student, he favoured the randy Ovid and the rebellious Lucan – he wrote translations of both. It appears (and this again seems so modern) that even while he was at Cambridge he had somehow been enlisted in political 'affaires'. In mid-1587 we find Christopher Morley on his way to Reims, working as one of Walsingham's spies, and posing as a recusant and would-be priest. How was he enlisted? One of his fellow agents, Richard Baines, quoted him as saying that 'all they that love not tobacco and boies were fooles'.[18] One of his Cambridge acquaintances, Thomas Fineux of Hougham, near Dover, attested that 'Marlowe made him an atheist'. Walsingham would have seen that Marlowe's lack of religious belief would have made him a very useful spy, when it came to posing as a Catholic: he need have no scruples that would interfere with his work. Perhaps the love of boys played a part in the story – either that Marlowe was involved with a world of homosexual spies, or that he had made himself open to blackmail.

Nobody knows exactly when Marlowe wrote *The Tragical History of Doctor Faustus*. It seems to be an early work, perhaps from 1588–9.[19] Clearly, on the heavily censored London stage, Marlowe could not be blatantly atheistical. Equally clearly, the 'hellish fall' of Dr Faustus, which the Chorus, at the end of the play holds up as an object-lesson in the consequences of seeking forbidden knowledge, is thrilling to both author and audience. We are as far as possible, in this play, from the medieval miracle plays in which Heaven and Hell are realities. Marlowe's Faustus is a rootless sensualist who comes unstuck. But though some members of the audience might have shuddered, as they would at a genuinely religious medieval cycle, the sophisticates among Marlowe's first audience would read all the signals. F.S. Boas, Marlowe's biographer, observed that:

> Marlowe must have recognised in Faustus his own counterpart. The Canterbury boy through the bounty of Archbishop Parker had reached

> Cambridge to qualify himself there for the clerical career. His studies had earned him the Bachelor's and the Master's degrees, but he had turned his back on the Church, and on arrival in London had gained a reputation for atheism. Similarly, Faustus through the bounty of a rich uncle had been sent to Wittenberg to study divinity, and had obtained with credit his doctorate in the subject. But his interests lay elsewhere, and he had turned secretly to the study of necromancy and conjuration.[20]

Faust is a mythic character who haunts the sixteenth century, and who finds his most eloquent incarnation in Marlowe's tragi-farce. Luther, in his *Table-Talk*, had spoken of Faust, the arrogant scholar-turned-necromancer, accompanied by a dog who was really the Devil. These early Protestant accounts of Faust speak of him having died when the Devil decided to wring his neck. Goethe's Faust is the spokesman of the Enlightenment free-thinker, *led eternally onwards* to greater intellectual and sexual satisfaction by his having cast aside dogmatic restraints. He is not damned: one of many factors that makes Gounod's rendering so ludicrous. For Luther and the other Reformers, however, Faust is a terrible warning of what happens to the unbaptised imagination. He deliberately lays aside divine knowledge and goes it alone in quest of knowledge-as-power. The 'original' or 'real' Faust appears to have been born at the little town of Kindlingen and to have studied at Krakow. Marlowe, by the time he had picked up on the legend, makes him a mainstream German: 'Of riper years to Wertenberg he went . . .'

It is astounding how fast the Faust story turned into legend, passing in oral tradition through Poland, France, Holland and England during the 1580s and 1590s. It was very much a current piece of popular lore when Marlowe first saw his play performed. It draws, consciously or otherwise, on many stories circulating in Europe about men selling themselves to Satan in exchange for immortality or secret knowledge. Luther's horror of the story – and Luther, who was very superstitious, would almost certainly have believed that the Devil could pop up and strangle his adepts on Earth – was based on the fear that in starting (in effect) the Reformation, he had begun something unstoppable, and something that would ultimately rebound against the pure word of God. Among intellectuals, as we have already noticed in our considerations of Dr Dee, the belief in magic was widespread. Marlowe probably did dabble in Satanism, and probably did express atheistic beliefs.

What he achieved in the theatre, however, was sheer thrill. It is neither more nor less 'deep' than a Graham Greene novel:

I do repent; and yet I do despair:
Hell strives with grace for conquest in my breast . . .

Such thrills, which are achieved largely through Marlowe's superb gifts of rhetoric, in the drama of Faustus, first grabbed the public attention in his bombastic *tour de force*, the *Tamburlaine* plays.

Greek tragedy began as part of religious ceremonial, plumbing deep familial, psychological fears. Tragedy in the English theatre had different wellsprings and found very different settings in which to expand and explore its own possibilities. It exploited the combined skills of travelling, vagabond-actors, singing-boys and comedians. It was staged for mobs hungry for sensation in new, purpose-built – with an emphasis on the *built*, the enclosed – arenas. In a violent, crowded city, it projected fantasies of power and violence and madness, which drowned the fears and sorrows of its audience with melodramatic horrors, exciting not so much the Fear and Pity that Aristotle had looked for in the poetic masterpieces of Euripides, as the sensationalism of the circus combined with the irrationality of nightmare. A favoured theme was revenge.

Theirs was a society that depended for its very preservation on the failure to finish what later psychiatric theory would call 'unfinished business'. There were so many stories in individual English lives at this date that cried for *vendetta*: the Catholics who resented losing position or land or money for the sake of faith; the old families yielding place to new money; the burgeoning petty-bourgeois Puritan-leaning class of merchants and tradesmen whose voice was unheeded in Church and state, as well as the thousand private causes for resentment in family feuds, street violence or rivalries, commercial or amorous. The law, with a justice so rough that our sensibility could hardly deem it justice at all, cut off a hand here, hanged a miscreant there; disembowelled a traitor, mangled a heretic, whipped a petty-criminal within inches of his life. In this world the story of the lurid murder, revenged after a convoluted story by killings no less bloody, was just what the collective psyche seemed to require.

Thomas Kyd (1558–94) was a pupil of Mulcaster's, and a contemporary of Spenser's, at the Merchant Taylors' School. His short life followed the pattern of nihilistic disillusion that can be found in the writings of Greene and Nashe or inferred from the death of Marlowe, and which seems to have been almost a *sine qua non* for theatrical poets: he was arrested on 12 May 1593, and when his rooms were searched, papers were found that allowed his prosecutors to accuse him of atheism. (The purport of these documents seems in fact to have been a rather mild form of Unitarianism.[21]) He was tortured and died not long afterwards:

What outcries pluck me from my naked bed,
And chill my throbbing heart with trembling fear,
Which never danger yet could haunt before? . . .

The audiences of Kyd's *Spanish Tragedy* enjoyed the gruesome killing of Horatio, the father – Hieronimo – going mad with grief, the staged 'play within a play' that helps to unmask the murderers, and the suicide of heroine and hero. The enthusiasm of the crowds for this extraordinary play would not have been lost on the fledgling dramatist Ben Jonson, who probably contributed some lines to it, or on another young man who had come up to London from Stratford-on-Avon, perhaps as a travelling player. This would have been in the late 1580s, and Shakespeare had left a Stratford in which he could still keenly remember the death of one Katherine Hamlett by drowning;[22] she was disinterred when it was feared she died by suicide – one of the many ingredients in his brain, presumably, together with the influence and excitement of Kyd's tragedy, that would one day fructify as his own complicated revenge-drama.

But if Kyd gave the crowds an intoxicating cocktail of poetry and gore, moral outrage fulfilled by violence, the emergence of Marlowe as tragedian was indeed a pyrotechnic fizz in the London sky. Tamburlaine gives voice to every mob's basest political fantasy: namely, that waiting among the crowds at any historical juncture is some Rienzi or Hitler who, regardless of lowly origins, and in defiance of any moral or social convention, can seize pure, naked, delectable power. Those who had felt the charm of Queen Elizabeth I precisely because, and not in spite of, the fact that many denounced her as a bastard; those who loved the piratical side of her nature, and cheered home the looted Spanish gold on Drake's or Hawkins's ships, or gathered excitedly to watch bears baited or papists disembowelled – all these would be enraptured by the story of a Scythian shepherd-robber's aggrandisement, set to a verse the like of which had never been heard in English:

Now hang our bloody colours by Damascus,
Reflexing hues of blood upon their heads,
While they walk quivering on their city-walls,
Half-dead for fear before they feel my wrath.
Then let us freely banquet, and carouse
Full bowls of wine unto the god of war,
That means to fill your helmets full of gold,
And make Damascus' spoils as rich to you
As was to Jason Colchos' golden fleece . . .

Marlowe himself, in his *The Massacre at Paris* – about St Bartholomew's Day, 1572 – was fully aware that there was nothing even the most sensation-hungry theatrical impresario could put on stage at the Rose or the Theatre that could match the drama of what was happening to England itself. The dramatists knew that there were rich mines to be plundered from native soil. This applied both to the small-town murder story, such as the 1585(?) *Arden of Faversham* (an anonymous play, which has been attributed variously to Kyd, Marlowe and Shakespeare, not in any of the three cases entirely convincingly), and to such historical dramas as the anonymous *Troublesome History of John, King of England* (1587?).

Clearly, in a world where an ill-judged comment in a political pamphlet could result in author and printer having hands chopped off, any written work that reflected on the current political scene needed to be crafted with great caution. The Tudor dynasty had emerged with dubious legality from a painfully protracted civil war. Anyone with political and historical intelligence in the 1580s knew that the drama of England itself, its evolution as a state, grew out of these civil wars and the contemporary wars with France in the reign of Henry VI. These problems in turn evolved from the succession-wrangles consequent upon Henry Bolingbroke having seized power from Richard II in 1399.

It was fascinating material for stage-drama: yet dangerous, for one of the repeated and demonstrable truths of English history in the fourteenth and fifteenth centuries was that no one holds power without consent; that even the most popular or absolute of monarchs can find power slipping, or being grabbed, from their fist. That is a story which all mobs, and no monarchs or tyrants, want to hear.

It is very unlikely that the play we often refer to as *Henry VI Part I* was the work of one hand. Authorship of plays was not, especially in the early days of the purpose-built theatres, displayed on billboards, nor did authors retain any rights in material that they would have sold outright to the impresario. Only later, in the unusual situation of an author publishing his play, do we get a sense of authorship in this modern sense. In any case, the first *Henry VI* play in chronological terms is unlikely to have been the first to have been performed. *The First Part of the Contention of the two Famous Houses of York and Lancaster with the Death of the Good Duke Humphrey* is what we call *Henry VI Part II*. Unlike *Part I*, which seems to have been a heavily collaborative work (scholars detect in it the hands of Thomas Nashe, Robert Greene, Marlowe and George Peele), *Part II* was largely Shakespeare's own work.

Whatever work Shakespeare (1564–1616) had previously done in the theatre, as an actor and as a collaborative playwright contributing to others' work, it is in the plays about Henry VI – whatever title you give them – that he emerges as a figure in the London theatre. When Shakespeare was in his mid-to-late twenties, *Henry VI Parts II and III* were complete. Robert Greene denounced the new arrival, with a clear parody of one of Shakespeare's lines in the play. 'For there is an upstart Crow, beautified with our feathers, that with his *Tygers heart wrapt in a Players hyde*, supposes he is as well able to bombast out a blanke verse as the best of you; and being an absolute *Johannes fac totum*, is in his owne conceit the only Shake-scene in a country.'

Here we have an obvious reference, by an *envious*, dying man (Greene died on 3 September 1592) to a new star. The 'Tygers heart' reference is to *Henry VI Part III, Act I, Scene 4*. The captive Duke of York stands, humiliated, on a molehill wearing a paper crown and being taunted by the terrifying Queen Margaret. She waves a napkin stained with the blood of York's son:

> Where are your mess of sons to back you now?
> The wanton Edward, and the lusty George?
> And where's that valiant crook-back prodigy,
> Dickie your boy, that with his grumbling voice
> Was wont to cheer his dad in mutinies?
> Or, with the rest, where is your darling, Rutland?
> Look, York: I stained this napkin with the blood
> That valiant Clifford, with his rapier's point
> Made issue from the bosom of the boy . . .

There had never been writing like this in the English theatre before, and the intimacy of the language – 'cheer his dad' – immeasurably adds to the menace and the torture. And here were the Kings and Queens of England, and the cartels of aristocrats who vied for power in the previous century and steeped the country in anarchy and blood, brought alive, in a language that is both realistic (to that degree demotic) and vividly poetic. More than any of the other dramatists, Shakespeare wrote evermore challenging roles for the boy actors playing formidable women. Queen Margaret is the first of them – a great line that will include Cleopatra, Goneril and Regan, Lady Macbeth and Gertrude. Margaret is denounced by York as the 'she-wolf of France' and as 'O, tiger's heart wrapped in a woman's hide'. So we can have no doubt that the University Wits, of whom Greene was one, saw Shakespeare the man of Stratford as an upstart. Greene's 'upstart Crow' joke is a reference to the Aesop fable in which the crow dresses in the brighter plumage of other birds. Poor Greene, only in his early thirties, was living in abject poverty as the lodger of a poor shoe-maker when he met his end. None of his Cambridge friends came near him in his dejection and sickness. (It appears to have been some sort of food poisoning – he fell ill after a dinner of pickled herring and Rhenish wine.)

Shakespeare's histories still work on the stage. The *Henry VI* plays have enjoyed a number of revivals in England in recent years. Can we hope to reconstruct what the original audiences made of them, or whether the cycle of English history plays – written by Shakespeare and others – conveys some overall shared political viewpoint? Probably not. It is no longer fashionable to suppose that Shakespeare set out to write a National Epic, in which the chronicles of Hall and Holinshed come to life as stage plays. But, as at other periods of history – one thinks of the Soviet theatre, or of the life of the theatre in Paris during the German occupation – the theatre is a flexibly creative outlet for political dissent.

The *Henry VI* plays, in particular, do not provide us with a homogeneous or obvious political message. They are not, as earlier generations of critics wanted to say, a finished piece of propaganda for the Tudor dynasty, or upholders of the Tudor myth, or even a consistent defence of privilege against the mob. On the contrary, in *Henry VI Part II*, for example, the rebellion of Jack Cade is viewed as a prelude to the anarchy that is going to engulf the whole of England during the Wars of the Roses. But Cade is not viewed as inferior to the aristocrats, whose behaviour is in many ways like his. Indeed, Cade inverts the chivalric code by asserting, 'The proudest peer in the realm shall not wear a head on his shoulders, unless he pay me a tribute; there shall not a maid be married, but she shall pay to me her maidenhead ere they have it . . .'[23] This *droit de seigneur* is no more than the medieval aristocracy demanded of the English people. Cade is not seen by Shakespeare as less noble than the murderous York family, the bloodthirsty Queen Margaret; or as more of an anarchist than Hotspur and Owain Glyndŵr and the 'rebels' of later plays. 'What, Buckingham and Clifford, are ye so brave? And you, base peasants, do ye believe him?'[24]

There is a deep-seated radicalism in the very idea of depicting English history as a stage play, and Shakespeare is by no means the arch-conservative, afraid of taking away 'degree', whom an earlier generation saw. By 'radicalism', however, I do not mean that Shakespeare – once thought to be right-wing – was really left-wing. I mean that he saw down to the roots of the political realities of his day, more intelligently and more subversively than that. Watching the history plays now is to feel what an extraordinarily explosive, changeable and dangerous period the later years of Queen Elizabeth's reign were. By looking back at the previous century, when contention about the Crown and the succession were the causes of civil war, the London audiences were looking at their own age – in which Ireland was, as ever, in a state of semi-anarchy and hostility to England; when, behind the doll-like figure of the ageing queen and her court of senescent sycophants, lurked the spectre of the Succession Question. London, in particular, where these plays were staged, was a place where we can meet factions just as likely to tear one another apart as the factions depicted in Shakespeare's sixteenth-century reconstructions. There were the Roman Catholics hoping for Elizabeth to be replaced by – whom? Arbella Stuart? There were the extreme radicals who wanted the Reformation to be finished. There were the merchants of the City, the money-men who were not sufficiently represented in the seats of power, and who would, together with the Puritans, come to see Parliament as the setting for challenging the royal prerogative. The struggles that turned into the English Civil War all lay ahead, but we can see them at work in Elizabethan London and we can read prophetic meditations upon the issues of that war in Shakespeare's plays. And we can also read his monumental distaste for politics, his assertion of the personal above the collective. By far the most sympathetic, as well as memorable, figure in all the history plays was not a king or a queen or a noble warrior, but a fat old man who wanted to waste his time (and everyone else's) in whorehouses and taverns, undermining a prince not for reasons of political anarchy, but because he loved young men and mischief and drink.

22

Marprelate and Hooker

Some of the funniest writing of Elizabeth's reign is to be found in the seven anonymous pamphlets of Martin Marprelate, published on a secret printing press between 1588 and 1589. The object of his satirical abuse is the Church of England, and its bishops in particular. Although the specific *matter* of the tracts would seem to a modern reader narrowly ecclesiastical – 'Martin' is arguing for the abolition of bishops and the setting up of a form of Presbyterianism in England – the pamphlets have a far wider importance in literary and political history. For a start, they are superbly inventive and surreal in their manipulation of language, standing worthy of comparison with the prose of Milton (which they plainly influenced), Dean Swift and – in their gleeful puns and coinages – James Joyce.

But they are also, from the midst of that repressively censored world, a cry for intellectual and political freedom. At the centre of his target is the Archbishop of Canterbury, John Whitgift, who in 1586 had persuaded the Council in the Star Chamber (it was not difficult!) to give to himself and John Aylmer, the bustling, aggressive, diminutive Bishop of London, the power of sole censors of all printed material. They had the power – if they did not like what the press was printing – to destroy the press, deface the type, disable the printer and imprison him for up to six months.[1] Marprelate cited the case of a Protestant painter, Robert Waldegrave, who:

> dares not show his face for the bloodthirsty desire you have for his life, only for printing of books which toucheth the Bishops' mitres. You know that Waldegrave's printing press and letters [i.e. type] were taken away. His press, being timber, was sawn and hewed in pieces. The iron work battered and made unserviceable, his letters melted, with cases and other tools defaced . . . and he himself utterly deprived forever [of] printing again, having a wife and six small children. Will this monstrous cruelty never be revenged, think you?[2]

Marprelate pretends to address the archbishop reverently as 'your Grace' and 'your Lordship', but it isn't long before the archbishop has become 'Master Whitgift' and 'your Paltripolitanship' (a coinage suggesting the paltriness of Whitgift and his claims to exercise authority from the Metropolitical See of Canterbury. Whitgift is also addressed as 'His Canterburinesse'. Doctors of Divinity become 'Doctors of Divillitie'. And the pamphlets fizz with imagined hecklers in the margins – 'M. Marprelate you put more then the question in the conclusion of your syllogisme' – with Marprelate then shouting back at the supposed interruption, 'This is a pretie matter that standers by must be so busie in other men's games.' He represents sniggering and laughter: 'Tse, tse, tse – hy, hy – py, py. Ha, ha ha.' No writing of this freshness and spontaneity had ever appeared in English prose, still less in a work whose primary function was religious.

Marprelate voiced the view, widespread among Puritans, that the laws and censors persecuted Protestantism more vigorously than it condemned papism. Compare the fate of poor Waldegrave having his press, and his livelihood, destroyed, with 'knave Thackwen the printer, which printed popish and traitorous Welsh books in Wales. Thackwen is at liberty to walk where he will and permitted to make the most he could of his press and letters . . .' As well as making a strong point about the perils of Protestantism, there was also a brave joke here since Waldegrave was, we presume, the printer of the tract itself. Two presses were involved in the series, one in the possession of John Penry, which was hidden by Elizabeth Crane, a London Puritan in her house in East Molesey, and another that was concealed by a Warwickshire squire called Roger Wigston.

We can hear in Marprelate the authentic voice of radicalism, who proclaims, 'Thought is free.' He is giving witty and fantastical voice to a constituency of opinion that would sail to America in the *Mayflower*; which would take up arms against Charles Stuart in the Civil Wars; which, among the nonconformists of the eighteenth century, would give birth to more robustly political forms of republicanism and egalitarianism in the writings of Blake and Paine and Shelley.

Likewise, the response of the Establishment to Marprelate was the classic establishment view that by pulling one thread, episcopacy, the Puritans would undo the whole fabric of society. 'If this outragious spirit of boldenesse be not stopped speedily,' opined Thomas Cooper, the Bishop of Winchester, 'I feare he wil prove himself to bee, not only *Marprelate* but *Mar-prince*, *Mar-state*, *Mar-lawe*, *Mar-magistrate*, and all together, until he bring it to an Anabaptisticall equalitie and communite.' Cooper had reason to complain of Marprelate, who in the tract entitled *An Epistle to the Terrible Priests* had denounced 'My Lord of Winchester' as 'a monstrous hypocrite' and 'a very dunce'.[3]

Marprelate, by contrast, saw the bishops themselves as 'not only traitors against God and His Word, but also enemies to the Prince and to the State'.[4]

Despite their best endeavours, they never did find out for certain who wrote the tracts. Nor did the literary historians and detectives of subsequent ages. At least twenty-two candidates have been suggested as the likely author. Leland H. Carlson makes strong claims for Job Throckmorton, an Oxford-educated (the Queen's College) country gentleman from Haseley in Warwickshire. From the 1570s onwards, Throckmorton wrote many letters and pamphlets insulting the bishops. Carlson makes out a convincing case for stylistic similarity between the anonymous Marprelate and works to which Throckmorton gave his name. He points to the number of allusions to betting and games of chance in both authors; to a similarly knowledgeable use of legal terminology. Both authors like coining words with the preface 'be' – Marprelate has 'bedeaconed, besir, becetyfull' and Throckmorton 'beglazed, beprouded, behackled'. Both, tellingly, refer to Dean Bridges of Salisbury as 'old Lockwood of Sarum'; both denounce the Archbishop of Canterbury as 'a giddie head' – and there are many other persuasive points of comparison.[5]

The most persuasive feature of Carlson's thesis is that, plainly, Marprelate was not representative of any faction. Though he sided with the Puritans, they distanced themselves from him: they disliked his ribaldry, his bawdry, his satire. Throckmorton, who was a Member of Parliament, believed passionately in free speech for those speaking in the House of Commons and those speaking from a pulpit. He was really a hundred years at least ahead of his time, advocating political ideals that were not achieved until the Bill of Rights and the Toleration Act in the reign of William and Mary.

Viewed as a campaign on behalf of the Puritans, the Marprelate tracts misfired. The authorities rumbled Throckmorton, but they could not prove his authorship. It may even be the case that the Queen herself was partly amused by the vigour of the tracts, and smiled upon a cousin of a lady-in-waiting, Elizabeth Throckmorton – who was a favourite of the Queen until it was discovered that she had secretly married Sir Walter Raleigh.[6]

One of the more remarkable features of the Marprelate controversy was how quickly it burst out of the confines of the Church and became a matter of general public interest. The prelates writhed beneath his lash, but they could not match his wit. The bishops engaged Gabriel Harvey and Thomas Nashe to answer Marprelate in kind. But in a sense this was just what was *not* needed. The mainstream Puritans shared Marprelate's view that contemporary Church order should be modelled as simply as possible on the elders, presbyters and deacons mentioned in the New Testament. But they knew that he was not really one of their number. Josias Nichols, a Puritan writing at the end of

Elizabeth's reign, said that the appearance of the Marprelate pamphlets 'did greatlie astonish us, & verie much demean the righteouesnesse of our cause'. Nichols would never have used Throckmorton's vivid turns of phrase, which were applied to Puritans as well as prelates. When he visited William Hacket, a self-proclaimed prophet, for instance, Throckmorton likened his prayer to 'the wildgoose chase, neither heade, nor foote, rime nor reason'. He was amused by 'the very puffing and swellinge of his face, the staring and goggling of his eies, with his gahstlie [*sic*] countenance'.[7]

The Marprelate episode revealed in stark and semi-comic clarity that, after thirty years, the Elizabethan Church was very far from being perfect. The experiment, of setting up a Church that was both Catholic and Reformed, might be seen, through Marprelate's eyes, as a pathetic failure. The bishops had the greatest difficulty in filling the 8,700 parishes of England with educated priests. Far from being good preachers, many of them had the greatest difficulty in reading from the Book of Common Prayer and the Book of Homilies.[8]

There is an understandable tendency among historians, particularly among those who are not themselves religious, to suppose that the serious contenders in the sixteenth-century debate were, on the one hand, the Puritans, or Calvinists, who wanted a wholesale Reformation; and on the other, the supporters of the Pope, the Counter-Reformation; and the Jesuits. Viewed from this perspective, the Queen's religion – Henrician Catholicism within a National Church – is seen as a quasi-political compromise, even an expression of religious indifferentism. And the defenders of the position which had been carefully worked out by the National Church, above all Richard Hooker, are seen as wishy-washies, or small-c conservatives who merely wanted to retain the status quo.

In the case of Richard Hooker (1554?–1600) no judgement could be less accurate or less fair. He is one of the few writers in the English language with claims to be an original theologian. And although the title of his most celebrated work makes it seem as if his interests were limited to the Church, *Of the Laws of Ecclesiastical Polity* is actually a carefully considered philosophical *Summa*, a great contribution to European thought, which is not merely a defence of the Church of England, but also a synthesis of medieval scholastic thought, radically reworked for the modern age. He was the English Aristotle, interested in everything, temperate, curious, profoundly learned and, by the way, a superb prose writer. In many respects it makes sense to read Hooker beside the *Principall Voyages* of Hakluyt or the *Arcadias* of Sidney. In all three writers, we sense the distinctiveness and isolation of England since the Reformation; and yet, with all three, we find acute minds aware of the greater world: in

Hakluyt's case, the larger geography and cosmography; in Sidney's, the whole world of European humanism and in particular the Italian poetic tradition; in Hooker's case, a sense of the vast continuing tradition of Christianity, from its earliest biblical origins and its Greek patristic literature through the Western traditions of the Roman Church. Nothing makes Hooker's Puritan opponents seem more petty-minded or parochial than their being scandalised by his view, expressed in *A Learned Discourse of Justification*, that Roman Catholics were actually Christians, even if they belonged to a branch of the Church that was flawed. ('But how many millions of them are known so to have ended their mortal lives, that the drawing of their breath hath ceased with the uttering of this faith, "Christ my Saviour, my Redeemer Jesus!" And shall we say that such did not hold the foundation of Christian faith?'[9]

Both to the papists, who considered that the Institution of the Church was of such godly perfection that it could not err, and to the Calvinists, who wanted to destroy all existent Christian traditions and start again in pursuit of some perfect image of the New Testament Church, Hooker wanted to say that all human institutions were by their very nature imperfect. Yet this deeply holy, humble, learned man had a view of the Church that was more philosophically coherent than either of the alternatives on offer. It was not a compromise – still less a fudge – his philosophy. Extremists on either side could dismiss him as 'Latitudinarian'. Readers of his charming biography by Isaak Walton will treasure the moment, when he was the vicar of Drayton Beauchamp in Buckinghamshire, when his two favourite pupils, Cranmer (great-nephew of the archbishop) and Sandys (son of the Archbishop of York), visited him in his rural fastness and found him in a field reading the odes of Horace while tending his sheep. Hooker belonged to that benign company described by William James as the 'once born'; and even so sympathetic a commentator as C.S. Lewis could write, 'Sometimes a suspicion crosses our mind that the doctrine of the Fall did not loom quite large enough in his universe.' Lewis's phrase – though he insists it is not his own view of Hooker – 'a mild eupeptic' stays in the mind.[10]

Hooker came from Exeter, as every visitor to that city, who passes his statue in the Cathedral Close will know. His great-grandfather had been a mayor of the city, but the family had fallen on hard times, and by the time Hooker was a boy, they were poor. His uncle, who somehow knew John Jewel when he was Bishop of Salisbury, asked Jewel to 'become his patron and prevent him from being a tradesman, for he was a boy of remarkable hopes'.[11]

Hooker thereby got a place at Corpus Christi College, Oxford, though making frequent return visits on foot to Exeter to visit his family. He was deeply learned in Hebrew and Greek, and in 1581 took Holy Orders. On 17 March 1584–5 Hooker was appointed as Master of the Temple. It was a baptism of fire. London and the Inns of Court were the centre of religious controversy in England. As we have already noted, the Inns were full of Catholic recusants and their sympathisers; but, on the other side, there were also many ardent Calvinists who wanted the Elizabethan Church rooted out, who objected, on a superficial level, to such things as set forms of liturgy, feast days of the Church other than the Sabbath (Christmas, Easter, and so on, they saw as popish) and the wearing of ceremonial robes such as surplices in church; and who believed that between Apostolic times and the present there had been an ecclesiastical Dark Age, in which the Holy Spirit had not breathed over the ecclesiastical waters. An ardent exponent of this extreme Calvinistic position, directly inspired by the French theologian from his Genevan theocracy, was Walter Travers, afternoon lecturer at the Temple, who had been hoping for the mastership and was angered at being passed over in favour of Hooker. Increasingly the two men appeared to be offering to the congregation of the Temple Church a critique of two opposing views of the sixteenth-century religious dilemma. It was probably painful to the mild-mannered Hooker, but he did not shrink from the controversy. An observer tells us that 'The pulpit spake pure Canterbury in the morning and Geneva in the afternoon.'[12]

But these engagements with Travers laid the foundation of Hooker's masterwork. When offered a country living – first at Boscombe in Wiltshire and later at Bishopsbourne near Canterbury – Hooker could retreat from the glare of public argy-bargy and concentrate upon his writing. (Friends pitied him for his ill-tempered wife – 'a clownish silly woman and withal a mere Xanthippe,' according to Anthony Wood, who is not always a reliable gossip.) There were children, but Hooker was never a healthy person, and this showed with his blotchy, spotty complexion. Presumably he ate unwisely.

The present book is not the sort of work where it would be appropriate to expound Hooker's philosophical and religious position in detail. He wrote, 'Though for no other cause, yet for this; that posterity may know we have not loosely through silence permitted things to pass away as in a dream'.[13]

Hooker did not share the Puritan fear of the secular *polis*. He believed that the state was a human construct, and that, while human beings were fallen creatures, they were capable of building rational, rich institutions that enable virtue to flourish. The fact that an institution is of human origin, and human beings are fallen, does not of itself logically demand that all human institutions are inherently evil. Therefore Hooker can reject both the theocracy of Geneva and of Rome. As a follower of Thomas Aquinas, he was dubious about absolute monarchy. He was no lickspittle for the Elizabethan Settlement. He saw the role of the Church, and of individual Christians, as the redemption of public life. Elizabeth was Governor of the Church of (and in) England, but the Church's life was given to it not by the Crown, but by God. He was 'High Church' in so far as he defended such traditions as going to confession, making the sign of the Cross and revering Christ in the Eucharist. But he recognised that *how* Christians organise their Church is determined by where they find themselves in history. Thus, although he took a high view of the episcopate, he saw bishops – the highest form of priests, since they can themselves make priests – as of the *bonum esse* of the Church, not of its *esse*, as a good thing, but they were not the essence of the thing. One could conceive, in other words, of being a Christian without bishops, though it was better to have them. That is, the Church is made by the people of God, in obedience to God; it is not made, as it were, by the magic of sacrament. The Roman Catholics of the Counter-Reformation appeared to be teaching that the priesthood and the Eucharist have, so to say, a life of their own – independent, almost of the people through whom they are mediated. Sacrament, in this view of things, can degenerate into something like magic. Similarly the hierarchical structure of society, in which Hooker deeply believed, can degenerate into tyranny if it is not seen as a contract between all peoples of goodwill.

The Puritans were especially scandalised by Hooker's high doctrine of the Eucharist, just as, no doubt, there were Roman Catholics who regarded as suspect his insistence that '*the soul of man* is the receptacle of Christ's presence' (Hooker's italics).[14] 'The fruit of the Eucharist is the participation of the body and blood of Christ.'[15] This statement, in the fifth of Hooker's books of *Laws*, actually lies at the heart of his whole philosophy of life. Far from being a compromiser who cobbled together a political justification for the Church of England, he saw the Church as emblematic of human society as a whole, men and women joined together for the common good to fulfil their destiny as children of God. He believed this to be the destiny of all human beings, regardless of whether they had the good fortune to have been born in England. In the England of Elizabeth, he believed this destiny was best fulfilled by an obedient membership of the National Church, whose faults he readily acknowledged. Indeed, the faults in part authenticated his viewpoint, since he believed that, this side of the grave, no institution – ecclesiastical, legal or political – could be perfect, and that wheat and tares would grow together in the Lord's field until the harvest.

E.M.W. Tillyard, in a book that was once very popular, called

The Elizabethan World Picture, demonstrated that the great writers of the age – Spenser, Sidney, Raleigh, Hooker, Shakespeare and Jonson – were all 'united in holding with earnestness and passion and assurance to the main outlines of the medieval world picture'.[16] Since this was true of the poets in their Neoplatonism, in their shared concepts of a 'chain of being', in their idea of order and hierarchy, it was inevitably true of the Elizabethan Church. As all the inspectors' and bishops' reports and visitations show, the majority of English men and women were wistful about the parting of the old order, missed many of the old ways, but did not want to follow the Jesuits into civil war and regicide. They found that, for all the hurly-burly of the Reformation years, the Catholic religion – as found in the formularies of the Church of England – was in essence what it had been before, with changes that were on the whole welcome: a vernacular liturgy, and a Bible you could read for yourself. Hooker spoke to this generation, but he was not merely the mouthpiece of the zeitgeist. He was the carefully considered philosophical expression of a fact: nothing in *essence* had altered about England or its Church. There had been a few local improvements.

Hooker's last years were clouded by illness, but brightened by the friendship of a Dutch priest, Dr Saravia, a prebend of Canterbury. They were one another's confessors. His life at Bishopsbourne – as an active parish priest, and as a scholar – was cut short when he was only forty-six, by what seems to have been pneumonia. As he lay on his final sickbed he heard that his house had been burgled. 'Are my books and written papers safe?' was his revealing response. As he became weaker, Dr Saravia came once more to hear his confession:

> and then the Doctor gave him, and some of those friends which were with him, the blessed sacrament of the body and blood of our Jesus. Which being performed, the Doctor thought he saw a reverend gaiety and joy in his face; but it lasted not long; for his bodily infirmities did return suddenly, and became more visible, insomuch that the Doctor apprehended death ready to seize him; yet, after some amendment, left him at night, with a promise to return early the day following; which he did and then found him better in appearance, deep in contemplation, and not inclinable to discourse; which gave the Doctor occasion to require his present thoughts. To which he replied, 'That he was meditating the number and nature of angels, and their blessed obedience and order, without which peace could not be in heaven: and Oh! That it might be so on earth.[17]

Part Four

The Close of the Reign

23

A Hive for Bees

The Accession Day Tilt on 17 November 1590 marked the retirement of Sir Henry Lee as the Queen's Champion. The whole ceremony was choreographed, as had been the previous twenty or so (opinion differs about the date of the first), by Lee himself. He was not only an inspired deviser of symbolic ceremonial. He was himself an embodiment of Elizabethan tastes, values, history and aspirations. He was Elizabeth's champion in far more than name only, and although he would live for another twenty years, his withdrawal from this particular role blew a chill wind. He was sixty. Some said that he was the Queen's half-brother, a by-blow of Henry VIII's. ('He ordered that all his family should be christened *Harry's*,'[1] gossiped John Aubrey). Whatever the truth of that, he was brought up as the child of gentry – of Sir Anthony Lee of Borston, Buckinghamshire – but entered royal service at the court of Henry VIII when he was fourteen. Aubrey tells us that Lee never married, but this is untrue: it was his (unhappy) marriage to the Catholic Anne Paget that saved this stoutly Protestant gentleman's bacon during the precarious reign of Mary Tudor.

Travelling through Europe as a diplomat in his mid-thirties, Lee visited Italy – Rome, Florence, Venice – Germany, and the Low Countries, and it was in Antwerp that he sat for his portrait to the Flemish artist Antonis Mor. The painter has captured with entire plausibility a clever upper-class English face whose type is still to be met to this day in certain diplomats, financiers, army officers, landowners. If you discount the high ruff (which became fashionable in the 1560s), the ribbed, padded velvet doublet and the goatee beard, and substitute a suit cut in twenty-first century Savile Row and a shirt made in Jermyn Street, you could easily be looking at a man who had solved *The Times* crossword in ten minutes and who, after a productive morning at the Foreign Office or in a merchant bank, was going to lunch at his club in St James's Street. The curly hair, high brow and ironical eyes are instantly familiar. So too is the deceptively thin-lipped smile, which just fails to conceal sensuality. After his wife died, and he had retired, Lee lived openly with his mistress, a raffish figure called Anne Vavasour, who had given birth to an illegitimate child by Lord Oxford. Active in all senses in his retirement, he farmed sheep on a vast scale, making himself heartily disliked in Oxfordshire for his ruthless enclosure of common land and rebuilding his seat – Ditchley Park – to make it a worthy place for his heroine, Elizabeth, to visit; which, in spite of the irregularity of his ménage, she did. (Lee was made a Knight of the Garter in 1597 – a very unusual honour for one who was not a peer.[2])

His flair for the pregnantly meaningful pageant had demonstrated year after year some aspect of their own mood or national aspiration to the courtly classes. One that stood out in memory was his tribute to his dead friend Sir Philip Sidney at the tilt for 1587, when lamentations were spoken over a riderless horse (perhaps an emblem that 350 years later inspired Yeats's lines about 'The high horse riderless / Though mounted in that saddle Homer rode'.[3]

And so his own last tilt as Queen's Champion spoke of the extraordinary generation that was now facing old age. They had been born into the England in which Henry VIII was just beginning his ruthless innovations. The monasteries were dissolved during their early childhoods, becoming 'Bare ruined choirs where late the sweet birds sang'.[4] Henry had strengthened the navy, reinvented the Church and raised up the new rich by giving them lands and revenues snatched from the Church. After his death, the country had lurched from the extreme Protestantism advocated by Edward VI's advisers to the Marian Counter-Reformation, with the screams of heretics coming from the bonfires of Smithfield. Then had come the relief: the young queen – who was *their age* – an incarnation of so many of their intellectual, religious and political values. And thirty years had passed, thirty years in which England itself had begun to establish the identity that it would retain for centuries to come: an England where the Inns of Court, the universities and the grammar schools, the Church, the landed gentry, the magistracy, provided the framework of life; an England expanding and looking overseas to mercantile, possibly imperial, futures; an England ruthlessly and intransigently embedded in Ireland, callously indifferent to the plight of its own poor, as rigidly hierarchical as the orders of angels contemplated by Hooker on his deathbed, but as socially flexible as the careers of the clever, grammar-school educated could make it. This – Sir Henry Lee's generation and that of the Queen herself – was the generation now growing old.

Would it age wisely and graciously? The great success of the early years of the reign was that it had been a country given into the hands of clever, imaginative young people. Would they – many of them still holding on to the reins of power – step down, like Sir Henry? Or would they hang on, and try to choke back new intellectual enquiry, new political or geographical endeavours? In the government-inspired murder of Christopher Marlowe, in the cool treatment meted out to their great epic poet Spenser, in their semi-cold-shouldering of Dr Dee, we get warning signals of a gerontocracy tightening its grip. Sir Francis Drake sailing round the world in the late

1570s was a cause for national pride; Raleigh's voyage to Guiana in 1595 was viewed with suspicion. The ageing queen's doting on the young Earl of Essex, far from bringing forward a generation of New Talent, was to end in disaster. So the autumn winds that blew through Whitehall, that November of 1590, were bringing troubled times to the closing years of the reign. Some modern historians have seen the 1590s as a 'second reign' of Elizabeth – one of meteorological disaster, economic hardship, religious anarchy, escalating crime, Irish horror, and something very close, with the calamity of the Essex rebellion, to the civil wars from which Elizabeth's 'good grandfather' had delivered the country in 1485.

The retirement tilt of Sir Henry Lee had some of the qualities of a glorious sunset flare. Lee could not possibly have guessed, but his imagination might somehow have intuited, what troubles lay ahead; now, therefore, in his scale of values, was a moment of undiluted triumphalism, and of uncritical worship of their Virgin Idol.

The pseudo-medieval knights who rode out into the tiltyard of Whitehall (roughly the site of Horse Guards Parade today) were now all long in the tooth. There was always an element of comedy, as well as of excitement, about these pageants, as a visiting German, Lupold von Wedel, had observed in 1584: 'When a gentleman with his servants approached the barrier, on horseback or in carriage, he stopped at the foot of the staircase leading to the queen's room, while one of the servants in pompous attire of a special pattern mounted the steps and addressed the queen in well-composed verses or with a ludicrous speech, making her and her ladies laugh.'[5] Now, mingled with the comedy, there was elegy, and as Sir Henry Lee took leave of the Queen, a choir sang verses of his own composing, which were absurd and touching in equal measure:

His golden locks time hath to silver turned
(O time too swift, O swiftness never ceasing!);
His youth gainst time and age hath ever spurned,
But spurned in vain; youth waneth by increasing.
Beauty, strength, youth are flowers but fading seen;
Duty, faith, love are roots, and ever green.

His helmet now shall make a hive for bees,
And lover's sonnets turn to holy psalms;
A man-at-arms must now serve on his knees,
And feed on prayers, which are age's alms.
But though from court to cottage he depart,
His saint is sure of his unspotted heart.[6]

Whereas other historians saw the last fifteen years of Elizabeth's reign as a tale of triumph, played out against the backdrop of Gloriana's golden sunset, we might see something rather different: an oligarchy of diminishing competence, presided over by an ageing and increasingly indecisive queen; an embattled island, continuously at war in Europe; an archipelago in effect at war with itself – with Ireland consumed by violence, with Catholics and Puritans in England at one another's throats, with the Queen's closest favourite, Essex, leading a failed coup against her. These are the realities to be set beside the literary glories of Shakespeare's plays and of Spenser's *Faerie Queene*. The expansion of Elizabethan England abroad, and the establishment of the colony at Virginia – causes of celebration as they might be, in one way of looking at things – can also be seen as laying the foundation for the most hateful economic and racial exploitations by European over non-European humanity.

But, then, if we are looking to suck the milk of human kindness, we have come to the wrong place in the England of Elizabeth. Thomas Nashe, as so often, sailed near the wind in his picaresque novel *The Unfortunate Traveller*, when he made the protagonist, Jack Wilton, recall the conversations of Erasmus in Rotterdam:

> This I can assure you, *Erasmus*, in all his speeches seemed so much to mislike the indiscretion of Princes in preferring of parasites and fools, that he decreed with himself to swim with the stream, and write a booke forwith in commendation of follie. Quick witted Sir *Thomas Moore* traueld in a cleane contrarie province, for he seeing most common-wealths corrupted by ill custome, & that principalities were nothing but great piracies which, gotten by violence and murther, were maintained by private vndermining and bloudshed, that in the cheefest flourishing kindgomes there was no equall or well decided weale one with an other, but a manifest conspiracie of rich men against poore men, procuring their owne vnlawfull commodities vnder the name and interest of the common wealth: hee concluded with himself to lay doune a perfect plot of a common-wealth or gouernment, which he would intitle his *Vtopia*.[7]

Nashe was bold enough to point out that More's satire of the England of 1516 had become a reality by the 1590s. Who, witnessing the Queen herself, and her Council members, cashing in on Hawkins's slave-trade, Drake's open acts of maritime theft or the enclosure by the New Rich of common land, could fail to see that the whole 'principality' was 'nothing but great piracie'?

Thomas Nashe's fictions, pamphlets and satirical journalism paint a completely devastating picture of how unremittingly horrendous life was for the majority of the rapidly expanding population. We do not know the exact figures, but during Elizabeth's reign the population of her kingdom expanded by 1 per cent *per annum* (more than 35 per cent for the period 1558–1603), and this in spite of repeated plagues and actual starvation.[8] The 1590s also saw those exceptionally bad weather conditions, attributed by the Fairy Queen Titania to the petulant whim of her husband Oberon:

> The ox hath therefore stretched his yoke in vain,
> The ploughman lost his sweat, and the green corn
> Hath rotted ere his youth attained a beard.
> The fold stands empty in the drownèd field . . .
>
> The spring, the summer,
> The chiding autumn, angry winter, change
> Their wonted liveries, and the mazèd world
> By their increase now knows not which is which.[9]

The years 1593 and 1594 had bad harvests, 1596 and 1597 actual dearth, with a great increase in the parish registers of burials. The poor and the starving took to crime. In September 1596 Edward Hext, a Justice of the Peace in Somerset, wrote to Lord Burghley to express his fear that social order was breaking down altogether. 'Rapynes and thefts . . . multiplye daylye.' The starving vagrants were seen by this gentleman as 'wicked and desparate' persons, who 'beinge putt to any hard labour, will greve them above measure, so as they will rather hazard their lives than work'. Hext reckoned that there were 300 or 400 'wandring souldiers and other stout roages' in every county in England.[10]

The paradox about the central economic idea of the Rev. Thomas Malthus, whose essay on population gave Charles Darwin the idea of Nature as an everlasting warfare for the survival of the fittest, was that the theory was true more or less until the moment in history when Malthus chose to write it. That is to say, there was a limited amount of edible matter and, when this had been consumed, the population adjusted itself by disease or starvation. Periods of great wealth were those, such as the fifteenth century in England following the Black Death, when the population fell in proportion to the amount of food. In the period following the Industrial Revolution, in spite of cataclysms such as the Irish Famine, Europeans began for the first time to produce enough for an *expanding* population to eat, thereby hugely increasing economic growth.

Elizabethan England, however, remained firmly trapped in the Malthusian lock. The middle decades of the reign were remarkably free from epidemics of plague. Life expectancy rose to an average of forty.[11] There was the inevitable increase in food prices and deflation of wages, and a desperate scramble both for foreign markets for English exports and for areas abroad where commodities could be had for cheap – or plundered for free. This is one explanation for the population explosion (from three million to four million during the reign[12]), which was only checked by outbreaks of plague. In a 'good' year, from a Malthusian viewpoint, such as 1593, London lost 23,236 through plague, a little over 10 per cent of its population.

One way of dealing with the problem of poor 'roages', apart from the Malthusian and obvious one of allowing them simply to starve to death, was to draft them into armed service. The wars in the Netherlands and in Ireland needed cannon-fodder. In the county of Kent alone, during the 1590s, 6,000 men were 'impressed' – that is press-ganged into the army. That is a huge proportion of the county's population, which stood at around 130,000.

Inevitably, the indigent drifted towards London. Nashe in *Christ's Teares over Iervsalem* comments upon the particular meanness of the English mercantile class and the nobility in giving to the poor:

> A halfe-penny a month to the poore mans boxe we count our vtter empouerishing. I have hearde trauailers of credite avouch, that in *London* is not gyuen the tenth part of that almes in a weeke, which in the poorest besieged City of Fraunce is gyuen in a day . . . Our dogges are fedde with the crumbes that fal from our Tables. Our Christian bretheren are famisht for want of the crumbs that fall from our tables. Take it from me, rich men expressly, that it is not your owne which you haue purchast with your industry: it is part of it the poores, part your Princes, parte your Preachers. You ought to possesse no more than will moderatly sustaine your house and your family.[13]

Pneumonic plague, carried by black rats, is a directly infectious disease that is sprayed into the air by coughing.[14] The burial records tell the story. 'A poor boy that died under St John's Wall', 'a poor wench died in the cage', 'a poor child found at Mistress Bake's door'.[15] People were alive and merry one hour, and dead the next.

In the principal towns the attempts to contain the plague were the responsibility of mayors. In London, the Lord Mayor made the constables, when they took office, swear to report the true numbers of plague victims, should the disease break out. Concealing plague-death was a serious offence punishable by heavy fines and imprisonment.

Dogs were thought to be especially infectious. Elizabethan London swarmed with dogs.[16] Special officers were appointed in 1563 to 'murder' and bury dogs found in the streets in plague-time. Many parishes paid dog-catchers – the dog-catcher for St Margaret's, Westminster, killed 656 in 1592, 502 in 1603. (Daniel Defoe, in his *Journal of the Plague Year, 1665* reports the killing of 40,000 London dogs.) Elizabethans tended to leave their dead animals – 'dead dogs, cats, whelps or kitlings' – in the street to rot. Plague-houses were marked with a red cross and 'Lord Have Mercy on Us'. Burials were perforce hugger-mugger. Few could afford coffins. Corpses, covered with a winding sheet, were flung into pest-pits without prayer or ceremony. In 1582 twenty-three parishes were trying to use St Paul's churchyard as their burying ground and corpses were bursting from the shallow site.

Few who have read Nashe's diatribe will ever be able to forget his picture of plague-victims in Gray's Inn, Clerkenwell, Finsbury and Moorfields. They were domestic servants who had been driven out of their masters' houses to die 'for want of reliefe and warme-keeping . . . Cursing and rauing by the high-way side have they expired, & theyr Maisters never sent to them nor succourd them.'[17]

The words of the clever, Cambridge-educated, Lowestoft-born Nashe were echoed in Kent by a farm labourer in 1598, who 'hoped to see such warre in this realme to afflicte the rich man of this countrye to requite their hardnes of heart towards the poore'.[18] Nashe's view survives because he was an incomparably powerful prose stylist. The labourer survives in an indictment.

One historian has written that 'the law of sedition in Elizabethan England provided that anyone who criticised the government, reported others' criticisms, or even speculated about when the government would change or when the queen died, was subject to crushing fines, and cruel corporal punishment, and even death itself'.[19] Nine years before audiences rocked with laughter at the antics on stage of Bottom the Weaver. Thomas Bird (a weaver from Sandwich) was arrested in 1586 for loose talk about a planned uprising of 800–900 men, who had declared their intention to 'hang up the rich farmers that had corn at their own doors'.[20]

The statute of 1581 against seditious words decreed that first offenders unable to pay the £200 fine should be set in the pillory and have their ears cut off. 'Seditious words' could mean whatever the magistrate chose them to mean. In 1596 James Bradshaw of Oxfordshire asked a fellow 'conspirator' 'whether there were not certain good fellows in Witney that wold ryse & knock down the gentlemen & riche men that take in the commons and make corne so dear'. George Binkes from Essex was overheard bragging that if pressed for military service against Spain it 'wold goe against his conscience'. He further said that 'capteyne Drake and his souldiers when they have gone forth into the prince's service do robbe and spoile the kynge of Spayne his goods which is the right Kyng of Ingland'.[21]

Dissent was by no means limited to religious minorities, such as the Anabaptists, or to Roman Catholics, who were probably very numerous. We find it everywhere we look. The government, both the central government in London and its provincial arms, the Justices of the Peace, were mercilessly efficient at silencing 'seditious words'. Seventy-eight people in Devon were killed in 1598 alone for sedition. When there was actual danger of starvation after poor harvests and a hike in grain prices, local corporations sold cheap bread: 725 people a week in Coventry were buying it during the dearths of 1597 and 1598. Add these to the miserable unpaid or impressed troops in Ireland and Holland, and a large proportion of the population are seen to be unhappy. Moreover, Elizabeth had succeeded politically by failing to give either side, in any of the great political questions of the day, what they wanted. The Roman Catholics were as displeased by the Established Church as were the Puritans. The Succession Question was unsatisfactory – especially to those who had hoped the Queen would marry and have children of her own. No one knew anything about James VI of Scotland, Elizabeth's heir. Elizabeth survived, and actually thrived, on ambiguity and unresolved questions. Her policy was *après moi, le déluge*. The establishment of a colonial bolthole in America, which became a place to which dissidents could imagine taking themselves, actually increased the strength of religious dissent at home. And population growth, especially in London, created social dislocation of all kinds. Crime and disease were only part of it. Deep-seated questions about the nature of authority, and clashes between monarch and parliament were laid down by Elizabeth for her successors to deal with. By the end of her reign the divisions in society, and the political divisions at its apex, had become incorrigible.

The 'cult of Elizabeth' – the exaggerated worship of Elizabeth as a goddess – was in part a ritual, limited to a small number of courtiers or would-be courtiers. There was no doubt that she *was* popular, and indeed loved, by much of the population throughout her reign. But the Queen and the people of England were like the cynical lovers in Shakespeare's sonnet (the first version printed in *The Passionate Pilgrim* in 1599, the second in *Shakespeare's Sonnets*, 1609):

> Therefore I lie with her, and she with me,
> And in our faults by lies we flattered be.[22]

Even in the most apparently basilolatrous of her poets, Spenser, Elizabeth could have read criticism: some have found in his work outright republicanism. Her dearest favourite of the late phase was the Essex who betrayed her. Ted Hughes, the late-twentieth-century Poet Laureate, made a rich imaginative reading of the sixteenth century's greatest writer, *Shakespeare and the Goddess of Complete Being*. Of course Hughes was not an Eng. Lit. don and his book would be eschewed by what Thomas Nashe in a different context called 'scholasticall squitter books'.[23] But Hughes was surely right to see that Shakespeare was a manner of prophet who saw into the life of what was happening to his society: 'The *Zeitgeist* itself, it seems, conscripted Shakespeare's synapses to rehearse all those regicides (malevolent and pitiless like Richard III; possessed yet noble like Macbeth; noble and selfless like Brutus; shrewd and evil like Edmund) before it finally stepped out (after quirkish flashes in the pan – the giddy Essex, its attempts to incriminate Raleigh) into flesh and blood and history. In about the year that Shakespeare wrote *Macbeth*, Oliver Cromwell (another apocalyptic dreamer) dreamed he would be King (and told his master and was whipped for it).[24]

Francis Walsingham, a lynchpin of the old regime, died in April 1590. In his final illness his duties as Secretary had passed back to the seventy-year-old hands of Burghley, who, in the atmosphere of court rivalry that grew ever more malicious and frenzied, was desperate to promote the interests of his clever, efficient, physically deformed and charmless son, Robert, against those of the rising Earl of Essex. What Elizabeth needed at this juncture was a new young adviser who combined Robert Cecil's administrative skills with the flair and sex-appeal of the young Earl of Essex – and without Essex's appallingly spoilt-brat displays of temperament. Instead, she held the two men endlessly at odds, undermining the stability of governance. It could be said that after the death of Walsingham the Elizabethan tapestry began to unravel. Its foreign policy came more confusedly to reflect the Queen's Hamlet-like indecisiveness. Its Church Settlement looked increasingly unsettled. And Ireland entered one of the saddest and bloodiest decades in its history, a situation exacerbated – but, in reality, almost entirely caused – by the meanness of the Queen and the corrupt dealings of the ageing Burghley.

It was the fall of Sir John Perrot that brought these unpalatable facts to the surface. Perrot, like Sir Henry Lee, with whose delightful pageants we began this chapter, was said to be yet another son of Henry VIII. It was a plausible speculation. Like the dead king, Perrot was a huge, angry ladies' man. He had been born in 1527, out of wedlock, and his mother, Mary Berkeley, married Thomas Perrot, esquire of Pembrokeshire, a rising star of the Tudor Taffia.

Between 1584 and 1588 Perrot had been one of those unfortunates who found himself Lord Deputy of Ireland. As the reader of this book will have discovered, I do not defend the Elizabethan policy in Ireland, which was not only unjust and unworkable in itself, but stored up misery for generations to come. Within the Elizabethan terms, however, Perrot was a good Lord Deputy. When he stood down, returning to his native Pembrokeshire and becoming MP for the fine old town of Haverfordwest, he left Ireland in peace. In that Armada year, had Ireland had a different Lord Deputy, the Spanish troops who came ashore might well have joined forces with one or another of the rival Irish clans and made war against the English. As it was – a terrible thing in human terms, but a stabilising one politically – the young Spaniards were massacred.

Perrot, brutal and choleric as he may have been, was a good administrator. He rode roughshod over various vested English interests in Ireland and fatally made enemies, but he had been a success. He was replaced by Sir William Fitzwilliam, a very different character, who happened to be a cousin of Mildred Cooke, who happened to be married to Burghley. As well as the feuds among the Irish themselves, and the everlasting hostility between the Irish and the English, the faction-fighting among the English administrators in Ireland helped to spoil any chance of happiness for that island. Perrot still had his supporters on the Irish Council and they did their best to make life difficult for William Fitzwilliam. He in turn decided to 'frame' Perrot as a traitor. First, he got one Sir Dennis O'Roughan, a double-agent Catholic priest who had been used by Perrot as a 'priest catcher', to write letters to the Queen, alleging that Perrot was a crypto-papist-Spanish spy. O'Roughan claimed he had said secret Masses for Perrot (highly unlikely) and (even less likely) that Perrot had negotiated with the King of Spain, offering Philip II support in exchange for an hereditary grant in Wales.

While Fitzwilliam was a cousin by marriage of Burghley, Perrot was loosely connected with Burghley's new bête noire, the Earl of Essex (Perrot's son was married to Essex's sister). Burghley persuaded the Queen to appoint a commission, consisting of himself, Sir Christopher Hatton, Lord Hunsdon, the Lord Chamberlain, Howard, the Lord Admiral, and Lord Buckhurst. Hatton was someone else who had it in for Perrot, as Burghley well knew that Perrot had seduced and impregnated Hatton's daughter. Burghley and Hatton breached protocol by using a servant of Fitzwilliam's, rather than the Queen's official messenger, to collect and deliver O'Roughan's very questionable written communications, none of which survive – another very suspicious fact.

O'Roughan came to England. There a woman in Chester who accused him of having married her bigamously, a charge he denied – but it gives us some flavour of this priest-spy's character. Perrot answered all O'Roughan's insinuations robustly: 'it is as possible for me to perform the contents of that forged letter as it is for me to dance around with Paul's steeple on my thumb'.[25]

The Crown prosecutors could see that Perrot would have no difficulty in refuting O'Roughan's lies, so they changed tack. They now turned to Sir Richard Bingham, the Chief Commissioner of Connaught. Burghley had come to hear that there were some rhymers in Connaught who had composed poems against the Queen and claimed that she was not the lawful Queen of England. The poems themselves were in Irish, but even here Perrot utterly denied the charge that he had been soft with these supposedly seditious verses. He had taken the trouble to have them translated, and the 'worst' of them, addressed to the O'Connor Don, expressed the wish that 'he should be a wise hungry greyhound and should drive all Englishmen over the salt sea'. So, there was nothing treasonable in the rhymes and Perrot had not, in any case, encouraged them. Perrot was then accused by Fitzwilliam of having encouraged the rebellion of Brian O'Rourke, Lord of West Breifne, recently shired as County Leitrim. In 1586 O'Rourke had set up an image of a woman, inscribed it with the name ELIZABETH and then got his gallowglasses to drag it through the mud and chop it up.

In fact, as Perrot was able to demonstrate, he had not known of this incident until three years after it happened – years in which he had had some dealings with O'Rourke. In 1591, when O'Rourke came to Scotland to recruit mercenaries, he was extradited to England. Meanwhile, hearsay evidence was being collected against Perrot, remarks that he had made about the Queen when Lord Deputy. Obviously Perrot *was* extremely intemperate in his remarks about the Queen. I have already quoted 'Silly woman, now she shall not curb me, she shall not rule me now', and his view that taking orders from Elizabeth was 'to serve a base bastard piss kitchen woman'. Those who knew Perrot were aware that he was quite capable of such outbursts. Quite whether they merited the expensive palaver of a trial for high treason, with its inevitable gruesome outcome, was another matter.

The trial began on 27 April 1592. Perrot was brought by barge from the Tower to a packed Westminster Hall. He defended himself with the utmost vigour. Essex tried in vain to get the Queen to stop the proceedings. Although he failed, the Queen stayed judgement against him six times. Lord Chief Justice Anderson condemned Perrot to hang at Tyburn, but Perrot in fact died in the Tower of natural causes. It was clear that the Queen did not believe his guilt, since it was normal for the Crown to confiscate the lands of traitors, and Sir Thomas Perrot inherited most of the Welsh estate from his father.

It would seem that Sir John Perrot was put through these proceedings solely because Sir William Fitzwilliam had concocted his foolish conspiracy. To admit the folly and malice of Fitzwilliam would be to discredit the cousin of Burghley's wife. Burghley's credit as a factional leader would thereby have been irreparably damaged. Perrot was condemned to death not because he was a traitor, but because Burghley needed to maintain his Polonius-grip on the tiller. It was an incident that revealed how wildly out of control English policy could fly after the death of Walsingham.

24

Sex and the City

For a society that worshipped its Head of State as an unblemished Virgin, Elizabethan England has left behind plenty of evidence of advanced, collective sexual obsession. Ben Jonson, gossiping in his cups after the reign was over, could speculate that Elizabeth had 'had a Membrana on her which made her uncapable of men, though for her delight she tryed many, at the comming over of Monsieur, there was a French Chirugion who took in hand to cut it, yett fear stayed her & his death.'[1] Perhaps the cult of Elizabeth's virginity by the politicians was fed by the fact that Elizabethan society was, by the standards of later ages, especially open in its use of sexual language and in its discussion of sex in its most detailed and physical aspects. In the second Queen Elizabeth's reign the BBC actually noted, with a horror that would have been excessive, had the person concerned actually performed the sexual act – the first time the word FUCK was used on television, and in the mid- to late twentieth century there were special organisations, such as Mary Whitehouse's Viewers' and Listeners' Association, that monitored the number of times lewd acts or sexually suggestive allusions intruded themselves into public broadcasts.

Had Mrs Whitehouse and her friends spent their evenings rereading the works of William Shakespeare, they would have found that almost every play and poem that he wrote was full of sexual allusion, much of it rather childish. A man's bauble – as in 'hide his bauble in a hole' (*Romeo and Juliet* II.iii.93) – his thing, his prick, dial, poperin pear, cod's head, capon, cock or holy thistle is hard to avoid. If a tail or a tale is mentioned, some character is bound to make a pun, such as Mercutio's 'Thou desistest me to stop in my tale against the hair' (from the same scene in *Romeo and Juliet*). Hair only sometimes in Shakespeare means the hair on someone's head. To meet with a pipe, a needle, a pig's tail or a parson's nose is to know that someone is on the lookout for a hole, a placket-hole, a sluice, a gate, a thing, an organ, an et cetera, or the 'dearest bodily part'. It would be fanciful to attribute the enormous population explosion during Shakespeare's lifetime to an increase in popularity in playing the beast with two backs, rutting, scrambling, mounting, riding, sluicing, ravening or picking the lock, but as any of Shakespeare's audiences knew, these were all synonyms that he enlisted in his fertile and varied sexual vocabulary.[2]

Shakespeare's work both mirrored and fed the erotic obsessions of the age. The Roman erotic poet, Ovid, was his inspiration, and Shakespeare soon became the Ovid of his own epoch. His two long poems dedicated to the Earl of Southampton feature on the one hand, Venus, the goddess of love, as an older woman attempting to initiate a coy and unwilling Adonis into her own sexual obsessions; and Lucrece, brutally raped by Tarquin. Many of his most popular plays reflect not merely an artist, but a society, obsessed by sex. *Romeo and Juliet*, the most triumphantly successful of his early erotic comedies, concerns a thirteen-year-old girl whose mother wishes her to marry:

> Younger than you,
> Here in Verona, ladies of esteem
> Are made already mothers.[3]

It was followed by *A Midsummer Night's Dream* with its Ovidian metamorphosis of a working-class buffoon into a donkey – notoriously the best-endowed of male beasts – drawing the Fairy Queen into a physical obsession that is hilarious, sexy, but also humiliating. For while being the Ovidian celebrant of the rites of Eros, Shakespeare is the ultimate sexual cynic, whose Thersites in *Troilus and Cressida* exclaims: 'Lechery, lechery, still wars and lechery, nothing else holds fashion. A burning devil take them!'[4] The same association between lechery and burning – lust and hell; sex and the scalding sensations of venereal disease – are expressed in the starkest and most personal form in Shakespeare's Sonnets. In those twenty-eight sonnets that reflect the twenty-eight days of his dark mistress's menstrual cycle, he berated her for having infected both him and his beautiful young male friend:

> I guess one angel in another's hell.
> Yet this shall I ne'er know, but live in doubt,
> Till my bad angel fire my good one out.[5]

Measure for Measure, that sex-obsessed play in which extramarital sex is a capital offence, and in which the man of power, Angelo – another angel like those of Comfort and Despair in the sonnet just quoted – is willing to commute Claudio's death-sentence in exchange for the nun-sister's maidenhead, enters into the darkest places of the human sexual life, and the blowsy bordello and tavern-life of Mistress Overdone, Lucio, a 'fantastic' (that is, an extravagant dresser), Pompey the Clown and friends is one not merely familiar to Shakespeare, but a world of lechery that was known to the theatre audiences; which, indeed, when the Globe theatre had been built on Bankside in the thick of the capital's brothels, was absolutely visible all around them.

When Pompey and Mistress Overdone bemoan, at the beginning of *Measure for Measure*, the possibility that the priggish Angelo is going to demolish the seedy 'suburbs' of the city and close the brothels, they are speaking of something that the Londoners of Shakespeare's day would know had been tried during the reign of Henry VIII.

Scholarly opinion divides between those who do and do not believe that the *morbus gallicus* of venereal syphilis was brought to Europe from the New World, and that this explains the rampant growth of the disease in the sixteenth century. If it were a consequence of the Old World's greed for the treasures of the New World, there would be an emblematic fittingness to the story that is perhaps too neat, and which explains perhaps why some medics believe a mild form of syphilis existed in Europe in the fifteenth century, but transmuted itself into the ravaging disease that so laid waste humankind until the discovery of penicillin.[6]

Henry VIII, who had attempted to enact the *Measure for Measure*-style anti-bordello laws himself, died in an agony of syphilitic periostitis at the age of fifty-five. This great ox of a man had survived smallpox, malaria and the tuberculosis that had killed his father; he had survived dangerous sports; but eventually the symptoms of syphilis became unmistakable: ulcers on both legs, a collapsed nose, an increasingly erratic mental state. When he died his vast corpse was put in a lead coffin and slowly transported from London to Windsor. It was rested overnight at Syon House, where the coffin split and leakage spattered on the floor, to be licked by the household dogs. If ever there was a character who exemplified the Divided Self, described by Friar Lawrence in *Romeo and Juliet*, it was Henry:

> Two such opposèd kings encamp them still
> In man, as well as herbs – grace and rude will.[7]

At war with his destructive sexual nature, Henry VIII had closed the brothels, which his son Edward VI reopened in 1550. 'For the Stews', as a priest said in a sermon at Paul's Cross, 'are so necessary in a commonwealth as a jaxe in a man's house.'[8]

Thomas Nashe's *The Choise of Valentines* – alternative title *Nash his Dildo* – is a poem with hilarious candour: the 'offertory', before entering the 'Oratorie' to the 'foggie three-chinnd dame' at the door; the choice of 'prettie Trulls' offered him; the eventual selection of 'gentle mistris Francis', who pretends she has only come to this 'dancing-schoole' 'to avoide the troblous stormy weather'; the slow undressing; the preliminary cunnilingus:

> his mouth beset with uglie bryers
> Resembling much a duskie nett of wyres –

The penis flagging until she:

> dandled it, and dance't it up and downe,
> Not ceasing, till she rais'd it from his swoune,
> And then he flue on hir as he were wood [mad],
> And on her breeche did thack, and foyne a-good

The age-old cry of womankind:

> Oh not so fast, my rauisht Mistriss cryes
> . . . Togeather let our equall motions stirr . . .
>
> . . . She ierks hir legs, and sprauleth with hir heeles,
> No tongue may tell the solace that she feeles . . .

The pleasure being over, despite Nashe's attempts to contain himself, in quarter of an hour, the 'gentle mistris' says that in future she will get more pleasure from her dildo:

> That bendeth not, nor fouldeth anie deale,
> But stands as stiff as he were made of steele,
> And playes at peacock twixt my legs right blythe.[9]

The brothels had to be painted white and to carry a particular sign: one of the most celebrated of which was the cardinals' hats suggested less by religious considerations than by the scarlet tip shared by both princes of the Church and excited male organs. The double-think of the human race with regard to this whole area of life was in abundant evidence, with, on the one hand, open patronage of prostitution by those in authority; and, on the other, merciless punishments meted out by the law upon the women caught up in this trade. Cardinal Wolsey reputedly had an inscription over one of the doors of his palace at Hampton Court, which read 'the rooms of the whores of my Lord Cardinal'. Queen Elizabeth's cousin, Lord Hunsdon, did not go so far, but he let out properties in Paris Gardens, Southwark, to Francis Langley, owner of the Swan theatre, fully aware of what took place in the region.

A Mirror for Magistrates in 1584 recorded that a young man might have to part with 'forty shillings or better' in 'some blind [obscure] house about the suburbs' for 'a pottle or two of wine, the embracement of a painted strumpet and the French welcome' – that is, venereal disease. A woman convicted of being a prostitute had to appease the convoluted perversity of male shame. She would have her head shaved, and would then be carted about the streets with a paper labelling her as a whore pasted to her forehead; accompanied by the banging together of barbers' basins clattering in mockery. Repeat offenders might be tied to the 'cart's arse' and dragged through the streets to the Bridewell prison, where they would receive a whipping. Bridewell was a house of correction, not a long-term prison. Mary Tudor had wanted to close the place down, since so many of the women whipped there revealed the sexual misdemeanours of the clergy; but it was given a reprieve and throughout Elizabeth's reign it witnessed the regular beatings and thrashings and hangings meted out to petty – and not so petty – criminals. WHIPPED AT THE BRIDEWELL FOR HAVING FORSAKEN HER CHILD IN THE STREETS was an inscription on one unhappy head, who had been put in the pillory at Cheapside and then dragged through the streets.[10]

The risks of such terrible punishments did not deter the 'Winchester geese', as the women were called, after the Bishop of Winchester who owned so much of the Southwark property in which they plied their profession, any more than the risk of venereal disease deterred their clients. The need to survive in the one case, to satisfy lust in the other, was stronger than the dictates of common sense. Shakespeare's sense that sex on such terms was an image of Hell was reflected in the writings of his contemporaries. In Thomas Dekker's *Lanthorn and Candlelight* (1608) a visitor from Hell 'saw the doors of notorious carted bawds like Hell gates stand night and day wide open, with a pair of harlots in taffeta gowns, like two painted posts, garnishing out those doors, being better to the house than a double sign'.

In *The Honest Whore*, also by Dekker, one of the characters says to Bellafont, the prostitute:

> The sin of many men
> Is within you; and thus much I suppose,
> That if all your committers stood in a rank,
> They'd make a lane in which your shame might dwell
> And with their spaces reach from hence to hell.[11]

Inevitably, in such a world, the doctor was in a position to see more than most. The sordid diaries and casebooks of Simon Forman (now in

Oxford's Bodleian Library), called by some, rather too generously, the Elizabethan Pepys, reveal not only the author's obsessive sexual pursuits and conquests, but the sexual lives of innumerable Londoners of both high and low degree. Forman practised as an astrologer and as a medic. He first practised medicine in Salisbury, and by the time he was established in London in the 1590s he was noticing whenever he had 'halek', his word for sexual congress. A regular mistress was one Avis Allen, the recusant wife of William Allen, who was prepared to pay the enormous sum of £100 to avoid attendance at church at St Botolph's, Bishopsgate. They first kissed on 20 November 1593, and a fortnight later, 'she rose and came to me, et halek Avis Allen' . . . She had come to him as a patient. The Allens, who entertained their doctor to dinner, were evidently in the shipping trade and resided in Thames Street near the river. Throughout the time of his affair with her, and its rather chillingly recounted adulterous encounters, Forman was advising clients about their astrological chances of good business deals, or the potential conception of children, as well as giving them cures for dropsy, venereal and other diseases. Men came to him to establish, via astrology, their chances of 'halek' with certain women, and 'whether she is honest or a harlot'. Forman himself had ample chances of 'halek' – in the street, in his consulting rooms and in the houses of his clients. Marriage did not change his habits, though he noted down in his illiterate Latin the occurrences of 'halek' '*cum uxore meo*' (*sic*, rather than *mea*; with my wife).

One of the women in Forman's casebooks was Emilia Lanier, daughter of Battista Bassano, a court musician. While her husband was away at sea with the Earl of Essex, Emilia consulted Forman about Mr Lanier's chances of a knighthood and professional promotion. She was a spirited, highly sexed woman, and Forman clearly came to know her tastes and habits intimately. She 'hath a mind to the quent, but seems she is or will be a harlot. And because . . . she useth sodomy' says a marginal note in his casebook (it might in fact refer to some other woman, but it gives the flavour of the levels of Forman's interests in his clients. Another entry speaks of a man who wanted to know his chances of 'halek' with a woman and sent his servant to explore her body. She did not allow the servant to 'halek', but it is clear – unless this is a lurid fantasy of Forman's – that the man 'felt all parts of her body willingly and kissed her often'.

Emilia Lanier was the woman who became the mistress of the Queen's cousin, Lord Hunsdon. What Forman's casebooks reveal so interestingly – and we derive exactly the same impression from Shakespeare's plays and poems – is a sexual free-for-all. The existence of syphilis and gonorrhoea with no real palliatives, and the fact that everyone in London was nominally Christian, did not diminish the rampant sexual energy of an expanding city. Forman happened to be there, with his inkhorn and his notebooks. But the men and women who pass through his pages, all sexually obsessed, are only a tiny fraction of the whole. No one especially expresses feelings of sexual guilt, and none are especially deterred by the morality propounded by the Puritans. Monogamy, chastity and even celibacy must have been practised by some Elizabethans, but one does not derive the impression from their writings that such conditions of life were the norm. As so often happens in a city where great cultural change is afoot, and where the population of immigrants from other lands, and from the country, is high, there is encountered this pulsating energy that irrepressibly takes sexual expression. The Berlin of the Weimar Republic, or the New York of Andy Warhol's generation, was perhaps comparable in this respect to Elizabethan London.

Whether it was especially homosexual, or simply highly sexual, is quite hard to assess. Was Shakespeare gay, or did he simply – as well as enjoying sex with women – fall for boy actors from time to time? The word 'Homosexuality', like the word 'Anglicanism', did not exist in sixteenth-century English. The two words are so closely associated in twenty-first-century parlance that it is inevitable that one should ask whether the *thing* existed, even if they had no word for it. I have suggested in an earlier chapter that the word 'Anglicanism' did not exist because the Elizabethans had no concept of it. They had Catholic or Protestant ideas about the Church, but their quarrels and debates centred around the extent to which they accepted the Church of England, not whether they believed in a thing called 'Anglicanism'. Modern readers will probably be less inclined to accept the idea that, because there was no word, there was also no 'homosexuality'. But the sexual climate was very different, as is demonstrated by the hundreds of thousands of confused words written about the sexuality of Shakespeare. But when we go back in time and say that Marlowe and James VI and I were gay, I suspect that we are committing an anachronism. We can say that if they were alive *nowadays* they would have been gay; or that, viewed by our way of classifying human beings, they were gay. But the idea of classifying human beings *at all*, still less of dividing them according to sexual preference (or, come to that, skin pigmentation), is a by-product of nineteenth-century science. Just as Victorian collectors wanted to classify different species of butterfly or beetle, so they divided the human race and invented words such as 'homosexual'.

One useful corrective to the idea that there were gay Elizabethans is the legal evidence. 'During the forty-five years of Queen Elizabeth's reign and the twenty-three years of King James I's reign only six men are recorded as having been indicted for sodomy in the Home Counties assizes, for example, with only one conviction.'[12]

It is an astonishingly low statistic, and when same-sex activity was punished by law, it was nearly always because some act of violence had accompanied it: buggery itself being in many cases a form of violence, whether performed upon a member of the same or the opposite sex. Rape, incest and adultery were the ingredients, for example, that made John Atherton's acts of buggery seem worthy of death. He was hanged in 1640. The case made something of a stir since he was Bishop of Waterford and Lismore, and the woodcuts show the Right Reverend gentleman being hanged in his bishop's outfit – Canterbury cap, rochet and chimere.

In questioning whether it is useful to use anachronistic words such as 'Anglican' or 'homosexual' in relation to the Elizabethans, I am not, of course, denying the obvious reason why such words *are* used; namely, that they are a clumsy shorthand designed to guide us through the alien world of a very different age. John Atherton was a bishop, and he did not acknowledge the authority of the Pope, and he dressed like twenty-first-century Anglican bishops: easier to call him an 'Anglican' or a promoter of 'Anglicanism' than to go back into his world and get the feeling of his religious milieu, which is something subtly different from what the word 'Anglican' implies. Likewise, it would be folly to deny that there were Elizabethan men who fell in love with one another, or with boys. The most famous of them quipped that 'All they that love not tobacco and boys are fools.' But sexual preferences need to be understood in social terms. Labels sometimes confuse as much as they illuminate. The emperor Claudius was considered a freak because he exclusively liked women and eschewed young male catamites. That fact stands out. To label all the other Roman Emperors as paederasts might be true, but only true nor' by nor'-west.

Undoubtedly Elizabethan England provided as much opportunity as any other society for gay love to flourish; possibly rather more, given the number of pretty boy actors, and the male fashions that exposed the legs so alluringly. Given the mode among modern 'gender studies' for exploring human character from this angle, however, it is remarkable how *little* mention there is of gay sex in Elizabethan pornography, or accounts of the Elizabethan underworld; equally remarkable is the fact that when men openly express their fondness for their own sex, it appears to have excited no particular shock. Richard Barnfield's *The Affectionate Shepheard: Containing The Complaint of Daphnis* [male] *for the love of Ganymede* (also male) was published in 1594. His work was quite popular. No printer had his hands chopped off for printing it. Nor did Barnfield, a Shropshire gentleman, graduate of Brasenose and friend of Shakespeare, seem to have ruffled many feathers by his candid sexual and emotional preference for his own sex (though the fact that he was disinherited by his father *could* indicate that what was unremarkable in Oxford and London upset the rustic sensibilities of Market Drayton, where he was buried). Barnfield was clearly one who enjoyed sex with boys. Equally obviously, Shakespeare (whose Sonnets are the only other such poems of the age that are addressed by a male to a male) was surprised by a joyous love for a beautiful youth, which developed into an all-consuming obsession that (in Sonnet 20) was specifically non-sexual. It was the boy's *youth* and his *face* that enchanted Shakespeare and the twentieth sonnet rather crudely but explicitly makes clear that there was no interest for Shakespeare below the Mason–Dixon line, to use the Duchess of Windsor's phrase.

What was new in the sixteenth century, and conceivably deserves a mention in this context, is the formulation of buggery as an offence in English law. It was in Henry VIII's reign that sodomy became a statutory felony, punishable by hanging. This was not because the King had a particular interest in the matter. It was instead almost accidental. Henrician law after 1540 transferred power and judicial authority from the Church of Rome to the Crown. The offence of sodomy had formerly been covered by Church law. When, therefore, Mary Tudor revoked all her father's law with a view to bringing everything back under papal control, she inadvertently brought in what was effectively a Buggers' Charter in 1553. It was ten years later, in 1563, that the anomaly was corrected in English law, though all case law subsequently – as has already been said – related to cases where other offences such as rape or incest were involved. It was Sir Edward Coke (1552–1634), a Norfolk gentleman, whose *Institutes of the Laws of England* (1600–15) defined the crime in the greatest detail – for example, including bestialism in its definitions and making the distinction that if the act took place between an adult and a minor, only the adult could be prosecuted. Coke, Speaker of the House of Commons (1593), Attorney General (1594), Chief Justice of the Common Pleas (1606), Chief Justice of the King's Bench and Privy Councillor (both in 1613), was one of the great English law-makers – dismissed by James VI and I for questioning the limits of royal power and prerogative. The language of Coke's *Institutes* in relation to buggery might make him sound prurient. It is true that he was probably a horrible man, but the description of this particular activity as 'detestable and abominable' was something he merely took over from the legislation of Henry VIII; and his concern, disgusting as may be the details that he spells out, was merely with legal definitions – extent of penetration, whether accompanied by emission, and so forth. In this area, as in all others, Coke was concerned to make laws that were clear and which could be established in evidence presented to a court. The language of the laws and statutes ('Amongst Christians not to be named'),[13] which clearly upsets some modern historians, overlooks the fact that when stray remarks made in the workplace about the Queen or the army could be viewed as dangerous acts of sedition; when membership of the Anabaptist sect could result in being publicly disembowelled; and when acts of petty theft could lead to the gallows – then the Elizabethans were very relaxed about same-sex encounters, only bothering to have a word for them when they involved anal rape. Compare this with the England of Elizabeth II, where prosecutions for homosexual behaviour in the early years of her reign were frequent: 480 men convicted for private acts between consenting adults during the period 1953–6.[14]

We have mentioned Christopher Marlowe's joke about tobacco and boys. It was inevitable, after Marlowe's violent death, that moralisers should have considered it was no more than he deserved. Thomas Beard, for instance, Oliver Cromwell's headmaster at Huntingdon Grammar School (the man who whipped Oliver for dreaming he was king), wrote of Marlowe in *The Theatre of God's Judgements*. Beard's book is a rich compilation of examples of the vindictiveness of the Deity, and in the chapter that gloats over the grisly ends 'of Epicures and Atheists':

> It is so fell out that in London streets, as he purposed to stab one whom he ought a grudge unto with his dagger, the other party perceiving, so avoided the stroke that withal catching hold of his wrist, he stabbed with his own dagger into his own head, in such sort that notwithstanding all the means of surgery that could be wrought, he shortly after died thereof.

This was written four years after Marlowe died. The next year, in 1598, Francis Meres, who had overlapped with Marlowe as an undergraduate at Cambridge, added the salacious detail that the poet was 'stabbed to death by a bawdy serving-man, a rival of his in his lewd love'. So it became a brawl in a gay bar. Gabriel Harvey, the gossipy Cambridge don who reckoned he knew what was happening in 'literary London', believed that Marlowe – 'He that not feared God, nor dreaded Devil' – had been punished by dying of the plague.

In one of the most scintillating works of historical detective work, *The Reckoning* (published in 1992, revised 2002), Charles Nicholl reconstructed the murder of Christopher Marlowe in Deptford, in the summer of 1593. He even speculated whether the misinformation that had been fed to the normally close watcher of events – Harvey – had been deliberately put about by Marlowe's seedy colleagues in the world of espionage.

Nicholl's book laid bare with devastating plausibility how close Marlowe's murderer was to the network of spies and government informers who were directly answerable to the Cecils, to Walsingham, to Essex. He unearthed what another historian has called 'the murky amoral world', the 'conspiratorial underbelly of Elizabethan politics'.[15] One detail alone convinced me of the plausibility of Nicholl's story: it was that when Ingram Frizier fatally stabbed Marlowe through the eye – an offence that would normally carry an automatic death-penalty – he did not go into hiding, but attended the inquest at Deptford on Friday, 1 June 1593. The inquest found that Frizier had killed the poet 'in the defence and saving of his own life'. Just four weeks later, on Thursday, 28 June, the Queen issued a formal pardon: it was a remarkably quick outcome of the case by Elizabethan standards. Frizier lived on – at Eltham in Kent – married, became a church warden and died in 1627.[16]

What Nicholl did in his 1992 book, and which had never been done before in anything approaching his level of detail, was to follow up the identities and careers of the three men who were with Marlowe in the Widow Bull's house at Deptford Strand on the day Marlowe met his end. For a start, Eleanor Bull herself. She was not some blowsy old publican. She was born Eleanor Whitney of a landed family in Herefordshire, known to Queen Elizabeth's confidante Blanche Parry, who made a number of bequests to the Whitneys. Her husband, Richard Bull, was a sub-bailiff at Deptford and he is styled a 'gentleman' in the parish register.[17] Marlowe was not visiting a low tavern or a bawdy-house on the day he died.

Deptford was a small village near Greenwich, on the Surrey side of the Thames. It was the site of great shipyards and docks: the Royal Dock for the navy, as well as commercial docks for innumerable merchant ships, with all the attendant sheds and warehouses. In the 1590s it had become a 'boom town', with as many as 4,000 new residents.

Deptford was full of a wide variety of foreign visitors, as well as those fringe members of the court who could not find anywhere to live at nearby Greenwich – minor courtiers, officials, choir members of the Chapel Royal. Records tell us that a French trumpeter, Pierre Rossel, a German singer, Dente Natrige, and a Welsh chorister, Wenfayd Royce, all lodged at Deptford.[18] In this polyglot, floating population it was not surprising that there were also found secret agents.

Ingram Frizier was a shady businessman: on the make, arraigned in the Exchequer court of 1591, but by 1593 described as a 'gentleman'. He was also a spy, and shared a spy-master – Thomas Walsingham – with Christopher Marlowe. Thomas was the young (Marlowe's age) kinsman of Francis Walsingham. Skeres, one of the others present when Marlowe was killed, appears to have been a 'fence' for stolen property. He was part of the Essex circle and part of the military expedition to France in 1592 to assist Henri of Navarre. He was involved in the entrapment of the Babington Plot, and the Babington accomplices had met in the lodgings of Robert Poley, the fourth man in the room when Marlowe was killed. Poley had been a government agent for two decades. He went to Denmark, France, Scotland and the Netherlands. He lurked in prisons and eavesdropped on conversations. He was known as 'the very genius of the Elizabethan underworld'. He tricked dozens of Catholics into indiscretion. Just back from the Low Countries, he was on government business that evening in Deptford.

It is not possible at this distance in time, and with three such rogues as the principal witnesses at the inquest, to reconstruct what, precisely, made Marlowe a potential object of embarrassment to the government. But knowing as we now do the background in sordid espionage, swindling and extortion in which his three Deptford companions moved, it is safe to suggest – more than to suggest, to state – that they were not gathered for a poetry-reading. Presumably (but it is a safe presumption) Poley, probably guided by Thomas Walsingham or Robert Cecil, wanted to have Marlowe's assurance of silence, or collaboration, or perhaps he was asked to part with some letters. The men were together for *eight hours* at the Widow Bull's house. Evidently, at some point, Marlowe lost his temper. Nothing unusual about that. In 1589 he was imprisoned after a sword-fight in Shoreditch, which had resulted in someone's death. In 1592, again in Shoreditch, Marlowe had been bound over to keep the peace. A few months later he had fought a tailor named Cortine 'with a staff and dagger'. He might well have drawn Frizier's dagger, as he asserted, and Frizier might well have reacted in self-defence, when he stabbed Marlowe through the eye.

There is no doubt that Marlowe was employed as an anti-Catholic spy, and that some of those in English Intelligence feared that he would 'go native' or become 'a practiser with them'. In the world of espionage, the double-agent becomes so accustomed to his duplicity that it is probably not even possible for himself, let alone his spy-masters on either side, to know where his loyalties lie. William Parry, hanged for treason in 1585 as a Catholic plotting against the government, maintained until his tearful end that he had been an agent provocateur working for the government.[19] Marlowe was enlisted into the secret service while still an undergraduate at Cambridge. As a double-agent, his work took him to the Low Countries and it was there in January 1592, the seventh year of the war, that he was arrested for 'coining' or counterfeiting money. A letter about it by the governor of Flushing – Sir Robert Sidney – to Lord

Burghley only came to light in 1976. The forging of Dutch shillings was revealed by Richard Baines, a spy who worked behind enemy lines for Walsingham, posing as a seminarian and keen Romanist for years. The man accused with Marlowe, John Poole, was known to hold subversive Catholic views. The Low Countries were Robert Poley's special area of intrigue and he knew all about Marlowe's activities in Flushing, his letter-drops, his Catholic contacts – Poley was especially interested, at this time of Marlowe's arrest, in a cell of Catholic plotters in Brussels. Accounts were also brought to Burghley about Marlowe's association with the spy-poet Matthew Roydon. Reading these stray bits of surviving evidence from the Public Record Office we can reconstruct Marlowe's life of spying and his involvement with the low-life world of crime.

Richard Baines was the author of the celebrated note, surviving in two manuscripts of the Harleian Collection in the British Library, that indicts 'Christopher Marly concerning his damnable judgment of religion and scorn of God's word'. This is the document that quotes Marlowe saying 'that Christ was a bastard and his mother dishonest' . . . 'that all the New Testament is filthily written' . . . that 'the sacrament . . . would have been much better being administered in a tobacco-pipe'. Similar charges to those against Marlowe were made against another spy, Richard Cholmeley – another hunter of 'papists & other dangerous men'. An informer against Cholmeley came up with charges of amazing similarity to those that Baines brought against Marlowe: 'That Jesus Christ was a bastard, St Mary a whore & the Angel Gabriel a bawd to the Holy Ghost' and that 'Moses was a juggler . . . for his miracles to Pharaoh to prove there was a God' (Cholmeley). 'That Moses was but a juggler . . . that it was an easy matter for Moses, being brought up in all the arts of the Egyptians, to abuse the Jews' (Marlowe, quoted by Baines).

In both cases, the atheism was regarded as subversive not only of religion, but of the government. The spy who denounced Cholmeley claimed that there was a gang of sixty such atheists, determined 'after her Majesty's decease, to make a King among themselves, & live according to their own laws'. It would easily be accomplished, thought Cholmeley, because there were 'as many of their opinion as of any other religion'.

Cholmeley was arrested on 28 June 1593, the very day that Ingram Frizier was pardoned for killing Marlowe. No one knows what happened to Cholmeley after he was taken off to prison, but it surely can be no coincidence that his recorded blasphemies are so similar in word and sentiment to Marlowe's. If Nicholl's (to me highly plausible) speculations are correct, all this 'evidence' was contrived to discredit Christopher Marlowe and, by association, Walter Raleigh. Nicholl's contention is that Marlowe had been working for Robert Cecil, who kept him out of prosecution for the coinage scam in Flushing, but was increasingly embarrassed by his connection with this flamboyant and outspoken troublemaker. Sir John Puckering, Lord Keeper of the Privy Seal, was also, like Mr Secretary Robert Cecil, embarrassed by how much the government agent Marlowe *knew*, and by how much could be said against the government if rumours of Marlowe's atheism spread.

'If an unfortunate accident were at this stage to befall Christopher Marlowe, neither his prosecutor Sir John Puckering nor his protector Sir Robert Cecil would be much displeased,' wrote Nicholl.[20] He did not produce enough evidence to convict Robert Cecil in a court of law. But the cumulative effect of *The Reckoning* is to see a world of corruption and intrigue and government-sponsored torture and murder, which undoubtedly *did* exist. Presumably, Marlowe's growing fame as a poet and a dramatist made him even more dangerous to the government. There can be no doubt that the death of this marvellous poet before he was thirty is one of the greatest calamities in the history of literature.

25

The Occult Philosophy

Marlowe's death stilled the voice of a young poet of unexampled resonance. The poetry, and the plays, would presumably have continued to rival those of Shakespeare. Had he lived, the 1590s and the Jacobean age would have left behind an even more stupendous dramatic legacy. The decade saw an enormous growth in the popularity and quality of the theatre. James Burbage had created the first building of that name in the 1570s, thereby deliberately creating a Roman word for a Roman concept, probably based (Burbage was first a joiner and would have studied the rudiments of architectural theory) upon the ideas of Vitruvius, the first century BC Roman architect whose book *De architectura* had so deep an effect upon Palladio and the other architects of the Italian Renaissance. These ideas were not 'random'. Their aesthetic was guided by notions about the world which to a modern mind might very likely seem bizarre, but which run through almost every aspect of Renaissance life – not merely its architecture, but also its poetry, its fashion sense, its politics. The Vitruvian theatre, for example, rested upon seven pillars, symbolising the 'seven pillars of Wisdom' of Solomon's Temple.[1] The shape and design of the building was conceived not simply to pack in as large an audience as possible, but actually, in a mystic-magical way, to stimulate memory. The philosopher Giulio Camillo, one of the most famous men of the Renaissance, constructed a wooden theatre in Venice that reflected the seven planets, with seven gangways or doors, and represented the universe expanding from First Causes through the stages of Creation. It is inconceivable that some such theories did not influence the design of the London theatres.

Visitors to the reconstructed Globe Theatre in London, a charming piece of fantasy, have an idea that they are seeing a re-creation of the very stage on which Shakespeare's plays were first performed. They do not necessarily realise that what they are seeing is a bit of mystic geometry. We do not actually know in precise detail what Shakespeare's Globe looked like. Much of what we know of Elizabethan theatre-design is based on one small sketch, made by John de Witt and copied by Arend van Buchell. The fact that he labels his sketch with classical terms – *proscaenivum*, *ingresus*, *orchestra*, *mimorum aedes*, and so on – shows that he was aware of the classical influences on the building.

Dr Johnson's friend, Hester Thrale, was married to a rich brewer,

Henry Thrale, who owned the land in Southwark that had housed the original Globe Theatre. She wrote:

> For a long time, then – or I thought it such – my fate was bound up with the old Globe Theatre, upon the Bankside, Southwark; the alley it had occupied having been purchased and thrown down by Mr Thrale to make an opening before the windows of our dwelling house. When it lay desolate in a Hack heap of rubbish, my Mother, one day, in a joke, called it the ruins of Palmyra, and after that they laid it down in a grass plot . . . But there were really curious remains of the old Globe Playhouse, which though hexagonal in form was round within.[2]

If you put a circle within a hexagon, you provide one of those spaces so beloved of the Renaissance, of an outstretched man within a square and a circle. The most famous of these survives in the notebooks of Leonardo, but we also find it as a frontispiece in a book by Dr Dee about the symbolic geometry of man's relationship to the Cosmos. Within that circle-in-a-hexagon, the seven triangular apices would have provided the seven gangways of the auditorium.

The first Globe Theatre was built on Bankside in 1599, partly from materials salvaged from the demolished theatre. The builder was Peter Street, and so successful was he with this venture for the Lord Chamberlain's company (for which Shakespeare wrote and acted) that he was employed by Philip Henslowe to build the Fortune Theatre in 1600. It was vast, the Globe. Its capacity might have been as great as 3,000–3,800 standing in the yard, and more than 2,000 in the three layers of covered galleries.[3]

There have been those who doubted whether Mrs Thrale's 'Palmyra' was really the old playhouse, rather than the remains of a tenement building.[4] But even if archaeology banished uncertainty, the work done by the great scholar of Renaissance thought, Frances Yates, remains invaluable, as a reminder to us of how different the Elizabethan mindset was from our own.

We have already encountered, in these pages, Dr Dee, the adept of occult philosophy, who was a pioneer of mathematics, and who cast the Queen's horoscope. We have alluded to the baffled, insular, narrow grammarians of Oxford, who laughed to scorn the idea of a Copernican universe, with the revolving Sun as its centre, and the Earth – far from being the still centre of the universe – being on the move. When this was expounded to them by the visiting Italian philosopher Giordano Bruno (1548–1600), George Abbott, later Archbishop of Canterbury, quipped, 'in truth, it was his owne head which rather did run round, & his braines did not stand stil'.[5] Abbott was a deeply Calvinist, Puritan undergraduate at Balliol at the time of Bruno's visit to the university in 1583. He disliked Bruno's way of pronouncing Latin: 'he had more boldly then wisely, got vp into the highest place of our best & most renowned schoole, stripping vp his sleeves like some Iugler, and telling vs much of *chentrum* & *chriculus* & circumferenchia (after the pronunciation of his Country language)'.[6]

Giordano Bruno's statue broods over the Campo dei Fiori in Rome on the site where he was burned alive at the stake by the Inquisition. The statue was erected in the nineteenth century with money raised from enthusiastic Italian liberals, non-believers and anti-papalists of varied lands, who saw Bruno as an early champion of their agnosticism or irreligion. Certainly Bruno can be profitably studied from varied standpoints, and he continues to attract a varied press. One book, published by a great academic press as recently as 1991, concludes with Bruno's gruesome fate and signs off with the words 'it served him right', which at least lets us know where the author stands. Yet this author, evidently a modern adherent of Counter-Reformation papalism, John Bossy, failed to convince one reader at least that Bruno was the 'mole' in the French Embassy in London, code-named Fagot, who shopped poor Francis Throckmorton. Nevertheless, if you look for books about Bruno in the London Library you will have an energetic time, moving between Biography, Occult Science and *Spies*.

Even if we believe that Bruno was employed, during his shortish sojourn in England, by Walsingham to 'shop' English Catholics in the early 1580s, it would be a skewed vision that saw this as his primary significance. For Bruno-enthusiasts, such as Philip Sidney or John Dee, as for hostile members of his lecture audience like the Puritan zealot George Abbott, the great significance of Giordano Bruno was as an exponent of the occult philosophy that underpinned so much of their lives.

The writings of Hermes Trismegistus (known in Latin as Mercurius Trismegistus) are, in the universal scale of things, as influential as any to emerge from late antiquity. In fact, as far as intellectuals of the Renaissance were concerned, Hermes Trismegistus was perhaps *the* most influential thinker-sage-magus of all time. Whether or not he existed, and whether his compilation of writings, sometimes known as the *Corpus Hermeticum*, was written by several hands, is of far less significance than the drift and influence of this body of writings.

You can see a representation of Hermes Trismegistus (meaning 'thrice-great') in the inlaid pavement of Siena's glorious cathedral, dating from the 1480s. Hermes, in his tall wizardy hat, receives the obeisance of Moses himself, who – it was believed in Renaissance times – was 'Hermes's contemporary'. We know now that the Hermetic writings, which are a mish-mash of late-Platonic 'uplift', numerology, astrology, Creation mythology, ethics and philosophical speculation, belong to the period AD 100–300, and that they were written in Greek. St Augustine (354–430), in *The City of God* (written 413–26), denounced 'Hermes', whom he read in a Latin translation, for a passage in which he described how the Egyptians could call down spirits by magic to animate the idols of their gods.

Denunciation is often a useful form of literary advertisement, and Augustine's condemnation ensured that Hermes Trismegistus was remembered by subsequent Christian generations. It also led to the muddle of supposing – because, in his rambling, encyclopaedic fashion, Hermes Trismegistus had alluded to the ancient Egyptians – that he actually *was* an ancient Egyptian; that his writings were, in fact, the very origin of theology and philosophy. Moses is bowing to Hermes in the Siena pavement because all religion, according to the Hermetic way of looking at life, derived from this ancient source of wisdom. Plato, who actually wrote 500 or 600 hundred years *before* Hermes, and some of whose myths and ideas form a substantial template for 'Hermetic' notions – of the superiority of Spirit over Matter, of God the remote and immovable Spirit producing the Demiurge who created matter, and many other influential notions – this Plato was conceived by those who revered Hermes to be, like Moses and Judaism, deeply in the ancient magus's debt.

The Renaissance in Europe is the name given to a series of intellectual and artistic developments which were in some ways innovatory, but which saw themselves as profoundly conservative. The so-called humanists rediscovered Greek, and tried to write Latin and Greek in a purity of style that matched that of the Classics, untainted by the monkish crudities of the Middle Ages. But, for a generation that grew up with the humanists as its masters, such striving after grammatical purity and formal correctness in language alone was arid and unprofitable. The Victorian poet Robert Browning, in his superb poem 'A Grammarian's Funeral', conveys the life-view of such a humanist scholar who has buried his whole existence in a devotion to the intricacies of Greek morphology. Even as he is dying, it is the death-rattle that is referred to:

> Still, thro' the rattle, parts of speech were rife.
>   While he could stammer
> He settled *Hoti*'s business – let it be! –
>   Properly based *Oun* – [Greek for therefore]
> Gave us the doctrine of the enclytic *De* . . . [Untranslatable little monosyllable used to create elegance in a Greek sentence]

Browning's grammarian is being buried in Italy, but this could be Sir John Cheke, who taught Burghley and others at Cambridge.

The Hermetic devotees – men such as Giordano Bruno or John Dee – deplored the humanist preoccupation with the structure of language, at the expense of the contents of ancient texts.

We live in the post-Romantic or post-Hegelian world, and are programmed by our collective myths to suppose that human history is a development, or evolution. We imagine ourselves moving onwards and upwards to sharper scientific understanding, ever more efficient or equitable political structures, a keener sense of The Good. Harbingers of this 'modern' outlook had dawned in the twelfth and thirteenth centuries, when Aristotle was rediscovered through Arabic and Syriac texts, when the European study of mathematics was pioneered, thereby allowing for such innovations as the pointed arch or the striking clock.

What we more commonly call the Renaissance, however, in the fifteenth and sixteenth centuries was a quest for the great values of antiquity. To this extent, it was largely reactionary. Far from believing, as Hegel or Darwin or Marx believed, that the Good Life was something to which they aspired in the future, when they had put behind them the crudities or injustices of the past, the wise men and women of the Renaissance looked backwards to a supposed Age of Gold. Both the Reformation and the Counter-Reformation were trying to assert what they believed to be the core values and practices of the earliest age of Christianity. A new nation, such as Elizabethan England, in which so many of the new rich and powerful families were of recent coinage, looked back to bogus reconstructions of Arthurian history, or links between Albion and Rome, between the Brute coming from Troy to found their Britannium. In the twenty-first century our most avant-garde philosophical movements would wish to claim to be the newest. Their most avant-garde thinkers, such as Giordano Bruno, believed that they tapped into a wisdom, for a time lost in the mists of antiquity and now rediscovered. It was this ancient wisdom that Giordano Bruno was eager to impart: he became, indeed, a sort of missionary for it, abandoning the Dominican Order to which he had committed his youth in Naples and, in 1576 (having been inevitably accused of heresy), wandering through Europe and preaching with zeal the Hermetic mysteries.

In March 1583 the English Ambassador in Paris, Henry Cobham, sent a dispatch to Walsingham: 'Doctor Jordano Bruno Nolano, a professor in philosophy, intends to pass into England, whose religion I cannot commend.[7] I have already alluded to the contribution Bruno might have made to Marlowe's representation of the Faust myth. Marlowe had an instinctive contempt for what could, if we wanted to be harsh, be called mumbo-jumbo, which was every bit as fierce as the scepticism of the Aristotelians of Oxford about Copernicus.

When Marlowe the contemptuous 'atheist' expresses views that coincide with orthodox English Calvinists, you can sense intellectual chauvinism. Here is a foreshadowing of 'Anglo-Saxon' philosophy's contempt for 'continental' thinking in the twentieth century: Bertrand Russell's dismissal of Hegelianism, later his quarrel with Wittgenstein. The studied refusal to discuss, let alone to read, Sartre or Heidegger or Derrida, by the main-stream analytical philosophical schools that exalted, on one side of the Atlantic, Ayer and Ryle, on the other Quine. But although the Hermetic philosophy offended theological Protestants and 'common-sense' satirists such as Marlowe, it had a huge influence upon the way men and women, born during and after the Renaissance, viewed the world.

What, perhaps, we need to remind ourselves, is that strong as its appeal might be to the inner coterie of intellectuals, to the would-be Fausts aspiring after knowledge-as-power, the Hermetic philosophy was also *part of the common currency of the way in which Elizabethans thought about the world*. It would be unsafe to press home with too great an emphasis analogies with modern thinkers. But for every dozen committed Darwinian scientists or scientifically minded philosophers, who had examined in learned detail the problems of the Natural Selection theory, there are, in our day in the Western world, millions of individuals who accept that Darwin has somehow or other 'explained' our life on this planet. Only one in a thousand students at universities a generation ago actually read Roland Barthes; but in our generation much of the Barthian language has filtered down into journalism, so that, for example, my last observation, about Darwinism, could be rephrased – 'We believe in a Darwinian *narrative*.' It is in this kind of way that we must see the importance of Giordano Bruno's missionary journey to England, and to the spread, generally, of Hermetic ideas. In rather the same way, in the mid-twentieth century, vaguely Marxian ideas about economic determinism, or vaguely Freudian beliefs that human beings had been programmed by early childhood trauma, were maps by which to read the life-journey.

An older generation of Elizabethan scholars liked to see coteries of heretics meeting in secret to expound their forbidden ideas. This could be exciting, but it could also blind us to the fact that such ideas, as well as being the secret preserve of adepts, were also part of the common currency.

The genius of Frances Yates rediscovered, for example, the fact that Spenser's *Faerie Queene* was a great magical poem, reflecting the ideas of Dee and Bruno. But this is not like discovering that Jane Austen was a secret Jacobin, infusing her novels with hidden revolutionary codes. It is not, in other words, a cranky conspiracy theory. It is a reminder that most intelligent readers of Spenser *at the time* would have responded cognitively to his astrological and numerological symbolism, just as when they saw the Globe Theatre, they would have realised that it had a symbolic architecture. Most Elizabethans, as well as the intellectuals, believed in magic, planetary influences and the package of Hermetic ideology. Not all had worked out the logical conclusions of such beliefs – if there were any – but such ideas were in the air. Shakespeare would throw such ideas about on the stage precisely because they were in the air. Edmund in *King Lear* would express the total scepticism about astrology that is probably shared by most twenty-first-century play-goers. But to Elizabethan audiences, his scepticism would be intentionally shocking:

> This is the excellent foppery of the world, that when we are sick in fortune – often the surfeits of our own behaviour – we make guilty of our disasters the sun, the moon, and stars, as if we were villains on necessity, fools by heavenly compulsion, knaves, thieves and treacherous by spherical predominance, drunkards, liars and adulterers by an enforced obedience of planetary influence.[8]

Much closer to what was generally thought, and much closer to the Hermetic philosophy, is the beautiful passage about the music of the spheres, and the soul's kinship with them, expressed by Lorenzo to Jessica in *The Merchant of Venice*:

> How sweet the moonlight sleeps upon this bank!
> Here will we sit and let the sounds of music
> Creep in our ears. Soft stillness and the night
> Become the touches of sweet harmony.
> Sit, Jessica. Look how the floor of heaven
> Is thick inlaid with patens of bright gold
> There's not the smallest orb which thou behold'st
> But in his motion like an angel sings,
> Still choiring to the young-eyed cherubins;
> Such harmony is in immortal souls,
> But whilst this muddy vesture of decay
> Doth grossly close it in, we cannot hear it.[9]

Hooker, contemplating the hierarchy of angels on his deathbed, would have shared the view (which had become a commonplace of the Italian Renaissance from the time that Marsilius Ficino translated Hermes Trismegistus into Latin for Cosimo de' Medici in the fifteenth century, and indeed among those who had read him since Dante Alighieri in the fourteenth century) that the planets and the angelic hierarchies were one.

The discovery by Copernicus that the Earth was part of a heliocentric planetary system was a revelation of the divinity of the universe. Far from banishing the angels, as a 'modern' space scientist might do in the imagination of some contemporaries, Copernicus brought them closer. The Copernican Sun, centre of the new system, had risen to bring light to the sixteenth century. That was how Giordano Bruno saw matters. Bruno viewed himself as the prophet of a new movement, a Gnostic rediscovery of ancient wisdom. In Cornelius Agrippa's book on occult magic/philosophy, *De occulta philosophia*, he speaks of an ascent of the soul: 'no one has such powers but he who has cohabited with the elements, vanquished nature, mounted higher than the heavens, elevating himself above the angels to the archetype itself, with whom he then becomes co-operator and can do all things'.[10]

Bruno contrasts the religious maniacs of his own day, killing one another for theories about Justification by Faith or incomprehensible definitions of the Eucharist, with the kindly, reasonable adepts of Hermetic philosophy:

> The question which we ought to ask ourselves is whether we are in the daylight with the light of truth rising above our horizon, or whether the day is within our adversaries in the antipodes; whether the shadows of error are over us or over them; whether we who are beginning to revive the ancient philosophy are in the dawn which ends the night or in the evening of a day which is closing . . .[11]

Bruno's enthusiasm for his beliefs was fatal to him in the end. His unguarded conversations in Venice with the aristocratic Giovanni Mocenigo were relayed to the Inquisition. After being tortured and cross-questioned in Venice he was passed on to Rome, where they eventually roasted him alive. Bruno, declared the Father Inquisitor, 'is no simple heretic, but the leader of heretics, an organiser, a rebel. He has consorted with Protestants, he is an apostate monk who has openly praised the heretic queen Elizabeth of England and has written occult works that attempt to undermine the sanctity of the Church'.[12] There was a measure of truth in the Inquisitor's words. Bruno had seen himself as the leader of a new movement, which might – by a discovery of the *Prisca Theologia*, the origins of Judaeo-Christian and Greek religion in the wisdom of ancient Egypt, and the *Prisca Sapientia*, the Ur-philosophy of the Pharaohs – save the sixteenth century from its barbarously cruel, murderously quarrelsome self. You might consider Bruno more than a little crazy.

Probably he was, but as he insisted in his writings and conversations, who would not prefer the gentleness of Trismegistus's ideas to the homicidal intolerance of Bruno's contemporaries? If – a very big if – he worked as a spy for Walsingham, his motivation would surely have been that he saw Elizabeth (who had patronised and befriended Dr Dee) as a potential ally against the disaster of the Inquisition. He had not calculated, in that event, upon Elizabeth's political callousness, her need to play safe and, *au fond*, her religious conservatism.

The Hermetic philosophy did not *catch on* in Elizabethan England in the sense that Bruno would have hoped. The Church of England did not 'go Rosicrucian'. And yet it was the generality of Hermetic philosophy, not its esoteric secrecy, that stands out as a mark of the age. Those who enjoyed discussions about the new philosophy were inevitably regarded with suspicion or derision by others – hence (some believe) Shakespeare's semi-humorous reference in *Love's Labour's Lost* to 'the school of night.' Whether such a group of intellectuals met formally we can take leave to question, though Marlowe, Thomas Harriot and others would appear to have belonged loosely to such a coterie. Notable among them was Harriot's patron Henry Percy, 9th Earl of Northumberland, sometimes known as 'the wizard earl'. He married Essex's sister, Dorothy Perrot (widow of Sir Thomas, daughter-in-law of Sir John). He was one of those who had a tempestuous relationship with Essex, sometimes his friend, sometimes very much not. In spite of deafness, Northumberland was a courtier, soldier, gambler and feuder. Yet such is the esteem in which he was held that when the Queen was dying in 1603 he was invited to join the Council and there was even a short period when he might have been asked to serve as Lord Protector of the Realm until James I succeeded. So Northumberland was not a man on the political fringe. Indeed, after the suicide of his recusant father in the Tower, Northumberland did his utmost to emphasise his conformity to the Church of England while admitting, like many members of that Church at the time and since, that he 'troubled not much himself' with religion. Yet this 'wizard earl' was – almost certainly unjustly – condemned by James I and his council for complicity in the Gunpowder Plot of 1605, and he remained a scholarly prisoner in the Tower for sixteen years. His reputation during Elizabethan times as an 'atheist' probably did not help him at the time of the plot.

At least Northumberland was eventually released and died in his bed, at Petworth, in 1632, aged sixty-eight. His friend Sir Walter Raleigh was not so lucky – thirteen years, 1603–16 in the Tower, falsely accused of treason; it was here that he wrote *The History of the World* before he was released to make his last fateful voyage to Orinoco. Raleigh was another 'atheist', according to the oafish Jesuit propagandist Robert

Parsons. In Parsons's propaganda, Raleigh presided over a 'schoole of atheism' in which, under Harriot's direction, 'both Moyses and our Savior, the olde, and the new testament are jested at, and the scholars taught among other things to spell God backwarde'. There is no evidence for these wild accusations, though we can tell that Raleigh's was an enquiring intelligence. During a supper at the house of Sir George Trenchard at Winterbourne, Dorset, in 1593, Raleigh and his brother Carew upset the vicar, Ralph Ironside, by enquiring what he meant by his *soul* and exposing his circular arguments.[13] As we have already seen throughout this book, the Elizabethan Age was not one of religious tolerance, and such talk was dangerous. In the twenty-first century, if a cleric had an argument with a distinguished poet, courtier, public man and explorer, he might well get the worse of it (assuming such a figure as Raleigh to be remotely imaginable outside his own times). Ironside, perhaps stung by his own poor performance in theological debate, insisted that Raleigh be investigated by the Court of High Commission in March 1594. Raleigh, for his part, felt he must prove his orthodox Protestant credentials by 'shopping' a recusant Mass priest at Chideock – John Cornelius, alias Mooney, chaplain to the Arundell family, 'a notable stout villain' according to Raleigh. Another account suggests that Raleigh spent a long time trying to convince Cornelius, and that he was impressed by the man's sincerity.[14]

Raleigh was not a secret adept of Giordano Bruno's Hermetic creed, or a secret unbeliever. As his brush with Parson Ironside showed, he was a thoughtful, humorous, but basically serious person. Absolutely typical of intellectuals of his age, he – in common with Montaigne, or with Philip Sidney – was impossible to pin down to a position. The characteristic of the age was uncertainty, which was perhaps what made the institutions of Church and state so merciless to minds that, inevitably, strayed outside the orthodoxies. But Europe was fighting wars about matters that, as Raleigh's playful Socratic dialogue in Winterbourne demonstrated to the foolish and vindictive clergyman, could not possibly be proved true or false. In the Preface to his *History of the World*, he wrote:

> Certainly there is nothing more to bee admired, and more to bee lamented, than the privat contention, the passionate dispute, the personall hatred, and the perpetuall warre, massacres, and murders, for Religion among *Christians*: the discourse whereof hath so occupied the World, as it hath well neare driven the practise thereof out of the world.

The appalling disparity between the bitterness of the quarrels and the message of Love that lay at the heart of the Christian message could not but induce an aghast cynicism: 'Wee are all (in effect) become Comoedians in religion: and while we act in gesture and voice, divine vertues, in all the course of our lives wee renounce our Persons, and the parts wee play.'[15]

If there was a School of Night, as opposed to a group of friends who felt free, when together, to air their thoughts without reference to thought-police, then Raleigh was the centre of it. The most fascinating and attractive character, he understandably drew to himself poets and philosophers, explorers and adventurers. He was much the most interesting of all Queen Elizabeth's favourites, and from 1582 to 1592 she showered him with honours: Lord Warden of the Stanneries, Lord Lieutenant of Cornwall, Vice Admiral of the Western Counties and, as Captain of the Queen's Bodyguard, a courtier who was all but unable to leave her side.

Sir John Harington, the Queen's godson and the translator of Ariosto, tells the story that when Raleigh was riding between Plymouth and the court, he fell in love with Sherborne Castle, the country seat of the Bishops of Sherborne. 'This Castle being right in the way, he cast such an eye upon it as Ahab did upon Naboth's vineyard, and once above the rest being talking of it, of the commodiousness of the place, and how easily it might be got from the bishopric, suddenly over and over came his horse, that his very face, which was then thought a very good face, ploughed up the earth where he fell.'

It was perhaps an unhappy omen of Raleigh's accident-prone career. At the time, the Queen was only too happy to force the Bishops of Sherborne to allow the Crown a ninety-nine-year lease upon the castle and estate, and to give the castle to Raleigh as his grace-and-favour residence. The favour did not last long. In the early days, when the Queen was still smarting from the marriage of her greatest love, Leicester, to Lettice Knollys, Raleigh's flattering attentions were a consolation. It is pointless to ask whether his protestations of love for Elizabeth were 'genuine'. Court life was an elaborate dance. The abject gestures and hyperbolic words of the successful courtier would be insanely sycophantic if translated into a modern context – if, for example, we were to imagine a modern male office worker addressing such words to his female boss as Raleigh wrote to Elizabeth:

> O princely form, my fancy's adamant,
>   Divine conceit, my pain's acceptance,
> Oh all in one, oh heaven on earth transparent,
>   The seat of joy's and love's abundance!

But the poem 'The Ocean to Scinthia' (that is, Raleigh to Elizabeth) subverts and extends many of the courtly conventions. Behind the ritualistic façade of the courtier's devotion to his jewel-encrusted monarch-doll there was a tempestuous, very often serious and unhappy friendship between two extremely strong characters. Raleigh, exceptionally tall and very good-looking, undoubtedly attracted the Queen sexually. He was also a match for her intellectually, which few people were. She must have relished the side of him that was cynical, enquiring and angry, and which surfaces from time to time in some of the very few poems agreed by scholars to be of his composition:

> Tell potentates, they live
>   Acting by others' action,
> Not loved unless they give,
>   Not strong but by affection.
> If potentates reply,
>   Give potentates the lie.

Raleigh's cleverness, his ability to read and converse in three modern European languages, his grace, his panache and his physical courage would all have been appealing to the Queen. But it was not to be expected that such a person would be sexless, and Ocean's (Walter's, or Wa'ter's) love for the Chaste Moon-Goddess could not be the whole of Raleigh's life. Elizabeth might try to hide this obvious fact from herself, but it could not be hidden from Raleigh.

Evidently there were always tensions in their relationship, and even before the 2nd Earl of Essex invaded her heart, she could be petulant and dismissive of Raleigh in his role of favourite. For a while, the two men were uneasy friends and rivals for the position of chief favourite at court. In 1588, after some petty squabble, Essex challenged Raleigh to a duel. Raleigh went to Ireland, and it was on this visit that he befriended Spenser, and read Spenser's work-in-progress, probably the first three books of *The Faerie Queene*. As well as being one of the poem's first great champions, Raleigh also became some of the characters within Spenser's fantasy: not only within *The Faerie Queene*, but in the charming *Colin Clouts Come Home Againe*. It tells the story of how Raleigh – the Shepherd of the Sea – came to Ireland, and persuaded Spenser to cross the sea to visit Cynthia (Elizabeth) and the beautiful ladies of her court. They left Kilcolman, Spenser's Irish seat, in the autumn of 1589; eighteen months later the Queen rewarded Spenser with an annual pension of £50 to complete his epic. The poem is dated 'the 27th of December 1591, from my house of Kilcolman'. So, for this London-born poet, Ireland had become home, even though England is represented as a land of peace and civilisation beside the tormented island:

For there all happie peace and plenteous store
Conspire in one to make contented blisse:
No wayling there nor wretchednesse is heard,
No bloodie issues nor no leprosies,
No grisly famine, nor no raging sweard,
No nightly bodrags [raids], nor no hue and cries . . .[16]

It is a glorious poem. The description of the sea-voyage to England is especially fine. The list of court beauties is in part poetry, in part the Elizabethan equivalent of a 'social diary' in a modern illustrated magazine, and in part an application for patronage. His praise of 'Amaryllis' – Alice Spencer, the recent widow of Ferdinando Stanley, Lord Strange – will catch the eye of literary historians, for this is the lady who would live well into the seventeenth century and would be the patroness – by then as the Countess of Derby – to whom Milton dedicated *Comus*. Her splendid tomb in Harefield, Middlesex, shows her golden hair streaming over her shoulders.

It is noticeable that Spenser singles out love, and the worship of the love-god Cupid, as the particular occupational hazard of the poet – 'For him the greatest of the gods we deem.' But the contrast between the rancorous, feud-ridden court and the idyllic rural delights of Kilcolman is the real theme of this extremely deft and backhanded piece of pastoral. Whereas the Shepherd of the Ocean has promised the simpleton-bard a journey to a place where there are no 'Troubles' of the classic Irish kind – midnight raids, fights, killings – he actually leads him into a court where the rivalries and feuds provide evidence of human depravity that is every bit as strong. In the dedication to Raleigh, Spenser alludes to the 'malice of evill mouthes, which are always wide open to carpe at and misconstrue my simple meaning. I pray continually for your happinesse'. The poem was not published until 1595, but this dedication is dated 1591, when Raleigh's happiness – and indeed his very life – was threatened by a situation that Spenser, in his apparently simple pastoral poem of two bumpkin shepherds, had so laid bare.

During the period of Spenser's visit back to England, and his excited taste of court life with its beautiful women – 'Beautie is the bayt, which with delight / Doth man allure'[17] – Raleigh fell in love with one of Elizabeth's ladies-in-waiting: Elizabeth Throckmorton. By the time Raleigh had taken possession of Sherborne Castle, and Spenser had gone back to Ireland, Bess Throckmorton was pregnant. The lovers were to grow into a devoted married couple, but they both knew the Queen and realised they were in deadly peril. Raleigh was thirty-six or thirty-seven. Bess was twenty-five when her baby was born. The child was hastily christened: the godparents were his uncle, Arthur Throckmorton, Anna Throckmorton and, of all people, the Earl of Essex. He was then hastily sent to a wet-nurse in Enfield. Raleigh was supposed to be planning a naval expedition against the Spanish, and Bess tried to return to court as if the marriage and the baby had never happened. There was no real hope of keeping their marriage a secret – not in such a court as that. For this reason, presumably, Raleigh attempted 'damage limitation': getting Essex as the godfather of the child, and a building-up of his own reputation as an indispensable sea-hero. But there was no denying what had happened. He, the favourite, or ex-favourite, had committed that unpardonable sin. Raleigh and Bess were sent to the Tower of London.

It was probably while he was in the Tower that Raleigh wrote his poem, the 'Book of the Ocean to Cynthia'. He let it be known that this was to be an extended work of twelve books, like *The Faerie Queene*. How seriously are we to take this? The first ten books are supposedly 'lost', but it is just as possible that he never wrote them. Given his friendship with Spenser, his sardonic nature, his anger with the Queen, is it not likely that he built up the idea of the long poem to Cynthia as a sort of bitter joke? There is certainly a great bitterness in the poem as he looks back on his twelve years as the companion-courtier of that impossible character 'Cynthia':

> Twelve years entire I wasted in this war,[18]
> Twelve years of my most happy younger days;
> But I in them, and they now wasted are,
> Of all which past the sorrow only stays.

At nearly forty, a sixteenth century man was entering, if not old age, then a period when the best of life is over. C.S. Lewis wrote that the quatrains 'vibrate with sombre passion', as well they might, as Raleigh reflected on his dangerous and emotionally upsetting relationship with the Queen. As it happened, he only had to spend five weeks in the Tower. His wife was imprisoned for rather longer, but although they were released, it was 'never glad confident morning again'. Raleigh's hey-day as a courtier was over. He now looked abroad for glory.

26

My America

Raleigh and his wife were sent to a prison where – had the Queen's whim so decreed – they might easily have been incarcerated for years, or until death. As things turned out, Raleigh did, under the next monarch, spend years of his life in the Tower, and was beheaded there in 1618. Prince Henry, James I's son, who loved Raleigh and admired his genius, said that 'no king but his father would keep such a bird in a cage' and blamed Robert Cecil (by then the Earl of Salisbury) for his sad fate. [1] Bess, as a maid of honour, had incurred the Queen's wrath for marrying without royal consent. But one gets an uncanny sense that the offence for which Walter and Bess Raleigh were sent down by Elizabeth in 1591 was that of consummating heterosexual love, procreating and marrying. In order to atone for these sins, Raleigh would have to commit 'virtuous' deeds – that is, sail out into the high seas, commit acts of piracy and mass murder on Spanish vessels and then sail to the New World to lay claim to land inhabited by other people. Such is the moral universe that the Elizabethans at court inhabited. No wonder, in order to compose his great moral epic *The Faerie Queene*, Spenser felt he had to return to the rural seclusion in Ireland, where human wrongdoing was daily manifest, but morality was perhaps a little less inverted.

While Raleigh was imprisoned in the Tower, his old friend Sir Richard Grenville was sent in his place, alongside Lord Thomas Howard, to capture the Spanish treasure-ships at sea. Grenville's ship was the *Revenge*. Three of the other vessels were captained by men who would be Raleigh's comrades on the later voyage to Guiana: Whiddon, Cross and Thynne. They loitered off the Azores, some sixteen English ships. By the end of August 1591, however, sailing off the coast of Portugal, the Earl of Cumberland got wind of what the Spanish intended – namely to send an Armada of fifty-three ships against the English state-sponsored pirates. Cumberland was able to reach the Azores just, but only just, before the arrival of the Spanish fleet. He found the English in a bad way – fever and sickness had weakened the men of six ships, and Lord Thomas Howard decided that it would be suicidal to engage with an enemy so hugely superior in strength and numbers. So he weighed anchor and took off to England. The Spanish had surrounded Grenville before he could pick up his men or rejoin the English fleet. Grenville disobeyed Howard's orders to rejoin the fleet. He was not an experienced sailor, and the loss of the *Revenge* and the men on it was his fault. Yet Raleigh saw the death of the stubborn Cornishman Grenville as heroic. Rather than surrender to the Spaniards, Grenville was prepared to die, with all his crew, and if necessary to destroy the ships that remained to them rather than allow them to fall into enemy hands. There is something undeniably impressive about this: in his defiance, his doughty Protestantism, his contempt for the enemy and his willing embrace of death, Sir Richard Grenville was an archetypical Elizabethan hero; and so the loss of the *Revenge* passed into historical legend, being seen as on the scale of the defence of the 300 at Thermopylae. Tennyson's version of the story, based on his reading of Froude, for a hundred years became part of the poetic repertoire of any English child:

> 'We die – does it matter when?
> Sink me the ship, Master Gunner – sink her, split her in twain!
> Fall into the hands of God, not into the hands of Spain!'

The patriotic Victorians, Tennyson and Froude, would have been unable to write about the loss of the *Revenge* in the way that they did, had it not been for Raleigh who first immortalised the legend in 'A report of the truth of the fight about the Isles of Azores, this last summer betwixt the Revenge, one of Her Majesties Shippes, and an Armada of the King of Spaine'. It is one of Raleigh's finest pieces of prose, violently partisan, crudely anti-Spanish, but essential reading if you want to capture the heroic Elizabethan mindset and their attitude to the Spanish Empire, which then dominated the world. It is one of the great pieces of battle-reportage in the English language:

> All the Powder of the Revenge to the last barrel was now spent, all her pikes broken, fortie of her best men slaine, and the most part of the rest hurt. In the beginning of the fight she had but one hundredth free from sicknes, and fourscore and ten sicke, laid in hold upon the Ballast. A small troop to man such a ship, and a weak Garrison to resist so mighty an Army. By those hundred all was sustained, the voleis, bourdings, and entrings of fifteen ships of warre, besides those which beat her at large. On the contrarie, the Spanish were always supplied with souldiers brought from everie squadron: all manner of Armes and pouder at wil.

Raleigh was insistent that the majority of the English fleet did not sail away for reasons of cowardice; but he was also anxious to absolve his old friend Grenville from any imputation of incompetence. There were men still stuck on the island and he could not leave them to the merciless fates of captives of Spain, which were by now notoriously commonplace throughout the world.

Raleigh was contemptuous of the religious arguments put forward by the King of Spain, and by 'their runnagate Jesuites', which place high on any Spanish agenda the wish to convert the world to Catholicism. 'Neither have they at any time as they protest invaded the kingdoms of the Indies and Peru and els where, but onely led thereunto, rather to reduce the people to Christianitie, then for either golde or empire.' Conquest and world domination were their aim and business, and Raleigh wanted no one – least of all English Catholics such as so many of his Throckmorton in-laws – to be deceived by any of the propaganda. The King of Spain 'useth his pretence of religion, for no other purpose, but to bewitch us from the obedience of our naturall Prince'.

Raleigh therefore felt perfectly within his rights, as an Englishman, to exact revenge for the *Revenge*. And since this venture stood to make its backers, including the Queen, a great deal of money, Raleigh was temporarily released from the Tower. The Queen adventured two ships, and £3,000. Raleigh gave his ship, the *Roebuck*, and a lot of borrowed money. The idea had been that Raleigh would accompany the fleet to the coast of Spain, and then return to England while they sailed on to Panama. As soon as he was at sea, however, Raleigh ignored all the orders from Frobisher to go home. He persuaded Frobisher to stay and watch the Spanish coast while he took his squadron to the Azores, where they commandeered two giant Spanish carracks from the East Indies. The *Santa Cruz*, having been plundered, they drove ashore and burned. The *Madre de Dios* – 1,600 tons, a huge ship – was boarded and taken. The sailors on board who took her back to England could not believe their luck and spent the whole voyage pilfering loot. Raleigh managed to get some small return on his investment, though he claimed he lost on the deal. (He and his partners put in £34,000, took £36,000 out, but had a lot of incidental expense.) The Queen took the bulk of the loot – valued at £82,666. 13s. 4d.

No wonder their friend and fellow 'Scholar of Night', George Chapman – famed as the translator whose version of Homer made Keats feel:

> like some watcher of the skies
> When a new planet swims into his ken

– should have seen the potentialities of Guiana as almost limitless. In that decade when the economy was in such a parlous state – rising food prices, failed crops, a fall in the real value of money, and inflation

– Guiana became a mythic source of betterment, which could return England to its wealth, and Elizabeth to the bright glory of her early years:

> Riches and conquest and renown I sing
> Riches with honour, conquest without blood,
> Enough to seat the monarchy of earth,
> Like to Jove's eagle on Eliza's hand.
> Guiana, whose rich feet are mines of gold,
> Whose forehead knocks against the roof of stars,
> Stands on her tiptoe at fair England looking,
> Kissing her hand, bowing her mighty breast,
> And every sign of all submission making,
> To be her sister and her daughter both
> Of our most sacred Maid . . .[2]

Although he had made the sacred Maid, the Queen, so spectacular a sum of money from the *Madre de Dios* raid, Raleigh was still in disgrace. He and his wife were released from the Tower, but retreated to Sherborne Castle, where they missed the court, and London, keenly. Raleigh planned another expedition. By 1595 the rather grandiose schemes had shrunk. The fleet of seven vessels became four, with his friends Lawrence Keymis, Jacob Whiddon and Douglas Master in charge of them. Keymis was an interesting man – a Fellow of Balliol College, Oxford, from 1583 to 1591, a good mathematician and geographer, a member of the group of friends who constituted (in so far as it existed) the 'School of Night', and a fast friend of Raleigh's. It would have been easy to desert Raleigh when he fell from the royal favour, but Keymis stayed loyal and, while Raleigh was in the Tower, acted as his agent and tried to keep his ever-interesting financial affairs in order. Raleigh attracted real devotion, and one still feels his attraction – of all the great Elizabethans, he is the most attractive.

As they reached Trinidad, Raleigh temporarily parted company from them to do a brief reconnaissance in the Orinoco delta in (modern-day) Venezuela. For it was on the banks of the Orinoco that he hoped to find gold. When he met the native caciques:

> I made them understand that I was a servant of a Queen, who was the great cacique of the north and a virgin . . . that she was an enemy to the Castellani [that is, the Spanish] in respect of their tyranny and oppression, and that she delivered all such nations about her, as were by them oppressed, and having freed all the coast of the northern world from their servitude had sent me to free them also, and withal

> to defend the country of Guiana from their invasion and conquest. I showed them her majesty's picture which they so admired and honoured, as it had been easy to have brought them idolatrous thereof . . . so as in that part of the world, her majesty is very famous and admirable, whom they now call Ezrabeta Cassipuna Aquerewana, which is as much as Elizabeth, the great princess or greatest commander.[3]

Raleigh was anxious that his sailors should not behave like the Spanish Conquistadors: there were to be no rapes, no violence, no plunder of the villages. He wanted the caciques to be on his side and to lead him to his obsession – the gold. Fatally, he did manage to find a few fragments of gold in the river, and this fed the mania that possessed him for the next twenty-three years: the belief that somewhere in the Orinoco he was going to find riches beyond avarice's wildest hope. It was the failure of that last expedition to Orinoco in 1618 that cost him his life. He lost his son on that final expedition, and when he came home it was to face trumped-up charges of treason and fraud.

The night before he died, he sat up in his cell in the Tower of London and wrote that mordant verse:

> Even such is Time, which takes in trust
> Our youth, our joys, and all we have,
> And pays us with but age and dust;
> Who in the dark and silent grave,
> When we have wandered all our ways,
> Shuts up the story of our days.

Did he pause there, as he wrote. And was that the whole of his faith, this enquiring, sceptical man who in the 1590s had been accused of being an atheist? No. It was not mere convention that made him add the next two lines. Raleigh did not give a fig for conventions. Like so many of the most interesting men and women of the age, he was very close to scepticism. His mind questioned everything. It was one of the things that he had in common, not only with raffish young intellectuals such as Marlowe, but with the Queen. But, like the Queen, he held fast to the faith:

> And from which earth, and grave, and dust,
> The Lord shall raise me up, I trust.[4]

Likewise, we find the sceptic Thomas Hariot reading aloud from the Scriptures to the Native Americans in Virginia in 1616.

And although the dreams of gold in Guiana turned out to be a dangerous fantasy, Raleigh's involvement with the fledgling colony of Virginia was not useless.

In his essay on 'Plantations', the malicious Francis Bacon wrote, 'it is the sinfullest thing in the world to forsake or destitute a plantation once in forwardness, for besides the dishonour, it is the guiltiness of blood of many commiserable persons'. It was clearly a dig against Raleigh, who had claimed that the voyage of 1595 had been to protect the new colony of Virginia, but he had become distracted by the prospect of finding gold in Guiana. Yet it was unfair to blame Raleigh for the financial setbacks of the early settlers in Virginia. He lived on borrowed money and, until he found his crock of Guianan gold, he could not subsidise Virginia. He did abandon the Roanoke settlers, but no one else helped them either in the 1580s or 1590s. 'I long since presumed to offer your Majesty my service in Virginia,' he wrote to James I, 'with a short repetition of the commodity, honour and safety which the King's Majesty might reap by that plantation, if it were followed to effect. I do still humbly beseech your Majesty, that I may rather die in serving the King and my Country than to perish here' (he was writing from the Tower).

Raleigh, however, was the pioneer who literally put Virginia on the map, and who, simply by his fame and colourful personality – smoking tobacco, cutting a figure – reminded people of the colony's existence. It was really Hakluyt who had the prescience to see Virginia's vast historical potential. We began this book with the observation that the world created by the Elizabethans had ended in our lifetime: and as far as England is concerned that is very largely true. The class who rose to eminence under Elizabeth as the governing class – the Cecils, the Cavendishes, the Herberts – were in positions of political power until the early to mid-twentieth century. Now, though they might still inhabit Hatfield, Wilton and Chatsworth, they are not in government. The Church of England still exists, and its bishops still wear Elizabethan lawn-sleeved rochets with gathered cuffs. But the claim of that Church to speak for England looks, in the multicultural atmosphere of twenty-first-century Britain, more notional than practical. The grammar schools created by Elizabethans to educate poor scholars either became private schools in the nineteenth century (Rugby, Harrow, and so on) or in the twentieth century were made into comprehensive schools and lost much of their distinction. So, as we began by saying, the Elizabethan world has gone.

But in one respect that generalisation is not true. Although Virginia has not been an English colony since 1776, the fact that the largest and most powerful nation in the world is English-speaking is the direct consequence of the Elizabethan view of things; and, in particular, it is the consequence of

Richard Hakluyt's vision of things. In 1587 Hakluyt produced a new edition of the *Decades* of Peter Martyr (1457–1526). Martyr was an Italian who went to Spain in his early twenties and was one of the leading humanists at Salamanca University. He was a geographer of great renown – he was the first person, for example, to understand the significance of the Gulf Stream – and he wrote about the transatlantic voyages and discoveries in a ten-part work known as the *Decades*.

At first sight, it would seem puzzling that Hakluyt should have re-issued this by now all-but-obsolete book, which dated from the very beginning of the century, and the beginning of Spanish and Portuguese conquest of the Americas. But that was the point. He published the book in Latin, and in Paris, because it was aimed at a European-wide market, and he dedicated this particular edition to Raleigh. Martyr had been a great geographer, and Hakluyt paid handsome tribute to this fact. He praised Martyr for his anthropological boldness in recounting the Spanish 'avarice, ambition, butchery, rapine, debauchery, their cruelty towards defenceless and harmless peoples'. It was Martyr who chronicled the Spanish conquest of 'vast regions of the New World'. In other words, what Hakluyt was doing by publishing this book in this particular way was saying to the world: 'although the Pope famously divided the New World between Portugal and Spain and told them to share it between them, he had no authority to do so'. Peter Martyr demonstrated that the Spaniards conquered *much*, but not all, of the Americas. The rest was waiting for new and more benignant conquerors. Geography is the eye of history, said Hakluyt – *Geographiam esse historiae oculus*. He hoped that this work by a foreigner might inspire 'our island race' . . . 'For he who proclaims the praises of foreigners rouses his own countrymen if they be not dolts.'[5]

Furthermore, Hakluyt urged Raleigh on to Virginia. The 'sweet nymph' needed to be pursued and wooed like any other woman. 'There yet remain for you new lands, ample realms, unknown peoples'. Moreover, the English efforts to colonise Virginia were sanctioned by Holy Scripture itself. Christ's command in St Matthew's Gospel to baptise and teach all people was understood by Hakluyt to mean 'to recall the savage and pagan to civility', a serious call, given the twin threats still posed to the world by Islam and Roman Catholicism.[6] If Raleigh had the boldness to pursue the colonisation of America, he would, Hakluyt promised him, 'find at length, if not a Homer, yet some Martyr – by whom I mean some happy genius – to rescue your heroic enterprises from the vast maw of oblivion'.[7]

Hakluyt's own multi-volume work is perhaps more comparable to the work of Herodotus than to that of Homer. It was a history of his own people, but written from the point of view of naval exploits, geographical curiosity and the new ideology of Empire. He announced the coming of the work in 1589 and it would include 'the most remote and farthest distant Quarters of the earth at any time within the compasse of these 1500 years'. So, from the journey of that Colchester girl, the Empress Helena, to find the relics of the True Cross in Jerusalem in the fourth century, to the circumnavigation of the globe by Francis Drake, was seen as one vast Bible of English world-exploration, an allegory of imperial expansionism. And it is worthy to be placed beside Herodotus as one of the most absorbing set of narratives ever collected in book form.

In 1590 Hakluyt was able to give up being the 'preacher' at the English Embassy in Paris and retire to the English countryside. His ambassador's wife, Lady Douglas Stafford, was the patron of the living of Wetheringsett in Suffolk. It was as the rector of All Saints' church there that Hakluyt could repair, and it is clear that he did not regard it simply as a sinecure. He was the resident parish priest. His son was christened there in 1593; his first wife was buried there in 1597.

When, as a sixteen-year-old Westminster schoolboy, Hakluyt had visited his namesake cousin in the Middle Temple and 'found lying open upon his boord certeine books of Cosmographie, with an universall Mappe', he had experienced something like an epiphany; and in the early years of his career it looked as if the Queen and her Council had seen the point of English expansionism. Rather than shoring up the creaking economy by occasional piratical forays to steal merchandise and gold and jewels from Spanish vessels, the English could think of themselves quite differently: as a small maritime power rather like Venice, capable – by a mixture of commercial enterprise and large-sightedness – of ruling other lands and other seas. To the young Elizabethans this had seemed like a realisable vision. To the Elizabethans grown old, to the court dominated by feuds between Cecil and Essex, to a queen who could allow Ireland to fall into bloody crisis because one arrogant young man had seen her in her nightie (as we shall see in the next chapter), the world had become a smaller place. Hakluyt's vision was not much heeded.

This did not deter him. He continued to use his compilations of geography and travellers' tales as a spur to colonial action.[8] Richard Mulcaster, whom we met earlier – first as the young man who described the elaborate ceremonies preceding Elizabeth's coronation in London, and next as the first headmaster of the Merchant Taylors' School and a noted grammarian – was someone who saw the point of Hakluyt. By now the High Master of St Paul's, a post he was granted in 1596, his sixty-sixth year, Mulcaster composed a long tribute to Hakluyt in Homeric Greek verse. The Fatherland, wrote Mulcaster, owed much to Hakluyt, 'since, for what reason does our England boast itself more than because, in addition to everything else, it becomes powerful through its fleet? Which fleet, before hidden in shadows, Hakluyt liberates, so that now everyone may know how noble is its activity. If we use it like Daedalus, we shall rise to the heights; if we are to be Icarus, then the sea will have something to swallow'.[9]

Hakluyt dedicated his *Principall Navigations* to Robert Cecil. No more forceful indication could be given of the book's political motivation – to spur the highest authorities to encourage colonialisation. And not just to America. Hakluyt led the life of a private scholar and we know little of his day-to-day life, but one of the few acts that we can date is in mid-October 1599, when he attended a meeting in London of the directors of the East India Company. A couple of years later, in January 1601, Hakluyt met them again to tell them the best places in the subcontinent where trade was 'to be had' and to assemble 'out of his notes & books divers instruccions for provisions of jewelles'.[10] After the debacle of the first attempts to settle Virginia, Hakluyt patiently continued to advocate the advantages of maintaining the colony there. 'To the southwest of our old fort in Virginia,' he reported, in 1609, there existed, 'a great melting of red metal, reporting the manner of working the same.' . . . Besides, 'our owne Indians have lately revealed either this or another rich mine of copper or gold in a towne called Ritanoe, near certain mountains lying West of Roanoac'.[11]

Hakluyt had deplored, in many of his writings, the cruelty of the Spanish Conquistadors towards the natives of invaded lands. He urged gentleness on the new colonists, but gentleness could – in his scale of values – have its limits. The Native Americans were, he decreed from his Suffolk parsonage, never having set foot in the new colonies, 'great liars and dissemblers' who could be 'as unconstant as a weathercock'. Yet Hakluyt did not advocate eliminating the Native Americans, as the Spanish had done in the Caribbean and elsewhere. The Algonquin and other peoples 'should be treated gently, while gentle courses may be found to serve'. If such a strategy were successful, 'then we shall not want hammerours and rough masons now, I meane our old souldiours trained up in the Netherlands, to square and prepare them to our Preachers hands'.

Hakluyt urged the Council to finance the new colony and to encourage English settlers there. As was to happen in India and Africa, the Imperial Idea was driven forward by a peculiar blend of avarice and piety. While hoping to find gold, pearls, copper and fertile land, Hakluyt also saw magnificent opportunities for missions among the Algonquin. 'The painfull Preachers shall be reverenced and cherished, the valiant and forward souldier respected, the diligent rewarded, the coward emboldened, the weake and the sick relieved, the mutinous suppressed, the reputation of the Christians among the Salvages preserved, our most holy faith exalted, all Paganisme and Idolatrie by little and little utterly extinguished'.[12] In 1618 Hakluyt was listed as one of the 'Adventurers to Virginia' and bought two shares in the venture, later valued at £21.

It is interesting, in his writing to Raleigh, that Hakluyt saw himself as conveying Homeric status on the explorers and settlers in the *Principall Navigation*. He could see that by establishing interests on the other side of the Atlantic, the Elizabethans had expanded much more than their investment portfolios.

The young John Donne, in one of the most beautiful, and witty, erotic poems – 'To his Mistris Going to Bed' – likened the experience of seeing her naked, and 'exploring' her with his hands, to the explorations of the transatlantic voyagers:

> License my roving hands, and let them go
> Before, behind, between, above, below,
> O, my America! My new-found land
> My kingdome, safeliest when with one man man'd,
> My mine of precious stones, My Emperie,
> How blest I am in this discovering thee![13]

Donne's poem is not describing a 'Special Relationship' of long-standing. It is not about warm-hearted, cosy or marital sex, or sex between two people whose bodies are familiar with one another. It is about the intense excitement of discovering new love, led on by mutual lust. 'How blest I am in this discovering thee!' By implication, the corollary is almost true: that the discovery of America for the English – the real discovery, which came into the Elizabethan Age, rather than the mere knowledge that America was 'there' – was as exciting as new love. We know what the American future held, which makes the early colonisation of Roanoke, and the far-sighted optimism of Raleigh and Hakluyt, all the more extraordinary to contemplate.

The refounding of Virginia, and the appointment of Lord de la Warr as the governor of the new colony – that is a story that belongs to the reign of James I. So, too, does the story of Pocahontas, a naked girl doing cartwheels to delight spectators in the new marketplace of Jamestown. This princess was the daughter of Chief Powhattan. The story, written up eight years after the event, was that she intervened with her father to prevent one of the English settlers, Captain John Smith, (1580?–1631) being brained with clubs by the braves. When she was about sixteen years of age she was taken hostage by Captain Samuel Argal, who was trading for corn along the Potomac, in exchange for 'good behaviour' by the indigenous inhabitants. The following year she was baptised Rebecca and married to the colonist John Rolfe. She went to England in 1616. Homesick for American soil, Pocahontas pined away, and in the parish registry in Gravesend can be read the stark entry, '1616, May 2j, Rebecca Wrothe, wyff of Thas Wroth, gent, a Virginia lady borne, here was buried in the chauncell.'

All this lay in the future.

27

Tyrone

Irish patriots needed a William the Silent, a man with the subtle intelligence of a politician and the courage of a military hero: one who could unite the warring factions on his own side, and enlist foreign support against the colonisation and appropriation of his native land. Thanks to the clumsiness of English policy in Ireland, the Irish William the Silent very nearly materialised in the person of Hugh O'Neill (*c*.1540–1616) (Aodh Ó Néill), who became 2nd Earl of Tyrone in 1587. He led the rebellion against Elizabethan authority that came closest to being successful. That such a man could have been provoked into this position was symptomatic of Elizabeth and her advisers having pathetically lost their grasp. O'Neill, after all – to whom, for the sake of clarity, we shall refer as *Tyrone* – had been bred to be an anglophone supporter of the Queen, and of the English in Ireland. He almost certainly grew up, for at least part of his childhood, in the household of the Lord Deputy, Sir Henry Sidney. (Sidney claimed he had 'bred' him 'from a little boy, then very poor of goods and full feebly friended'.[1]) Throughout the 1570s – during his thirties – the English had given him more and more land, commensurate with his status. The 1st Earl of Essex made him colonel of a cavalry regiment. Tyrone supported some of the most bloodthirsty and futile campaigns by English planters against Irish chiefs in Munster. The Queen advised the 1st Earl of Essex to 'use all good means to nourish [his] good devotion towards us'.

It was the two English rivals, Sir John Perrot and Sir William Fitzwilliam, who succeeded in antagonising Tyrone. The English had hitherto supported his claim to the earldom – it had been hotly contested, not least because he was only the second son, and a second son at that of Matthew O'Neill, whose legitimacy as an O'Neill was questioned by other O'Neills. As the lord and ruler of Ulster, Tyrone wanted to make it his task to drive out the Scottish settlers and rule the area with trusted English and Irish administrators. But neither Perrot nor Fitzwilliam fully trusted him. Perrot wanted to divide the O'Neill lordship into two units and deprive Tyrone of half his power and wealth; Fitzwilliam wanted to devote his final term as Lord Deputy (1588–94) to dividing Ulster into English-style shires. Tyrone resented both procedures and seized the lands that Perrot had assigned to his rival, Turlough Luineach O'Neill. Elizabeth initially conceded Tyrone's claim. He reciprocated by massacring 500 Spanish Armada survivors and by pursuing his deadly rivals, the MacShanes, who were still importing Scottish mercenaries into Ulster.

The English administrators, however, were suspicious of Tyrone's enormous power. Sir Henry Bagenal, Marshal of the army, succeeded his father (Sir Nicholas – of Newry in Ulster) as an Irish privy councillor in 1590. He wanted to check Tyrone's dynastic and political power, not least because there was strong personal antipathy between the two men. Tyrone had been married to a kinswoman by whom he had several children, but this union was put aside on the grounds of consanguinity and he horrified Sir Henry Bagenal by eloping with Bagenal's sister, Mabel. The pair were married on 3 August 1591 by Thomas Jones, Bishop of Meath, in the house of a friend in County Dublin.

The elopement provoked some psychologically interesting reactions. Tyrone's former brother-in-law, Hugh Roe O'Donnell, became his ally; Sir Henry Bagenal, his new brother-in-law, became his inveterate foe. O'Donnell escaped from confinement in Dublin Castle and formed a new alliance with Tyrone. In the opening years of the 1590s a number of factors came together, which made it almost inevitable that Tyrone would become the figurehead of anti-English resistance. His refusal to check his Irish allies (new and old) in their attacks on English soldiers was outraging the authorities at the same time as the Counter-Reformation was making inroads in Ireland. Tyrone – in spite of what the English alleged – was not at first involved with this, but some of his allies (the O'Donnells and Hugh Maguire, for instance) backed the appointment of Counter-Reformation bishops who actively encouraged their people to support the deposition of Elizabeth I in support of Philip II. A generation earlier, when Maryborough and Philipstown were established in County Offaly, the patriotic Irish position was to oppose Philip; and had his Catholic English queen, Mary, lived and produced heirs, the land of Ireland would no doubt have rivalled Holland and Switzerland in its collective devotion to the tenets of the Reformation. From the 1590s onwards, however, loyalty to the Church of Rome became part of the heady mix of Irish nationalist mythology, and Tyrone and friends were seen as champions of 'Christ's Catholic religion'.[2]

The incendiary moment occurred in 1594. Fitzwilliam had been replaced as Lord Deputy by Sir William Russell, and a number of Tyrone's allies resented having English garrisons planted on their land. The garrison at Enniskillen, County Fermanagh, was attacked and routed by Maguire and Macbarron. Even at this late stage Tyrone attended upon Russell in Dublin and presented him with a petition for the garrisons to be removed. Elizabeth told Russell not to concede. The Irish then laid siege to a few more garrisons, including Blackwater Fort on Tyrone's own land. Then his brother-in-law, Sir Henry Bagenal, was attacked at Clontibret, County Monaghan, and his 1,750 men were forced into retreat by a large Irish army headed by Tyrone himself. His William the Silent moment had come.

In English and in Irish, Tyrone was formally declared a traitor on 24 June 1595 at Dundalk, County Louth. The English, who had been more than happy to support his claim to the earldom when he was on their side, then issued statements about the bastardy of Tyrone's father. But Tyrone now had the loyalty of thousands of Irish fighters from his own lands, and he also petitioned for 600 or 700 Spanish soldiers to help. Mercenaries were engaged from the Scottish islands. The English now had a major Irish resistance on their hands. On 14 August 1598 Bagenal was killed and thousands of his army were scattered or killed at the Battle of Yellow Ford, between Armagh and Blackwater. It was a major victory for the Irish from a military and a propaganda point of view. And it left Tyrone, in effect, the Lord of all Ireland.

What was Elizabeth to do? What was Philip of Spain to do? What would Lord Burghley advise? These are the familiar questions, which, for the previous forty years of the reign, would have been asked at any time of national emergency. But the old players were no longer able to take the stage. Philip II was dying as he heard the news of Tyrone's victory at Yellow Ford. He died on 13 September – he was seventy-one years old. Old Burghley had died ten days before Tyrone's triumph. Elizabeth in her old age must overcome her indecisiveness and face the Irish crisis by herself, and choose a course between the warring factions of her younger courtiers. None of them would be surprised when she chose, as the English hero to defeat the Irish William the Silent, her favourite, the young Earl of Essex.

By the time she was in her mid-sixties the Queen had grown prematurely old, with a 'goggle throat, a great gullet hanging out'.[3] When the new French Ambassador, André Hurault, Sieur de Maisse, arrived at her court in November 1597, he described an England and a queen long past their springtime. The country between Dover and London was 'poor and for the most part wild and untilled, and the Spanish could not easily make their entrance, for owing to the scarcity of provisions it would be necessary to bring them from Spain'.[4] De Maisse arrived at Whitehall by barge. He found 'the entrance on the riverside . . . very small and inconvenient; it is a covered alley and rather dark. Thence one enters a low hall, and then by a staircase of fifteen or twenty steps to the rooms above. It is very low and has no great appearance for a royal house.'[5] On his first visit, de Maisse was led down a dark corridor where the Queen was sitting in a low chair, all by herself.[6] Bishop Goodman (1583–1656) noted that six years later she died 'very much neglected, which was an occasion of her melancholy'.[7]

When de Maisse was shown into the Preserve, Elizabeth excused herself for still being in her nightgown and said, gesturing to the ambassador's entourage, 'What will these gentlemen say to see me so attired? I am much disturbed that they should see me in this state.'[8]

She was wearing a dress:

> of silver cloth, white and crimson, or silver 'gauze' as they call it. This dress had slashed sleeves lined with red taffeta, and was girt about with other little sleeves that hung down to the ground, which she was forever twisting and untwisting. She kept the front of her dress open, and one could see the whole of her bosom, and passing low, and often she would open the front of this robe with her hands as if she was too hot.[9]

On a later visit de Maisse noted that 'when she raises her head she has a trick of putting both hands on her gown and opening it insomuch that all her belly can be seen'.[10] Her long, thin face was lined. Her 'teeth were very yellow and unequal'.[11] On either side of her ears hung two great curls of hair, which hung down to her shoulders. On top of the head was a somewhat fantastical red wig. She was festooned with jewels. A chain of rubies and pearls encircled the turkey-throat. Spangles of gold and silver and more pearls were in the wig. She had six or seven rows of pearl bracelets on each wrist.

This extraordinary apparition was accompanied, when de Maisse called again, by Burghley. The Frenchman thought Burghley was eighty-two. In fact he was only seventy-eight, but stone-deaf and apparently unable to hear, however loud de Maisse shouted. England, which at the beginning of the reign had been a young country, had decayed into a gerontocracy.

Burghley continued to keep his all-but-totally-deaf ear to the ground, attending Council meetings, pushing his son Robert forward, intriguing, weighing, interfering as much as always. In the summer of 1598 he at last began to fail. Elizabeth visited him on his sickbed and spoon-fed him with partridges sent by his son Robert. He had always been there – working as her Secretary at Hatfield before the death of her sister Mary, masterminding her accession and directing her policy, first as Secretary, later as Treasurer.

On his bed of sickness, which turned into a deathbed, he manifested two of his most marked characteristics: physical toughness and piety.

'Oh, what a heart have I that will not die!' he complained. He said the Lord's Prayer in Latin. No one had more consummately played, as with kite-strings, the Queen's moods and vagaries. He had not always achieved his aims: most notably he had failed to persuade her, in those early days, to marry. When she rebuked him, he did not pretend to be indifferent – 'I am so wownded in my hart with the late sharp and percyng speeches of hir Majestie to my self in ye hearing of my L of Lecester . . .'[12] Some would raise an eyebrow at his claim that he submitted everything that he did to the Christian Gospel: everything? Every piece of intrigue, every word of back-stairs gossip, every piece of evidence falsified against enemies such as Sir John Perrot? Maybe these tainted deeds flitted through his sharp mind as he prayed for the pardon of his enemies, even as he forgave them. The be-all and end-all of his political standpoint had been the strengthening and preserving of Queen Elizabeth; and chief among his reasons for supporting her against all her enemies had been his belief that she was the strongest possible protectress of the Reformed Christianity in which he believed. Had she died before Mary, Queen of Scots, or had the Spaniards been successful in their forwarding of some rival claimant – Arbella Stuart, for example – much more would have been lost than one clever, vain woman in a red wig.

Elizabeth had become the embodiment, for Burghley, of that Reformation in which Sir John Cheke had taught him, at Cambridge, to believe. Therefore, he had served her. At the time of the Treaty of Edinburgh in 1560, when Elizabeth was in full flight of hysterical rage against him, he had quoted the Greek verse 'Blessed is he who serves the blessed ones.' For the best part of forty years, he had made the motto his life.

'Serve God,' he wrote to his son Robert in those last weeks, 'for all other service is indeed bondage to the devil.'[13] They would have been good last words. Not uncomically, however, five days later he had risen from his bed and was attending yet another meeting of the Council. Only at the beginning of August did he go back to bed and resume the Latin prayers, finally yielding up the ghost 'mildly' during the night of 3rd–4th of that month.

There is no doubt that, viewed in some lights, Burghley possessed all the virtues that were attributed to him by his friend William Camden: 'a most excellent man . . . moderation . . . singular piety . . . so great a Councillor . . . and to his wholesome counsels the state of England for ever shall be beholden'.[14] Another way of looking at Burghley's record in old age was that he was working for the interests of a faction within the court, and that factionalism enormously diminished the political life of late-Elizabethan England. Such was the strength of the *regnum*

Cecilianum that old Burghley was prepared to stop the careers of talented men in their tracks – such as those of Sir Thomas Bodley, Henry Unten, Anthony Standen and Sir William Russell. More than just the careers of courtiers was at stake. The Irish situation became so particularly horrible because of the factionalism at court. Without the *regnum Cecilianum*, there might have been a chance for a less wild creature than the Earl of Essex to come forward as the young head on the old Elizabethan shoulders. As things turned out, the antiquity of the court, and of his enemies within it, were an essential part of the Essex tragedy.

A quarrel in which old people are struggling victoriously against young people is a dismaying archetype to contemplate. Essex was no wounded Balder or Adonis: he had brought his troubles on himself, all right. But those of his generation who watched and followed his career could hardly feel – as a younger generation evidently had felt – that Queen Elizabeth and her councillors were on their side. No wonder Shakespeare (born three years before Essex) could view the old queen's death with complete equanimity:

> The mortal moon hath her eclipse endured
> And the sad augurs mock their own presage . . .

and could proclaim, in his Sonnets, the strength of personal relationships and the inner life:

> When tyrants' crests and tombs of brass are spent.[15]

Robert Devereux was born on 10 November 1567, the child of that beautiful, sexy Lettice Knollys who would capture the fancy of the Queen's favourite, Leicester, and Walter Devereux. They were at the heart of the story that we have been telling in this book. Whatever master-dramatist was staging the reign of Elizabeth cast Robert Devereux in the supreme role of tragic hero for the closing scenes.

The parents – Walter and Lettice – settled first at Chartley, their Staffordshire seat, which was doomed to be Mary, Queen of Scots' prison. Walter was caught up in the Irish tragedy and died of illness contracted there. Their daughter Penelope was the 'Stella' of Sir Philip Sidney's 'Astrophil', the beautiful inspiration for a sonnet-sequence that in some ways outmatches Shakespeare's for technical accomplishment, though not for psychological interest. Lettice had been having an affair with the Earl of Leicester before her husband died, and it was her hold over Leicester that always had the power to reduce the Queen to frenzies of jealous fury. For one woman to have such power over *any* other is heady; to exercise it over an absolute monarch who wielded an axe must have induced a heroin-high of some potency. Elizabeth called her the 'She-Wolf'.

Her son Robert inherited the gift for mayhem. Without remotely suggesting that he was the man to whom Shakespeare wrote any of his sonnets, we could say to Essex – who possessed Lettice's curly auburn hair, dark eyes, curling satirical mouth, fiery temper and total selfishness:

> Thou art thy mother's glass and she in thee
> Calls back the lovely April of her prime . . . [16]

Essex (the Queen's kinsman via his Boleyn-descended mother) first appeared at court at the age of ten – at Christmas 1577. From the first, his relationship with his monarch was arch and combatively flirtatious. He refused to allow her to kiss him, and kept his hat on in her presence. As Burghley's ward, he was sent to Cambridge as early as possible – he matriculated aged thirteen at Trinity – and from the first he wished to combine, as Philip Sidney had done, the Renaissance qualities of book-learning, military heroism and the exercise of statecraft. At eighteen he was accompanying his stepfather Leicester as 'general of the horse' on the Netherlands campaign. By twenty he had returned and become the whirlwind success as a courtier. 'When she is abroad,' noted another courtier wistfully on 3 May 1587, 'nobody with her but my Lord Essex, and at night my lord is at cards, or one game or another with her, that he cometh not to his own lodging till birds sing in the morning.'

He knew how to play the game, and how to flatter the wrinkled old crone for her beauty, whisper in her ear and lead her round the dance floor in the elaborate steps of the galliard. At the same time, there was something new in this last attachment of the Queen's. Essex behaved with the conscious bullying of the toy-boy towards a pathetically older woman who was grateful for his love. She in turn, having allowed him to get away with outbursts of rage or with disobedience that would have cost others their liberty, or their head, would then check herself and insist upon his penitence – or even banish him for a while from her favours. He liked living dangerously, and he did not guard his tongue. He became a Knight of the Garter aged twenty-two and when, a few months later, his stepfather Leicester died, he let it be known that he thought he should succeed him as Chancellor of Oxford University (the Queen gave the honour to the faithful Sir Christopher Hatton). Essex made no secret of his contempt for her other favourite courtiers, and since Raleigh had been the greatest of these before Essex's star rose in the sky, it was not to be wondered at that Essex reserved some of his bitterest expressions of contempt for Raleigh.

He was also determined to prove himself as great a hero as the brave Sir Walter. In 1589 he defied the Queen by persuading the captain of a ship called the *Swiftsure* to follow Drake and Norris on their madcap raid on Lisbon, in support of Don Antonio's claim to the Portuguese throne. Elizabeth sent after him an imperious letter: 'Essex, your sudden and undutiful departure from our presence and your place of attendance, you may easily conceive how offensive it is' . . . She even called for Sir Roger Williams, the Falstaffian soldier who accompanied Essex on his Portuguese adventure, to be punished by death. But by the time Essex came back from Portugal, having stuck his lance in the city gates of Lisbon, and left Drake and his mates to plunder the port of Vigo, Elizabeth had forgiven him.

Inevitably, as a heterosexual who wished to found a dynasty, Essex knew that sooner or later he would have to commit what – in a favourite of Elizabeth's – was the ultimate betrayal. He showed the direction of his ambition by marrying Philip Sidney's widow Frances, the daughter of Francis Walsingham. Essex was in many ways a brilliant person, but he was not in the league of Sidney. The ersatz Renaissance hero that he needed to become was a reflection of a decline at court. He left behind no sonnet sequence, still less a masterpiece to compare with *Arcadia*. He lacked any of Sidney's philosophical reserve or moral depth, though, as his noble death showed, Essex shared with Sidney a deep piety that must have surprised some of his enemies. Frances Sidney and Essex had five children, of whom the firstborn, Robert, became the 3rd Earl and a parliamentary general in the Civil War – surely a reflection, among other things, of the 2nd Earl's fate at the hands of the elderly Queen Elizabeth.

The Queen did forgive him for committing the sin of matrimony, but only just, and only on condition that his wife should live 'very retired in her mother's house'.[17]

Throughout the nineties, Essex punctuated his attentions to the Queen at court with displays of derring-do on the international scene. In 1591 he led 4,000 men into France to support Henri of Navarre in his struggle against the Catholic League. In 1596 he advocated a raid on the Spanish ports as the best way of dampening Spanish aggression. Raleigh was leading the attack – to Essex's intense annoyance – but Essex himself had command of a squadron and, when the English ships inflicted utter defeat upon the Spanish, Essex could then upstage Raleigh, Lord Howard of Effingham and the other English officers by entering Cadiz and planting his standard on the citadel. During the service of thanksgiving for this campaign, which was held in St Paul's Cathedral, the congregation burst into applause when Essex was eulogised from the pulpit.

Essex, who was a highly motivated and ambitious politician, was not simply anxious to be regarded as the daredevil of the decade; nor, with all his elaborate courtship of Elizabeth on the dance-floor, and his bravery, kitted out with the Queen's glove on his arm and hundreds of pounds' worth of elaborately tailored clothes and armour on the rest of his person, as a latterday piece of camp, court decoration. The Queen was an ageing woman. The overwhelming likelihood was now that she would be succeeded by the King of Scotland, but under this capricious and pathologically indecisive tyrant, anything could happen and no one knew exactly when the yellow-toothed, wrinkly, sad old woman, who had all but given up food and drink, would quit the scene.

Essex, as her 'favourite', was openly jockeying for position as the most powerful man, politically, in England. Who would be the man who would exercise power as the Queen slipped into her dotage? Who would have his hand on the tiller when the new captain, whoever that turned out to be, took over? Who would guarantee that the takeover would continue the Protestant, anti-Spanish, university-dominated regime that had been the political creation of William Cecil? Or would it take off in a new direction, with a greater toleration for the papists? In 1593, having accepted military aid from England to maintain his Protestant powerbase, Henri IV of France had become a Catholic for the eminently sensible reason that 'Paris is worth a Mass' – that is, control of the French capital, and friendship with the largely Catholic governing classes, were more important than narrow theological principle; Elizabeth was disgusted and called Henri 'an AntiChrist of ingratitude' – but Essex would have understood, and so would many of the young noblemen in the Essex circle. Not just the Catholic Earl of Southampton, and not just the young – for Lettice Essex, the young earl's mother, had married for the third time to Sir Charles Blount (future Lord Mountjoy), one of the pivotal senior Catholics in England. In short, anything could happen; and Essex was determined, when the time came, that he would be in a position of supreme power.

It was a cataclysmic blow to his schemes that, while he was away in Cadiz, performing deeds that would win him the applause of the crowd in St Paul's Cathedral, his old rival Robert Cecil should be appointed as Secretary. Old Burghley was still alive at this juncture. Elizabeth had chosen wisely. The Cecils were not merely astute politicians in their own interest; it was very largely because of the *regnum Cecilianum* that Elizabeth had maintained a stable government for so long. Robert Cecil, in spite of his physical deformity, and his personal sorrows in the early years of high office (his wife died that year when he was only thirty-three, as did his father-in-law Lord Cobham, leaving him with his daughter Frances, who had inherited her father's deformity, and a frail son William[18]), was able to guide the Queen with great astuteness during the few years left to her. Nor did he make the mistake of underestimating Essex's considerable power-base, with allies in the Privy Council, at court and in the country at large.

Essex's power was extended by his sister Dorothy Perrot (married to Sir John Perrot's son, Tom), later to become Countess of Northumberland; and by their mother with all the Blount/Mountjoy lands and connections. This took in much of Wales, a crucially important power-base in Elizabethan England, especially since the Irish situation was so uncertain. Essex had suffered not merely a great personal blow when Sir John Perrot was condemned for treason; it also meant a loss of land and influence for his sister, since a traitor's lands reverted to the Crown, and it was a great coup for Essex the flatterer that he managed to persuade Elizabeth to allow him and Dorothy to recover so much of the Perrot land in Pembrokeshire. Much of Carmarthenshire, the Welsh country immediately to the east, belonged to the Devereux interest: the fine church of St Peter's, Carmarthen, was a traditional burying place for the Devereux, and Essex was Constable of Carmarthen Castle. These were not mere sinecures, however rarely Essex visited south Wales. What he was controlling here was, besides much fertile and well-fortified land, the high road between England and Ireland.

As lord of Chartley, the Devereux seat near Stafford where Mary, Queen of Scots had been imprisoned, Essex was also the master of much of the land through which any army, discontented or otherwise, would have to march (north or south) in the event of a great civil disturbance. The North of England was still broadly speaking Catholic – the religion of the Blounts (Essex's new in-laws) of his sister, Penelope Rich, and of so many of the northern families who supported the Earl of Northumberland, whom Dorothy Devereux (Lady Perrot) had married in 1594.[19] Essex had a huge territorial power-base, which Robert Cecil – however much he detested his political rival – was not such a fool as to ignore.

Nor was it a merely territorial strength that Essex possessed. Enough has already been written here to demonstrate that he was a difficult, indeed in many respects an odious, young man. But quite apart from his considerable skills at wowing the public and wooing private political allies, Essex, with all the quarterings of his Devereux forebears and extended relations, was related by blood to a high proportion of the tiny peerage of England. Many of them might cordially loathe him, but they were bound to him by kinship. Through his own marriage, Essex was bound to the Sidneys, and to the Earl of Pembroke (who, it must be said, hated him).

Either through kinship or old family association, Essex was close to the Earls of Worcester and Sussex, Rutland and Southampton, Lords Lumley, Eure, Willoughby d'Eresby and Lord Henry Howard. 'This glittering circle of friends was as impressive a grouping of noblemen as any seen in the sixteenth century'.[20]

Of course, there was a sense in which all these connections and influences were only of use to Essex – and of threat to his rivals at court – for as long as he enjoyed the favour of the Queen. But were the Queen seriously to antagonise a great power-base like this, the country would be facing more than a little local difficulty. What began at the start of the decade as a very embarrassing crush formed by a lonely old woman on someone almost young enough to be her grandson would develop into the greatest political threat that had endangered Elizabeth since the execution of Mary, Queen of Scots. The steely way in which she dealt with the threat, when it came to the point of crisis, showed that for all her foolish capacity to dote on her favourites, and her physical decrepitude, she had actually lost none of her ruthlessness, none of that political cunning, which, after nail-bitingly long periods of dither, so often served her.

And so we return to the Battle of Yellow Ford, on 14 August 1598, when the Earl of Tyrone, antagonised needlessly but beyond endurance by the English administration, had killed his brother-in-law Sir Henry Bagenal, routed thousands of English soldiers and proclaimed himself the lord of Ulster and the champion of Christ's Catholic religion. In this moment of supreme national crisis, a crisis almost as serious as the arrival of the Armada ten years before, the Queen forgave Essex – they were in the middle of one of their tiffs – summoned him back from his Achilles-sulk and made him Lord Lieutenant of Ireland. 'By God,' he declared, 'I will beat Tyrone in the field.'

He could not have been more wrong. The losers in the tale would be Essex (the most disastrous loser), the people of Ireland – if they had hoped for the freedom to return to the old Gaelic ways of life, independent of English bossing – and the poor English foot-soldiers who followed Essex on his lacklustre campaign. The victor was the Earl of Tyrone, for the time being. In the end, by 1603, the Ulster rebellion would totally collapse. English law would be enforced (by Essex's successor in Ireland, his Catholic uncle-in-law Mountjoy) upon the whole land of Ireland and, under James VI, the Scottish planting of Ulster would begin, which would lead, in the nineteenth and twentieth centuries, to so bloody and so catastrophic a cohabitation of irreconcilable peoples and cultures. Essex set off to confront Tyrone with the largest army[21] ever to leave English shores during the entire reign – 16,000 foot and 1,300 horse.

In the time it took to assemble this force, Tyrone's triumph at Yellow Ford had led to a virtual collapse of the state's authority throughout Connaught and Munster and parts of Leinster.

As far as posterity cares about Tyrone's short-lived victories, the worst consequence was a literary one. *The Faerie Queene*, the greatest English epic, was everlastingly interrupted, and its author destroyed. Two months after Yellow Ford, Tyrone sent an expedition into Munster and the whole province rose up against the English. Spenser, who was by now Sheriff of Cork, was living in his beautiful seat at Kilcolman with his wife and family when the mob arrived. The house was sacked and burned to the ground. The poet escaped to Cork with his wife and what was left of the family – some say he lost a child in the fire. Sir John Norreys, President of the Province of Munster, gave the Spensers hospitality in Cork, and by the time of Christmas, Spenser was in London, able to present to the Queen his *View of the Present State of Ireland*, whose genocidal proposals – never to be forgotten or forgiven by Irish scholars of Spenser – can be understood in their political context. He died shortly after reaching the age of forty-seven. He was buried next to Chaucer in Westminster Abbey and Essex paid for the funeral.[22] It is a loss to literature comparable only to the murder of Marlowe and the premature death of Sidney that *The Faerie Queene* remained only half-finished.

Essex's campaign in Ireland was totally ineffectual. He spent twenty-one weeks in the country where his father had died. Unlike Spenser, who was so deeply versed in Irish lore and language and topography, he knew nothing of the place. Unlike his successor Mountjoy, who did manage to subdue Ulster, and with it the whole of Ireland, Essex had no idea of tactics. Mountjoy subdued Ireland by utter ruthlessness, spoiling crops, wrecking land and houses, clocking up small victory after small victory from a military point of view, while applying relentless political pressure on Tyrone. Essex allowed Tyrone to run rings round him. The 16,000-strong English army consisted largely of untrained raw recruits. Essex approached each skirmish and battle, each local uprising in dribs and drabs, rather than having a ruthless policy for Ireland as a whole. In Wicklow, Louth, Kildare and Roscommon the Queen's armies were humiliatingly defeated. Essex scarcely moved from the Pale. Exasperated, the Queen sent messages telling him to move north. 'If we had meant that Ireland, after all the calamities in which they have wrapped it, should still have been abandoned,' she witheringly wrote, 'then it was very superfluous to have sent over a personage such as yourself.'

On 7 September Tyrone persuaded Essex to meet him for a negotiated truce, at Carrickmacross. Tyrone extracted from Essex the most astonishing concessions. The English would establish no more garrisons or forts. The truce would last six weeks, extendable at further six-weekly intervals until May 1600 – in other words, to give time for Tyrone to receive the invading Spanish reinforcements that he had been promised. Or so it was surmised. Essex made the further blunder of parleying with Tyrone alone, without witnesses or secretaries.

'We never doubted,' Elizabeth wrote sarcastically:

> but that Tyrone, whensoever he saw any force approach either himself or any of his principal partisans would instantly offer a parley, specially with our supreme general of that Kingdom, having done it with those of subaltern authority, always seeking these cessations with like words, like protestations, and upon such contingents as we gather these will prove. It appeareth by your journal that you and the traitor spoke half an hour together without anybody's hearing, wherein though we trust you are far from mistrusting you with a traitor, yet both for comeliness example and your own discharge, we marvel you would carry it no better.[23]

Essex realized that he had blundered, and he then made matters worse by playing the lover's card. Had he stayed at his post in Ireland and begun to pull off genocidal acts of retribution against the Irish, he might have saved his English political career. Instead he panicked, and hurried back to London, hoping to make a personal appeal to Elizabeth. He rode without interruption as soon as he got to England and, covered with mud and sweat, reached Nonsuch on 28 September at ten in the morning, having been in the saddle all night.

Brooking no warning signals from flunkies, he brushed past the ladies-in-waiting and did what no man had ever done for years – he walked straight into the Queen's bedroom apartments. He saw the old lady with her 'grey hairs about her ears', and the wig several feet away on its stand. She was not dressed. At first, however, it looked as if his gamble had paid off. She patted him softly on the head and told him to return when they had time to prepare themselves. He was able to say, to the awestruck gaggle of courtiers who had assembled in the public rooms, that 'though he had suffered much trouble and storms abroad he found a sweet calm at home'.[24]

When he returned at eleven, clean and dressed, his sovereign had also had time to array herself in her accustomed finery. They spoke for more than an hour, during which he tried to justify himself. Cecil, Raleigh, Grey and the Howards waited while the colloquy took place. When the Queen and Essex emerged, they explained to Cecil and the others how the truce with Tyrone had been negotiated. Essex had no idea how badly he had blundered – blundered in conducting such a truce, blundered in leaving his post in Ireland and perhaps, above all, blundered in having seen Elizabeth without a wig, make-up or day-clothes. Only when he came back for a third audience in the afternoon, by which time Elizabeth had had time to consult Robert Cecil, did Essex realise that he had cooked his goose.

In the morning, a swaggering, mud-spattered young horseman, exhausted by his ride, but a fully powerful, sexually active man in his thirties, had confronted a poor, withered old lady. By the evening, an incompetent public servant who had outlived his usefulness and overstepped every boundary of royal protocol faced his bejewelled, intelligent, ruthless head of state. Elizabeth, in the presence of her councillors, mercilessly confronted Essex with what he had done. The more she spelt it out to him – his military failure, his diplomatic idiocy in seeing Tyrone without accompaniment, his concession of the truce, his desertion of his post – the more stammeringly inadequate were Essex's responses. Then the blow fell. She dismissed him from all his offices and placed him under the surveillance of Lord Keeper Egerton at York House. She would never set eyes upon him again.

28

Essex and the End

For a year – the year of 1600 to 1601 – both Elizabeth and Essex remained in an inanition, stunned by what had happened; hoping, perhaps, that it had not happened. Essex sank into illness and religious melancholy under house-arrest. Elizabeth sent him broth and a consortium of doctors. Apart from political disgrace, he faced financial ruin. He was £16,000 in debt, and by depriving him of office she removed from him – as privy councillor, Master of the Ordinance, Master of the Queen's Horse and Earl Marshal of England – innumerable opportunities to take bribes in exchange for favours and jobs. One great source of income remained to him. On Michaelmas Day (29 September) 1590, in their happy golden days, she had bestowed upon him the lucrative Farm of Sweet Wines, the sinecure – worth well over £3,000 per annum – that had been enjoyed by his stepfather Leicester. Should she renew it? Or, tempting prospect to that parsimonious old lady, keep it herself? It was obvious which course would be recommended by Mr Secretary Robert Cecil. Friends tried to put in good words for Essex. 'This day se' night,' he wrote desperately in September 1600:

> the lease which I hold by your Majesty's beneficence expireth, and that farm [of sweet wines] is both my chiefest maintenance and mine only means of compounding with the merchants to whom I am endebted . . . If my creditors will take for payment as many ounces of my blood, or the taking away of this farm would only for want finish me of this body, your Majesty should never hear of this suit. For in myself I can find no boldness to importune, and from myself I can draw no argument to solicit.[1]

It was a useless letter. Essex was finished. Such was his personal magnetism, however, and such was the personal detestation in which Robert Cecil was held, that a significant number of Essex's friends joined with him in a rebellion, even though it was plainly a madcap scheme – and they were a formidable collection of people.

This was a sign not only of Essex's extraordinary charisma, but also of how desperate things had become at court, and at the heart of the Elizabethan machine. In the glory days there had been terrible factions at court, but William Cecil, Robert Dudley, Francis Walsingham, Nicholas

Bacon and the rest had, *in extremis*, been prepared to sink their differences for a common purpose. Not only were they devoted to a young queen: their political lives depended upon her survival. Now things were very different. It was inevitable that the old Queen would die – perhaps soon. The Essex faction saw no possibility of being reconciled with the Cecil faction, short of actually taking up arms.

Or perhaps they needed to focus their feelings of dissatisfaction upon Robert Cecil, rather than admit to themselves that the real reason for discontent was the Queen – increasingly indecisive, irascible, parsimonious, capricious. One of Essex's friends, who did not desert him in his troubles, was the Earl of Southampton. Like Essex, he had been a ward of Burghley and brought up at Cecil House, that strange aristocratic boarding school in the Strand. Southampton was now one of those, with Lord Mountjoy, who began to hatch the crazy plan of an armed coup *d'état*. Already, Essex and Mountjoy had been in secret correspondence with King James VI of Scotland, assuring him of their loyalty and hoping to assure him that, in the event of his succeeding, it was to them, and not to Cecil, that he should look for support. Compared with Sidney, Marlowe and Spenser, William Shakespeare, of all the great Elizabethan writers, cultivated a superb detachment from political involvement. But with his patron Southampton so deeply involved with Essex, total disengagement was not entirely possible.

In 1599 one Dr John Hayward had written a book, which he dedicated to Essex, on the subject of Henry IV. The dedication compared Essex with Bolingbroke, the man who successfully overthrew Richard II and made himself King. When the time of the rebellion approached, Essex's Chief Steward, a fiery Welshman called Sir Gelli Meyrick, was also happy to remember how the Welsh had rallied to Bolingbroke's cause. Among notable supporters of the Essex rebellion were John and Owen Salusbury, who had accompanied Essex on the Cadiz expedition. Sir John Salusbury's coat of arms bears the motto 'posse et nolle nobile'. 'To be able to do harm, but to abstain from doing so, is noble' would be one rendering; another 'They that have power to hurt and will do none' – the first line of Shakespeare's Sonnet 94. It is all but inconceivable that this is a coincidence, though exactly what it suggests or proves (beyond some connection between Shakespeare and the Salusburys) is another matter. Salusbury was admitted to the Middle Temple in 1595. We know that Shakespeare had many associations with that Inn, where *Twelfth Night* was first performed in 1602. There is abundant evidence in his plays of Shakespeare's affectionate, sometimes humorous feeling for the Welsh. He would certainly have appreciated it, had he been a witness, when Sir John Salusbury celebrated his readmission to the Inn, after his elder brother Thomas's involvement in the Babington Conspiracy, and a royal pardon, with 'seven bards, four harpists and two crowthers to Lleweni to celebrate his newly recovered status.'[2]

The Salusburys of Lleweni were cousins of Queen Elizabeth, yet here was *their* cousin Owen involving himself with the Essex rebellion. Any analogy between themselves and the fiery Owain Glyndŵr uniting with Bolingbroke to overthrow Richard II would not have been lost on anyone at Lleweni. Before the rising, Lord Mounteagle, Sir Charles Percy, Sir Jocelyn Percy and others of Percy's friends took a barge over the river to Bankside to the Globe Theatre. They offered a supplement of forty shillings if the Lord Chamberlain's company would put on a production of Shakespeare's *Richard II*. It was an old play, so the actors could self-protectively claim that the public had no particular interest in it any more; they had forgotten the lines, it would not be popular. But in the end they relented. Was Shakespeare among them? On the afternoon of Saturday, 7 February 1601 an enthusiastic audience of Essex supporters watched the play: it was the eve of the rebellion. To William Lambarde, one of her more learned courtiers, when 'caterpillars of the kingdom' were making their obeisance to her, Elizabeth had once remarked, 'I am Richard II. Know ye that?'[3]

One of the functions of court rituals, of Coronation Day tilts, of bowing before the monarch and walking backwards – as of all the quasi-ritualised Platonic adoration of the monarch in Spenser's poetry, in the formalised portraiture of the Queen and in the clothes with which she was decked out – was to disguise from monarch and people alike the uncomfortable truths that *Richard II* so mercilessly exposes. At the beginning of the play it is Richard who is the dressed doll at the centre of the power-game; by the third act, he is ironically enquiring, 'What says King Bolingbroke? Will his Majesty/Give Richard leave to live till Richard die?'[4] Elizabeth had known as a young girl that the division between absolute power and absolute ruin was no wider than the blade of an axe. Richard, in Shakespeare's masterpiece, asks the existential question:

> I live with bread, like you, feel want,
> Taste grief, need friends – subjected thus,
> How can you say to me, I am a king?[5]

More than 400 years after it happened, the Essex rebellion still almost beggars belief – both that they thought they could get away with it and that so many powerful men, with so much to lose, were prepared to take part. The Earls of Southampton, Rutland, Sussex and Bedford, as well as Lords Mounteagle, Cromwell and Sandys, were all part of it. And the roll-call shows that Essex was (potentially) uniting malcontents from across the whole politico-religious spectrum. On the one hand, the Cromwells represented extreme Puritan opinion (an opinion with which Essex himself personally sympathised); on the other hand – fatally to Essex himself – there were Catholics here, such as Southampton, who would as lief place Arbella Stuart on the throne of England as the Presbyterian Scottish king. Lord Mounteagle, who half-heartedly supported Essex, would also be in the secret of the Gunpowder Plot of 1605, and it was he who betrayed the conspirators on that occasion. Some of them, such as Francis Tresham and Robert Catesby, joined Essex evidently in the hope that they could produce, if not an actually Catholic monarch, a regime more favourable to their recusant standpoint.

So, all sorts of grievances came together at the time of the Essex rebellion, and not least the grievances of the London mob, who felt impoverished by years of bad crops and rising food prices. Eighteen months after the whole fiasco was over, and Essex was dead, a German visitor to the English capital found Londoners still singing the ballad 'Essex's Last Good-Night' and pointing out the spot in the Tower where 'the brave hero' perished.

The actual rebellion lasted only for twelve hours. If, on 8 February 1601, Essex and his friends had marched directly on Whitehall, they might have stood a chance of apprehending the Queen and taking the Great Seal. Instead, they marched eastwards up the Strand. 'To the Court! To the Court!' shouted the mob: they had the right idea. But Essex had been promised support by the Lord Mayor of London. He hoped to find 1,000 armed men waiting for him in Fenchurch Street, but this was fantasy. By the time they turned back towards Westminster, his followers were in disarray.

There was fighting in the streets and not a few casualties. Cavalry, under the command of the Earls of Cumberland and Lincoln, with Lord Burghley (Robert Cecil's dim-witted elder brother), Lord Thomas Howard and Lord Compton, blocked the Strand. Between Essex House and the river, Sir Robert Sidney, Sir Fulke Greville, Sir John Stanhope and Lord Cobham had entrenched in the Embankment Gardens. A few, including one of Southampton's footmen, were shot. Southampton came out on to his roof to declare that they meant no harm to the Queen: they had merely taken up arms to deliver her from the atheists and – that word from *Richard II* – 'caterpillars' who clustered around the throne: that is, Cecil and the Privy Council. Within hours, however, the thing had collapsed, the principal insurgents were behind bars and London was placed under martial law: 500 soldiers were stationed at Charing Cross, 400 men guarded the City, another 300 on the Surrey side of the river in

Southwark. Within a week twenty-five peers of the realm had been summoned to try Essex and Southampton.

In addition to the twenty-five peers, nine judges had been appointed for what was, in effect, a show trial. Essex demanded the right to challenge three of the judges on the grounds of their known personal enmity to himself, but this demand was refused. When Lord Grey de Wilton, with whom he had quarrelled publicly in Ireland, was called as a witness, Essex let out a loud, contemptuous laugh.

Cynical old Coke, one of the judges, remarked on the extraordinary verbal similarity in the testimony, extracted in the Tower of London, from Essex's companions Sir Charles Danvers, Sir Christopher Blount, the Earls of Bedford and Rutland, Lord Sandys and Lord Mountjoy. Of friends who turned in evidence against Essex, the most shockingly disloyal was Francis Bacon (1561–1626), destined in the next reign to become the Viscount St Albans and Lord Chancellor of England.

The two Bacon brothers, Francis and Anthony, were the sons of the former Lord Keeper. Essex had striven to get Francis Bacon the office of Attorney General, which had gone to Coke. Cecil wondered that Essex should wish to promote 'so raw a youth to so great a place'. Essex had fired back, with an insult that was not forgotten by Cecil, 'I have made no search for precedents of young men who have filled the office of Attorney General, but I could name to you, Sir Robert, a man younger than Francis [that is, Cecil himself], less learned and equally inexperienced, who is suing and striving with all his might for an office of far greater weight' – that is, the Secretaryship, which Cecil soon got.

It ill became Bacon to testify against his friend and protector, but Bacon had a career to think of. He was one of the most remarkable intellects of his age. In 1597 he had published a tiny octavo volume entitled (copying Montaigne, whose *Essais* were published in Bordeaux in 1580) *Essays*: the first time the word was used in English in that sense. Bacon the philosopher was the first Englishman to express what we mean by a modern scientific outlook – to distinguish between inductive and intuitive processes of reading information, to distinguish really between 'Art' and 'Science', to use our terminology. For this reason, William Blake, in his copy of Bacon's Essays, wrote the words 'Good Advice for Satan's Kingdom'.

As Francis spoke for the prosecution in Westminster Hall, Essex often interrupted his protégé with reproaches. To those who wished to believe some of the wilder assertions made against Essex (for example, that he had aspired to make himself the King of England), it was all the more damaging that his friend Bacon should have been prepared so fully to denounce him.

Essex must have known that he had no chance of persuading the peers and judges to acquit him. He asserted, as he had done before, that he had heard Cecil dispute the succession and express the wish for the Spanish Infanta to become Queen when Elizabeth died. This Cecil hotly repudiated. Cecil was unlike his father – who, in these circumstances, would have allowed Essex to condemn himself out of his own mouth and would not have descended to verbal exchanges with the prisoner. But Robert Cecil, who was physically deformed and acutely conscious that the comparatively new family of Cecil could not match the high lineage of the Devereux, could not resist a response to the years of swagger and bullying that he had endured at Essex's hands in the heyday of the Queen's crush on the young aristocrat:

> For wit I give you the pre-eminence – you have it abundantly. For nobility also I give you place – I am not noble, yet a gentleman; I am no swordsman – there also you have the odds: but I have innocence, conscience, truth and honesty to defend me against the scandal and sting of slanderous tongues, and in this court I stand as an upright man, and your lordship as a delinquent.[6]

Essex and Southampton were returned in procession to the Tower of London, with the axe's blade pointed towards them. At the age of thirty-four, on 25 February 1601, Essex was beheaded in the courtyard. He had asked the Queen for the privilege of a private death, and she had spared him the crowds on Tower Green. His last days were spent in fervent prayer with his chaplain, Mr Ashton. Southampton remained in the Tower, with the black-and-white cat made famous by the portrait of him there. When James I came to the throne, Southampton was released at once, and he went on to have a life full of honours – being made Knight of the Garter almost instantaneously, as well as Lord Lieutenant of Hampshire. His Catholicism weakened with age, and he became a Protestant. Much of his public life was devoted to the defence of the Virginia Company – though he could not stop its Charter being withdrawn in 1624. Much of his time, as in the years before and during his imprisonment, was devoted to study and to literature, and he presented a fine collection of books to the library at St John's College, Cambridge.

Essex's memory transmuted into that of folk-hero.

> Sweet England's pride is gone!
> *welladay! welladay!*

In 'Essex's Last Good-Night' as we have seen, they were still singing of the trial when a foreign visitor heard them in 1603:

All you that cry O hone! O hone!
come now and sing O Lord! With me.
For why? Our Jewel is from us gone,
the valiant Knight of Chivalry.

Little Cecil trips up and down,
He rules both Court and Crown,
With his brother Burghley Clown,
In his great fox-furred gown;
With the long proclamation
He swore he saved the Town
Is it not likely.[7]

So Essex lived on in drinking song and legend, everlastingly preserved in his youth, the victim of the old lady that no one could quite admit was the real cause of the rebellion. For it was not the machinations, real or imagined, of the Cecil faction that caused the atmosphere of frustration in 1600–1 so much as the sense that the country's head of state was too old, too stubborn, too stingy, too indecisive to be a great national leader any more.

Essex's circle had an interesting afterlife in the seventeenth century. Frances, the widow both of Philip Sidney and of Essex, married the Earl of Clanricard in 1603 and became a Roman Catholic. Penelope, Essex's sister and Sidney's 'Stella', divorced Lord Rich and she too became a Roman Catholic. She died in 1607. The old 'she-Wolf' – the beautiful Lettice – who had so excited Queen Elizabeth's jealousy when she married the Earl of Leicester lost her third husband, Sir Christopher Blount, who was executed for his part in the Essex rebellion. Thus she lost both son and husband, but it appeared not to diminish her energies. She lived to the age of ninety-four in 1634. What a very different world it would have been, had Elizabeth been spared for a comparable span!

When her godson Sir John Harington tried to cheer her up by reading to her some of his epigrams, the Queen replied, 'When Thou dost feel creeping Time at thy gate, these fooleries will please thee less.'

Yet despite the ravages of time, and the sadness of her life after the death of Essex, Elizabeth retained much of her old physical vigour. She enjoyed dancing almost to the end. Right up to her sixty-ninth birthday she could still ride ten miles in a day and go hunting afterwards. Her mental faculties were undiminished and she retained her linguistic skills.

In February 1603 the Doge and Senate of Venice sent Giovanni Scaramelli as ambassador to the English court, the first official Venetian Ambassador since her accession.

She received him at Richmond. The clothes-conscious Italian noted that she no longer dressed fashionably, but the overall effect of her outfit and appearance was overwhelming:

> Her skirts were much fuller and began lower down than is the fashion in France. Her hair was of a light colour not made by nature, and she wore great pearls like pears round the forehead. She had a vast quantity of gems and pearls upon her person; even under her stomacher she was covered with golden-jewelled girdles and single gems, carbuncles, balas-rubies and diamonds. Round her wrists in place of bracelets she wore double rows of pearls of more than medium size.[8]

On her head was an imperial crown. Here was Astraea indeed, a walking emblem.

Scaramelli was awestruck and knelt to kiss the hem of her garment. She offered her right hand to kiss and spoke to him in Italian: 'Welcome to England, Mr Secretary, it was high time that the Republic sent to visit a Queen, who has always honoured it on every possible occasion.' The ambassador then made a formal complaint to the Queen about the behaviour of English corsairs in the Adriatic, looting and attacking Venetian and Spanish vessels. Elizabeth haughtily countered with:

> I cannot help feeling that the Republic of Venice during the forty-four years of my reign has never made herself heard by me except to ask for something, nor, for the rest, prosperous or adverse as my affairs have been, never has she given a sign of holding me or my Kingdom in that esteem which other princes and other potentates have not refused. Nor am I aware that my sex has brought me this demerit, for my sex [she said confidently] cannot diminish my prestige, nor offend them who treat me as other Princes are treated to whom the Signory of Venice sends its ambassadors.[9]

Then she added, 'I will do all in my power to give satisfaction to the serene Republic.'

That was all the Venetians heard on the subject of English pirates. Playfully, she concluded, 'I do not know if I have spoken Italian well; I think so, for I learned it as a child and believe I have not forgotten it.'

The Venetian was impressed, as well he might be.

About many of her utterances in her latter years there was a hint of valediction, as if she knew that they might be her last great speech on the stage. When she had addressed Parliament the previous November she had said:

> I have ever used to set the Last Judgement Day before mine eyes and so to rule as I shall be judged to answer before an higher judge, and now if my kingly bounties have been abused and my grants turned to the hurt of my people contrary to my will and meaning, and if any in authority under me have neglected or perverted what I have committed to them, I hope God will not lay their culps and offences in my charge. I know the title of a King is a glorious title, but assure yourself that the shining glory of princely authority hath not so dazzled the eyes of our understanding, but that we well know and remember that we also are to yield an account of our actions before the great judge. To be a king and to wear a crown is a thing more glorious to them that see it than it is pleasant to them that bear it. For myself I was never so much enticed with the glorious name of a King or royal authority of a Queen as delighted that God hath made me his instrument to maintain his truth and glory and to defend this kingdom as I said from peril, dishonour, tyranny and oppression. There will never Queen sit in my seat with more zeal to my country, care to my subjects and that will sooner with willingness venture her life for your good and safety than myself. For it is my desire to reign no longer than my life and reign shall be for your good. And though you have had, and may have, many princes more mighty and more wise sitting in this seat, yet you never had nor shall have any that will be more careful and loving.[10]

From an English perspective, the news from Ireland had improved. Lord Mountjoy won a resounding victory over the Earl of Tyrone and his thousands of Spanish mercenaries, and brought an end to any hope of an independent Ireland. At least Elizabeth could die with that perennial problem, the Irish situation, in a quiescent phase.

But she could not die happy. She was too introspective, too solitary, too intelligent a being for that. At the end of February 1603, Kate Carey, one of her favourite Boleyn cousins – married to Admiral Charles Howard, Earl of Nottingham, died. It was a bereavement that prostrated her. The loss of a much-loved kinswoman exacerbated the solitude of the motherless, childless woman. The first Boleyn bereavement she had suffered had been that of her mother. She was too young to remember Anne Boleyn with her conscious mind, but events such as this register in a person's psyche. When Kate's younger boy Robert Carey was admitted to see the

Queen some days after Kate's death, he kissed her hand and she held on to it; wrung it. He said that he was glad to find her better and she replied, 'No, Robin, I am not well.' She let out a groan such as had not been heard since her bout of hysteria following the death of the Scottish queen.

She developed a throat infection, and was perpetually thirsty. She would eat nothing. She was sleepless, and restless. Robert Cecil told her that she must go to bed. 'Little man, little man,' she replied, '*must* is not to be used to princes. If your father had lived, ye durst not have said so much.'

On 21 March, Carey at length persuaded her to take to her bed. One gruesome and emblematic detail was that her finger had swollen, so that the Coronation Ring had eaten into her flesh. The ring had to be sawn off. Only by such means could she be separated from her hold on power. The woman and the office had become so deeply enfleshed and entwined. And still, with only days of life to run, she gave no certain indication about her choice of successor. Cecil came into the bedchamber, where she was by now silent, and tried to get her to make a formal assent to the succession of James VI of Scotland. She held up both her hands and made her fingers into the shape of a crown and held them to the sides of her head.

Presently she asked for John Whitgift, the Archbishop of Canterbury. The great royal bedchamber was now filled with people, who kept a discreet distance. At the bedside were only the archbishop on his knees and Robert Carey. Whitgift prayed for about half an hour and then made to rise, but one of the ladies-in-waiting, Philadelphia Carey, gestured to him that he should continue. So the prayers went on. Again, his knees and his voice weary, the archbishop attempted to bring his part of the proceedings to an end, but this time an arm-gesture from the silent royal form on the bed prevented him from rising, and he continued to utter prayers until the Queen appeared to sink into unconsciousness. As deep night fell, all but the ladies-in-waiting left the bedroom. Midnight chimed. It was now 24 March, the eve of Lady Day. At quarter to three the watchers approached the bed and stared at the figure who lay there. She was lying with her head on her right arm. Her Welsh chaplain, Dr Parry, said that she had slipped away 'mildly, like a lamb, easily, like a ripe apple from the tree'. But these gentle, pastoral images were not really appropriate. A twentieth-century biographer, Elizabeth Jenkins, captured the moment more aptly when she wrote that 'her warfare was accomplished'.

29

Hamlet: One Through Two

If there was one linguistic quirk that the Church of England had given the world, it was hendiadys. The Greek word means 'one through two'. Like a stammer or a second thought, hendiadys suggests that the first word needs amplification or qualification. 'Law and order' is a typical example of the genre. Queen Elizabeth's godfather, Thomas Cranmer, died at the stake in Oxford when he refused to abjure his Protestant heresy. But before he allowed himself to be thrust bodily into the flames, he put out his own right hand to be burned. For, with this right hand, he had, in fact, abjured his 'heresy' and proclaimed his belief in Catholicism. He was not only Elizabeth's godfather; he was, spiritually speaking, the godfather of the Church of England, the Church whose *raison d'être* was holding together two points of view that many Christians considered irreconcilable: the Church of Reform, and of Catholicism – the Church of hendiadys. By the end of Elizabeth's reign that Church had provided the official national religion for forty years. It had been of very limited success. There were still plenty of Catholic recusants, particularly in the North, who would not accept the new rites as acceptable to their tastes; just as there were ever-growing numbers of Puritans who believed that Cranmer's liturgy was the old popish Mass-book done into euphonious English – 'the Pope's dregs', as the scornful Cambridge Puritans called it.[1]

But Cranmer's words had entered the language. For forty years now, English men and women had attended Morning and Evening Prayer, and the Communion, and baptisms, and weddings, with the Prayer Book as the libretto of their life-experiences. And Cranmer's hendiadys had become music inside their heads: 'Almighty and most merciful father; We have erred and strayed from thy ways like lost sheep. We have followed too much the devices and desires of our own hearts . . . Almighty God . . . hath given power, and commandment, to his Ministers, to declare and pronounce . . .' 'Behold our most gracious sovereign lady Queen Elizabeth . . . grant her in health and wealth long to live; strengthen her that she may vanquish and overcome all her enemies; and finally after this life she may attain everlasting joy and felicity.'

Hamlet, too, is a play that would be half the length were it not for Shakespeare's addiction to Cranmerian hendiadys. 'It harrows me with fear and wonder' . . . 'Without the sensible and true avouch / Of mine own eyes' . . . 'this same strict and most observant watch' . . . 'of unimproved mettle, hot and full'. . . 'Of this post-haste and rummage in the land' . . . 'In the most high and palmy state of Rome . . .' 'Did squeak and gibber in the Roman streets' . . 'If thou hast any sound or use of voice', and so on, and so on.

Cranmer's distinctive stylistic tic reflected the core modernity of the Reformation. We might think that existential angst began with the nineteenth century, perhaps with Kierkegaard's idea of the self divided against itself. But Kierkegaard was a Lutheran, albeit a very eccentric one, and Luther – the mastermind of the Reformation – was *simul justus et peccator*, as he described himself: both justified and a sinner. He was both the genius who invented the modern Protestant mind and the inevitable mouthpiece of history. Had he not existed, Time would have invented other Luthers, who threw off the collective wisdom of the Church in order to become the soliloquist alone with God – if there was a God. And even Luther was perpetually visited by the temptation to turn away from God or to deny him, or to mistake His presence for that of the Devil. Wittenberg was the German town where it all began, where Luther taught in the university. King Claudius of Denmark was a monarch who, in history, was supposedly living in the Dark Ages. Yet in Shakespeare's version of the events he enjoins his nephew:

For your intent
In going back to school in Wittenberg
It is most retrograde to our desire . . .

If the Book of Common Prayer was the libretto for English national self-consciousness, not only in Elizabeth's reign but for centuries afterwards, *Hamlet* is its psychodrama, its portmanteau work of art that contains everything. Indeed, *Hamlet* is without parallel in any other literature in the world, in many ways of greater significance in the English language and culture than the Bible. Shakespeare's first plays for the London theatres had been reconstructions of English national history, portrayals of the dynastic and internecine struggles, through the fifteenth century, that led to the power-seizure of the Tudors. Midway through the journey of this our life, when Shakespeare was thirty-five, he wrote a different sort of play: a rehash of an old revenge theme, which had been doing the highly successful theatrical rounds for at least a decade. But into this reworking of a popular piece of theatrical hackwork he poured everything – the national identity-crisis, as London awaited the death of one monarch and the arrival of another; the mood of public disillusion as Elizabeth's reign ended; the doubts and anxieties that thoughtful men and women felt about politics, religion and philosophy. But if politics were in crisis, the court riven with faction, the Church Settlement unsettled, the public raucous and drunken and often disease-ridden and hungry, the culture was still fructiferous.

Note the very fact that *Hamlet* contains more coinages than any other Shakespeare play, or than any other work of English literature. Shakespeare's work is the strongest example of what happens when a culture is still growing and alive and, for all its misgivings about itself, in a position of strength. The old Greek word *poet* was rendered by Middle English in its literal sense – 'Maker'. When the culture has life in it, the Makers are quite literally helping to fashion it. Thirty per cent of the words current in the Italian language were coined by Dante. Shakespeare did not perhaps actually invent the English language in the way that Italian was invented by Dante. Nor did he – as did Luther, using his own version or dialect of German to translate and interpret the Bible – determine the variety of his native language that would be spoken by men and women in after-generations. But Shakespeare, more than any other Elizabethan, stretched and expanded the English language and therefore (since the playhouses were so hugely popular and drama was in no sense an esoteric art-form) he gave to all speakers of English a larger vocabulary and hence a larger capacity to describe experience.

Hamlet was written some time (probably) before the death of Essex. The Stationers' Register records '*A Book Called the Revenge of Hamlett*' on 26 July 1602, and the date on the First Quarto version of the printed play is 1603. Although the First Quarto is the famously bad version, presumably based on a poor actor's memory – 'To be or not to be – ay, there's the point, / To die to sleep – is that all?' – it clearly is our play, and represents therefore the *terminus a quo* for Shakespeare's *Hamlet*, however much he revised or cut or retouched it for performance. We know that there was an earlier Hamlet play, not by Shakespeare, which was going the theatrical rounds in the 1590s, since Thomas Lodge in *Wit's Misery* (1596) alludes to the pale-vizarded ghost 'which cried so miserably at the Theatre, like an oyster-wife, *Hamlet, revenge*!' (this is not a phrase that occurs in Shakespeare's play).

And one of the things that makes Shakespeare's *Hamlet* so modern, so almost modern*ist,* in texture is that it seems so closely and so relaxedly to admit its own staginess. The Players not only perform a play within the play. They are recognisably part of the London theatre world of 1600–1. Hamlet asks Rosencrantz of his friends the actors (I quote from the First Folio text of 1623), 'Do they hold the same estimation they did when I was in the city?' Now, which city is that? We are meant to be in a Danish castle. Yet it is obvious that Rosencrantz (Rossencraft in the First Quarto) is telling Hamlet about the theatrical spats in London between the Children of the Chapel, who were used as actors by Ben Jonson at the Blackfriars Theatre towards the end of 1600, and the adult actors of the Lord Chamberlain's Men.

'There is, sir, an eyrie of children, little eyases that cry out on the top of question and are most tyrannically clapp'd for it. These are now the fashion, and so berattle the common stages (so they call them) that many wearing rapiers are afraid of goose-quills and dare scarce come hither.'[2]

Shakespeare is actually making the London theatre audiences part of the drama that they are themselves watching. A supposedly medieval Danish prince in an embattled royal court in the Dark Ages is, with casual and deliberate anachronism, pulsating with topical Elizabethan allusions. In the Second Quarto, of 1604–5, we find that the tragedians have lately been censored or inhibited – 'I think their inhibition comes by the means of the late innovation': enough time has elapsed since the play's first performance to put into print this possible allusion to the Essex rebellion. Even if it is not an allusion to the Essex rising, it is clearly a topical allusion of some kind. From the beginning, then, *Hamlet* was not a drama staged in some reconstructed past: it is not a 'history' play; it is a play by and about Elizabethans. The First Quarto title-pages tells us that The Tragicall Historie 'hath beene diuerse times acted by his Highnesse Seruants in the Cittie of London: as also in the two Vniuersities of Cambridge and Oxford and elsewhere'. There is no reason to doubt this claim that *Hamlet* was, from the beginning, an extremely popular play. Richard Burbage is traditionally supposed to have made the role his own at the Globe, and the theatre tradition is that Shakespeare himself played father Hamlet's Ghost. The first record we possess of a performance of *Hamlet* was not, as it happens, in a theatre or a university, but on board ship. In the journal of Captain William Keeling, captain of the *Red Dragon*, anchored off the coast of Sierra Leone in 1607, we read, on 5 September, 'We gave the Tragedy of Hamlet' and, on 31 September, 'I invited Captain Hawkins to a ffishe dinner and had Hamlet acted abord whiche I permit to keepe my peple from idleness and unlawful games or sleepe.'[3] There are many allusions to *Hamlet* in the popular playwrights of Jacobean London – Middleton, Marston and Dekker – and it is impossible to escape the conclusion that this was a play that was quickly established as part of the inner life of English-speakers and play-goers.

There is a peculiar aptness, then, about it being a play that entered anglophone consciousness at about the time that the Elizabethan Age was coming to an end. Of all great works of art of the Elizabethan period, *Hamlet* speaks to us most eloquently about the Elizabethans' inner lives and concerns – political, philosophical, religious, social. There is, on a simple and superficial level, the fact that it is a play about royal succession. We begin the play by regarding Fortinbras as a threat, and we end it by seeing Fortinbras as the saviour of a state that had gone rotten. The Elizabethan statesmen, led by William Cecil, began their era regarding the Scottish monarch as the ultimate threat, and ended it with Cecil's son Robert seeing the arrival of James VI as the best hope for stability.

Schoolteachers ask their pupils why Hamlet delays his revenge. The play begins like any good old-fashioned Revenge Tragedy, with a Ghost calling for his son to 'revenge his foul and most unnatural murder'.[4] But already audiences of the play know that they are in a world quite other than the blood and spooks of the old Hamlet play, or of Kyd's *Spanish Tragedy*. For one thing, they have been turned to gooseflesh by poetry. The guard on watch on the battlements at Elsinore have delivered themselves of some of the most beautiful lines of English verse ever written, about the fading of the ghost at cock-crow, about the legends surrounding Christmas, and about the coming of the dawn, which:

> in russet mantle clad
> Walks o'er the dew of yon high eastward hill.[5]

Already, we have been plunged into a profoundly interesting psychological situation in which the young Prince is deeply disturbed by the hasty remarriage of his mother to his uncle, and already the Prince has treated us to one of his great soliloquies:

> How weary, stale, flat and unprofitable
> Seem to me all the uses of this world![6]

Already, we are in a poem of profound psychological depth, and philosophical puzzlement. Already, we have plunged into the deepest metaphysical speculations about the pointlessness of existence itself on this planet. Already, as we have said, King Claudius and Hamlet are shown to belong not to Denmark in the Dark Ages, but to sixteenth-century Europe, with Luther's university of Wittenberg the Prince's alma mater. And already, as is shown by one of Shakespeare's most masterly examples of stagecraft and scenic compression, we have entered the claustrophobic, violent and feud-ridden Renaissance court of Elsinore. Elsie is a popular diminutive of the name of Elizabeth. Elsinore is immediately recognisable as an alternative Elsie-world, or Elizabethan Universe. It is nothing so crude as a *pièce-à-clef*, or a coded metaphor or a piece of political satire, with Polonius standing for Burghley, for example – even though Polonius's mixture of deviousness and wordiness and dry-stick pomposity were recognised as an allusion to Burghley. *Hamlet* is not a work of ephemeral satire. Elsinore, rather, is the inner workings of Elsie-Elizabeth's London and England. It is a portrait of the Elizabethans in all their responses to life.

Hence, we should not expect this particular Prince to exact revenge in the manner of the conventional blood-and-guts stage hero of a revenge drama. For forty-four years England had been ruled over by a Hamlet-like queen, thinking too precisely upon the event. The two Revenge moments of the reign – the death of Mary, Queen of Scots and the death of the Earl of Essex – were both psychological crises for her. This was because Elizabeth, like Hamlet, could see the calamitous effects of too great a precision and too great a decisiveness in political life.

Ever since Elizabeth stepped onto the stage in November 1558, her advisers and courtiers had been urging her to make decisions: to be Catholic or to be Protestant; to marry; to fight a decisive and expensive war in Ireland or in the Low Countries. In almost all cases Elizabeth had dithered, Hamlet-like; and dithering had been, if not the right policy, then at least not the wrong policy. This god-daughter of Cranmer, the liturgical master of hendiadys, had seen the wisdom of double-think.

Hamlet depicts a society that is 'out of joint', a 'Denmark' that is 'rotten', a political system that is completely corrupt and based upon murder and intrigue. There is, therefore, far more in it of subversively profound political disillusion than in any other 'revenge tragedy'. The play contains the hope for a new beginning with a new reign, which must have been a collective desire in 1603. The ambiguities and 'unfinished' quality of *Hamlet* are what make it so resonantly intelligent.

Many of those who have criticised *Hamlet* as fuzzy, incoherent, have failed to attend to the kind of work of art it is. Interestingly, two of the play's most intelligent readers in the twentieth-century English world, C.S. Lewis and T.S. Eliot, both made this misjudgement. Lewis, who contrasted the Prince and the Poem, and Eliot, who dismissed the play as an artistic failure, were looking for a work of art that was finished and coherent. Shakespeare, on the other hand, presented his contemporaries, and us, with a work of art that is disturbingly incoherent, which has been on all available journeys. *Hamlet* is full of loose ends. It positively depends on its inconsistencies. As for its length, as it appears in the Second Quarto or the First Folio, it would have taken well over four hours to perform, scarcely a possibility in the pre-electrical age. So, it even outsoars its own borders, ceasing to be a play and becoming a book, a sort of novel, in which the experiences of Shakespeare's own life – the drowning of Ophelia-like Katherine Hamlett in Warwickshire, the death of his own son Hamnet – blend into the preoccupations of the London theatre audiences in the last years of Elizabeth's reign and together they enter into Elsie-nor. It is the first modern novel, the first work of psycho-analysis, the first great Romantic poem of the Inner Life – while continuing to be, as generations of theatre-goers ever since can testify, an electrifying drama that stretches and tests the capacities of the actor who plays the role. Scholars have noted affinities with Montaigne's *Essays*, which Shakespeare probably knew in the translation of John Florio. Like Montaigne, it provides the companionable mystery, not of the author's biography, but in exploring what it was like inside the author's head. While Europe fought wars about theology, many individual men and women must themselves have been inwardly divided about the change that had come upon the European consciousness with the Reformation. The careful Protestant response to a ghost – 'Stay, illusion!' – is what many of them were saying to the old religious certainties. As a Protestant, Horatio technically believed that ghosts were either non-existent or illusory tricks played on the eyes by the Devil. Yet instinct makes him old-fashioned enough to believe in the Catholic soul discontented with Purgatory and 'doomed for a certain term to walk the night'. But – a war between people who believed that the Eucharistic elements actually changed into flesh and blood and those who believed that God had predestined them to everlasting salvation? 'Stay, illusion!' You feel the gentle scepticism in Shakespeare and in Montaigne. Neither man was an unbeliever in the post-Victorian way. Montaigne was a practising Catholic, and Shakespeare allows his characters purely Christian sentiments:

> Why all the souls that were, were forfeit once,
> And He that might the vantage best have took
> Found out a remedy.[7]

But neither man could have felt at home in the insanity of contemporary religious controversy. *Hamlet* was full of the Elizabethan division – the division in individual minds between the old world and the new, between the old geocentric universe and the new worlds opened up by Copernicus; between Catholic and Protestant; between worship of Gloriana and discontent with the way in which politics had led England into wasteful wars.

There could have been no more appropriate play for the London audiences to have seen performed in Elizabeth's last days, unless it had been *Julius Caesar*, written a little earlier, perhaps in 1599, with its devastating reminder of the human frailty of monarchs:

He had a fever when he was in Spain.
And when the fit was on him, I did mark
How he did shake; 'tis true, this god did shake.
His coward lips did from their colour fly,
And that same eye, whose bend doth awe the world,
Did lose his lustre; I did hear him groan;
Ay, and that tongue of his that bade the Romans
Mark him, and write his speeches in their books,
'Alas!' it cried, 'Give me some drink, Titinius',
As a sick girl.[8]

Elizabeth Tudor had been neither so vain nor so foolish as to be blind to the brutal truth contained in Cassius's republican speech. She knew her own bodily frailty. She had specified one last message to her nation and people, the sepulchral equivalent of hendiadys.

Her dead body was brought by Thames boat from Richmond. The coffin was sealed and covered, but, as was the custom with funerals of the great, there was a wax effigy of the Queen. William Camden, who walked in the procession as Clarenceux King of Arms tells us:

> The City of Westminster was surcharged with multitudes of all sorts of people, in their streets, houses, windows, leads and gutters, that came to see the obsequy; and when they beheld her statue or picture, lying upon the coffin, set forth in royal robes, having a crown upon the head thereof, and a ball and sceptre in either hand, there was such a general sighing and groaning, and weeping, as the like has not been seen or known in the memory of man; neither doth any history mention any people, time or state, to make like lamentation for the death of their sovereign.[9]

The funeral sermon was preached by the great Lancelot Andrewes, Dean of Westminster. Sir Walter Raleigh was present as captain of the guard. It was his last public act. Elizabeth was carried to the north aisle of Henry VII's chapel, and it was here that she made her last statement to the world. She was buried at her request in the unmarked grave of her half-sister, Mary I. Later, the great tomb that we see today in the Abbey was erected over the sisters. Was it Andrewes himself who devised the perfect epitaph – *Regno consortes et urna, hic obdormimus Elizabetha et Maria sorores, in spe resurrectionis*: we sisters, sharers in reigning, in a burial place and in the hope of the resurrection are here fallen asleep? One of the sisters had never tried to live with Doubt. Mary Tudor was as far as possible from the intellectual world of Montaigne and *Hamlet*.

But the other sister, in her burial – which was both a humble nod to her Roman Catholic subjects and a pious aspiration for the flourishing of truth, unity and concord – was different. Elizabeth in her burial held out the hope that the English people might learn the lessons she imparted. To judge from the first fifty-seven years after her death, it would seem as if they were slow to learn the lesson – with the clumsy Stuart experiment in absolute monarchy on a continental pattern, with the Civil Wars, with the triumphs of Puritan absolutism and the abolition of Parliament. But history is a long game. Perhaps some of the factors that made Britain emerge, in the post-1660 era, as a country of such enormous intellectual, commercial, scientific and political resource derived in part from the legacy of her most distinguished monarch, and the evolved experience of the Elizabethan Age.

Notes

Preface

1 Lewis, p. 378.
2 Ciarán Brady 'The Road to the View. On the Decline of Reform Thought in Tudor Ireland,' in Coughlan (ed.), p. 40.

1 The Difficulty

1 The phrase is the title of an invaluable study by Nicholas Canny (2001) of a history of Ireland from 1580 to 1650.
2 Ranelagh, p. 48.
3 Rowse, (1955), p. 120.
4 Ibid., p. 120.
5 Ranelagh, p. 50.
6 Ciaran Brady, 'The Road to the View', in Coughlan (ed.), p. 35.
7 Brady (1994) p.96.
8 Ciaran Brady, (1994), p. 273.
9 Ibid., p. 17.
10 Hiram Morgan, 'The Fall of Sir John Perrot', in Guy (ed.) p. 121.
11 Quoted Canny (2001), pp. 62–3.
12 See Brendan Bradshaw, 'Robe and Sword in the Conquest of Ireland' in Cross, Loades and Scarisbrick (eds).
13 For example, Coughlan (ed).
14 Ibid., pp. 18ff.
15 Moryson, 'The Manners and Customs of Ireland', quoted Canny, *Making Ireland British* p. 7.
16 Graves, 'Edmund Campion', *ODNB*, 9, p. 872.
17 Edmund Campion, *A Historie of Ireland*, quoted McGuire, p. 15.
18 Canny Ibid., p. 30.
19 William Butler, p. xi.
20 Rev Paul Walsh, *Gleanings from Irish Manuscripts*, 2nd edition, Dublin, Colm & Lochlainn 1933, p. 182.
21 Ibid., pp. 189–90.
22 Moryson, II. i. 77.
23 Shakespeare, *Macbeth*, III.iv. 1.152.
24 Canny (2001), p. 132.

2 The New World

1 J. A. Williamson (1949), p. 309.
2 '*Un Cassario Ingles, Uamado Juan Achines, que he andado en las Indias con quarto navios de armade, haziendo robos y dãnos harto grandes a mis subditos* . . . quoted Kelsey (2002), pp. 76 and 325.
3 Ibid., p. 75.
4 Ibid., p. 27.
5 Hugh Thomas p. 21.
6 Ibid., p. 38.
7 Ibid., p. 180.
8 Ibid., pp. 203 and 219.
9 Laughton, 'Sir John Hawkins or Hawkyns', *DNB*, IX, p. 212.
10 Hugh Thomas, p. 88.
11 Shakespeare, *The Tempest,* I. ii. 389 . . . 403.
12 Hakluyt (1903–5), pp. 520–1.
13 Kelsey (2002), p. 11.
14 Ibid., p. 13.
15 Ibid., p. 268.
16 Williamson (1949), p. 69.
17 Hugh Thomas, p. 156.
18 Kelsey (2002), p. 68.
19 BL Cotton MS, Otho E, viii, modernised by Williamson (1949), p. 133.
20 Hakluyt – the remark is omitted in the narrative in BL Cotton, MS Otho E, viii.
21 Testimony of Gregorio de Sias, quoted Kelsey (2002), p. 96.

3 Ceremonial – Twixt earnest and twixt game

1 Rowse (1950), pp. 301–2.
2 Goodman, p. 76.
3 William Camden, p. 18.
4 Black, p. 1.
5 Challis, *The Tudor Coinage*, Manchester, Manchester University Press, 1978, pp. 119–28.
6 Jenkins (1958), p. 66.
7 Maria Perry, p. 133.
8 Hunt, *The Drama of Coronation*. Unless otherwise stated, all that follows about Elizabeth's coronation and the ceremonies proceeding from it derive from Dr Hunt's highly recommended and original study.
9 Hunt, p. 79.
10 Spenser, *The Faerie Queene*, I.xii.8.

11 Hunt, p. 162.
12 Starkey, p. 274.
13 Spenser, *Mutabilitie*, Canto VII, 37.
14 Yates (1975/1985).
15 Arnold, p. 107.
16 Sidney (1912–26), p. 283.

4 Men in Power

1 Ridley, p. 115.
2 Dawson, 'John Knox', *ODNB*, 32, p. 17.
3 Ridley, p. 188.
4 Knox p. 66.
5 Ibid., p. 45.
6 For an exploration of these themes, see Jansen.
7 Lewis, p. 200.
8 Knox, p. 71.
9 Williams, pp. 1–4.
10 Rowse (1950), p. 331.
11 See Kinney, p. 86.
12 Ibid., p. 2.
13 Creighton, p. 45.
14 CSP Spanish, VI, p.18.
15 Loades, p. 51.
16 The title of Derek Wilson's excellent study of the Dudleys (2005). See also his *Sweet Robin*.
17 Wilson (2005), p. 257, and Wilson (1981), p. 81.
18 CST Dom. Addenda, XXVI.9.
19 Q. Jenkins 49, *De la Forêt, Dépêches*, quoted by Van Rauner, *Elizabeth and Mary Stuart*.
20 Wilson (1981), p. 18.
21 Ibid., p. 47.
22 CSP Venetian, VII, p. 81.
23 CSP Spanish, p. 57.
24 The point is emphasised in Aird, *English Historical Review*.
25 Sidney (1905), pp. 8–9 *passim*.
26 Wilson (1981), p. 118.
27 CSP Spanish, I, p. 175.
28 Ibid., p. 177.
29 Ibid., p. 262.
30 Ibid., p. 176.
31 BL Harley MS 6286, ff. 37–39.
32 CSP Spanish, I, p. 213.

33 Violet Alice Wilson, p. 78.
34 Read, (1925) p. 212.
35 Ibid., p. 215.
36 A.F. Pollard, 'Sir Edward Seymour', *DNB*, XVII, 1249.
37 BL Harleian MS 6286, f. 22.
38 Borman, p. 247.
39 The National Archives, State Papers, 12/159, f. 38v.
40 Wilson (1981), p. 139.
41 Shakespeare, *Macbeth*, I. iii. 69.
42 Bate and Rasmussen, p. 1862.
43 Wilson (1981), p. 146.

5 Which Church?

1 Donne, Poem p. 15; Gardner's gloss, p. 127.
2 Black, p. 8.
3 CSP Venetian, VII, p. 94.
4 Ibid., p. 57.
5 Perry, pp. 52 and 68.
6 *Publications of the Cambridge Antiquarian Society*, Vol. I (1840–6), p. 23.
7 An excellent account of the whole ceremony and its significance is written by a former librarian of St Hugh's College, Oxford, Beatrice M. Hamilton Thompson, *The Consecration of Archbishop Parker*, with a foreword by no less a scholar than B.J. Kidd, Warden of Keble College.
8 Creighton, p. 70.
9 Ibid., p. 70.
10 Carleton, p. 186.
11 Haugaard, p. 246.
12 Williams, p. 455.
13 Ibid., p. 460.
14 Edith Weir Perry, p. 235.
15 Ibid., p. 254.
16 Ibid., p. 29.
17 Ibid., p. 151.
18 Ibid., p. 33.
19 Ibid., p. 140.
20 Ibid., p. 87.
21 Ibid., p. 89.
22 Duffy, p. 569.
23 Cosin, 'Notes and Collections on the Book of Common Prayer', *Works*, VI, pp. 1145ff.

24 Vernon Johnson, p. 7.
25 Ibid. p. 10.
26 Creighton, p. 68.
27 Patrick Collinson in Tyacke, p. 172.
28 Manning, p. 76.
29 Ibid., p. 46.
30 Duffy, p. 593.
31 Manning, p. 32.
32 Creighton, p. 117.

6 The New Learning

1 Barker, 'Richard Mulcaster', *ODNB,* 39, p. 697.
2 Shakespeare, *Henry VIII*, I. ii. 171–5.
3 Alford, p. 10.
4 Brodie, p. 47.
5 J.F. Nicholls, *The Free Grammar School of Bristol,* St Peter Port, Toucan Press, 1984, p. 2.
6 Bennett, p. 16.
7 And Marian Oxford provided the backbone of Catholic missionary resistance to the Elizabethan Church and state. 'Throughout the 1560s and 1570s a steady stream of Oxford men left for the seminaries of Louvain, Douai and Rheims.' Loach, p. 381.
8 *Articles of Visitation*, quoted Stowe, pp. 147–8.
9 Milton, 'A Book Was Writ of Late Called *Tetrachordon.*'
10 Draper, p.13.
11 Ibid., p. 33.
12 Shakespeare, *As You Like It*, II. vii. 149.
13 Hinde, p. 17.
14 Brown, p.19.
15 Draper, p. 32.
16 Brown, p. 25.
17 Mulcaster's Elementarie, edited with introduction by E.T Campagnac, Oxford at the Clarendon Press, 1925.
18 Jones p. 172.
19 Introduction to Roger Ascham, *The Schoolmaster,* London, Cassell & Company, 1909.
20 Starkey p. 80.
21 Ibid., p. 81.
22 Dobson, I. 39.
23 Strang, p. 110.
24 Greenough and Kittredge, p. 106. Strang, 129, to whom I am indebted for the examples of loan words, *passim.*

7 A Library at Mortlake

1 Kesten, p. 299.
2 Ibid., p. 310.
3 Ibid., p. 10.
4 British Library Catalogue. But Kesten ignored, also, the work of Thomas Digges, whose *A Perfect Description of the Caelestiall Orbes* (1576) contains substantial portions of Copernicus's Book I in translation.
5 Woolley, p. 155.
6 Johnson and Larkey, p. 115.
7 See E.M. Butler (1948), pp. 121–3.
8 *The Works of Christopher Marlowe*, ed. C.F. Tucker Brooke, Oxford, at the Clarendon Press, 1910, p. 142.
9 Aubrey p. xxxviii.
10 Ibid., p. 89.
11 Woolley, p. 14.
12 Aubrey, p. 89.
13 Woolley, p. 63.
14 Sherman, p. 8.
15 L. & P. Henry VIII. ix.350 quoted Jennifer Loach, 'Reformation Controversies', in *The History of the University of Oxford, Vol. III: The Collegiate University*, Oxford at the Clarendon Press, 1986 p. 365.
16 Woolley, p. 308.
17 M.R. James.
18 Yates (1969), p. 12.
19 Sherman, p. 29.
20 Shakespeare, *The Tempest*, I.ii.110.
21 An influential short book with this title, by E.M.W. Tillyard, was published in 1943.

8 The Northern Rebellion

1 PRO SP/12/20/5 and PRO SP/12/20/25, quoted David Marcombe, 'A Rude and Heady People. The local community and the Rebellion of the Northern Earls' in David Marcombe (ed.): *The Last Principality: Politics, Religion and Society in The Bishopric of Durham 1494–1660*, Nottingham, Nottingham University Press, 1987.
2 Church Comm. Durham MS, Survey of the Bishopric 1588, quoted Mervyn James, p. 30.
3 Fletcher, p. 45.
4 Palliser, p. 263.

5 Kesselring, p. 2.
6 Palliser, p. 270.
7 Haigh (1975), pp. 333–4.
8 Ibid., p. 217.
9 Ibid., p. 219.
10 Neale (1934), p. 141.
11 Ibid., p. 159.
12 Jenkins (1958), p. 134.
13 Neale (1934), p. 185.
14 Kesselring, p. 21.
15 D. Carcombe, 'A Rude and Healthy People', in Marcombe, p. 195.
16 Mervyn James, p. 51 and *passim*.
17 Anthony Fletcher and Diarmaid Mac Culloch, *Tudor Rebellions*, Revised 5th Edition, Harlow, Pearson Longman, 2008, p. 106.
18 Kesselring, p. 143.
19 Penry Williams, p. 262.
20 Fletcher, p. 114.
21 Penry Williams, p. 265.
22 Quoted Creighton, p. 122.

9 St Bartholomew's Day Massacre

1 Ranke, p. 220.
2 Freiherr von Pastor, XVIII, p. 36.
3 Derek Wilson (1997), p. 75.
4 Read (1925), I, p. 110.
5 Derek Wilson, *Sir Francis Walsingham*, London, Constable, 2007, p. 79.
6 Hutchinson, p. 51.
7 See, for instance, '*Détails de l'horrible massacre des Protestants arrivé a Montauban; ou la Nouvelle Saint-Barthélemy*', Chez Garnéry Libraire, Paris, 1790.
8 Sidney (1985), p. 225.
9 Hutchinson, p. 50.
10 Duncan-Jones (1991), p. 60.
11 Derek Wilson (2007), p. 81.
12 Quoted, 2007 p. 80.
13 Hutchinson, p. 51.
14 Derek Wilson, (2007) p. 83.
15 Quoted ibid., p. 83.
16 Read (1925) I, p. 239.
17 Lionel Henry Cust, 'Sir Thomas Gargrave', *DNB*, VII, p. 875.
18 CSP (Domestic) 1566–1579, p. 425.

19 Neale (1934), p. 225.
20 Ibid., p.226.
21 CSP (Domestic) 1566–1579, p. 439.
22 Simon Adams, 'Robert Dudley, earl of Leicester, *ODNB*, 5, p. 101.
23 The phrase is from Yates' (1985), p. 101.
24 Duncan-Jones, (1991), p. 36.
25 Michael Graves, 'Edmund Campion', *ODNB*, III, p. 851.
26 Translated by Richard Simpson, Campion's biographer, and quoted Duncan-Jones (1991), p. 126.
27 Ackroyd, p. 704.
28 Loades, p. 124.
29 Quoted Loades, p. 144.
30 David Loades, *The Cecils*, p. 123.
31 Loades, p. 145.
32 Alan Clark, *The Tories: Conservatives and the Nation State 1922–1997*, London Weidenfeld and Nicolson, 1998, p. 312.
33 Alford (2008), p. 146.
34 Ibid., p. 207.
35 Aubrey, p. 305.
36 Alford (2008), p. 240.

10 Elizabethan Women

1 Shakespeare, *Richard* II.i.50.
2 See Carroll Camden, p. 58.
3 Shakespeare, *Romeo and Juliet*, I.iii.14.
4 Camden, p. 93.
5 See Laslett, p. 90.
6 Shakespeare, *Twelfth Night*, IV.iii.22–8.
7 Anne Laurence, in Tittler p. 385.
8 Campion, p. 25.
9 Ibid., pp. 21–2.
10 Camden, p. 105.
11 Jonson, *Epicoene*, IV.ii.60–5.
12 Quoted William Camden, p. 112.
13 Baker, p. 21.
14 Carroll Camden, p. 99.
15 Ibid., p. 100.
16 Lovell, p. 28.
17 Ibid., p. 9.
18 Ibid., p. 147.
19 Ibid., p. 205.
20 Ibid., p. 207.

21 Ibid., p. 209.
22 Fraser, p. 489.
23 Zulueta, p. 5.
24 Lovell, p. 217.
25 Ibid., p. 315.
26 Rowse (1950), p. 160.
27 Girouard (1989), p. 16.
28 Ibid., p. 15. There is no absolute proof that Smythson provided designs for Hardwick.
29 Ibid., p. 18.
30 Ibid., p. 36.
31 See Levey, p. 17.
32 Girouard (1966), p. 59.
33 Cheetham and Piper, p. 185.
34 Stone, p. 31.
35 Richard Mulcaster, *Positions* (1581), p. 198, quoted ibid., p. 50.
36 Ibid., p. 49.
37 Allen D. Boyer, 'Sir Edward Coke', *ODNB*, 12, pp. 451–3.
38 Rowse (1950), p. 230.
39 Ibid., p. 242.
40 Stone, p. 38.
41 Cliffe, p. 63.
42 Ibid., p. 28.
43 Ibid., pp. 28–9.
44 Anthony Wagner (1967), p. 206.
45 Stone, p. 578.
46 Ibid., p. 578.
47 BL Lansdowne MS 18, f.5, quoted Anthony Wagner (1967), p. 202.
48 Anthony Wagner (1967), p. 200.

11 Histories

1 See Duncan-Jones 'Afterword: Stow's Remains' in (ed.) Ian Gadd and Alexandra Gillespie, *John Stow (1525–1605) and the Making of the English Past*, London, British Library, 2004, p. 157.
2 Lewis, p. 299.
3 Daniel Woolf, 'Senses of the Past in Tudor Britain', in Tittler and Jones, p. 415.
4 Lewis, p. 300.
5 See Knapp, p. 155.
6 Lewis, p. 302.
7 Patterson, p. viii.
8 Ibid., p. 151.

9 E.g. Tillyard (1944).
10 Holinshed *Chronicles*, 4.405–6, quoted Patterson, p. 129.
11 Patterson, p. 133.
12 Bale, pp. 56–7.
13 McKisack, p. 18.
14 Aston, p. 58.
15 Quoted Patterson, p. 137.
16 David Scott Kastan, *King Henry IV Part I*, London, the Arden Shakespeare, 2002, p. 76.
17 Spenser, *A View of the Present State of Ireland*, Oxford at the Clarendon Press, 1970, pp. 84–5.
18 McCabe, p. 146.
19 Doyle, 'William Hakewill', *ODNB*, 24, p. 495.
20 Duncan-Jones and Van Dorstern, p. 84.
21 Ibid., p. 92.
22 Ibid., p. 106.
23 Spenser, *The Faerie Queene*, VI.xii.1.
24 Ibid., III. i.13.
25 Ibid., III. iii.49.

12 Kenilworth

1 Machyn, p. 293.
2 Biographical details from the introduction to Gascoigne, pp. xii–xliii.
3 Gascoigne, p. 40.
4 Austen, pp. 105–15.
5 Read (1960), pp. 122 and 429.
6 Simon Adams, 'Robert Dudley, earl of Leicester', *ODNB*, 5, p. 101.
7 Sass, p.119.
8 Jenkins (1961), p. 238.
9 Kuin, p. 56.
10 Sass, p. 45.
11 Ibid., p. 51.
12 Ibid., p. 53.
13 Duncan-Jones (2001), p. 9.
14 Gascoigne, p. 116.
15 Dunlop, p. 147.
16 Gascoigne, p. 128.
17 Jenkins (1961), p. 40; Kuin, p. 57.
18 Shakespeare, *A Midsummer Night's Dream*, II.i. 150–6 and 157–164.
19 See the following chapter.

20 Quoted Simon Adams, 'Robert Dudley, earl of Leicester' *ODNB*, 5, p. 102.
21 Attributed to Matthew Arnold by *The Times Book of Quotations*, p. 40. I had always thought it was said by Disraeli.
22 MacCaffery, 'Sir Christopher Hatton,' *ODNB*, 25, p. 818.
23 Ibid., p. 820.
24 See chapter 3.
25 Nichols, p. 562.
26 Yates (1975/1985), pp. 97–8.
27 *A Proper New Ballad, initiated The Fairies Farewell, or God-a-Mercy will*, H.T.C. Grierson and G. Bullough, *The Oxford Book of Seventeenth Century Verse*, Oxford at the Clarendon Press, 1934, p. 206.
28 Yates (1975/1985), p. 113.
29 Ibid., p. 115.
30 Ibid., p. 117.

13 Ireland

1 G.A. Hayes McCoy, 'Tudor Conquest and Counter-Reformation', in Moody, Martin and Byrne (eds), vol. III, p. 105.
2 Rowse (1955), p. 127.
3 Wallace T. MacCaffery, 'Sir Henry Sidney, *ODNB*, 50, p. 549.
4 Ibid., p. 549.
5 Thomson, p. 96.
6 Canny (1976), p. 67.
7 Ibid., p. 83.
8 Williams, p. 293.
9 Ibid., p. 292.
10 Osborn, p. 439.
11 Sidney (1985), p. 178.
12 Osborn, p. 442.

14 Sir Francis Drake's Circumnavigation

1 Williamson (1951), p. 29.
2 Coote, p. 59.
3 Ibid., p. 76.
4 Quoted from BL Cotton MS, Otho E.viii, in Coote, p. 89.
5 Williamson (1951), p. 64.
6 Ibid., p. 65.
7 From Ringrose, *History of the Buccaneers*, quoted Laughton, Sir 'Francis Drake', *DNB*, V, p. 1336.
8 Coote, p. 172.

9 Ibid., p. 175.
10 Williamson, (1938) p. 194.
11 Quoted Coote, p. 179.
12 Ibid., p. 188.
13 Henry Raup Wagner, pp. 204–5; Gibbs, pp. 117–18.
14 Yates (1975/1985), p. 55.

15 A Frog He Would A-wooing Go

1 John Lothrop Motley, *The Rise of the Dutch Republic* (Everyman), London, 3 Vols, 1966, vol 1, p. 217.
2 Worden, p. 79.
3 Quoted ibid., p. 73.
4 CSP Foreign, xiii, p. 487.
5 Jenkins (1958), p. 219.
6 Somerset, p. 312.
7 Ibid., p. 311.
8 Jenkins (1958), p. 223.
9 Duncan-Jones and Van Dorsten, Philip Sidney, *Miscellaneous Prose*, p. 48.
10 Black, p. 350.
11 CSP Spanish, III, p. 266.

16 Religious Dissent

1 Smithson, pp. 200–1.
2 Quoted ibid., p. 202.
3 Nichols, I, p. 438.
4 Fellowes, p. 39.
5 Monson, 'William Byrd', *ODNB*, 9, 327.
6 Haugaard, p. 317.
7 Francis Mills to Walsingham, 23 July 1586, in Froude (1881), XII, p. 110.
8 Parmiter, p. 23.
9 Ibid., p. 32.
10 Patrick Collinson, 'The Church and the New Religion', in Haigh (1984) p. 127.
11 Quoted Haigh, 'Church Catholics and People', in *The Reign of Elizabeth I*, p. 205.
12 Haugaard, p. 311.
13 Ibid., p. 319.
14 Waugh, p. 55.
15 Mush, p. 398.
16 Ibid., p. 432.

17 Walker, 'Margaret Clitherow', *ODNB*, 12, p. 159.
18 Ibid.
19 John Donne, 'Pseudo Martyr', quoted Bald, p. 23.
20 Fellowes, p. 39.
21 Haugaard, p. 327.
22 Elzinga, 'Philip Arundel', *ODNB*, 28, p, 408.
23 By Katherine Duncan-Jones: 'Sir Philip Sidney's Debt to Edmund Campion', in McCoog (ed.), p. 116.
24 Shakespeare, Sonnet 124.

17 Sir Philip Sidney

1 Wedgwood, p. 250.
2 Rowse (1955), p. 375.
3 Froude (1881), XI, p. 12.
4 Ibid., p. 13.
5 Ibid., p. 25.
6 Ibid., p. 35.
7 Philip Sidney, *Arcadia*, II (Baker 158–9) London, Routledge, 1907.
8 CSP Foreign 1585–6, pp. 23–4, quoted Duncan-Jones (1991), p. 274.
9 Ibid., p. 334.
10 Israel, p. 229.
11 Ibid., p. 230.
12 Froude (1881), XI, p. 58.
13 Woudhuysen, 'Philip Sidney', *ODNB*, 50, p. 564.
14 Duncan-Jones (1991), p. 295.
15 Quoted ibid., p. 295.
16 Philip Sidney, *Arcadia*, III.12 (ed. Maurice Evans, London, Penguin, 1977, p. 504).
17 III.2. (p. 441).
18 III.8 (p. 473).
19 II.15 (p. 116).
20 Woudhuysen, 'Philip Sidney', *ODNB*, 50, p. 565.
21 Nashe, Vol II, p. 253.
22 Buxton (1964), p. 140.
23 Judson, p. 200.
24 C.H. Herford and others, *Ben Jonson* (1925–52) in Plays, I, p. 137.

18 Hakluyt and Empire

1 Shakespeare, *Othello*, I.iii. 147–58.
2 *Encyclopoedia Britannica*, 11th edition, 'Calendar'.

3 Marlowe, *Tamburlaine*, V.iii.124–5.
4 Lynam p. 13.
5 Hakluyt (1903–5) p.17.
6 Mancall, p. 25, for the date, but he doesn't make the connection. Woudhuysen, 'Sir Philip Sidney', *ODNB*, 50, p. 557, tells us that Sidney's three earliest surviving letters, written between 12 March 1569 and 26 February 1570, were all written from Oxford.
7 See Buxton (1964), p. 42.
8 Hakluyt (1935), II, pp. 396–7.
9 CSP Foreign, 29 December 1558, p. 68.
10 Sidney Lee, 'Walter Raleigh', *DNB*, XVI, p. 631.
11 Milton p. 204.
12 Rowse (1959), pp. 50–1.

19 The Scottish Queen

1 Froude (1881), XII, p. 488.
2 Fraser, p. 582.
3 Harrington, 'Helena, Lady Gorges', *ODNB*, 22, p. 994.
4 Fraser, p. 586.
5 Quoted in Froude (1881), XII, p. 164.
6 Quoted ibid., p. 243.
7 Ibid., p. 168.
8 Ibid., p. 195.
9 Ibid., p. 183.
10 Ibid., p. 107.
11 Neale (1953), p. 105.
12 Ibid., p. 107.
13 Froude (1881), XII, p. 251.
14 Ibid.
15 Fraser, pp. 651–2.
16 Froude (1881), XII, p. 259.

20 The Armada

1 Fernández-Armesto, p. 12.
2 Exhibit 4.16.
3 Quoted Fernández-Armesto, p. 101.
4 Ibid., p. 56.
5 Mattingley, p. 242.
6 Ibid., p. 242.
7 Thomas Babington Macaulay, 'The Armada' who based his poem on Froude, VIII, p. 72.
8 Basil Morgan, *ODNB*, 25, p. 923.

9 Ibid.
10 Rodger, p. 270.
11 Mattingley, p. 304.
12 Maria Perry, p. 282.
13 Ibid., p. 211.
14 Froude (1895).
15 David A. Thomas, pp. 209ff.
16 Froude (1881), XII, p. 449.
17 CSP Ireland, 1588–92, p. 98.

21 London and Theatre

1 P. Arrowsmith, *The Population of Manchester from* AD *79 to 1801*, Manchester, Manchester University Press, 1987, p. 100.
2 Rowse (1950), p. 187.
3 P.M. Tillott, *A History of the County of York: The City of York*, London, Institute of Historical Research, Oxford University Press, 1961.
4 Inwood, p. 158.
5 Ibid., p. 160.
6 Quoted by Inwood, and annoyingly unnamed.
7 Ackroyd, p. 608.
8 Francine, Gottlieb, *Plague and Poverty in Elizabethan England*, New Haven, Yale University Press, 1972.
9 I am grateful to Katherine Duncan-Jones for these insights.
10 Gair, p. 3.
11 Gibson, p. 27.
12 Ibid., p. 56.
13 Charles Nicholl. 'Christopher Marlowe', *ODNB*.
14 Lewis p. 401.
15 G.K. Hunter, *English Drama, 1586–1642*, Oxford, Clarendon Press, 1997, p. 10.
16 Ibid., p. 16.
17 Nicholl *ODNB*, quoting Hazlitt, *Literature of the Age of Elizabeth*.
18 *ODNB* – Bodley, Harley MS 6848, fol. 185.
19 In the opinion, for example, of Charles Nicholl, *ODNB*, see p. 177.
20 Boas, p. 208.
21 Andrew S. Cairncross, preface to Thomas Kyd, *The Spanish Tragedy*, London, Edward Arnold, 1967, p. xii.
22 Duncan-Jones (2001), p. 23.
23 Shakespeare, 2 *Henry VI*, IV. vii. 92.
24 Ibid., IV. viii. 20.

22 Marprelate and Hooker

1 Green, p. 27.
2 Pierce, p. 64.
3 Ibid., p. 72.
4 Ibid. p. 238.
5 Carlson, *passim*.
6 Ibid., p. 115.
7 Jesse M. Lunder, 'Martin Marprelate', in *The Oxford Encyclopedia of British Literature*, 3, p. 409.
8 Carlson, p. 114.
9 Hooker, I, p. 32.
10 Lewis, pp. 461 and 453.
11 Sir Sidney Lee, 'Richard Hooker', *DNB*, IX, p. 1184.
12 Izaak Walton, *The Lives of Dr John Donne, Sir Henry Wotton, Mr Richard Hooker and Mr George Herbert*, London, Menston Scolar Press, 1969, p. 112.
13 Hooker, I p. 77.
14 Hooker, II, p. 320.
15 Ibid., p. 323.
16 Tillyard, p. 115.
17 Walton, p. 76.

23 A Hive for Bees

1 Aubrey p. 189.
2 Fernie, 'Sir Henry Lee', *ODNB*, 33, p. 73.
3 Ibid., p. 72, for the riderless horse. Yeats's poem 'Coole Park and Ballylee, 1931'.
4 Shakespeare, Sonnet 73.
5 Strong, p. 134.
6 *The New Oxford Book of Sixteenth Century Verse*, ed. Emrys Jones, Oxford, Oxford University Press, 1991, p. 432.
7 Nashe (1958), II, pp. 245–6.
8 Jim Sharpe, 'Social strain and social dislocation, 1585–1603', in Guy, pp. 192–5.
9 Shakespeare, *A Midsummer Night's Dream*, II.i. 94–7, 111–14.
10 Sharpe, in Guy, p. 192.
11 Wrigley and Schofield, p. 469.
12 Ibid., p. 531.
13 Nashe (1958), III, p. 161.
14 For this and most plague details, see F.P. Wilson.
15 Ibid., p. 97.
16 Ibid., p. 37–9.

17 Nashe (1958) III, p. 160.
18 PRO Clerks of Assize Records, Home Circuit Indictments ASSI 40/4147 quoted by Sharpe in Guy, p. 200.
19 Joel Sumatra, 'Gleanings form Local Criminal Court Records: Sedition amongst the "Inarticulate" in Elizabethan England', *Journal of Social History*, 8 (Summer 1975), p. 65.
20 Sharpe, p. 198.
21 Ibid., p. 199.
22 Shakespeare, Sonnet 138.
23 Nashe (1958), p. 248.
24 Hughes, p. 86.
25 Northumberland Papers VI, no. 1, ff. 1–6, quoted by Hiram Morgan in Guy, p. 117.

24 Sex and the City

1 Jonson, (1981) I. i. 142.
2 See Partridge, and William C. Carroll, 'Language and Sexuality in Shakespeare', in Alexander and Wells, pp. 14–34.
3 Shakespeare, *Romeo and Juliet,* I.iii.70–2.
4 Shakespeare, *Troilus and Cressida,* V.ii.204.
5 Shakespeare, Sonnet, 144. ii. 12–14.
6 *The Cambridge World History of Human Disease*, ed. Kenneth F. Kiple et. al., Cambridge, Cambridge University Press, 1993, p. 1027.
7 Shakespeare, *Romeo and Juliet*, II.iii.27.
8 Linnane, p. 13.
9 Nashe (1958), III, pp. 403–16.
10 Salgado, p. 187.
11 *The Dramatic Works of Thomas Dekker, Vol. II*, ed. Fredson Bowers, Cambridge, Cambridge University Press, 2009, p. 279.
12 Smith, p. 48.
13 Borris, pp. 94–9.
14 A.N. Wilson, *Our Times*, London, Hutchinson, 2009, p. 188.
15 Hiram Morgan in Guy, p. 109.
16 Nicholl, pp. 423–4 and *passim.*
17 Nicholl's word, ibid., p. 13.
18 Ibid., p. 14.
19 Ibid., p. 112.
20 Ibid., p. 408.

25 The Occult Philosophy

1 Yates (1966), p. 137.
2 Quoted Chambers II, p. 428.

3 Shakespeare, *Complete Works*, p. 24.
4 Hodges, p. 7.
5 Quoted Yates (1964), p. 277.
6 Quoted ibid, pp. 229–30.
7 Ibid., p. 225.
8 Shakespeare, *King Lear*, I.ii.93–7.
9 Shakespeare, *The Merchant of Venice* V.i.60–70.
10 Agrippa, *De occulta philosophia*, II, 30, quoted Yates (1964), p. 263.
11 Ibid., p. 262.
12 Michael White, p. 124.
13 BL, Harley MS 6849, ff. 184r–190r.
14 Nicholls and Williams, 'Sir Walter Raleigh', *ODNB*, 45.
15 Walter Raleigh, *History of the World*, Preface. London, William Jaggard, 1621.
16 Spenser, *Colin Clouts Come Home Againe*, II. 310–15.
17 Ibid., 871–2.
18 'Wasted' just means 'spent' in sixteenth-century English, but it was beginning to acquire its modern meaning of spending time pointlessly.

26 My America

1 Aikin, I, p. 346.
2 P. B Bartlett, *The Poems of George Chapman*, New York, Modern Language Association of American, 1941, p. 165.
3 Ibid.
4 *The Poems of Walter Raleigh*, ed. A.M.C. Latham, London, Muses Library, 1951, p. 122.
5 Mancall, p. 176.
6 Ibid., p. 177.
7 Ibid., p. 177.
8 Ibid., p. 221.
9 Ibid., p. 226. I have emended Mancall's version.
10 Ibid., p. 238.
11 Ibid., p. 271.
12 'Hakluyt Chronology', I. 323–4, quoted ibid., p. 272. See Susan M. Kingsbury (ed.), *Records of the Virginia Company of London*, 4 vols, Washington, DC, 1906–35, 384, 326.
13 *Donne's Poetical Works*, I, 52, ed. Herbert Grierson, Oxford at the Clarendon Press, 1913.

27 Tyrone

1 Canny, 'Hugh O'Neill', *ODNB*, 41, p. 837.

2 G.A. Hayes-McCoy in Moody and others (eds), p. 123.
3 Court of King James I, p. 163, quoted Geoffrey Soden, *Godfrey Goodman, Bishop of Gloucester 1853–1656*, London, SPCK, 1953, p. 27.
4 Maisse, p. 10.
5 Ibid., p. 27.
6 Ibid., p. 23.
7 Soden, p. 55.
8 Maisse, p. 24.
9 Ibid., p. 25.
10 Ibid., p. 37.
11 Ibid., p. 26.
12 BL Lansdowne MS 102, f.10.
13 Read (1960), p. 545.
14 Ibid., p. 546.
15 Shakespeare, Sonnet 107.
16 Shakespeare, Sonnet 3.
17 Goodman, I, p. 147.
18 Loades, pp. 205–7.
19 Hammer, p. 283 and *passim*.
20 Ibid., p. 288.
21 Neale (1934), p. 353.
22 Spenser, *Poetical Works*.
23 Lacey, p. 240.
24 Lacey, p. 242.

28 Essex and the End

1 CSP Domestic, p. 468.
2 See Katherine Duncan-Jones and Henry Woudhuysen (eds), *Shakespeare's Poems*, London, Arden Shakespeare, 2007, p. 104.
3 Nichols, III, p. 552.
4 Shakespeare, *Richard II*, III.iii.172–3.
5 Ibid., III.ii.175.
6 Jardine, I, p. 321.
7 Neale (1934), p. 377.
8 Maria Perry, p. 211.
9 Ibid.
10 Ibid., p 313.

29 *Hamlet*: One Through Two

1 Procter, p. 124.
2 Shakespeare, *Hamlet*, II.ii.337.

3 Thompson and Taylor, *Hamlet* (Second Quarto), London, The Arden Shakespeare, 2006, p. 54.
4 Shakespeare, *Hamlet*, I.v.25.
5 Ibid.
6 Ibid.
7 Shakespeare, *Measure for Measure*, II.ii. 92–4.
8 Shakespeare *Julius Caesar*, I.ii.125ff.
9 William Camden, *The Funeral Procession of Queen Elizabeth I*, London, British Library, 2006.

Bibliography

Ackroyd, Peter, *London – The Biography*, London, Chatto & Windus, 2000

Adams, Simon, *Leicester and the Court*, Manchester and New York, Manchester University Press, 2002

Aikin, Lucy, *Memoirs of the Court of James I*, 2 volumes, London, Longmans, 1822

—— *Memoirs of the Court of Queen Elizabeth*, London, Longmans, 1864

Aird, Ian, 'The Death of Amy Robsart', *The English Historical Review*, vol. LXXI, January 1956, London, Longmans

Akrigg, G.P.V., *Shakespeare and the Earl of Southampton*, London, Hamish Hamilton, 1968

Alexander, Catherine M.S., and Wells, Stanley, *Shakespeare and Sexuality*, Cambridge, Cambridge University Press, 2001

Alford, Stephen, *The Early Elizabethan Polity, William Cecil and the British Succession Crisis, 1558–1569*, Cambridge, Cambridge University Press, 1998

——*Burghley, William Cecil at the Court of Elizabeth I*, New Haven and London, Yale University Press, 2008

Appleton, Elizabeth, *An Anatomy of the Marprelate Controversy, 1588–1596, Lewiston-Queenston-Lampeter*, Lewiston, N.Y/ Lampeter, The Edwin Mellen Press, 2001

Arnold, Janet, *Queen Elizabeth's Wardrobe Unlock't*, Leeds, London and Washington, DC, Public Record Office, Folger Shakespeare Library, 1988

Aston, Margaret, *Lollards and Reformers*, London, Hambledon Press, 1984

Aubrey, John, *Brief Lives*, ed. O. Lawson Dick, London, Secker & Warburg, 1949

Austen, Gillian, *George Gascoigne*, Cambridge, D.S. Brewer, 2008

Baker, Margaret, *Discovering the Folklore and Customs of Love and Marriage*, Aylesbury, Shire Publications, 1974

Bald, R.C., *John Donne, A Life*, Oxford, Clarendon Press, 1970

Bale, John, *Select Works*, Cambridge, Parker Society, 1849

Barker, William, 'Richard Mulcaster', *ODNB*, Oxford, Oxford University Press, 2004, vol. 39, pp. 697–9

Batho, G.R. (ed.), *The Household Papers of Henry Percy, Ninth Earl of*

Northumberland (1564–1632), London, Royal Historical Society (Camden Third Series, vol. XCIII), 1962

Bennett, Walter, *A History of Burnley and the Grammar School during the Sixteenth Century*, Burnley, pub, 1930

Betteridge, Thomas, *Tudor Histories of the English Reformations, 1530–83*, Aldershot, Ashgate, 1999

Black, J.B., *The Reign of Elizabeth*, 2nd edition, Oxford, Clarendon Press, 1963

Boas, Frederick S., *Christopher Marlowe*, Oxford, Clarendon Press, 1940

Boorde, Andrew, *The Fyrst Boke of the Introduction of Knowledge*, London, Early English Text Society, 1870

Booth, Stephen, *The Book called Holinshed's Chronicle*, San Francisco, Book Club of California, 1968

Borman, Tracy, *Elizabeth's Women: The hidden story of the Virgin Queen*, London, Jonathan Cape, 2009

Borris, Kenneth (ed.), *Same-Sex Desire in the English Renaissance*, New York and London, Routledge, 2004

Bossy, John, *Giordano Bruno and the Embassy Affair*, New Haven and London, Yale University Press, 1991

—— *Under the Molehill, An Elizabethan Spy Story*, New Haven and London, Yale University Press, 2001

Bradbrook, M.C., *The School of Night*, Cambridge, Cambridge University Press, 1936

Bradbrook, Muriel, 'Princely Pleasures at Kenilworth', *Rice Institute Pamphlet*, 46, Houston, 1959

Brady, Ciaran, *The Chief Governors, the Rise and Fall of Reform Government in Tudor Ireland, 1536–1588*, Cambridge, Cambridge University Press, 1994

Bray, Alan, *Homosexuality in Renaissance England*, Boston, MA, The Gay Men's Press, 1988

Brett, Philip, *William Byrd and His Contemporaries*, Berkeley, LA, and London, University of California Press, 2007

Bridgett, T.E., and Knox, T.F., *The True Story of the Catholic Hierarchy Deposed by Queen Elizabeth*, New York and London, Burns & Oates, 1889

Brodie, John, *The Story of our School, the Royal Grammar School, Newcastle-upon-Tyne*, Newcastle-on-Tyne, Northumberland Press, 1924

Brown, Pamela Allen, *Better a Shrew than a Sheep*, Ithaca and London, Cornell University Press, 2003

Burnett, David, *Longleat, The Story of an English Country House*, London, William Collins, 1978

Butler, E.M., *The Myth of the Magus*, Cambridge, Cambridge University Press, 1948

—— *Ritual Magic*, Cambridge, Cambridge University Press, 1949

Butler, William, *Gleanings from Irish History*, London, Longmans, 1925

Buxton, John, *Elizabethan Taste*, London, Macmillan 1963

—— *Sir Philip Sidney and the English Renaissance*, London, Macmillan, 1964

Byrne, M. St Clare, *Elizabethan Life in Town and Country*, London, Methuen, 1950

Calendar of Letters and State Papers relating to English Affairs Preserved Principally in the Archives of Simancas, ed. Martin A.S. Hume, London, Her Majesty's Stationery Office, 1892 (CSP Spanish), vol. I, Elizabeth 1558–1567

Calendar of State Papers and Manuscripts Relating to English Affairs existing in the Archives and Collections of Venice and other libraries of Northern Italy, ed. the late Rawdon Brown and the Right Hon. G. Cavendish Bentinck, MP, 1890 (CSP Venetian), vol. VII, 1558–1580

Calendar of State Papers, Foreign Series of Elizabeth, ed. J. Stevenson et. al., London, Longmans, 1863

Calendar of State Papers, Ireland, Tudor Period, ed. Bernadette Cunningham, Revised ed., – Dublin, Irish Manuscripts Commission, 2009

Camden, Carroll, *The Elizabethan Woman*, Mararoneck, NY, Paul P. Appel, 1975

Camden, William, *The Historie of the most renowned and victorious princesse Elizabeth, the late Queene of England*, London, Benjamin Fisher, 1630

Campion, Edmund, *Two Bokes of the Histories of Ireland* (1571), ed. A.F. Vossen, Assen, Van Gorcam, 1963

Canny, Nicholas, *The Elizabethan Conquest of Ireland*, Hassocks, Harvester Press, 1976

—— *Making Ireland British*, Oxford, Oxford University Press, 2001

—— 'Henry O'Neill', *ODNB*, Oxford, Oxford University Press, 2004, vol. 41, pp. 837–45.

Carey, Vincent P., *Surviving the Tudors*, Dublin, Four Courts Press, 2002

Carleton Kenneth, *Bishops and Reform in the English Church, 1520–1559*, Woodbridge, The Boydell Press, 2001

Carlson, Leland H., *Martin Marprelate, Gentleman*, San Marino, Huntington Library, 1981

Carpenter, S.C., *The Church in England*, London, John Murray, 1954

Carter, Sydney, *The English Church and the Reformation*, London, Longmans Green & Co., 1925

Chambers, E.K., *The Elizabethan Stage*, 4 vols, Oxford, Clarendon Press, 1923 (reprinted 2009)

Cheetham, J.H., and Piper, John, *Wiltshire: A Shell Guide*, London, Faber & Faber, 1968

Ciliberto, Michele, *Giordano Bruno*, Roma-Bari, Editori Laterza, 1990

Cliffe, J.T., *The Yorkshire Gentry: From the Reformation to the Civil War*, London, The Athlone Press, 1969

Collier, J. Payne (ed.), *Fools and Jesters, with a reprint of Robert Armin's Nest of Ninnies, 1608*, London, The Shakespeare Society, 1842

Coote, Stephen, *Drake: The Life and Legend of an Elizabethan Hero*, London, Simon & Schuster, 2003

Corbett, Julian S., *Drake and the Tudor Navy*, London, Longmans, Green & Co., 1898

Cosin, John, *The Works of John Cosin, Five Volumes*, Oxford, Clarendon Press, 1843–55

Coughlan, Patricia (ed.), *Spenser and Ireland*, Cork, Cork University Press, 1989

Creighton, Mandell D.D., *Queen Elizabeth*, London, New York and Bombay, Longmans Green and Co., 1901

Cross, Clare, Loades, David, and Scarisbrick, J.J. (eds.), *Law and Government under the Tudors: Essays presented to Sir Geoffrey Elton*, Cambridge, Cambridge University Press, 1988

CSP Spanish, see *Calendar of Letters and State Papers . . .*

CSP Venetian, see *Calender of State Papers and Manuscripts . . .*

Dawson, Jane E.A., 'John Knox', *ODNB*, Oxford, Oxford University Press, 2004, vol. 32, pp. 15–30

Dean, Christopher, *Arthur of England: English Attitudes to King Arthur and the Knights of the Round Table in the Middle Ages and the Renaissance*, Toronto, Buffalo and London, University of Toronto Press, 1987

Dictionary of National Biography, XXII volumes, ed. Sir Leslie Stephen and Sir Sidney Lee, Oxford, Clarendon Press, 1917

Dobson, E.J., *English Pronunciation, 1500–1700*, Oxford, Clarendon Press, 1957

Dobson, Michael, and Watson, Nicola J., *England's Elizabeth: An Afterlife in Fame and Fantasy*, Oxford, Oxford University Press, 2002

Donne, John, *The Divine Poems*, 2nd edition, ed. Helen Gardner, Oxford, Clarendon Press, 1978

Doran, Susan, and Freeman, Thomas S., *The Myth of Elizabeth*, London, Palgrave Macmillan, 2003

Doyle, Sheila, 'William Hakewill', *ODNB*, Oxford, Oxford University Press, 2004, vol. 24, pp. 493–5

Draper, Frederick William Marsden, London, Oxford University Press, 1962

Duffy, Eamon, *Stripping of the Altars – traditional religion in England, 1400–1580*, New Haven, Yale University Press, 1994.

Duncan-Jones, Katherine, *Sir Philip Sidney, Courtier Poet*, London, Hamish Hamilton, 1991

—— (ed.), *Shakespeare's Sonnets*, London, The Arden Shakespeare, 1997.

—— *Ungentle Shakespeare*, London, The Arden Shakespeare, 2001

Duncan-Jones, Katherine, and Van Dorsten, Jan (eds), *Miscellaneous Prose of Sir Philip Sidney*, Oxford, Clarendon Press, 1973

Dunlop, Ian, *Palaces and Progresses of Queen Elizabeth*, London, Jonathan Cape, 1962

Erlanger, Philippe, *St Bartholomew's Night*, trans. from the French by Patrick O'Brian, London, Weidenfeld & Nicolson, 1960

Fellowes, Edmund H., *William Byrd*, London, New York and Toronto, Oxford University Press, 1948

Ferguson, Arthur B., *Clio Unbound, Perception of the social and cultural past in Renaissance England*, Durham, NC, Duke University Press, 1979

Fernández-Armesto, *The Spanish Armada: The Experience of War in 1588*, Oxford, Oxford University Press, 1988

Fernie, Ewan, 'Sir Henry Lee', *ODNB* Oxford, Oxford University Press, 2004, vol. 33, pp. 72–3

Fletcher, Anthony, *Tudor Rebellions*, London, Longmans, 1968

Fraser, Antonia, *Mary Queen of Scots*, London, Weidenfeld & Nicolson, 1969

Freiherr von Pastor, Ludwig, *The History of the Popes* (ed. Ralph Francis Kerr), vols XVII and XVIII, London, Routledge & Kegan Paul, 1952; St Louis, MO, B. Herder Book Co., 1952

Froude, James Anthony, *Short Studies on Great Subjects*, 2 vols, London, Longmans, 1867

—— *History of England: From the fall of Wolsey to the defeat of the Spanish Armada*, 12 vols, London, Longmans, 1881

——*English Seamen in the 16th Century*, London, Longmans, 1895

Gadd, Ian, and Gillespie, Alexandra, *John Stow (1525–1605) and the Making of the English Past*, London, British Library, 2004

Gair, Reaveley, *The Children of Paul's*, Cambridge, Cambridge University Press, 1982

Gascoigne, George, *A Hundredth Sundrie Flowres*, ed. G.W. Pigman III, Oxford, Clarendon Press, 2000

Gibbs, Lewis, *The Silver Circle*, London, Dent, 1963

Gibson, Joy Leslie, *Squeaking Cleopatras: The Elizabethan Boy Players*, Stroud, Sutton Publishing, 2000

Girouard, Mark, *Robert Smythson and the Architecture of the Elizabethan Era*, London, Country Life Ltd, 1966

—— *Hardwick Hall*, London, The National Trust, 1989

Goodman, Godfrey, *The Court of James the First*, London, R. Bentley, 1839

Goodwin, the Rev. James B.D., *The Rites and Ceremonies which took place at the Consecration of Archbishop Parker*, Cambridge, J. & J.J. Deighton and T. Stevenson, 1841

Graham, Timothy, and Watson, Andrew G., *The Recovery of the Past in Early Elizabethan England*, Cambridge, Cambridge Bibliographical Society, Cambridge University Library, 1998

Graves, Michael A.R., 'Edmund Campion', *ODNB*, Oxford, Oxford University Press, 2004, vol. 9, pp. 872–6

Green, Maria Giannina, *The Marprelate Tracts*, Kelowna, BC, Devere Press, 1990

Greenough, James, and Kittredge, George, *Words and their ways in English speech*, New York, Macmillan, 1901

Guy, John (ed.), *The Reign of Elizabeth I: Court and culture in the last decade*, Cambridge, Cambridge University Press, 1995

Haigh, Christopher, *Reformation and Renaissance in Tudor Lancashire*, Cambridge, Cambridge University Press, 1975

——(ed.), *The Reign of Elizabeth I*, Basingstoke, Macmillan, 1984

Hakluyt, Richard, *The Principall Navigations, Voyages, Traffiques & Discoveries of the English Nation*, 12 vols, Glasgow, James MacLehose and Sons, 1903–5

—— *The Original Writings and Correspondence of the two Richard Hakluyts*, 2 vols, with Introduction and Notes by E.G.R. Taylor, London, The Hakluyt Society, 1935

Hammer, Paul, *The Polarisation of Elizabethan Politics*, Cambridge, Cambridge University Press, 1999

Harrington, Paul, 'Helena, Lady Gorges, née Snakenborg', *ODNB*, Oxford, Oxford University Press, 2004, vol. 22, pp. 994–5

Haugaard, William P., *Elizabeth and the English Reformation*, Cambridge Cambridge University Press, 1968

Herbert, Mary Sidney, Countess of Pembroke, *The Collected Works, Volume I: Poems, Translations and Correspondence*, Oxford, Clarendon Press, 1998

Hinde, Sir Thomas, *Highgate School*, London, James and James, 1993

Hodges, C. Walter, *The Globe Restored*, London, Ernest Bann, 1953

Hooker, Richard, *Of the Laws of Ecclesiastical Polity*, 2 vols, London, Everyman's Library, 1907

Hotson, Leslie, *Mr W.H.*, London, Rupert Hart-Davis, 1964

Hughes, Ted, *Shakespeare and the Goddess of Complete Being*, London, Faber & Faber, 1991

Hunt, Alice, *The Drama of Coronation: Medieval Ceremony in Early Modern England*, Cambridge, Cambridge University Press, 2008

Hutchinson, Robert, *Elizabeth's Spy Master: Francis Walsingham and the Secret War that Saved England*, London, Weidenfeld & Nicolson, 2006

Inge-Soden, *Godfrey Goodman, Bishop of Gloucester, 1583–1656*, London, SPCK, 1953

Inwood, Stephen, *A History of London*, London, Macmillan, 1998

Israel, Jonathan, *The Dutch Republic*, Oxford, Clarendon Press, 1995

James, Mervyn, *Family, Lineage and Civil Society*, Oxford, Clarendon Press, 1974

James, M.R., *Lists of Manuscripts formerly owned by Dr John Dee*, Oxford, printed at the Oxford University Press of the Bibliographical Society, 1921

Jansen, Sharon L., *Debating Women, Politics and Power in Early Modern Europe*, New York, Palgrave Macmillan, 2008

Jardine, David, *Criminal Trials*, 2 vols, London, Society for the Diffusion of Useful Knowledge, 1832

Jenkins, Elizabeth, *Elizabeth the Great*, London, Victor Gollancz, 1958

—— *Elizabeth and Leicester*, London, Victor Gollancz, 1961

Johnson, Francis R., and Larkey, Sanford V., *Thomas Digges, the Copernican System, and the Idea of the Infinity of the University in 1576*, Huntingdon Library Bulletin, April 1934

Johnson, Vernon S.D.C., *The English Church always Catholic*, London, The Society of SS. Peter & Paul, 1925

Jones, Norman, *The Birth of the Elizabethan Age*, Oxford, Blackwell, 1993

Jonson, Ben, *The Complete Plays of Ben Jonson*, XI vols, ed. C.H. Herford and Evelyn Simpson, revised by G.A. Wilkes, Oxford, Clarendon Press, 1981

Judson, Alexander Corbin, *The Life of Edmund Spenser*, Baltimore, Johns Hopkins Press, 1947

Keith, Thomas, *The Perception of the Past in Early Modern England*, London, University of London, 1983

Kelly, J.N.C., *The Oxford Dictionary of Popes*, Oxford and New York, Oxford University Press, 1986

Kelsey, Harry, *Sir John Hawkins: Queen Elizabeth's Slave Trader*, New Haven and London, Yale University Press, 2002

—— 'Sir Francis Drake', *ODNB*, Oxford, Oxford University Press, 2004, vol. 16, pp. 858–69

Kesselring, K.J., *The Northern Rebellion of 1569*, Basingstoke, Palgrave Macmillan, 2007

Kesten, Hermann, *Copernicus und seine Welt*, Vienna, Munich and Basel, Verlag Kurt Desch, 1948

Kewes, Paulina (ed.), *The Uses of History in Early Modern England*, San Marino, CA, California Huntington Library, 2006

Kilroy, Gerard, *Edmund Campion: Memory and Transcription*, Aldershot, Ashgate, 2005

Kinney, Arthur F., *Titled Elizabethans*, Hamden, CN, Archon Books, 1973

Kiple, Kenneth F. (ed.), *The Cambridge World History of Human Disease*, Cambridge, Cambridge University Press, 1993

Knapp, James, *Illustrating the Past in Early Modern England*, Aldershot and Burlington, VT, Ashgate, 2003

Knox, John, ed. Martin A. Breslow, *The Political Writings of John Knox*, Washington, DC, Folger Books, 1985

Kuin, J.R.P. (ed.), *Robert Langham: A Letter*, Leider, Brill, 1983

Lacey, Robert, *Robert Earl of Essex*, London, Weidenfeld & Nicolson, 1971

Laslett, Peter, *The World We Have Lost*, London, Methuen, 1965

Laughton, John Knox, 'Sir Francis Drake', in *DNB*, Oxford, Oxford University Press, 1917, vol. V, pp. 1331–47

Leahy, William, *Elizabethan Triumphal Processions*, Aldershot, Ashgate, 2005

Levey, Santina, *The Embroideries at Hardwick Hall*, London, The National Trust, 2007

Levin, Carole, Carney, Jo Eldridge, and Barrett-Graves, Debra, *Elizabeth I, always her own free woman*, Aldershot, Ashgate, 2003

Lewis, C.S., *English Literature in the Sixteenth Century Excluding Drama*, Oxford, Clarendon Press, 1954

Linnane, Fergus, *London: The Wicked City*, London, Robson Books, 2003

Loades, David, *The Cecils, Privilege and Power Behind the Throne*, Kew, Richmond, The National Archives, 2007

Lovell, Mary S., *Bess of Hardwick, First Lady of Chatsworth, 1527–1608*, London, Little, Brown, 2005

Lynam, Edward, *British Maps and Map Makers*, London, Collins, 1944

McCabe, Richard A., *Spenser's Monstrous Regiment: Elizabethan Ireland and the Poetics of Difference*, Oxford, Oxford University Press, 2002

MacCaffery, Wallace T., 'Sir Christopher Hatton', *ODNB*, Oxford, Oxford University Press, 2004, vol. 25, pp. 817–23

McConica, James (ed.), *The History of the University of Oxford, Vol. III: The Collegiate University*, Oxford, Clarendon Press, 1986

McCoog, Thomas M. (ed.), *The Reckoned Expense*, Rome, Institutum Historicum Societatis Iesu, 2007

Macfarlane, Alan, *Witchcraft in Tudor and Stuart England*, London, Routledge & Kegan Paul, 1970

Machyn, Henry, *The Diary of Henry Machyn*, ed. J.G. Nichols, London, Camden Society, Old Series V.42, 1848

McKisack, May, *Medieval History in the Tudor Age*, Oxford, Clarendon Press, 1971

Maisse, André Huralut, sieur de, *A journal of all that was accomplished by Monsieur de Maisse, ambassador in England from King Henri IV to Queen Elizabeth, anno domini, 1597*, trans. by G.B. Harrison and R.A. Jones, London, Nonesuch Press, 1931

Mancall, Peter C., *Hakluyt's Promise*, New Haven, Yale University Press, 2007

Manning, Roger, *Religion and Society in Elizabethan Sussex*, Leicester, Leicester University Press, 1969

Marcombe, David, *The Last Principality*, Nottingham, University of Nottingham, 1987

Mathew, David, *Catholicism in England*, London, Eyre & Spottiswode, 1948

Mattingley, Garrett, *The Defeat of the Spanish Armada*, London, Jonathan Cape, 1959

Milton, Giles, *Big Chief Elizabeth*, London, Hodder & Stoughton, 2000

Monson, Craig, 'William Byrd', *ODNB*, Oxford, Oxford University Press, 2004, vol. 9, pp. 325–9

Moody, T.W., Martin, F.X., and Byrne, F.J. (eds), *A New History of Ireland, III: Early Modern Ireland*, Oxford, Clarendon Press, 1991

Morey, Adrian, *The Catholic Subjects of Elizabeth I*, London, Allen & Unwin, 1978

Morris, John (ed.), *The Catholics of York under Elizabeth*, London, Burns and Oates, 1891

Moryson, Fynes, *An itinerary written by Fynes Moryson gent. . . .*, 4 vols, Glasgow, James Maclehose & Sons, 1907

Mush, John, *Life and Death of Margaret Clitherow, the Martyr of York*, ed. William Nicholson, London, Richardson & Co., 1849

Nashe, Thomas, *The Works of Thomas Nashe*, 5 vols, ed. Ronald B. McKerrow (revised by F.P. Wilson), Oxford, Basil Blackwell, 1958

—— *The Unfortunate Traveller and Other Works*, introduced and edited by J.B. Steane, Harmondsworth, Penguin, 1978

Neale, J.E., *Queen Elizabeth*, London, Jonathan Cape, 1934

——*Queen Elizabeth and her Parliaments, 1559–1581*, London, Jonathan Cape, 1953

—— *Queen Elizabeth and her Parliaments, 1584–1601*, London, Jonathan Cape, 1957

Nicholl, Charles, *The Reckoning*, revised edition, London, Vintage, 2002

Nichols, John, *The Progresses and Public Processions of Queen Elizabeth*, 3 vols, London, Society of Antiquaries, 1823; New York, Arms Press, and Kraus Reprint Corporation, 1968

Nicholls, Mark, and Williams, Penry, 'Sir Walter Ralegh', *ODNB*, Oxford, Oxford University Press, 2004, vol. 45, pp. 278–91

ODNB Osborn, James M., *The Young Philip Sidney, 1572–1577*, New Haven and London, Yale University Press, 1972

Palliser, D.M., *Tudor York*, Oxford, Oxford University Press, 1979

Parmiter, Geoffrey de, *Elizabethan Popish Recusancy in the Inns of Court – London*, Bulletin of the Institute of Historical Research, 1976

Partridge, Eric, *Shakespeare's Bawdy*, London, Routledge, 1947

Patterson, Annabel, *Reading Holinshed's Chronicles*, Chicago and London, University of Chicago Press, 1994

Payne, Anthony, *Richard Hakluyt: A guide to his books and those associated with him 1580–1625*, London, Quaritch, 2008

Peacock, Edward (ed.) *English Church Furniture, Ornaments and the Decorations at the Period of the Reformation*, London, John Camden Hotten, 1866

Pearce, William, *An Historical Introduction to the Marprelate Tracts*, London, Archibald Constable, 1908

Percy, Martyn, *Introducing Richard Hooker and the Laws of Ecclesiastical Polity*, London, Darton, Longman and Todd, 1999

Perry, Edith Weir, *Under Four Tudors, being the story of Matthew Parker, sometime Archbishop of Canterbury*, London, Allen & Unwin, 1964

Perry, Maria, *Elizabeth I, the word of a Prince*, London, Folio Society, 1990

Picard, Liza, *Elizabeth's London*, London, Weidenfeld & Nicolson, 2003

Pierce, William (ed.), *The Martin Marprelate Tracts*, 1588, 1589, London, James Clarke & Co., 1911

Pritchard, Arnold, *Catholic Loyalism in Elizabethan England*, London, Scolar Press, 1979

PRO Proctor, Francis, *A New History of the Book of Common Prayer*, revised by W.H. Frere, London, Macmillan, 1902

Prouty, Charles T., *George Gascoigne, Elizabethan Courtier, Soldier and Poet*, New York, Columbia University Press, 1942

Ranelagh, John, *A Short History of Ireland*, Cambridge, Cambridge University Press, 1983

Ranke, Leopold von, *Die Römischen Päpste in den letzten vier Jahrhunderten*, 2 vols, Leipzig, Verlag von Duncker & Humblot, 1878

Read, Conyers, *Mr Secretary Cecil and the Policy of Queen Elizabeth*, 3 vols, Cambridge, MA, and Oxford, Harvard University Press and the Clarendon Press, 1925

—— *Lord Burghley and Queen Elizabeth*, London, Jonathan Cape, 1960

Reynolds, E.E., *Campion and Parsons. The Jesuit Mission of 1580–1*, London, Sheed and Ward, 1980

Ridley, Jasper, *John Knox*, Oxford, Clarendon Press, 1968

Robertson, Jean (ed.), *Sir Philip Sidney: The Countess of Pembroke's Arcadia (The Old Arcadia)*, Oxford, Clarendon Press, 1973

Rodger, N.A.M., *The Safeguard of the Sea: A Naval History of Great Britain. Volume One, 660–1649*, London, HarperCollins, in association with the National Maritime Museum, 1997

Rodriguez-Salgado, M.J., and others, *Armada, 1588–1988*, London, Penguin Books in association with the National Maritime Museum, 1988

Rowse, A.L., *The England of Elizabeth*, London, Macmillan, 1950

—— *Ralegh and the Throckmortons*, London, Macmillan, 1952

—— *The Expansion of Elizabethan England*, London, Macmillan, 1955

—— *The Elizabethans and America*, London, Macmillan, 1959

—— *Shakespeare's Southampton*, London, Macmillan, 1965

—— *Simon Forman, Sex and Society in Shakespeare's Age*, London, Weidenfeld & Nicolson, 1974

—— *Homosexuals in History*, London, Weidenfeld & Nicolson, 1977

Salgdao, Gamini, *The Elizabethan Underworld*, Gloucester, Alan Sutton, 1984

Sass, Lorna, *To the Queen's Taste*, London, John Murray, 1976

Schoenbaum, S., *William Shakespeare: A Compact Documentary Life*, Oxford, London and New York, Oxford University Press, 1977

——*Shakespeare's Lives*, Oxford and New York, Oxford University Press, 1993

Secor, Philip B., *Richard Hooker, Prophet of Anglicanism*, Tunbridge Wells and Toronto, Burns & Oates/The Anglican Book Centre, 1999

Shakespeare, William, *Complete Works*, ed. Jonathan Bate and Eric Rasmussen, London, Macmillan, 2007

Shapiro, James, *1599, A Year in the Life of William Shakespeare*, London, Faber & Faber, 2005

Sherman, William, *John Dee*, Amherst, University of Massachusetts Press, 1995

Sidney, Philip, *Amy Robsart at Cumnor*, Oxford, Alden & Co., Bocardo Press, 1905

—— *The Complete Works of Sir Philip Sidney*, ed. Albert Feuillerat,

Cambridge, Cambridge University Press, 1912–1926
——*The Countess of Pembroke's Arcadia* (*The Old Arcadia*), ed. Katherine Duncan-Jones, Oxford and New York, Oxford University Press, 1985
Sitwell, Edith, *The Queens and the Hive*, London, Macmillan, 1962
Slack, Paul, *The Impact of Plague in Tudor and Stuart England*, Oxford, Clarendon Press, 1985
Smith, Bruce R., *Homosexual Desire in Shakespeare's England*, Chicago, University of Chicago Press, 1991
Smithson, R.J., *The Anabaptists, Their Contribution to our Protestant Heritage*, London, James Clarke & Co., 1935
Somerset, Anne, *Elizabeth I*, London, Weidenfeld & Nicolson, 1991
Spencer, Colin, *Homosexuality: A History*, London, Fourth Estate, 1995
Spenser, Edmund, *The Poetical Works*, ed. J.C. Smith and E. De Selincourt, London, Oxford University Press, 1940
Starkey, David, *Elizabeth: Apprenticeship*, London, Chatto & Windus, 2000
Stone, Laurence, *The Crisis of the Aristocracy, 1558–1645*, Oxford, Clarendon Press, 1965
Stone, Laurence, and Stone, Jeanne C. Fawtier, *An Open Élite? England 1540–1880*, Oxford, Clarendon Press, 1984
Stow, John, *Survey of London*, London, Dent, 1960
Stowe, A. Monroe, *English Grammar Schools in the Reign of Queen Elizabeth*, Darby, PA, Darby Books, 1908
Strachey, [Giles] Lytton, *Elizabeth and Essex*, New York, Crosby Gaige, 1928
Strang, Barbara, *A History of English*, London, Methuen, 1970
Strong, Roy, *The Cult of Elizabeth*, London, Thames and Hudson, 1977
Thomas, David A., *The Illustrated Armada Handbook*, London, Harrap, 1988
Thomas, Hugh, *The Slave Trade*, London, Picador, 1997
Thomson, George Malcolm, *Sir Francis Drake*, Secker & Warburg, 1972
Thompson, Beatrice M. Hamilton, *The Consecration of Archbishop Parker*, London, Faith Press, 1934
Tillyard, E.M.W., *The Elizabethan World Picture*, London, Chatto & Windus, 1943
——*Shakespeare's History Plays*, London, Chatto & Windus, 1944
Tittler, Robert, and Jones, Norman, *A Companion to Tudor Britain*, Oxford, Blackwell Publishing, 2004
Trevelyan, G.M., *Illustrated English Social History. Volume Two: The Age of Shakespeare and the Stuart Period*, London, Longmans, Green & Co., 1950

Tyacke, Nicholas (ed.), *England's Long Reformation*, London, UCL, 1998
——*Aspects of English Protestantism c. 1530–1700*, Manchester and New York, Manchester University Press, 2001
Van Es, Bart, *Spenser's Form of History*, Oxford, Oxford University Press, 2002
Wagner, Sir Anthony, *English Genealogy*, Oxford, Clarendon Press, 1960
—— *Heralds of England: A History of the Office and College of Arms*, London, HMSO 1967
Wagner, Henry Raup, *Sir Francis Drake's Voyage around the world*, San Francisco, John Howell, 1926
Walker, Claire, 'Margaret Clitherow', *ODNB*, Oxford, Oxford University Press, 2004, vol. 12, pp. 159–160
Walton, Izaak, The Lives of Dr John Donne, Sir Henry Wotton, Mr Richard Hooker, Mr George Herbert, 1670, London, Menston Scolar Press, 1969
Waugh, Evelyn, *Edmund Campion*, London, Longmans, 1961
Wedgwood, C.V., *William the Silent*, London, Jonathan Cape, 1944
White, F.O., *The Lives of the Elizabethan Bishops*, London, Skeffington and Son, 1898
White, Michael, *The Pope and the Heretic*, London, Little, Brown, 2002
Williams, Penry, *The Later Tudors, England 1547–1603*, Oxford, Clarendon Press, 1995
Williamson, James A., *The Age of Drake*, London, Adam & Charles Black, 1938
—— *Hawkins of Plymouth*, London, Adam and Charles Black, 1949
—— *Sir Francis Drake*, London, Fontana Books, 1951
Wilson, C. Anne, *Food and Drink in Britain*, London, Constable, 1973
Wilson, Derek, *Sweet Robin: A Biography of Robert Dudley, Earl of Leicester, 1533–1588*, London, Hamish Hamilton, 1997.
—— *The Uncrowned Kings of England*, London, Constable, 2005.
Wilson, F.P., *The Plague in Shakespeare's London*, London, Oxford University Press (1927) Oxford Paperbacks, 1963
Wilson, J. Dover, *Martin Marprelate and Shakespeare's Fluellen*, London, Alexander Moring, 1919
Wilson, Jean, *Entertainments for Elizabeth I*, Woodbridge, D.S. Brewer, 1980
Wilson, Violet Alice, *Elizabeth's Maids of Honour*, London, S.I., 1923
Woolley, Benjamin, *The Queen's Conjuror*, London, HarperCollins, 2002
Worden, Blair, *The Sound of Virtue. Philip Sidney's Arcadia and Elizabethan Politics*, New Haven and London, Yale University Press, 1996

Woudhuysen, Henry, 'Sir Philip Sidney', *DNB*, Oxford, Oxford University Press, 2004, vol. 50, pp. 556–68,

Wrigley, E.A., and Schofield, R.S., *The Population History of England, 1541–1871*, London, Edward Arnold, 1981

Yates, Frances A., *Giordano Bruno and the Hermetic Tradition*, Routledge, 1964

—— *The Art of Memory*, Routledge, 1966

——*Theatre of the World*, London, Routledge & Kegan Paul, 1969

——*The Rosicrucian Enlightenment*, London, Routledge & Kegan Paul, 1972

—— *Astraea: The Imperial Theme in the Sixteenth Century*, London, Routledge & Kegan Paul, 1975; Ark Poperbacks, 1985

Yarwood, Doreen, *The Architecture of England*, London, B.T. Batsford, 1963

Zulueta, Francis de, *Embroideries of Mary Stuart & Elizabeth Talbot at Oxburgh Hall*, Oxford, Oxford University Press, 1923

Index